Adobe® InDesign® CS5
The Professional Portfolio

AGAINST THE CLOCK
mastering graphic technology

Managing Editor: Ellenn Behoriam
Cover & Interior Design: Erika Kendra
Copy Editor: Angelina Kendra
Printer: Prestige Printers

The fonts utilized in these training materials are the property of Against The Clock, Inc., and are supplied to the legitimate buyers of the Against The Clock training materials solely for use with the exercises and projects provided in the body of the materials. They may not be used for any other purpose, and under no circumstances may they be transferred to another individual, nor copied or distributed by any means whatsoever.

A portion of the images supplied in this book are copyright © PhotoDisc, Inc., 201 Fourth Ave., Seattle, WA 98121, or copyright ©PhotoSpin, 4030 Palos Verdes Dr. N., Suite 200, Rollings Hills Estates, CA. These images are the sole property of PhotoDisc or PhotoSpin and are used by Against The Clock with the permission of the owners. They may not be distributed, copied, transferred, or reproduced by any means whatsoever, other than for the completion of the exercises and projects contained in this Against The Clock training material.

Against The Clock and the Against The Clock logo are trademarks of Against The Clock, Inc., registered in the United States and elsewhere. References to and instructional materials provided for any particular application program, operating system, hardware platform, or other commercially available product or products do not represent an endorsement of such product or products by Against The Clock, Inc.

Photoshop, Acrobat, Illustrator, InDesign, PageMaker, Flash, Dreamweaver, Premiere, and PostScript are trademarks of Adobe Systems Incorporated. Macintosh is a trademark of Apple Computer, Inc. QuarkXPress is a registered trademark of Quark, Inc. Word, Excel, Office, Microsoft, and Windows are either registered trademarks or trademarks of Microsoft Corporation.

Other product and company names mentioned herein may be the trademarks of their respective owners.

10   9   8   7   6   5   4   3   2   978-1-936201-03-7

4710 28th Street North, Saint Petersburg, FL 33714
800-256-4ATC • www.againsttheclock.com

Acknowledgements

ABOUT AGAINST THE CLOCK

Against The Clock, long recognized as one of the nation's leaders in courseware development, has been publishing high-quality educational materials for the graphic and computer arts industries since 1990. The company has developed a solid and widely-respected approach to teaching people how to effectively utilize graphics applications, while maintaining a disciplined approach to real-world problems.

Having developed the *Against The Clock* and the *Essentials for Design* series with Prentice Hall/Pearson Education, ATC drew from years of professional experience and instructor feedback to develop *The Professional Portfolio Series*, focusing on the Adobe Creative Suite. These books feature step-by-step explanations, detailed foundational information, and advice and tips from industry professionals that offer practical solutions to technical issues.

Against The Clock works closely with all major software developers to create learning solutions that fulfill both the requirements of instructors and the needs of students. Thousands of graphic arts professionals — designers, illustrators, imaging specialists, prepress experts and production managers — began their educations with Against The Clock training books. These professionals studied at Baker College, Nossi College of Art, Virginia Tech, Appalachian State University, Keiser College, University of South Carolina, Gress Graphic Arts Institute, Hagerstown Community College, Kean University, Southern Polytechnic State University, Brenau University, and many other educational institutions.

ABOUT THE AUTHOR

Erika Kendra holds a BA in History and a BA in English Literature from the University of Pittsburgh. She began her career in the graphic communications industry as an editor at Graphic Arts Technical Foundation before moving to Los Angeles in 2000. Erika is the author or co-author of more than twenty books about Adobe graphic design software. She has also written several books about graphic design concepts such as color reproduction and preflighting, and dozens of articles for online and print journals in the graphics industry. Working with Against The Clock for more than ten years, Erika was a key partner in developing *The Professional Portfolio Series* of software training books.

CONTRIBUTING AUTHORS, ARTISTS, AND EDITORS

A big thank you to the people whose artwork, comments, and expertise contributed to the success of these books:

- **Bill Carberry**, ACI4hire.com
- **Beth Rogers**, Nossi College of Art
- **Randy Anderson**, Oklahoma City Community College
- **Jordan Cox**, Against The Clock
- **Debbie Davidson**, Sweet Dreams Design

Finally, thanks to **Angelina Kendra**, editor, for making sure that we all said what we meant to say.

Project Goals

Each project begins with a clear description of the overall concepts that are explained in the project; these goals closely match the different "stages" of the project workflow.

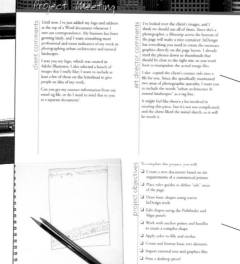

The Project Meeting

Each project includes the client's initial comments, which provide valuable information about the job. The Project Art Director, a vital part of any design workflow, also provides fundamental advice and production requirements.

Project Objectives

Each Project Meeting includes a summary of the specific skills required to complete the project.

Real-World Workflow

Projects are broken into logical lessons or "stages" of the workflow. Brief introductions at the beginning of each stage provide vital foundational material required to complete the task.

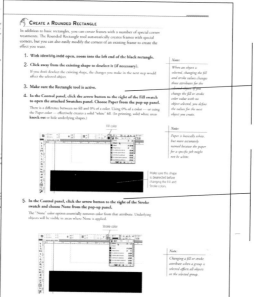

Step-By-Step Exercises

Every stage of the workflow is broken into multiple hands-on, step-by-step exercises.

Visual Explanations

Wherever possible, screen shots are annotated so you can quickly identify important information.

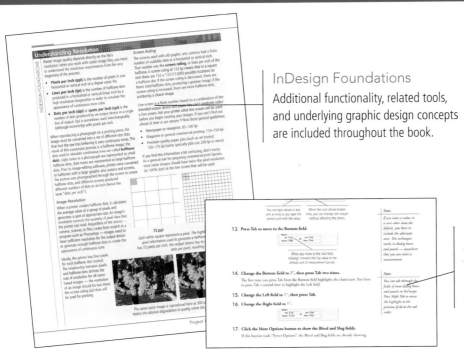

InDesign Foundations

Additional functionality, related tools, and underlying graphic design concepts are included throughout the book.

Advice and Warnings

Where appropriate, sidebars provide shortcuts, warnings, or tips about the topic at hand.

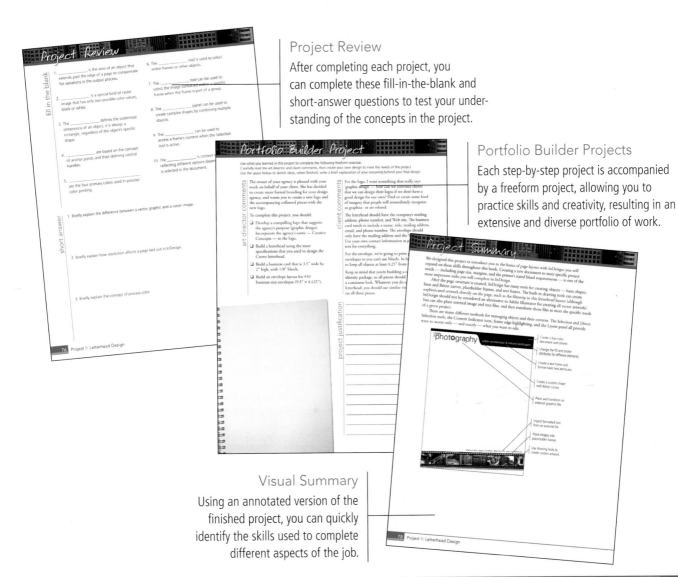

Project Review

After completing each project, you can complete these fill-in-the-blank and short-answer questions to test your understanding of the concepts in the project.

Portfolio Builder Projects

Each step-by-step project is accompanied by a freeform project, allowing you to practice skills and creativity, resulting in an extensive and diverse portfolio of work.

Visual Summary

Using an annotated version of the finished project, you can quickly identify the skills used to complete different aspects of the job.

The Against The Clock *Portfolio Series* teaches graphic design software tools and techniques entirely within the framework of real-world projects; we introduce and explain skills where they would naturally fall into a real project workflow.

The project-based approach in *The Professional Portfolio Series* allows you to get in depth with the software beginning in Project 1 — you don't have to read several chapters of introductory material before you can start creating finished artwork.

Our approach also prevents "topic tedium" — in other words, we don't require you to read pages and pages of information about text (for example); instead, we explain text tools and options as part of larger projects (in this case, beginning with placing text on a letterhead).

Clear, easy-to-read, step-by-step instructions walk you through every phase of each job, from creating a new file to saving the finished piece. Wherever logical, we also offer practical advice and tips about underlying concepts and graphic design practices that will benefit students as they enter the job market.

The projects in this book reflect a range of different types of InDesign jobs, from creating a client letterhead to implementing a newsletter template to compiling a multi-chapter book. When you finish the eight projects in this book (and the accompanying Portfolio Builder exercises), you will have a substantial body of work that should impress any potential employer.

The eight InDesign CS5 projects are described briefly here; more detail is provided in the full table of contents (beginning on Page viii).

project 1

Letterhead Design

- ❏ Setting up the Workspace
- ❏ Creating Basic Page Elements
- ❏ Placing External Images
- ❏ Creating and Formatting Basic Text
- ❏ Printing InDesign Files

project 2

Festival Poster

- ❏ Building Graphic Interest
- ❏ Importing and Formatting Text
- ❏ Graphics as Text and Text as Graphics
- ❏ Outputting the File

project 3

HeartSmart Newsletter

- ❏ Working with Templates
- ❏ Working with Styles
- ❏ Working with Tables
- ❏ Preflighting and Packaging the Job

Some experts claim most people use only a small fraction — maybe 10% — of their software's capabilities; this is likely because many people don't know what is available. As you complete the projects in this book, our goal is to familiarize you with the entire tool set so you can be more productive and more marketable in your career as a graphic designer.

It is important to keep in mind that InDesign is an extremely versatile and powerful application. The sheer volume of available tools, panels, and features can seem intimidating when you first look at the software interface. Most of these tools, however, are fairly simple to use with a bit of background information and a little practice.

Wherever necessary, we explain the underlying concepts and terms that are required for understanding the software. We're confident that these projects provide the practice you need to be able to create sophisticated artwork by the end of the very first project.

Contents

Contents

Contents

Project 7   NATIONAL PARKS INFO PIECES   375

PREREQUISITES

The Professional Portfolio Series is based on the assumption that you have a basic understanding of how to use your computer. You should know how to use your mouse to point and click, as well as how to drag items around the screen. You should be able to resize and arrange windows on your desktop to maximize your available space. You should know how to access drop-down menus, and understand how check boxes and radio buttons work. It also doesn't hurt to have a good understanding of how your operating system organizes files and folders, and how to navigate your way around them. If you're familiar with these fundamental skills, then you know all that's necessary to use the Portfolio Series.

RESOURCE FILES

All of the files you need to complete the projects in this book — except, of course, the InDesign application files — are on the Student Files Web page at www.againsttheclock.com. See the inside back cover of this book for access information.

Each archive (ZIP) file is named according to the related project (e.g., **ID5_RF_Project1.zip**). At the beginning of each project, you must download the archive file for that project and expand that archive to access the resource files that you need to complete the exercises. Detailed instructions for this process are included in the Interface chapter.

Files required for the related Portfolio Builder exercises at the end of each project are also available on the Student Files page; these archives are also named by project (e.g., **ID5_PB_Project1.zip**).

ATC FONTS

You must download and install the ATC fonts from the Student Files Web page to ensure that your exercises and projects will work as described in the book. Specific instructions for installing fonts are provided in the documentation that came with your computer. You should replace older (pre-2004) ATC fonts with the ones on the Student Files Web page.

SYSTEM REQUIREMENTS

The Professional Portfolio Series was designed to work on both Macintosh or Windows computers; where differences exist from one platform to another, we include specific instructions relative to each platform. One issue that remains different from Macintosh to Windows is the use of different modifier keys (Control, Shift, etc.) to accomplish the same task. When we present key commands, we always follow the same Macintosh/Windows format — Macintosh keys are listed first, then a slash, followed by the Windows key command.

Minimum System Requirements for Adobe InDesign CS5:

Windows

- Intel® Pentium® 4 or AMD Athlon® 64 processor
- Microsoft® Windows® XP with Service Pack 2 (Service Pack 3 recommended); Windows Vista® Home Premium, Business, Ultimate, or Enterprise with Service Pack 1; or Windows 7
- 1 GB of RAM (2 GB recommended)
- 1.6 GB of available hard-disk space for installation; additional free space required during installation
- 1024×768 display (1280×800 recommended) with 16-bit video card
- DVD-ROM drive
- Adobe® Flash® Player 10 software required to export SWF files

Macintosh OS

- Multicore Intel processor
- Mac OS X v10.5.7 or v10.6
- 1 GB of RAM (2 GB recommended)
- 2.6 GB of available hard-disk space for installation; additional free space required during installation
- 1024×768 display (1280×800 recommended) with 16-bit video card
- DVD-ROM drive
- Adobe Flash Player 10 software required to export SWF files

Adobe InDesign is a robust desktop-publishing application that allows you to integrate text and graphics, prepared in the program or imported from other sources, and produce files that can be printed to a local or networked printer, taken to a commercial printer, or published digitally. This book is designed to teach you how InDesign can be used to complete virtually any type project, from a 1-page flyer to a 500-page book.

The sheer volume of available options in InDesign means there are numerous tools and utilities that you need to learn to make the most of the application. The simple exercises in this introduction are designed to let you explore the InDesign user interface. Whether you are new to the application or upgrading from a previous version, we strongly encourage you to follow these steps to click around and become familiar with the basic workspace.

EXPLORE THE INDESIGN INTERFACE

The user interface (UI) is what you see when you launch the application. The specific elements that you see — including which panels are open and where they appear on the screen — depend on what was done the last time the application was open. The first time you launch InDesign, you see the default workspace settings defined by Adobe. When you relaunch the application after you or another user has quit, the workspace defaults to the last-used settings.

1. **Create a new empty folder named WIP on any writable disk (where you plan to save your work in progress).**

2. **Download the ID5_RF_Interface.zip archive from the Student Files Web page.**

3. **Macintosh users: Place the ZIP archive in your WIP folder, then double-click the file icon to expand it.**

    This **Interface** folder contains all the files you need to complete this introduction.

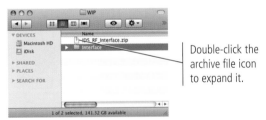

Double-click the archive file icon to expand it.

Windows users: Double-click the ZIP archive file to open it. Click the folder inside the archive and drag it into your primary WIP folder.

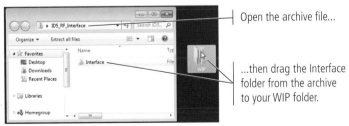

Open the archive file...

...then drag the Interface folder from the archive to your WIP folder.

4. **Macintosh users: While pressing Command-Option-Control-Shift, start InDesign. Click Yes when asked if you want to delete preference files.**

Windows users: Launch InDesign, and then press Control-Alt-Shift. Click Yes when asked if you want to delete preference files.

This step resets InDesign to the preference settings that are defined by Adobe as the application defaults. This helps to ensure that your application functions in the same way as what we show in our screen shots.

On Windows, each running application is contained within its own frame; all elements of the application — including the Menu bar, panels, tools, and open documents — are contained within the Application frame.

Adobe also offers the Application frame to Macintosh users as an option for controlling your workspace. When you activate the Application frame, the entire workspace shifts into a self-contained area that can be moved around the screen. All elements of the workspace (excluding the Menu bar) move when you move the Application frame.

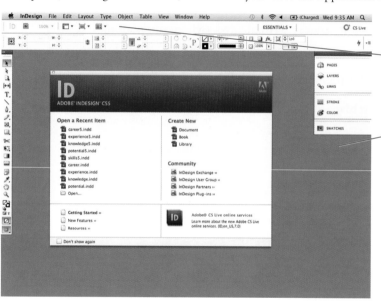

When the Application frame is not active, the Application bar appears below the Menu bar; in this case, the Application bar can be moved or turned off.

When the Application frame is not active, the desktop is visible behind the workspace elements.

5. Macintosh users: Open the Window menu and choose Application Frame to toggle that option on.

This option should be checked.

On Macintosh systems, the Application bar includes a number of buttons for accessing different view options. On Windows systems, those same options are available on the right side of the Menu bar.

The default workspace includes the Tools panel on the left side of the screen, the Control panel at the top of the screen, and a set of panels attached to the right side of the screen. (The area where the panels are stored is called the **panel dock**.)

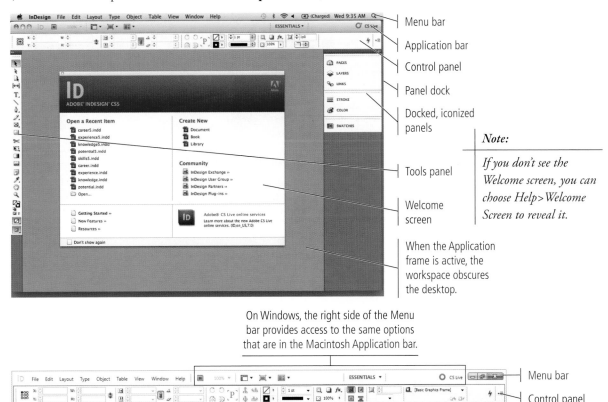

Menu bar

Application bar

Control panel

Panel dock

Docked, iconized panels

Tools panel

Welcome screen

When the Application frame is active, the workspace obscures the desktop.

Note:

If you don't see the Welcome screen, you can choose Help>Welcome Screen to reveal it.

On Windows, the right side of the Menu bar provides access to the same options that are in the Macintosh Application bar.

Menu bar

Control panel

6. Control/right-click the title bar above the panel dock. Choose Auto-Collapse Iconic Panels in the contextual menu to toggle on that option.

As we explained in the Getting Started section, when commands are different for the Macintosh and Windows operating systems, we include the different commands in the Macintosh/Windows format. In this case, Macintosh users who do not have right-click mouse capability can press the Control key and click to access the contextual menu. You do not have to press Control *and* right-click to access the menus.

(If you're using a Macintosh and don't have a mouse with right-click capability, we highly recommend that you purchase one. They're inexpensive, they're available at almost any retail store, and they save significant amounts of time accessing contextual options.)

Control/right-clicking a dock title bar opens the dock contextual menu, where you can change the default panel behavior. If you toggle on the Auto-Collapse Iconic Panels option (which is inactive by default), an open panel collapses as soon as you click away from it.

Note:

The Auto-Collapse Iconic Panels option is also available in the User Interface pane of the Preferences dialog box, which you can open directly from the dock contextual menu.

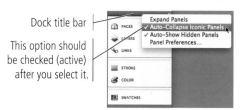

Dock title bar

This option should be checked (active) after you select it.

7. In the panel dock, click the Color button to expand the panel, and then click away from the expanded panel.

By default, expanded panels remain open until you manually close them or expand another panel in the same dock column. When Auto-Collapse Iconic Panels is toggled on, the expanded panel collapses as soon as you click away from it.

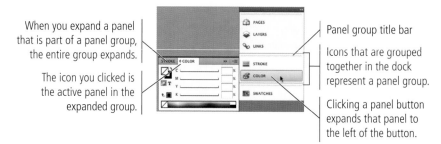

When you expand a panel that is part of a panel group, the entire group expands.

The icon you clicked is the active panel in the expanded group.

Panel group title bar

Icons that are grouped together in the dock represent a panel group.

Clicking a panel button expands that panel to the left of the button.

Note:

*Collapsed panels are referred to as **iconized** or **iconic**.*

8. Click the left edge of the docked panels and drag right.

When panels are iconized, you can reduce the button size to show icons only. Doing so can be particularly useful once you are more familiar with the application and the icons used to symbolize the different panels.

Click here...

...and drag right to hide the panel names.

9. **Double-click the title bar above the column of docked panels.**

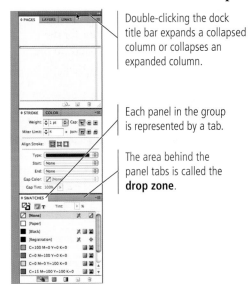

Double-clicking the dock title bar expands a collapsed column or collapses an expanded column.

Each panel in the group is represented by a tab.

The area behind the panel tabs is called the **drop zone**.

10. **On the left side of the workspace, double-click the title bar of the Tools panel.**

The Tools panel can't expand, but it can display as either one or two columns; clicking the Tools panel title bar toggles between the two modes.

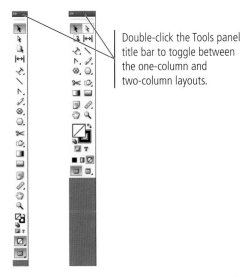

Double-click the Tools panel title bar to toggle between the one-column and two-column layouts.

Deciding whether to use the one- or two-column format is a purely personal choice. The one-column layout takes up less horizontal space on the screen, which can be useful if you have a small monitor; the two-column format fits in a smaller vertical space, which can be especially useful if you have a laptop with a widescreen monitor.

The Tools panel can also be floated (moved out of the dock) by clicking its title bar and dragging away from the edge of the screen. To re-dock the floating Tools panel, simply click the panel's title bar and drag back to the left edge of the screen; when a blue line highlights the edge of the workspace, releasing the mouse button places the Tools panel back in the dock. If the Tools panel is floating, you can toggle through three different modes — one-column vertical, two-column vertical, and one-row horizontal.

11. **Continue to the next exercise.**

InDesign CS5 includes 32 tools — a large number that indicates the real power of the application. In addition to the basic tool set, the bottom of the Tools panel includes options that control the foreground and background colors, as well as the preview mode you're using. You will learn how to use these tools as you complete the projects in this book. For now, you should simply take the opportunity to identify the tools.

Nested Tools and Keyboard Shortcuts

Any tool with an arrow in the bottom-right corner includes related tools below it. When you click a tool and hold down the mouse button (or Control/right-click a tool), the **nested tools** appear in a pop-up menu. When you choose one of the nested tools, that variation becomes the default choice in the Tools panel.

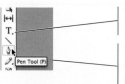
This arrow means the tool has other nested tools.

When you hover the mouse cursor over the tool, a tool tip shows the name of the tool.

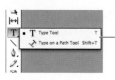
Click and hold down the mouse button (or Control/right-click a tool) to show the nested tools.

Most of the default InDesign tools can be accessed with a keyboard shortcut. When you hover the mouse cursor over a tool, the pop-up **tool tip** shows the name of the tool and a letter in parentheses. Pressing that letter on the keyboard activates the associated tool (unless you're working with type, in which case pressing a key adds that letter to your text). If you don't see tool tips, check the Interface pane of the Preferences dialog box; the Show Tool Tips check box should be active.

Finally, if you press and hold a tool's keyboard shortcut, you can temporarily call the appropriate tool (called **spring-loaded keys**); after releasing the shortcut key, you return to the tool you were using previously. For example, you might use this technique to switch temporarily from the Brush tool to the Eraser tool while painting.

Tools Panel Options

In addition to the basic tool set, the bottom of the Tools panel includes options that control the fill and stroke colors (as well as options for what attribute is being affected by color changes), and which screen preview mode to use.

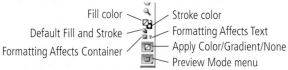
Fill color
Stroke color
Default Fill and Stroke
Formatting Affects Text
Formatting Affects Container
Apply Color/Gradient/None
Preview Mode menu

Tool Hints

The Tool Hints panel (Window>Utilities>Tool Hints) provides useful tips about the active tool, including a brief description of the tool; an explanation of the tool's behavior when you press one or more modifier keys; and the tool's keyboard shortcut.

The following image offers a quick reference of nested tools, as well as the keyboard shortcut for each tool (if any). Nested tools are shown indented and in italics.

- Selection tool (V)
- Direct Selection tool (A)
- Page tool (Shift-P)
- Gap tool (U)
- Type tool (T)
  - *Type on a Path tool (Shift-T)*
- Line tool (\)
- Pen tool (P)
  - *Add Anchor Point tool (=)*
  - *Delete Anchor Point tool (-)*
  - *Convert Direction Point tool (Shift-C)*
- Pencil tool (N)
  - *Smooth tool*
  - *Erase tool*
- Rectangle Frame tool (F)
  - *Ellipse Frame tool*
  - *Polygon Frame tool*
- Rectangle tool (M)
  - *Ellipse tool (L)*
  - *Polygon tool*
- Scissors tool (C)
- Free Transform tool (E)
  - *Rotate tool (R)*
  - *Scale tool (S)*
  - *Shear tool (O)*
- Gradient Swatch tool (G)
- Gradient Feather tool (Shift-G)
- Note tool
- Eyedropper tool (I)
  - *Measure tool (K)*
- Hand tool (H)
- Zoom tool (Z)

EXPLORE THE ARRANGEMENT OF INDESIGN PANELS

As you gain experience and familiarity with InDesign, you will develop personal artistic and working styles. You will also find that different types of InDesign jobs often require different but specific sets of tools. Adobe recognizes this wide range of needs and preferences among users; InDesign includes a number of options for arranging and managing the numerous panels so you can customize and personalize the workspace to suit your specific needs.

We designed the following exercise to give you an opportunity to explore different ways of controlling InDesign panels. Because workspace preferences are largely a matter of personal taste, the projects in this book instruct you to use certain tools and panels, but where you place those elements within the interface is up to you.

1. **With InDesign open, choose Window>Color>Color.**

   All panels can be toggled on and off from the Window menu.

   - If you choose a panel that's already open but iconized, the panel expands to the left of its icon.

   - If you choose a panel that's already open in an expanded group, that panel comes to the front of the group.

   - If you choose a panel that isn't currently open, it opens in the same place as it was when it was last closed.

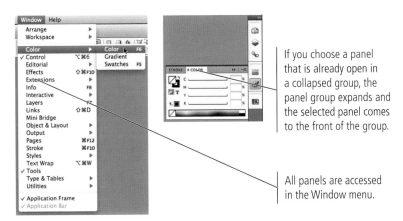

If you choose a panel that is already open in a collapsed group, the panel group expands and the selected panel comes to the front of the group.

All panels are accessed in the Window menu.

2. **Control/right-click the panel group drop zone (to the right of the panel tabs) and choose Close Tab Group from the contextual menu.**

   You can also Control/right-click a panel tab and choose Close to close only one panel in a group.

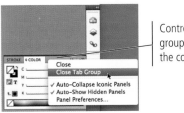

Control/right-click the panel group's drop zone to access the contextual menu.

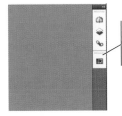

The closed panel group is removed from the panel dock.

Note:

You can click and drag a panel group's drop zone to float or move the entire group.

3. **Double-click the title bar of the panel dock to expand the dock column.**

4. Click the Links panel tab in the top panel group and drag away from the panel dock.

Panels can be **floated** by clicking a panel tab and dragging away from the dock.

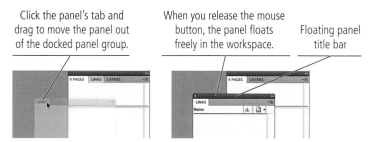

Click the panel's tab and drag to move the panel out of the docked panel group.

When you release the mouse button, the panel floats freely in the workspace.

Floating panel title bar

5. Click the Links panel tab and drag to the dock, between the Pages and Swatches panels. When you see a blue line between the existing docked panels, release the mouse button.

Panels and panel groups can be dragged to different locations (including into different groups) by dragging the panel's tab; the target location — where the panel will reside when you release the mouse button — is identified by the blue highlight.

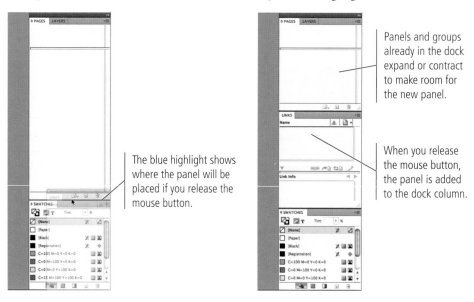

Panels and groups already in the dock expand or contract to make room for the new panel.

The blue highlight shows where the panel will be placed if you release the mouse button.

When you release the mouse button, the panel is added to the dock column.

6. Click the Layers panel tab and drag left until the blue highlight shows a second column added to the dock.

As we mentioned earlier, you can create multiple columns of panels in the dock. This can be very useful if you need easy access to a large number of panels and have a monitor with enough available screen space.

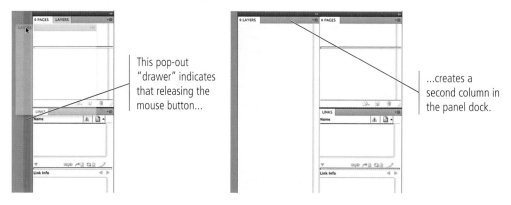

This pop-out "drawer" indicates that releasing the mouse button...

...creates a second column in the panel dock.

7. **Double-click the title bar of the left dock column to iconize that column.**

You can independently iconize or expand each column of docked panels and each floating panel (group).

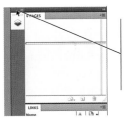

Double-click the title bar at the top of the dock column to collapse or expand it independently of other dock columns.

Note:

Each dock column, technically considered a separate dock, can be expanded or collapsed independently of other columns.

8. **Double-click the drop zone behind the Swatches panel tab to collapse the panel group.**

When a group is collapsed but not iconized, only the panel tabs are visible. Clicking a tab in a collapsed panel group expands the group and makes the selected panel active. You can also expand the group by again double-clicking the drop zone.

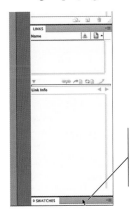

Double-click the panel group drop zone to collapse the group to show only the panel tabs.

Note:

Each column of the dock can be made wider or narrower by dragging the left edge of the column.

Dragging the left edge of a dock column changes the width of all panels in that column.

9. **In the right dock column, click the bottom edge of the Pages panel group and drag down until the Pages panel occupies approximately half of the vertical dock space.**

When you drag the bottom edge of a docked group, other panels in the same column expand or contract to fit the available space.

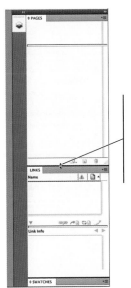

Dragging the bottom edge of a docked panel (or group) changes the height of that panel (or group). Other panels in the same column expand or shrink as necessary to fit the column.

Note:

Most screen shots in this book show floating panels so we can focus on the most important issue in a particular image. In our production workflow, however, we make heavy use of docked and iconized panels and take full advantage of saved custom workspaces.

10. **Continue to the next exercise.**

CREATE A SAVED WORKSPACE

By now you should understand that you have extensive control over the appearance of your InDesign workspace — what panels are visible, where and how they appear, and even the size of individual panels or panel groups.

Over time you will develop personal preferences — for example, the Colors panel always appears at the top — based on your work habits and project needs. Rather than re-establishing every workspace element each time you return to InDesign, you can save your custom workspace settings so you can recall them with a single click.

1. **Click the Workspace switcher in the Application/Menu bar and choose New Workspace.**

   Again, keep in mind that we list differing commands in the Macintosh/Windows format. On Macintosh, the Workspace switcher is in the Application bar; on Windows, it's in the Menu bar.

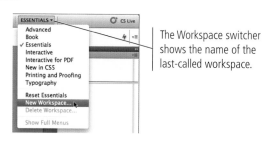

The Workspace switcher shows the name of the last-called workspace.

Note:

The Delete Workspace option opens a dialog box where you can choose a specific user-defined workspace to delete. You can't delete the default workspaces that come with the application.

2. **In the New Workspace dialog box, type** `Portfolio`. **Make sure the Panel Locations option is checked and click OK.**

   You didn't define custom menus, so that option is not relevant in this exercise.

After saving the current workspace, the Workspace switcher shows the name of the newly saved workspace.

Customizing InDesign Preferences

INDESIGN FOUNDATIONS

You can customize the way many of the program's tools and options function. On Macintosh, the Preferences dialog box is accessed in the InDesign menu. Windows users access the Preferences dialog box in the Edit menu.

The list of categories on the left side of the Preferences dialog box allows you to display the various sets of preferences available in InDesign. As you work your way through the projects in this book, you'll learn not only what you can do with these different collections of preferences, but also *why* and *when* you might want to use them.

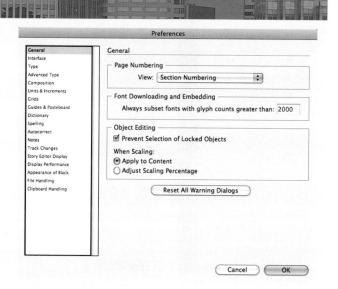

---

3. **Open the Window menu and choose Workspace>Essentials.**

Saved workspaces can be accessed in the Window>Workspace submenu as well as the Workspace switcher on the Application/Menu bar.

Options in this submenu are the same as those in the Workspace switcher.

Keyboard shortcuts (if available) are listed on the right side of the menu.

The checkmark indicates that an option is visible or toggled on.

If an option is grayed out, it is not available for the current selection.

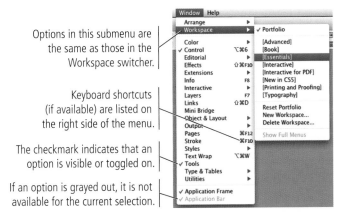

Calling a saved workspace restores the last-used state of the workspace. You made a number of changes since you launched InDesign with the default Essentials workspace, so calling the Essentials workspace restores the last state of that workspace — in essence, nothing changes from the saved Portfolio workspace.

The only apparent difference is the active workspace name.

Customizing Keyboard Shortcuts and Menus

People use InDesign for many different reasons, sometimes using only a specific, limited set of tools to complete a certain project. InDesign has built in several sophisticated options for customizing the user interface, including the ability to define the available menu options and the keyboard shortcuts associated with menu commands, panel menus, and tools.

At the bottom of the Edit menu, you can open the Keyboard Shortcuts and Menus dialog boxes to define custom sets. (If you don't see the Keyboard Shortcuts or Menus options in the Edit menu, choose Show All Menu Items to reveal the hidden commands.) Once you have defined custom shortcuts or menus, you can save your choices as a set so you can access the same choices again without having to redo the work.

Click here to access existing saved sets.

Use this menu to access different sets of commands.

Select a specific command here...

...view the associated keyboard shortcut here...

...and assign a new shortcut here.

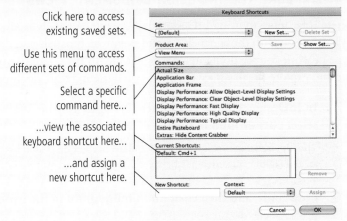

Click here to access existing saved sets.

Use this menu to access different sets of commands.

Click in this column to hide or show a specific menu command.

Click in this column to add a highlight color to the menu command.

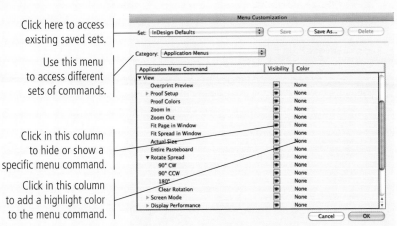

4. **Choose Window>Workspace>Reset Essentials (or click the Workspace switcher and choose Reset Essentials).**

Remember: calling a workspace again restores the panels exactly as they were the last time you used that workspace. For example, if you close a panel that is part of a saved workspace, the closed panel will not be reopened the next time you call the same workspace. To restore the saved state of the workspace, including opening closed panels or repositioning moved ones, you have to use the Reset option.

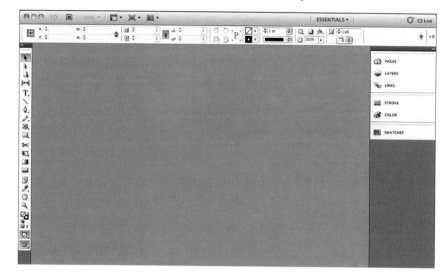

Note:

If you change anything and quit the application, those changes are remembered even when InDesign is relaunched.

5. **Continue to the next exercise.**

 ## EXPLORE THE INDESIGN DOCUMENT VIEWS

There is far more to using InDesign than arranging panels around the workspace. What you do with those panels — and even which panels you need — depends on the type of work you are doing in a particular file. In this exercise, you open an InDesign file and explore the interface elements you'll use to create documents.

Note:

Press Command/ Control-O to access the Open dialog box.

1. **In InDesign, choose File>Open. Navigate to your WIP>Interface folder and select career.indd in the list of available files.**

The Open dialog box is a system-standard navigation dialog box. This dialog box is one area of significant difference between Macintosh and Windows users.

2. **Press Shift, and then click knowledge.indd in the list of files.**

Pressing Shift allows you to select multiple contiguous (consecutive) files in the list.

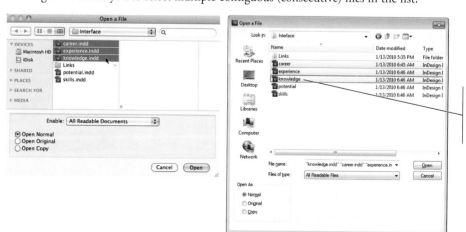

On Windows, the file extensions are not visible in the Open dialog box.

3. **Press Command/Control and click `potential.indd` and `skills.indd` to add those files to the active selection.**

One final reminder: we list differing commands in the Macintosh/Windows format. On Macintosh, you need to press the Command key; on Windows, press the Control key. (We will not repeat this explanation every time different commands are required for the different operating systems.)

Pressing Command/Control allows you to select and open non-contiguous files. (Depending on how files are sorted in your operating system, folders might be listed before other files — as shown in the Windows screen shot below. If that's the case on your system, you can press Shift or Control to select all five files.)

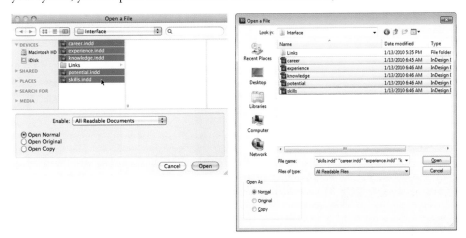

4. **Click Open to open all five selected files.**

InDesign files appear in a **document window**.

Each open document is represented by a separate tab.

The **document tabs** show the file name and current view percentage.

The active file tab is lighter than other tabs.

5. **Click the experience.indd tab to make that document active.**

6. Click the Zoom Level field in the Application/Menu bar and change the view percentage to 200.

Different people prefer larger or smaller view percentages, depending on a number of factors (eyesight, monitor size, and so on). As you complete the projects in this book, you'll see our screen shots zoom in or out as necessary to show you the most relevant part of a particular file. In most cases we do not tell you what specific view percentage to use for a particular exercise, unless it is specifically required for the work being done.

Note:

You can set the viewing percentage of an InDesign document to any value from 5% to 4000%.

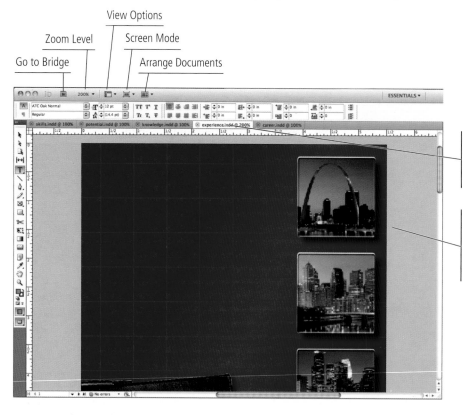

Go to Bridge

Zoom Level

View Options

Screen Mode

Arrange Documents

Click the tab to activate a specific file in the document window.

Changing the view percentage of the file does not affect the size of the document window.

7. Choose View>Fit Page in Window.

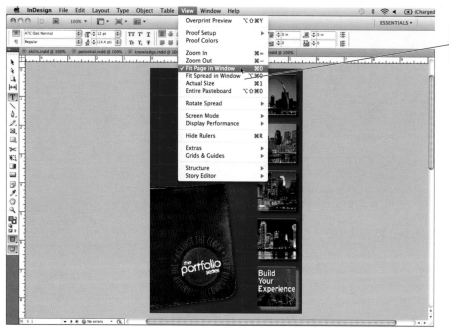

These six options affect the view percentage of a file.

Note:

Fit Page in Window automatically calculates view percentage based on the size of the document window.

Note:

Fit Spread in Window relates to documents that have left- and right-facing pages, such as a book. You build this kind of document in Project 4.

8. Click the Zoom tool in the Tools panel. Click in the document window and drag a marquee around the logo on the portfolio.

Dragging a marquee with the Zoom tool enlarges the selected area to fill the document window.

Note:

All open files are listed at the bottom of the Window menu.

Zoom tool cursor

The area of the marquee enlarges to fill the document window.

9. With the Zoom tool selected, Option/Alt-click in the document window.

Clicking with the Zoom tool enlarges the view percentage in specific, predefined steps. Pressing Option/Alt while clicking with the Zoom tool reduces the view percentage in the reverse sequence of the same percentages.

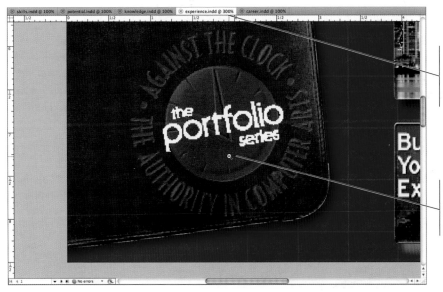

Option/Alt-clicking with the Zoom tool reduces the view percentage in the predefined sequence of percentages.

With the Zoom tool active, pressing Option/Alt changes the cursor to the Zoom Out icon.

10. Click the Hand tool near the bottom of the Tools panel.

11. Click in the document window, hold down the mouse button, and drag around.

The Hand tool is a very easy and convenient option for changing the visible area of an image in the document window.

Hand tool cursor

Note:

Press the Z key to access the Zoom tool.

Press the H key to access the Hand tool.

12. Choose View>Display Performance>High Quality Display.

You might have noticed that the images in this file look very bad (they are badly bitmapped). This is even more evident when you zoom in to a high view percentage. By default, InDesign displays a low-resolution preview of placed images to save time when the screen redraws (i.e., every time you change something). Fortunately, however, you have the option to preview the full-resolution images placed in a file.

Note:

The Fast Display option replaces all placed images with a solid medium gray (in other words, no preview image displays).

Using the High Quality Display, images do not show the bitmapping of the default low-resolution previews.

13. **Using the Selection tool, click the bottom-right image (the one with the text) to select it. Control/right-click the selected image and choose Display Performance>Typical Display from the contextual menu.**

In the View menu, the Allow Object-Level Display Settings option is active by default (see the image in the prevous step); this means you can change the display of individual objects on the page.

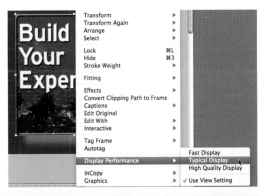

High-Quality Display is especially evident where sharp lines exist.

Typical Display uses a low-resolution preview of placed images.

14. **Choose View>Fit Page in Window to see the entire page.**

15. **Double-click the title bar above the docked panels to expand the panels.**

16. **In the Pages panel, double-click the Page 2 icon to show that page in the document window.**

The Pages panel is the easiest way to move from one page to another in a multi-page document. You will use this panel extensively as you complete the projects in this book.

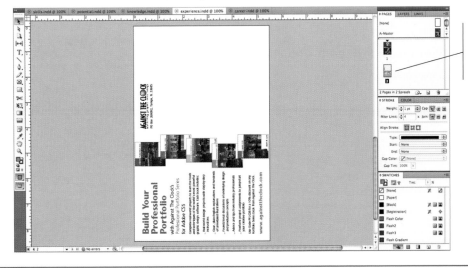

Double-click a page icon to display that page in the document window.

17. Control/right-click the Page 2 icon in the Pages panel and choose Rotate Spread View>90° CW from the contextual menu.

Rotating the view only changes the display of the page; the actual page remains unchanged in the file. This option allows you to work more easily on objects or pages that are oriented differently than the overall document. In this example, the front side of the postcard has portrait orientation, but the mailer side has landscape orientation.

Note:

You can also rotate page views using the options in the View>Rotate Spread menu.

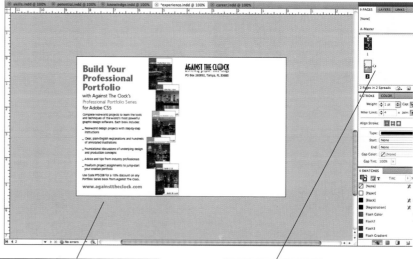

The rotated display makes it easier to work on pages with orientations different from the document definition.

Pages with a rotated view are identified in the Pages panel.

18. Continue to the next exercise.

Summing up the InDesign View Options

INDESIGN FOUNDATIONS

Most InDesign projects require some amount of zooming in and out to various view percentages, as well as navigating around the document within its window. As we show you how to complete various stages of the workflow, we usually won't tell you when to change your view percentage because that's largely a matter of personal preference. But you should understand the different options for navigating an InDesign file so you can easily and efficiently get to what you want.

View Menu

The View menu provides options for changing the view percentage. You should also become familiar with the keyboard shortcuts for these commands:

Zoom In	Command/Control-equals (=)
Zoom Out	Command/Control-minus (-)
Fit Page in Window	Command/Control-0 (zero)
Fit Spread in Window	Command-Option-0/Control-Alt-0
Actual Size (100%)	Command/Control-1
Entire Pasteboard	Command-Option-Shift-0/ Control-Alt-Shift-0

Zoom Level Field/Menu

You can use the Zoom Level field in the Application/Menu bar to type a specific view percentage, or you can use the attached menu to choose from the predefined view percentage steps.

Zoom Tool

You can click with the **Zoom tool** to increase the view percentage in specific, predefined intervals (the same intervals you see in the View Percentage menu in the bottom-left corner of the document window). Pressing Option/Alt with the Zoom tool allows you to zoom out in the same predefined percentages. If you drag a marquee with the Zoom tool, you can zoom into a specific location; the area surrounded by the marquee fills the available space in the document window.

Hand Tool

Whatever your view percentage, you can use the **Hand tool** to drag the file around in the document window, including scrolling from one page to another. The Hand tool only changes what is visible in the window; it has no effect on the actual content of the file.

EXPLORE THE ARRANGEMENT OF MULTIPLE DOCUMENTS

In many cases, you will need to work with more than one layout at the same time. InDesign CS5 incorporates a number of options for arranging multiple documents. We designed the following simple exercise so you can explore these options.

1. **With experience.indd active, choose Window>Arrange>Float in Window.**

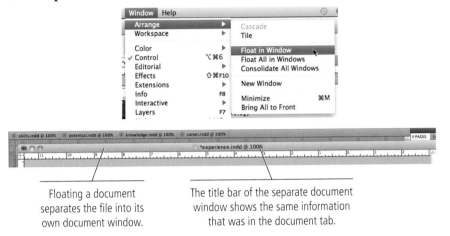

Floating a document separates the file into its own document window.

The title bar of the separate document window shows the same information that was in the document tab.

Note:

When multiple document windows are open, two options in the Window>Arrange menu allow you to cascade or tile the document windows. You can separate all open files by choosing Window>Arrange>Float All in Windows.

2. **In the Application/Menu bar, click the Arrange Documents button to open the panel of defined arrangements.**

3. **Click the 2 Up button in the Arrange Documents panel.**

The defined arrangements provide a number of options for tiling multiple open files within the available workspace; these arrangements manage all open files, including those in floating windows.

The Consolidate All button (top left) restores all floating documents into a single tabbed document window. The remaining buttons in the top row separate all open files into separate document windows and then arrange the different windows as indicated.

The lower options use a specific number of floating documents (2-Up, 3-Up, etc.); if more files are open than an option indicates, the extra files are consolidated as tabs in the first document window.

Note:

On a Macintosh, the Application bar must be visible to access the Arrange Documents button.

The Arrange Documents panel includes a number of tiling options for arranging multiple open files in the workspace.

The appearance of each icon suggests the result of that option.

Rolling your mouse cursor over an icon shows the arrangement name in a tool tip.

The 2-Up arrangement divides the document window in half, as indicated by the button icon.

Extra documents remain as tabs in the left document window.

4. **Click the experience.indd document tab and drag left until a blue highlight appears around the document tabs in the other panel.**

When you release the mouse button, all of the open files are again part of the same document window.

5. **Using the Pages panel, navigate to Page 1 of the file. Choose View>Fit Page in Window to show the entire page.**

The files you explored in this project were saved in Preview screen mode, which surrounds the page with a neutral gray background. Page guides, frame edges, and other non-printing areas are not visible in the Preview mode.

6. **Click the Screen Mode button in the Application/Menu bar and choose Bleed.**

The Bleed screen mode is an extension of the Preview mode; it shows an extra area (which was defined when the document was originally set up) around the page edge. This bleed area is a required part of print document design — objects that are supposed to print right up to the edge of the page must extend past the page edge, usually 1/8″ or more. (Bleed requirements and setup are explained in Project 1.)

Page edge

In Bleed mode, you can see a defined amount of space around the page edge.

7. **Click the Screen Mode button at the bottom of the Tools panel and choose Normal from the pop-up menu.**

   This menu has the same options as the button in the Application/Menu bar. As you will learn throughout this book, there is almost always more than one way to accomplish a same goal in InDesign.

   In Normal mode, you can see all non-printing elements, including guides and frame edges (if those are toggled on). You can now also see the white pasteboard surrounding the defined page area; your development work is not limited by the defined page size.

   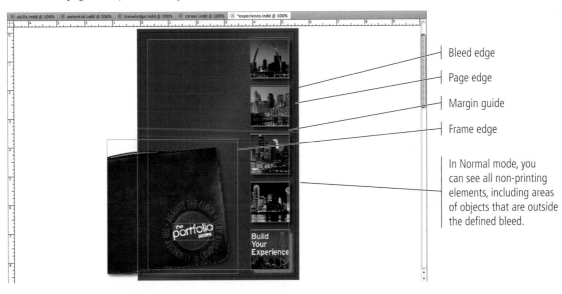

   Bleed edge

   Page edge

   Margin guide

   Frame edge

   In Normal mode, you can see all non-printing elements, including areas of objects that are outside the defined bleed.

8. **Using either Screen Mode button, choose the Presentation mode.**

   Presentation mode fills the entire screen with the active spread. By default, the area around the page is solid black; you can press W to change the surround to white or press G to change it to neutral gray. In Presentation mode, clicking anywhere on the screen shows the next spread; Shift-clicking shows the previous spread.

   In Presentation mode, the page, surrounded by solid black, fills the entire screen.

9. **Press ESC to exit Presentation mode.**

10. **Click the Close button on the active document tab.**

When multiple files are open, clicking the close button on a document tab closes only that file.

11. **Click Don't Save when asked if you want to save changes to experience.indd.**

By rotating the spread view on Page 2, the file has technically been changed. InDesign automatically asks if you want to save any file that has been changed before closing it.

12. **Macintosh users: Click the Close button in the top-left corner of the Application frame.**

Closing the Macintosh Application frame does not quit the application.

On Macintosh, closing the Application frame closes all files open in that frame.

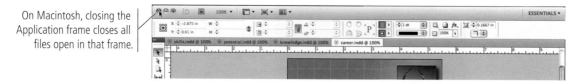

Windows users: Click the Close button on each open document tab to close the remaining files.

Clicking the Close button on the Windows Application frame (Menu bar) closes all open files *and* quits the application. To close open files *without* quitting, you have to manually close each open file.

Clicking the Close button on a document tab closes that particular file.

Clicking the Menu bar Close button closes all open files, and also quits the application.

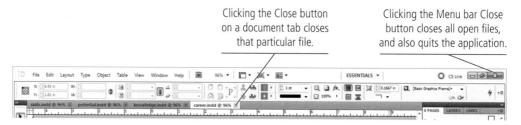

Letterhead Design

Your client, Amelia Crowe, is a local photographer. She hired you to create a letterhead design that incorporates her personal logo and a set of images representing the kind of work she does. She is going to have the letterhead printed commercially so she can use it to print letters, invoices, and other business correspondence.

This project incorporates the following skills:

❏ Creating a new file to meet defined project requirements

❏ Using the basic InDesign drawing tools to develop visual interest

❏ Selecting objects and object contents

❏ Creating and formatting basic text attributes

❏ Placing and manipulating external graphics files

❏ Printing a desktop proof sample

Project Meeting

client comments

Until now, I've just added my logo and address at the top of a Word document whenever I sent out correspondence. My business has been growing lately, and I want something more professional and more indicative of my work in photographing urban architecture and natural landscapes.

I sent you my logo, which was created in Adobe Illustrator. I also selected a bunch of images that I really like; I want to include at least a few of those on the letterhead to give people an idea of my work.

Can you get my contact information from my email sig file, or do I need to send that to you as a separate document?

art director comments

I've looked over the client's images, and I think we should use all of them. Since she's a photographer, a filmstrip across the bottom of the page will make a nice container; InDesign has everything you need to create the necessary graphics directly on the page layout. I already sized the photos down to thumbnails that should be close to the right size, so you won't have to manipulate the actual image files.

I also copied the client's contact info into a file for you. Since she specifically mentioned two areas of photographic specialty, I want you to include the words "urban architecture & natural landscapes" as a tag line.

It might feel like there's a lot involved in creating this piece, but it's not too complicated; and the client liked the initial sketch, so it will be worth it.

project objectives

To complete this project, you will:

- ❏ Create a new document based on the requirements of a commercial printer.
- ❏ Place ruler guides to define "safe" areas of the page.
- ❏ Draw basic shapes using native InDesign tools
- ❏ Edit shapes using the Pathfinder and Align panels
- ❏ Work with anchor points and handles to create a complex shape
- ❏ Apply color to fills and strokes
- ❏ Create and format basic text elements
- ❏ Import external text and graphics files
- ❏ Print a desktop proof

Stage 1 **Setting up the Workspace**

The best way to start any new project is to prepare your workspace. As you learned in the Interface chapter, InDesign gives you extensive control over your workspace — you can choose where to place panels, whether to collapse or expand open panels, and even to save workspaces with sets of panels in specific locations. Because workspace issues are largely a matter a personal preference, we tell you what tools to use but we don't tell you where to keep the various panels. Many of our screen captures show floating panels so we can maximize the available space and clearly focus on a specific issue. Likewise, we typically don't tell you what view percentage to use; you should use whatever you are comfortable with to accomplish the specific goal of an exercise.

DEFINE A NEW LAYOUT FILE

Some production-related concerns will dictate how you design a letterhead. In general, there are two ways to print letterhead: one-offs on a desktop laser or inkjet printer, or commercially in large quantities. (The first method typically involves creating a letterhead template, which you then use to write and print letters from directly within InDesign — a fairly common practice among graphic designers.)

If letterhead is being printed commercially, it's probably being printed with multiple copies on a large press sheet, from which the individual letterhead sheets will be cut. Most commercial printing happens this way. This type of printing typically means that design elements can run right off the edge of the sheet, called **bleeding**.

If you're designing for a printer that can only run letter-size paper, you have to allow enough of a margin area for your printer to hold the paper as it moves through the device (called the **gripper margin**); in this case, you can't design with bleeds.

The most basic process in designing a layout is creating a new InDesign file. The New Document dialog box has a large number of options, and the following exercise explains all of those. Don't be overwhelmed by the length of this process; in later projects, we simply tell you what settings to define without re-explaining every field.

Note:

Older desktop printers typically have a minimum margin at the page edges; you're usually safe with 3/8". Many newer inkjet printers have the capability to print 8.5 × 11" with full bleed. Consult your printer documentation to be sure.

1. **Download ID5_RF_Project1.zip from the Student Files web page.**

2. **Expand the ZIP archive in your WIP folder (Macintosh) or copy the archive contents into your WIP folder (Windows).**

   This results in a folder named **Crowe**, which contains all of the files you need for this project. You should also use this folder to save the files you create in this project.

   If necessary, refer to Page 1 of the Interface chapter for specific information on expanding or accessing the required resource files.

3. **In InDesign, choose File>New>Document.**

   The New Document dialog box always defaults to the last-used document preset; if no presets exist, the dialog box opens with the settings that are stored in the Default preset. Some of the options we define in the following steps might already be reflected in the dialog box, but we can't be sure because someone might have modified the default settings on your computer. If something is already set to the value we define, simply leave that value as is.

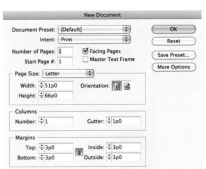

Note:

You can create a new file by pressing Command/Control-N.

4. Choose Print in the Intent menu.

InDesign uses picas as the default unit of measurement for print documents; measurements in this dialog box are shown in picas and points, using the "ApB" notation (for A picas and B points). Colors in a print-intent document default to the CMYK color model (see Page 56 in this project).

If you choose Web, InDesign changes the default unit of measurement to pixels, which is more appropriate for Web design. Colors in a Web-intent document default to the RGB color model.

5. Set the Number of Pages field to 1.

A letterhead is a single page, usually printed on only one side. A one-sided, one-page document needs only a single layout page in the InDesign file.

6. Set the Start Page # field to 1.

This option is useful when you work with multi-page files. Odd-numbered pages always appear on the right, as you see in any book or magazine; you can define an even-numbered starting page number to force the first page of a layout to the left. (This will make more sense when you begin working with longer documents in Project 4.)

7. Uncheck the Facing Pages check box.

Facing pages are used when a printed job will be read left to right like a book — with Page 1 starting on the right, then Page 2 facing Page 3, and so on. Facing-page layouts are based on **spreads**, which are pairs of left-right pages as you flip through a book (e.g., Page 6 facing Page 7).

8. Uncheck the Master Text Frame option.

When this option is checked, InDesign creates a text frame that automatically fills the area created by the defined page margins. A letterhead design primarily focuses on the area outside of the margins, so you don't need to add a master text frame to this file.

9. Choose Letter in the Page Size menu.

This menu includes a number of common sizes based on the selected intent. Choosing any of these options automatically changes the width and height fields to match the selected size.

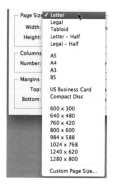

Note:

Picas are the measuring units traditionally used in typography; they are still used by many people in the graphic communications industry.

1 point = 1/72 inch

12 points = 1 pica

1 pica = 1/6 inch

6 picas = 1 inch

Note:

You work extensively with facing pages starting in Project 4.

Note:

Choosing Custom in the Page Size menu has no real effect. This setting is automatically reflected as soon as you change the Width or Height field from the standard measurements.

10. Choose the Portrait Orientation option.

Portrait documents are higher than they are wide; **landscape** documents are wider than they are high. If you click the orientation option that is not currently selected, the Width and Height values are automatically reversed.

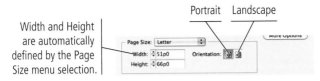

Width and Height are automatically defined by the Page Size menu selection.

Portrait Landscape

11. If the chain icon between the Margin fields shows two connected links, click the icon to break the link between the fields.

When the chain icon is active (connected links or highlighted dark gray), all four margin fields will be the same; changing one field changes all margin values to the same value. For this project, you need to define different values for the top and bottom than for the left and right, so you need to unlink (unconstrain) the margin fields if they are currently linked.

12. Highlight the first Margins field (Top) and type 1.25″.

Even though the default measurement is picas, you can type values in any unit as long as you type the appropriate unit along with the value; InDesign makes the necessary conversion for you so the values will still bedisplayed in the default units.

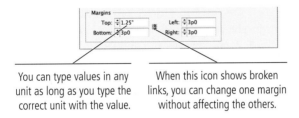

You can type values in any unit as long as you type the correct unit with the value.

When this icon shows broken links, you can change one margin without affecting the others.

13. Press Tab to move to the Bottom field.

When you move to the next field, InDesign converts the Top value to the default unit of measurement (picas).

14. Change the Bottom field to 2″, then press Tab two times.

The first time you press Tab from the Bottom field highlights the chain icon. You have to press Tab a second time to highlight the Left field.

15. Change the Left field to 1″, then press Tab.

16. Change the Right field to 1″.

17. Click the More Options button to show the Bleed and Slug fields.

If this button reads "Fewer Options", the Bleed and Slug fields are already showing.

Note:

When you work with non-facing pages, the Inside and Outside margin fields change to Left and Right respectively. Technically, non-facing pages do not have an inside (spine edge) or outside (face or trim edge), so there are only left and right sides.

Note:

If you enter a value in a unit other than the default, you have to include the alternate unit. This technique works in dialog boxes and panels — anywhere that you can enter a measurement.

Note:

You can tab through the fields of most dialog boxes and panels in InDesign. Press Shift-Tab to move the highlight to the previous field in the tab order.

18. Make sure the chain icon to the right of the Bleed fields is active (unbroken links), then change the first Bleed field to 0.125″ (the decimal equivalent of 1/8). Press Tab to apply the new Bleed value to all four sides.

The letterhead for this project will be printed commercially; the printer said the design can safely bleed on all four sides, and their equipment requires a 1/8″ bleed allowance. In this case, you want all four edges to have the same bleed, so the chain icon should be active to constrain all four Bleed fields to the same value.

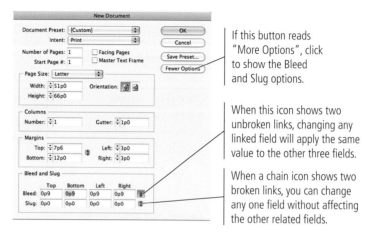

If this button reads "More Options", click to show the Bleed and Slug options.

When this icon shows two unbroken links, changing any linked field will apply the same value to the other three fields.

When a chain icon shows two broken links, you can change any one field without affecting the other related fields.

19. Make sure the chain icon to the right of the Slug fields is active, and then change the first Slug field to 0.

A **slug** is an area outside of the bleed, where designers typically add job information that will not appear in the final printed piece. (You'll use this slug area in Project 4.)

You don't need to type the full "0p0" notation when you change measurements using the default units. Zero pica is still zero, so you don't need to worry about converting units.

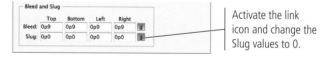

Activate the link icon and change the Slug values to 0.

20. Click OK to create the new document.

The document appears, filling the available space in the document window. Your view percentage might appear different than what you see in our images.

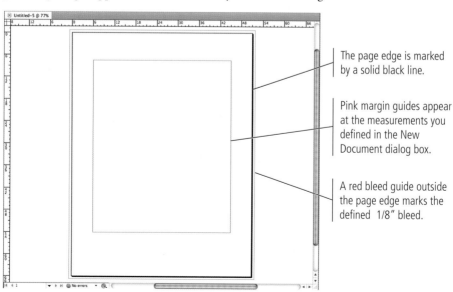

The page edge is marked by a solid black line.

Pink margin guides appear at the measurements you defined in the New Document dialog box.

A red bleed guide outside the page edge marks the defined 1/8″ bleed.

Note:

*A **slug** is an element entirely outside the page area, but included in the final output. The slug area can be used for file/plate information, special registration marks, color bars, and/or other elements that need to be printed on the press sheet, but do not appear within the job area.*

21. **Choose File>Save As. In the Save As dialog box, navigate to your WIP>Crowe folder as the target location for saving the file.**

The Save As dialog box follows a system-standard format. Macintosh and Windows users see slightly different options, but the basic InDesign functionality is the same.

22. **Change the file name (in the Save As field) to identity.indd and click Save.**

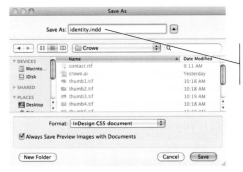

The extension ".indd" is automatically added to the file name.

Note:

The first time you save a file, the Save command opens the same dialog box as the File>Save As command. After saving the file once, you can use Save to save changes to the existing file, or use Save As to create an additional file under a new file name.

23. **Continue to the next exercise.**

Understanding Document Presets

INDESIGN FOUNDATIONS

A **preset** stores groups of common settings; you define a preset once, and then you can access the same group of settings later with a single click. You'll often use this concept while building InDesign documents — when you use text style, table styles, object styles, and output documents for printing.

If you frequently define the same document settings, you can save those choices as a preset so you can create the same document settings with minimal repetition. Clicking the Save Preset button in the New Document dialog box opens a secondary dialog box where you can name the preset. When you return to the New Document dialog box, your new preset appears as the selection in the Document Preset menu. Any time you need to create a file with the same settings, you can choose the saved preset from this menu.

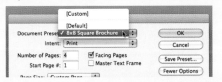

You can access and manage document presets in the File menu. If you choose one of the existing presets in the menu, the New Document dialog box opens, defaulting to the values in the preset that you called (instead of defaulting to the application-default letter-size page). All the settings you saved in the preset automatically reflect in the dialog box. You can also create, edit, and manage presets by choosing Define in the Document Presets submenu; this opens a dialog box that lists the existing presets.

- Click New to open the New Document Preset dialog box, which is basically the same as the New Document dialog box, except the Preset menu is replaced with a field where you can type the preset name instead of clicking the Save Preset button.
- Select a preset and click Edit to change the preset's associated options.
- Select a preset and click Delete to remove the preset from the application.
- Click Load to import presets created on another computer.
- Click Save to save a preset (with the extension ".dcst") so it can be sent to and used on another computer.

CREATE RULER GUIDES

In addition to the margin and bleed guides that you defined when you created the document, you can also place ruler guides to mark whatever other positions you need to identify in your layout.

The **live area** is the "safe" area inside the page edge, where important design elements should reside. Because printing and trimming are mechanical processes, there will always be some variation — however slight. Elements placed too close to the page edge run the risk of being accidentally trimmed off. The printer for this job recommended a 1/8″ live-area margin. You defined the margins for this file to describe the area that would typically occupy the content of a letter; in this exercise you will create ruler guides to mark the live area.

1. **With identity.indd open, choose View>Show Rulers if you don't see rulers at the top and left edges of the document window.**

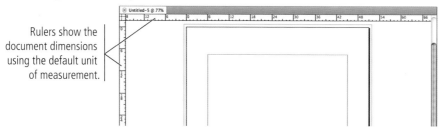

Rulers show the document dimensions using the default unit of measurement.

Note:

You should become familiar with the common fraction-to-decimal equivalents:

1/8 = 0.125

1/4 = 0.25

3/8 = 0.375

1/2 = 0.5

5/8 = 0.625

3/4 = 0.75

7/8 = 0.875

2. **Open the Units & Increments pane of the Preferences dialog box (from the InDesign menu on Macintosh or the Edit menu on Windows).**

   Since most people (in the United States, at least) think in terms of inches, we use inches throughout the projects in this book.

3. **In the Ruler Units area, choose Inches in both the Horizontal and Vertical menus, and then click OK.**

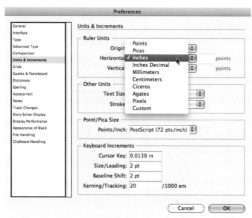

When you return to the document window, the rulers now display in inches.

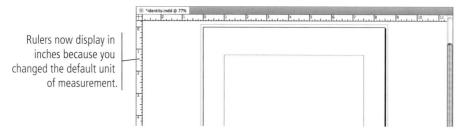

Rulers now display in inches because you changed the default unit of measurement.

4. **Click the horizontal page ruler (at the top of the document window) and drag down until the cursor feedback indicates that the guide is positioned at Y: 0.125″. With the cursor inside the page area, release the mouse button.**

As you drag, cursor feedback shows the current position of the guide you are placing; this makes it very easy to precisely position guides.

Note:

Y values define vertical (top-to-bottom) position; X values define horizontal (left-to-right) position.

Click and drag from the horizontal ruler to add a horizontal guide.

The Control panel, ruler, and cursor feedback all show the location of the guide you're dragging.

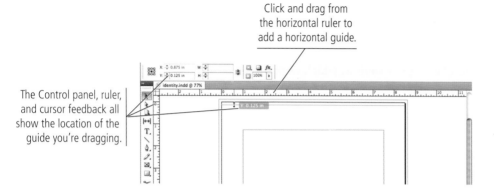

5. **Click the horizontal page ruler again and drag a guide to Y: 10.875″.**

Note:

If you drag a guide outside of the page edge, the guide will extend across the entire pasteboard. You can also press Command/Control while dragging a guide onto the page to extend the guide the entire width of the pasteboard.

6. **Click the vertical ruler and drag a guide to X: 0.125″.**

Watch the marker on the horizontal ruler to judge the guide's position.

Note:

If the Control panel is not visible, you can show it by choosing Window>Control.

Drag from the vertical ruler to add a vertical guide.

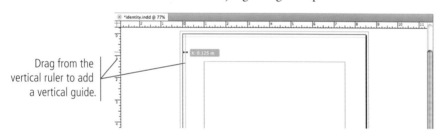

7. **Click the vertical ruler again and drag a second vertical guide to X: 8.375″.**

Note:

You can click the intersection of the rulers and drag to reposition the zero point away from the top-left corner of the page. If you do reposition the zero point, you can double-click the ruler intersection to reset the original zero point.

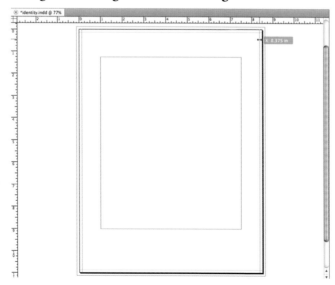

8. **Save the file and continue to the next stage of the project.**

Stage 2 Creating Basic Page Elements

Based on the approved sketch, the client's letterhead includes several elements:

- A "filmstrip" graphic to frame a number of thumbnails of the client's work

- A logo that was created in Adobe Illustrator

- A tag line, separated from the logo with a curved line

- Contact information, which was provided to you as a rich-text file

- Actual thumbnails of the client's photographs, which were supplied to you as ready-to-print TIFF files.

Other than the logo and the supplied photos, you need to create these elements directly in the InDesign file. Fortunately, the software includes sophisticated drawing tools that can create everything you need. Before you begin, however, you should understand the different types of elements that you will encounter when you design files in InDesign.

Vector graphics are composed of mathematical descriptions of a series of lines and shapes. Vector graphics are resolution independent; they can be freely scaled, and they are automatically output at the resolution of the output device. The shapes that you create in Adobe InDesign, or in drawing applications such as Adobe Illustrator, are vector graphics.

Raster images, such as photographs or files created in Adobe Photoshop, are made up of a grid of independent pixels (rasters or bits) in rows and columns (called a bitmap). Raster files are resolution dependent — their resolution is determined when you scan, photograph, or otherwise create the file. You can typically reduce raster images, but you cannot enlarge them without losing image quality.

Line art is a type of raster image that is made up entirely of 100% solid areas; the pixels in a line-art image have only two options: they can be all black or all white. Examples of line art are UPC bar codes or pen-and-ink drawings.

CREATE BASIC FRAMES

Although much drawing and illustration work is done in a dedicated illustration program such as Adobe Illustrator, you can use the drawing tools in InDesign to create vector artwork. In fact, the drawing tools in InDesign are actually a limited subset of the more comprehensive Illustrator toolset, which means you can create fairly sophisticated artwork entirely within the layout application. In this exercise, you are going to use the basic InDesign drawing tools to create a filmstrip graphic, which will serve as the background for the client's image samples.

1. **With identity.indd open, choose View>Grids & Guides>Smart Guides to make sure this option is toggled on. If the option is already checked, move the cursor away from the menu and click to dismiss it.**

   Smart guides are a useful function of the application, making it easy to create and precisely align objects. Smart guides show the dimensions of an object when you create it; the position of an object when you drag it; the edge and center position of nearby objects; and the distance between nearby similar objects.

   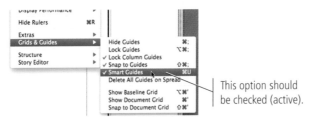

   This option should be checked (active).

Note:

You can turn off specific Smart Guide functions in the Guides & Pasteboard pane of the Preferences dialog box.

Raster image quality depends directly on the file's resolution; when you work with raster image files, you need to understand the resolution requirements from the very beginning of the process:

- **Pixels per inch (ppi)** is the number of pixels in one horizontal or vertical inch of a digital raster file.

- **Lines per inch (lpi)** is the number of halftone dots produced in a horizontal or vertical linear inch by a high-resolution imagesetter in order to simulate the appearance of continuous-tone color.

- **Dots per inch (dpi)** or **spots per inch (spi)** is the number of dots produced by an output device in a single line of output. Dpi is sometimes used interchangeably (although incorrectly) with pixels per inch.

When reproducing a photograph on a printing press, the image must be converted into a set of different-size dots that fool the eye into believing it sees continuous tones. The result of this conversion process is a halftone image; the dots used to simulate continuous tone are called **halftone dots**. Light tones in a photograph are represented as small halftone dots; dark tones are represented as large halftone dots. Prior to image-editing software, photos were converted to halftones with a large graphic-arts camera and screens. The picture was photographed through the screen to create halftone dots, and different screens produced different numbers of dots in an inch (hence the term "dots per inch").

Image Resolution

When a printer creates halftone dots, it calculates the average value of a group of pixels and generates a spot of appropriate size. An image's resolution controls the quantity of pixel data that the printer can read. Regardless of the source — camera, scanner, or files create from scratch in a program such as Photoshop — images need to have sufficient resolution for the output device to generate enough halftone dots to create the appearance of continuous tone.

Ideally, the printer has four pixels for each halftone dot created. The relationship between pixels and halftone dots defines the rule of resolution for all raster-based images — the resolution of an image should be two times the screen ruling (lpi) that will be used for printing.

Screen Ruling

The screens used with old graphic-arts cameras had a finite number of available dots in a horizontal or vertical inch. That number was the **screen ruling**, or lines per inch of the halftone. A screen ruling of 133 lpi means that in a square inch there are 133×133 (17,689) possible locations for a halftone dot. If the screen ruling is decreased, there are fewer total halftone dots, producing a grainier image; if the screen ruling is increased, there are more halftone dots, producing a clearer image.

Line screen is a finite number based on a combination of the intended output device and paper. You can't randomly select a line screen. Ask your printer what line screen will be used before you begin creating your images. If you can't find out ahead of time or are unsure, follow these general guidelines:

- Newspaper or newsprint: 85–100 lpi

- Magazine or general commercial printing: 133–150 lpi

- Premium-quality-paper jobs (such as art books): 150–175 lpi (some specialty jobs use 200 lpi or more)

If you find this information a bit confusing, don't worry. As a general rule for preparing commercial print layouts, most raster images should have twice the pixel resolution (at 100% size) as the line screen that will be used.

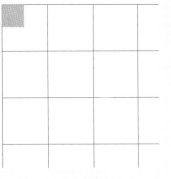
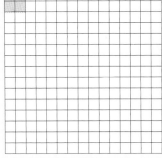

72 ppi   300 ppi

Each white square represents a pixel. The highlighted area shows the pixel information used to generate a halftone dot. If an image only has 72 pixels per inch, the output device has to generate four halftone dots per pixel, resulting in poor printed quality.

The same raster image is reproduced here at 300 ppi (left) and 72 ppi (right). Notice the obvious degradation in quality when the resolution is set to 72 ppi.

2. **Click the button at the right end of the Control panel to open the panel Options menu.**

3. **If the Dimensions Include Stroke Weight option is checked, choose that item to toggle the option off.**

When this option is active, the size of an object's stroke is factored as part of the overall object size. Consider, for example, a frame that is 72 points wide by 72 points high with a 1-point stroke. If you remove the stroke from the frame, the frame would then be only 70 points by 70 points.

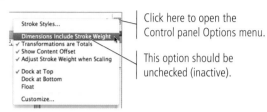

Click here to open the Control panel Options menu.

This option should be unchecked (inactive).

Note:

This option remembers the last-used setting. In many cases, you actually want the stroke weight to scale proportionally, so make sure you confirm the setting of this option if something looks wrong.

4. **Choose the Rectangle tool in the Tools panel.**

If you don't see the Rectangle tool, click and hold the default shape tool until the nested tools appear; slide over and down to select the Rectangle tool.

Note:

Tools with nested options default to show the last-used variation in the main Tools panel.

5. **Click the Default Fill and Stroke button at the bottom of the Tools panel.**

In InDesign, the default fill is None, and the default stroke is 1-pt black.

6. **Click anywhere on the page, and drag down and right to draw a rectangle that is about 1″ high and 2″ wide.**

As you draw, cursor feedback shows the size of the shape you are creating.

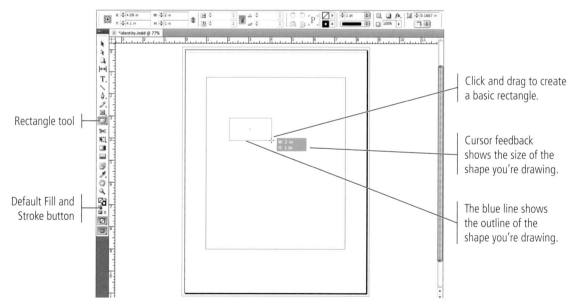

Rectangle tool

Default Fill and Stroke button

Click and drag to create a basic rectangle.

Cursor feedback shows the size of the shape you're drawing.

The blue line shows the outline of the shape you're drawing.

7. Release the mouse button to create the rectangle.

Every shape you create in an InDesign document has a **bounding box**, which is a non-printing rectangle that marks the outer dimensions of the shape. (Even a circle has a square bounding box, marking the largest height and width of the object.) The bounding box has eight handles, which you can drag to change the size of the rectangle. If you can see an object's bounding box handles, that object is selected.

Note:

Press Shift while drawing a frame to constrain the horizontal and vertical dimensions of the shape (in other words, to create a perfect square or circle).

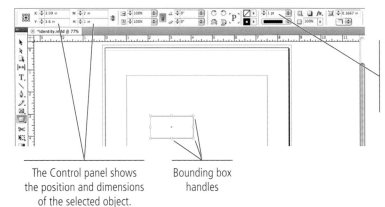

The shape has a 1-pt black stroke because you recalled the default fill and stroke values before creating the shape.

The Control panel shows the position and dimensions of the selected object.

Bounding box handles

8. At the bottom of the Tools panel, click the Swap Fill and Stroke button.

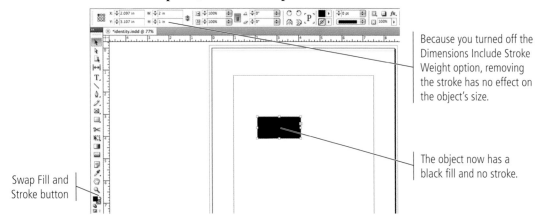

Because you turned off the Dimensions Include Stroke Weight option, removing the stroke has no effect on the object's size.

The object now has a black fill and no stroke.

Swap Fill and Stroke button

9. At the left end of the Control panel, select the top-left reference point.

The Control panel is context-sensitive, which means different options are available depending on what is selected in the document. This panel consolidates the most common options from multiple InDesign panels.

The **reference point** determines how transformations will occur (in other words, which point of the object will remain in place if you change one of the position or dimension values). These points correspond to the object's bounding box handles, as well as to the object's exact center point.

Constrain object width and height   Constrain object scale

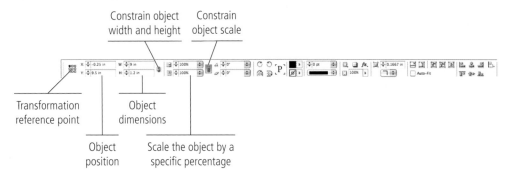

Transformation reference point

Object dimensions

Object position

Scale the object by a specific percentage

The Control panel is one of the most versatile, productive tools in the InDesign workspace, combining all of the most common formatting options into a single, compact format across the top of the workspace. It is context sensitive, which means different options are available depending on what is selected in the layout. Finally, it is customizable, which means you can change the options that are available in the panel.

It is also important to note that the options available in the Control panel might be limited by the active workspace, as well as by the width of your monitor or Application frame.

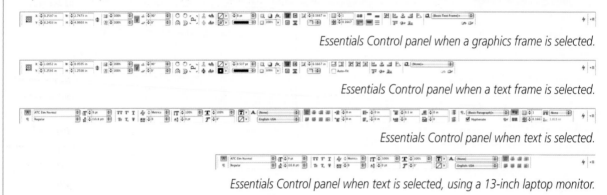

Essentials Control panel when a graphics frame is selected.

Essentials Control panel when a text frame is selected.

Essentials Control panel when text is selected.

Essentials Control panel when text is selected, using a 13-inch laptop monitor.

The panel Options menu includes options for controlling the position of the panel (top, bottom, or floating), as well as how transformations affect selected objects:

Quick Apply button

Click here to open the panel Options menu.

- **Stroke Styles.** This opens a dialog box where you can edit or define custom styles for lines and object strokes.

- **Clear Transformations.** Choosing this option resets an object to its original position (including rotation).

- **Dimensions Include Stroke Weight.** When checked, width and height values include the object width as well as the defined stroke width. For example, if this option is checked, a square that is 72 points wide with a 1-pt stroke would be 73 points wide (using the default stroke position that aligns the stroke on the center of the object edge).

- **Transformations are Totals.** When checked, transformations to an object's contents reflect the object's transformations plus transformations applied to the content within the frame. For example, if an object is rotated 10°, and the graphic within the object is rotated 5°, the object's rotation displays as 15° when this option is checked.

- **Show Content Offset.** When checked, the Control panel shows X+ and Y+ values for a graphic placed within a frame when the actual graphic (not the frame) is selected.

- **Adjust Stroke Weight when Scaling.** When checked, resizing an object changes the stroke weight proportionally. For example, resizing an object with a 1-pt stroke to 50% results in a 0.5-pt stroke.

Choosing **Customize** in the panel Options menu opens a dialog box where you can define the available options in the panel; anything with a checkmark will be available when it's relevant to the selection in the document.

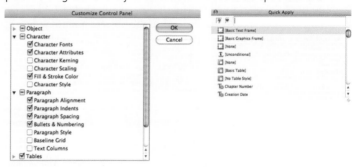

Clicking the Quick Apply button (to the left of the panel Options button) opens a special navigation dialog box. This feature enables you to easily find and apply what you want (menu commands, user-defined styles, and so on) by typing a few characters in the text entry field, and then clicking the related item in the list.

10. **Highlight the X field in the Control panel and type** -0.25**, then press Tab to move the highlight to the Y field.**

As in dialog boxes, you can use the Tab key to move through the fields in the Control panel. The X and Y fields determine the position of the selected object. X defines the horizontal (left-to-right) position and Y defines the vertical (top-to-bottom) position.

11. **With the Y field highlighted, type** 9.5 **and then press Return/Enter.**

Pressing Return/Enter applies your changes in the Control panel. You can also simply click away from the object to apply the changes, but then you would have to reselect the object to make further changes.

Note:

Because inches are now the default unit of measurement for this file, you don't need to type the unit in the field.

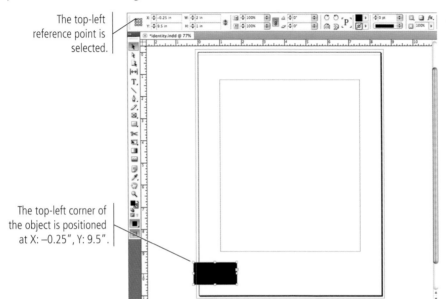

The top-left reference point is selected.

The top-left corner of the object is positioned at X: −0.25″, Y: 9.5″.

Note:

You can use math operators to add (+), subtract (-), divide (/), or multiply (*) existing values in the Control panel. This is useful when you want to move or change a value by a specific amount.

Type −.5 after the value to move the object up half an inch.

12. **In the Control panel, make sure the chain icon for the W and H fields is inactive (not linked). Change the W (width) field to** $9″$**, change the H (height) field to** $1.2″$**, and then press Return/Enter to apply the change.**

Remember, you don't need to type the units if you are working with the default units.

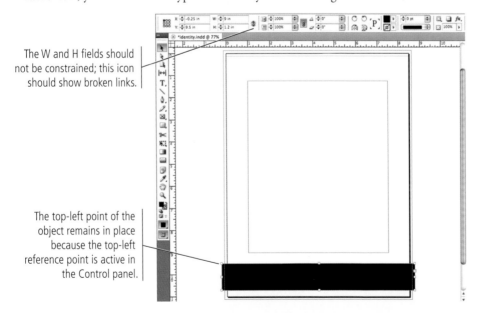

The W and H fields should not be constrained; this icon should show broken links.

The top-left point of the object remains in place because the top-left reference point is active in the Control panel.

Note:

The Transform panel (Window>Object & Layout>Transform) includes the same options that are available in the Control panel when an object is selected with the Selection tool. You can change an object's position or dimensions, scale an object to a specific percentage, and apply rotation or shear to the selected object. The Transform panel Options menu includes the same options that are available in the Control panel Options menu, as well as commands to rotate and flip the selected object.

13. **Save the file and continue to the next exercise.**

CREATE A ROUNDED RECTANGLE

In addition to basic rectangles, you can create frames with a number of special corner treatments. The Rounded Rectangle tool automatically creates frames with special corners, but you can also easily modify the corners of an existing frame to create the effect you want.

1. **With identity.indd open, zoom into the left end of the black rectangle.**

2. **Click away from the existing shape to deselect it (if necessary).**

   If you don't deselect the existing shape, the changes you make in the next step would affect the selected object.

3. **Make sure the Rectangle tool is active.**

4. **In the Control panel, click the arrow button to the right of the Fill swatch to open the attached Swatches panel. Choose Paper from the pop-up panel.**

   There is a difference between no fill and 0% of a color. Using 0% of a color — or using the Paper color — effectively creates a solid "white" fill. (In printing, solid white areas **knock out** or hide underlying shapes.)

Fill color

Make sure this shape is deselected before changing the Fill and Stroke colors.

5. **In the Control panel, click the arrow button to the right of the Stroke swatch and choose None from the pop-up panel.**

   The "None" color option essentially removes color from that attribute. Underlying objects will be visible in areas where None is applied.

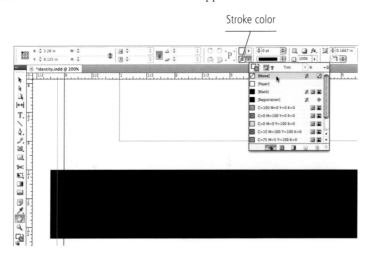

Stroke color

6. **Click once on the page to open the Rectangle dialog box.**

   Single-clicking with a shape tool opens a dialog box where you can define specific measurements for the new shape.

7. **In the Rectangle dialog box, set the Width to** `0.125"` **and the Height to** `0.08"`**, and then click OK.**

   The new rectangle is placed with the selected reference point where you clicked.

8. **Zoom in so you can more clearly see the small rectangle you just created.**

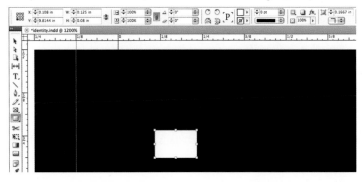

9. **With the new rectangle selected, open the Corner Shape menu in the Control panel and choose the rounded option.**

   Even though the object now has rounded corners, the **bounding box** still marks the outermost corners of the shape. (You might need to zoom in to see the effect of the new corner shape.)

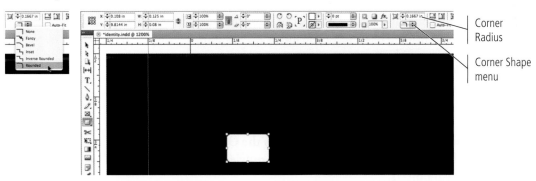

Corner Radius

Corner Shape menu

A rounded-corner rectangle is simply a rectangle with the corners cut at a specific distance from the end (the corner radius). The two sides are connected with one-fourth of a circle, which has a radius equal to the amount of the rounding.

Radius

10. **Save the file and continue to the next exercise.**

When a rectangular frame is selected in the layout, a small yellow square appears on the right edge of the shape's bounding box. You can click this button to enter Live Corner Effects edit mode, where you can dynamically adjust the appearance of corner effects for all corners (by simply clicking a corner diamond) or for one corner at a time (by pressing the Shift key when you click). Simply clicking away from the object exits the edit mode.

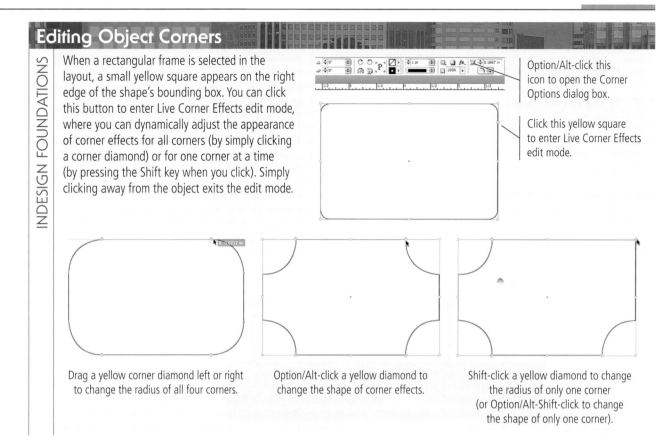

Option/Alt-click this icon to open the Corner Options dialog box.

Click this yellow square to enter Live Corner Effects edit mode.

Drag a yellow corner diamond left or right to change the radius of all four corners.

Option/Alt-click a yellow diamond to change the shape of corner effects.

Shift-click a yellow diamond to change the radius of only one corner (or Option/Alt-Shift-click to change the shape of only one corner).

CLONE, ALIGN, AND DISTRIBUTE MULTIPLE OBJECTS

As you should have already noticed, there is often more than one way to accomplish the same task in InDesign. Aligning multiple objects on a page is no exception. In fact, InDesign offers a number of methods for aligning objects, both to the page and to each other. In this exercise you will explore a number of those options as you create sprocket-hole shapes that will turn the black rectangle into a strip of film.

1. **With identity.indd open, choose the Selection tool in the Tools panel.**

   The Selection tool is used to select entire objects; the Direct Selection tool is used to select parts of objects or the contents of a frame.

2. **Click inside the area of the rounded rectangle, press the Option/Alt key, and drag right. Release the mouse button when the preview shows a small space between the two objects.**

   Pressing Option/Alt as you drag moves a copy of the selected object (called **cloning**). As you drag, a series of green lines mark the top, center, and bottom of the original object. These green lines are a function of InDesign's Smart Guides, which make it easy to align objects to each other by simply dragging.

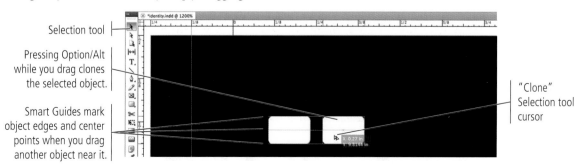

Selection tool

Pressing Option/Alt while you drag clones the selected object.

Smart Guides mark object edges and center points when you drag another object near it.

"Clone" Selection tool cursor

3. **Click the second shape, press Option/Alt, and drag right. Release the mouse button when you see opposing arrows below/between the first and second pair, and the second and third pair of shapes.**

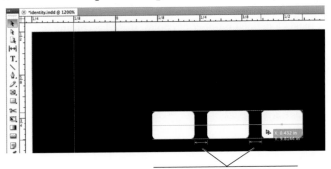

Smart Guides identify equal
spacing between multiple objects.

Note:

Smart Guides also identify equal dimensions when you create a new object near an existing one.

4. **Press Shift and then click the first and second shapes to add them to the current selection.**

   You can Shift-click an object to select it in addition to the previously selected object(s), or Shift-click an already selected object to deselect it without deselecting other objects.

5. **Click inside the area of any of the selected shapes. Using the following image as a guide, drag the selected objects to the top-left corner of the black rectangle.**

Leave a small
amount of space
above and to the left
of the left shape.

Click inside the area of
any selected object to
drag all selected objects.

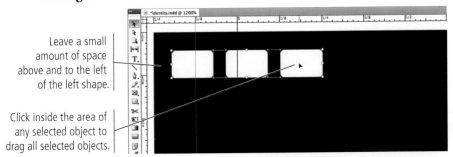

6. **Click away from the active objects to deselect them, then click only the third rounded rectangle. Option/Alt-click and drag right; release the mouse button when the fourth object is evenly spaced with the first three.**

   This step re-establishes the cloning movement as the last-applied transformation.

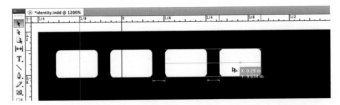

7. **With the fourth object still selected, choose Object>Transform Again> Transform Again.**

   This command applies the last-used transformation to the selected object. Because you used the cloning movement in the previous step, the result is a fifth copy that is spaced at the same distance you moved the copy in Step 6. (The Transform Again command can be used to re-apply rotation, scaling, sizing, and other transformations.)

Note:

You could also choose Edit>Duplicate, which makes a copy of the selected object using the last-applied movement distance.

8. With the new fifth object selected, choose Edit>Step and Repeat.

9. Activate the Preview option in the resulting dialog box, and type 45 in the Count field.

The Step and Repeat dialog box makes a defined number of copies, spaced according to the defined Offset values. By default, these values are set to the last-used movement that you applied in the layout. As you can see, the 50 copies (the original 5 and the 45 that will result from the Step and Repeat process) are all equally spaced, but not enough to fill the filmstrip.

10. Click OK to make the copies, then click away from the resulting shapes to deselect them.

11. Zoom in to the right end of the black rectangle, and select only the right-most rounded rectangle.

12. Press Shift, then drag to the right until the center of the object snaps to the bleed guide.

Because this object ends up entirely outside the page edge, the Smart Guides no longer appear to mark exact horizontal movement. Pressing Shift while dragging constrains the movement to 45° angles.

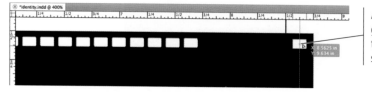

As you drag, the bleed guide acts as a magnet; the object's center point snaps to that guide.

13. Zoom out so you can see the entire page width, then choose Edit>Select All.

14. Press Shift and click the black rectangle to deselect only that object.

When you are working with a large number of objects, it is often easier to deselect what you don't want than to select the ones you do want. Steps 13 and 14 show a very easy way to select most, but not all, of the objects on a page.

All of the rounded rectangles should be selected.

The black rectangle should not be selected.

15. Open the Align panel (Window>Object & Layout>Align).

In addition to aligning objects with the assistance of Smart Guides, you can also use the Align panel to align multiple objects relative to one another, to the page margins, to the page, or to the spread.

The Align Objects options are fairly self explanatory; when multiple objects are selected, the objects align based on the edge(s) or center(s) you click.

The Distribute Objects options enable you to control the positions of multiple objects relative to each other. By default, objects are equally distributed within the dimensions of the overall selection; you can check the Use Spacing option to space edges or centers by a specific amount.

The Distribute Spacing options place equal space between the overall selected objects. You can also check the Use Spacing option to add a specific amount of space between the selected objects.

Below the Distribute Objects option, you can choose from the menu to determine how objects will align. (Because you can align objects relative to the document, the align buttons are also available when only one object is selected, allowing you to align any single object to a precise location on the page or spread.)

Many of the options from the Align panel are also available in the Control panel; the Align options are also available in all of the built-in workspaces. If you are using the Essentials workspace, the Distribute options are not available in the Control panel; you can turn them on by customizing the panel or by choosing the Advanced workspace option.

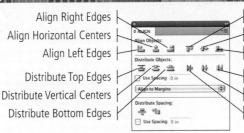

Align Right Edges
Align Horizontal Centers
Align Left Edges
Distribute Top Edges
Distribute Vertical Centers
Distribute Bottom Edges

Align Top Edges
Align Vertical Centers
Align Bottom Edges
Distribute Right Edges
Distribute Horizontal Centers
Distribute Left Edges

By default, the Distribute Objects options equally space the selected objects within the outermost dimensions of the selection.

The Use Spacing option places a specific amount of space between the selected edges (or centers) of selected objects.

The Distribute Spacing options place a specific amount of space between selected objects.

16. With all of the rounded rectangles selected, click the Distribute Horizontal Centers button in the Align panel.

This button places an equal amount of space between the center points of each selected object. The two outer shapes in the selection act as the anchors; all other objects between the outer objects are repositioned.

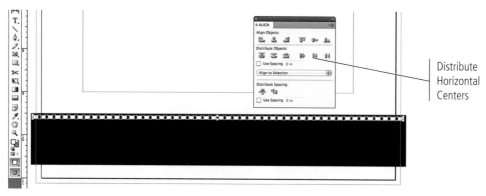

Distribute Horizontal Centers

17. Click any of the selected shapes, press Option/Alt-Shift, and drag down.

This creates a second row of rounded rectangles that is automatically aligned below the top row.

18. Save the file and continue to the next exercise.

 CREATE A COMPOUND PATH

Many shapes are composed of more than one path. The letter "O", for example, requires two separate paths — the outside shape and an inner shape to remove the area inside of the letter; without either path, the shape would be incomplete — just a circle instead of a recognizable letter. In this project, you will combine all of the existing shapes so the filmstrip is treated as a single object rather than 101 separate shapes.

1. With identity.indd open, deselect all objects on the page and then click to select only the black rectangle.

2. In the Control panel, click the Drop Shadow button.

This button applies a drop shadow to the selected object using the default effect settings. As you can see, the shadow is not visible through the sprocket holes because you filled them with the Paper color — which knocks out all underlying color (including the applied shadow). To make the graphic work properly, you have to remove the areas of the rounded rectangles from the black rectangle.

Note:

You will learn how to change these effect settings in Project 2.

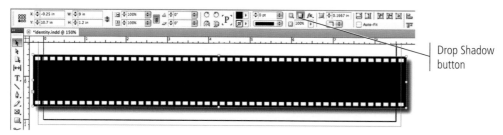

Drop Shadow button

3. **Using the Selection tool, click and drag a marquee that touches all objects that make up the filmstrip graphic.**

Using the Selection tool, any object that is at least partially surrounded by the selection marquee will be included in the resulting selection.

The gray line identifies the selection area.

Objects even partially selected by the marquee are selected.

4. **Open the Pathfinder panel (Window>Object & Layout>Pathfinder).**

The Pathfinder Panel in Depth

You can apply a number of transformations to objects using the Pathfinder panel. (The options in the Pathfinder panel are the same as those in the Object>Paths, Object>Pathfinder, Object>Convert Shape, and Object>Convert Point submenus.)

- Join Path
- Open Path
- Close Path
- Reverse Path

- Add
- Subtract
- Intersect
- Exclude Overlap
- Minus Back

- Rectangle
- Rounded Rectangle
- Beveled Rectangle
- Inverse Rounded Rectangle
- Ellipse
- Triangle
- Polygon
- Line
- Horizontal/Vertical Line

- Plain Point
- Corner Point
- Smooth Point
- Symmetrical Point

Path options break (open) a closed path, connect (close) the endpoints of an open path, or reverse a path's direction (start becomes end and vice versa, which is relevant if you use stylized end treatments).

Pathfinder options create complex objects by combining multiple existing objects. When you use the Pathfinder options (other than Subtract), the attributes of the front object are applied to the resulting shape; the Subtract function maintains the attributes of the back object.

- **Add** results in the combined shapes of all selected objects.
- **Subtract** returns the shape of the back object minus any overlapping area of the front object.
- **Intersect** results in the shape of only the overlapping areas of selected objects.
- **Exclude Overlap** results in the shape of all selected objects minus any overlapping areas.
- **Minus Back** results in the shape of the front object minus any area where it overlaps other selected objects.

Convert Shape options change the overall appearance of an object using one of the six defined basic shapes, or using the default polygon settings; you can also convert any existing shape to a basic line or an orthogonal (horizontal or vertical) line.

Convert Point options affect the position of direction handles when a specific anchor point is selected.

- **Plain** creates a point with no direction handles.
- **Corner** creates a point that produces a sharp corner; changing the direction handle on one side of the point does not affect the position or length of the handle on the other side of the point.
- **Smooth** creates a point with opposing direction handles that are exactly 180° from one another; the two handles can have different lengths.
- **Symmetrical** creates a smooth point with equal-length opposing direction handles; changing the length or position of one handle applies the same change to the opposing handle.

5. Click the Subtract button in the Pathfinder panel.

This button removes the area of front objects from the area of the backmost object. The result is a **compound path**, which is a single shape that is made up of multiple paths; interior paths are removed from the background shape, allowing underlying elements to show through.

Note:

It might take a while for the process to complete because InDesign has a lot of information to process to create a compound shape from 101 different paths.

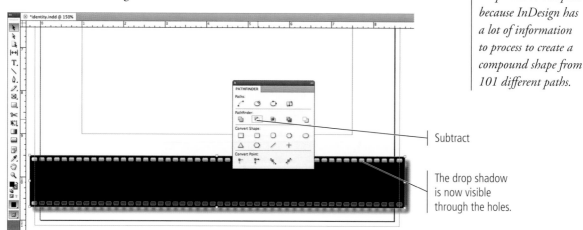

Subtract

The drop shadow is now visible through the holes.

6. Save the file and continue to the next exercise.

 CREATE AND TRANSFORM MULTIPLE FRAMES

Many layouts have defined space requirements for various elements. This letterhead layout, for example, requires eight thumbnail images across the filmstrip graphic, evenly spaced and equally sized — just as you would see on a traditional piece of photographic film. Rather than simply placing the images and resizing the resulting frames for all eight images, you can speed up the process by first creating empty graphics frames that will contain the images when you place them.

1. With identity.indd open, arrange your document window and view percentage so you can see the entire filmstrip at the bottom of the page.

2. Choose the Rectangle Frame tool in the Tools panel.

The frame tools work the same as the basic shape tools; the only difference is that the resulting shape automatically becomes a container for imported graphics or images.

3. Click the left edge of the filmstrip graphic just below the top row of holes, then drag down and right until cursor feedback shows W: 9″, H: 0.8″.

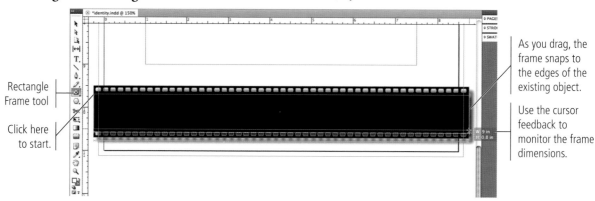

Rectangle Frame tool

Click here to start.

As you drag, the frame snaps to the edges of the existing object.

Use the cursor feedback to monitor the frame dimensions.

4. While still holding down the mouse button, press the Right Arrow key.

If you press the arrow keys while creating a frame, you can create a grid of frames within the area that you drag.

- Press the Right Arrow key to add columns.
- Press the Left Arrow key to remove columns.
- Press the Up Arrow key to add rows.
- Press the Down Arrow key to remove rows.

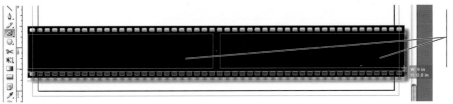

Note:

*This method of creating multiple frames, called **gridified tools**, works with any of the frame or basic shape tools.*

Pressing the Right Arrow key splits the area you draw into two equal-sized frames.

5. Press the Right Arrow key six more times to create a total of eight frames, then release the mouse button.

The resulting frames are equal in size, and have the same amount of space between each.

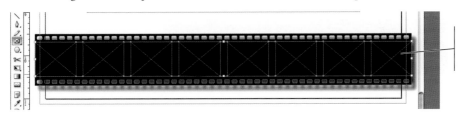

Crossed diagonal lines indicate that these are empty graphics frames.

6. With the eight resulting frames selected, choose the Selection tool.

As we stated previously, the Selection tool is used to access and manipulate entire objects. Using the Selection tool, you can:

- Click and drag a handle to resize selected objects.
- Shift-click and drag to resize objects proportionally.
- Command/Control-click and drag to scale selected objects.
- Command/Control-Shift-click and drag to scale selected objects proportionally.
- Press Option/Alt with any of these to apply the transformation around the selection's center point.

Note:

In previous versions of InDesign, you had to group multiple objects before you could transform them as a single unit. In CS5, you can resize, rotate, or scale multiple objects at once without first grouping them.

7. Click the right-center bounding box handle of the active selection. Press and hold the Spacebar, then drag left.

As you drag, the space between the selected objects changes; the size of the actual objects is not affected. This method is called **live distribution**; to work properly, you must click the handle before pressing the Spacebar.

The Selection tool is active.

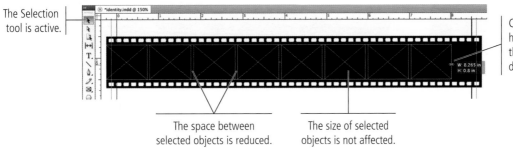

Click the center handle, then press the Spacebar and drag left.

The space between selected objects is reduced.

The size of selected objects is not affected.

8. **Click the right-center handle again. Without pressing the Spacebar, drag right until the handle snaps to the right edge of the filmstrip.**

   Simply dragging the handle resizes the entire selection; the spacing and position of various selected objects relative to one another is not affected.

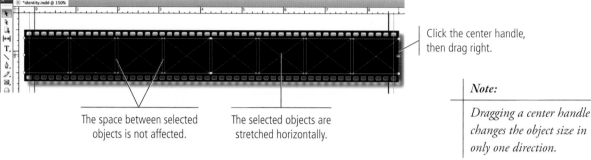

Click the center handle, then drag right.

The space between selected objects is not affected.

The selected objects are stretched horizontally.

9. **With the eight empty frames selected, choose Object>Group.**

   Grouping multiple objects means you can treat them as a single unit. This is necessary when you want to use the align options to position the group of frames relative to other objects without affecting the positioning of the placeholder frames relative to one another.

After grouping, a single bounding box outlines the entire group.

10. **Press Shift, and click the filmstrip graphic to add it to the active selection.**

11. **Using the Align panel or the Control panel, click the Align Horizontal Centers and Align Vertical Centers buttons.**

    Depending on how precisely you created and transformed the frames, this might have a very noticeable effect; it ensures that the frames are centered to the filmstrip graphic.

12. **In the Control panel, choose the center reference point.**

13. **Place the Selection tool cursor just outside the top-right handle of the selection. When you see the Rotate cursor, click and drag up until the cursor feedback shows 3°.**

The rotation is applied around the selected reference point.

Rotation Angle field

The orange lines show the angle compared to the horizontal plane.

Cursor feedback shows the degree of rotation.

Place the Selection tool cursor just outside a corner handle to rotate the selection.

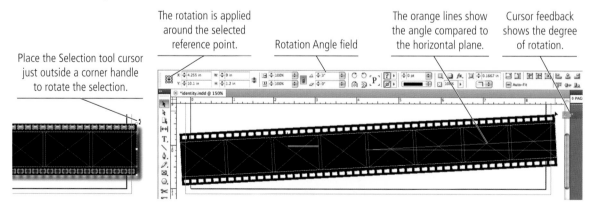

14. **Save the file and continue to the next exercise.**

CREATE A SIMPLE LINE

InDesign includes two tools for creating lines: the Line tool for creating straight lines and the Pen tool for creating curved lines called **Bézier curves** (although you can also create straight lines with the Pen tool). In this exercise, you create the most basic element possible: a straight line; you then add anchor points to the line to create a multi-segment path.

Every line is composed of anchor points and line segments that connect those points. Even a simple straight line has two points, one at each end. More sophisticated shapes can be created by adding anchor points, and manipulating the direction handles of those points to control the shape of segments that connect the different points.

This concept is the heart of Bézier curves and vector-based drawing, and can be one of the most challenging skills for new designers to master. The Pen tool (and its variations) is extremely powerful, but also very confusing for new users. The best way to understand this tool is simply practice. As you gain experience, you will become more comfortable with manipulating anchor points, handles, and line segments.

Note:

Bézier curves can be difficult to master without a relatively deep understanding of geometry or trigonometry. The best training is to practice until you can recognize and predict how moving a point or handle will affect the connected segments.

1. **With identity.indd open, choose the Line tool in the Tools panel.**

2. **Click the Default Fill and Stroke button at the bottom of the Tools panel.**

   The default options for the Line tool are a 1-pt black stroke with no fill.

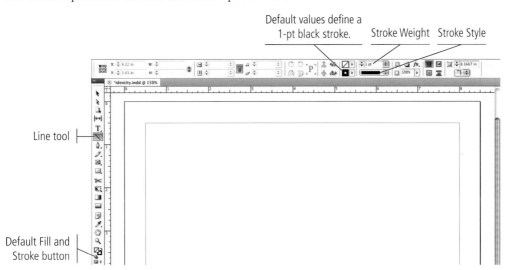

3. **At the top of the page, click at the left bleed guide and drag to the right bleed guide. Press Shift, and then release the mouse button.**

   As you drag, the cursor feedback shows the length of the line you are drawing. The blue line previews what will appear when you release the mouse button. Pressing Shift as you draw forces or constrains the line to exactly 45° angles — including exactly horizontal.

Note:

When drawing lines, cursor feedback shows the length of the segment you are drawing.

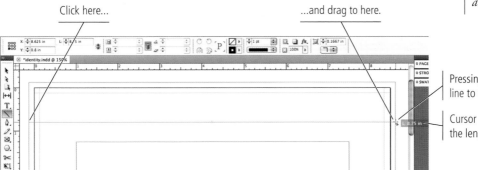

Pressing Shift snaps the line to the horizontal.

Cursor feedback shows the length of the line.

4. **In the Control panel, open the Stroke Weight menu and choose 2 pt.**

   You can choose one of the stroke weight presets from this menu, or simply type any value in the field.

5. **At the left end of the Control panel, change the Y field to 1″ and press Return/Enter to apply the change.**

   Because you constrained this line, changing the Y field moves the entire line.

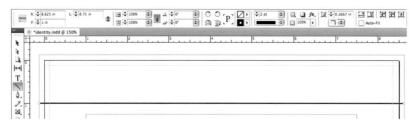

Note:

Remember, you do not need to type the units if you are entering a measurement in the default unit of measurement. We include the units in our steps for the sake of clarity.

6. **Choose the Pen tool in the Tools panel.**

7. **Move the cursor over the line you just created.**

   When the Pen tool is over an existing selected line, it automatically switches to the Add Anchor Point tool cursor; clicking adds a new point to the selected line.

   If the Pen tool is over a specific point on a selected line, it automatically switches to the Delete Anchor Point tool cursor; clicking removes that point from the line.

Pen tool

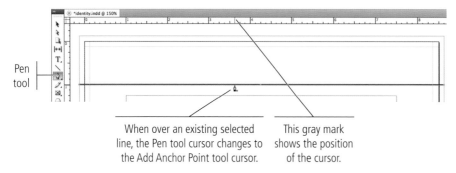

When over an existing selected line, the Pen tool cursor changes to the Add Anchor Point tool cursor.

This gray mark shows the position of the cursor.

8. **When the cursor is at the 3.625″ mark of the horizontal page ruler, click to add a point to the line.**

   The visible center point of the selected line is a bit deceptive. This simply marks the center of the shape (a line, in this case); it is not an actual point on the line.

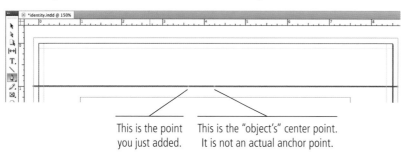

This is the point you just added.

This is the "object's" center point. It is not an actual anchor point.

9. **Move the cursor right to the 4.375″ mark and click to add another point.**

   All vector objects are composed of anchor points and connecting line segments, even if you don't create each point manually. The original line had two regular points, one at each end, and a straight connecting segment. You added two new points, for a total of four points and three connecting segments.

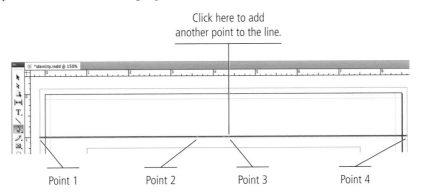

Click here to add
another point to the line.

Point 1   Point 2   Point 3   Point 4

10. **Choose the Direct Selection tool in the Tools panel, and click away from the line to deselect it.**

    The Direct Selection tool is used to select individual pieces of objects, such as a specific point on a line, or a specific line segment between two points. However, you have to first deselect the entire line before you can select only part of it.

11. **Move the cursor over the left part of the line.**

    When the Direct Selection tool cursor shows a small line in the icon, clicking will select the specific segment under the cursor.

Direct
Selection
tool

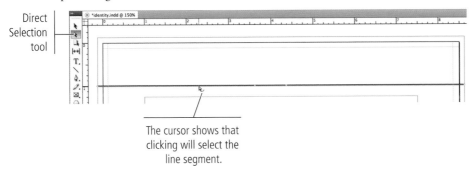

The cursor shows that
clicking will select the
line segment.

12. **Click anywhere between the first and second points on the line. Press Shift, and drag up until the cursor feedback shows the Y position of 0.19″.**

    The segment you selected moves, and the segment between points 2 and 3 adjusts as necessary to remain connected. The segment between points 3 and 4 is not affected.

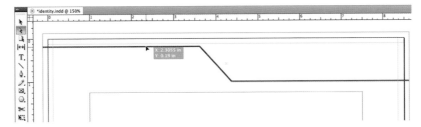

13. **Using the Direct Selection tool, click the second point from the left (Point 2).**

    When the Direct Selection tool cursor shows a small circle in the icon, clicking will select the specific point under the cursor.

14. **In the Control panel, change the X position of the selected point 3.625".**

As you can see, you can control the precise position of every point in a shape.

You can define the exact position of the selected point.

The cursor shows that clicking will select the point.

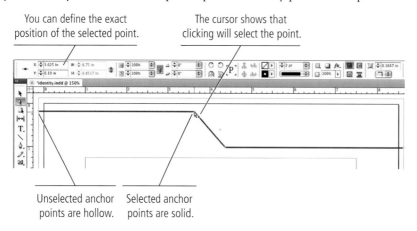

Unselected anchor points are hollow.   Selected anchor points are solid.

15. **Save the file and continue to the next exercise.**

CREATE BÉZIER CURVES

In this exercise you will make very simple manipulations to the straight line you just created. In Project 2, you will use the Pen tool to create a new curved line. We also encourage you to practice as much as possible using the Pen tool until you are more proficient; for example, try copying the outlines of various shapes in photographs.

1. **With identity.indd open, make sure the line at the top of the page is selected.**

2. **Choose the Convert Direction Point tool nested under the Pen tool.**

The Convert Direction Point tool changes a corner point to a smooth point. **Smooth points** have handles that control the size and shape of curves connected to that point. You can use the Direct Selection tool to drag handles for a selected anchor point.

Note:

Using the Convert Direction Point tool, you can click an existing point and drag to add handles to the point, converting the point to a smooth point.

3. **Click the second point on the line, press Shift, and drag right until the ruler shows that the cursor is at 4.125".**

When you click a point with the Convert Direction Point tool and immediately drag, you add direction handles to the point. Those direction handles define the shape of the line segments that are connected to the point. As you drag farther away from the point, the affected segment's curve increases.

Pressing Shift constrains the new direction handles to 45° angles — in this case, exactly horizontal. If you look closely, you can see that the direction handle on the left side of the point is exactly on top of the line.

By default, clicking and dragging creates a smooth, symmetrical point, in which equal-length handles are added to each side of the point directly opposite each other. As long as a point is symmetrical, changing the angle of one handle also affects the handle on the other side of the point.

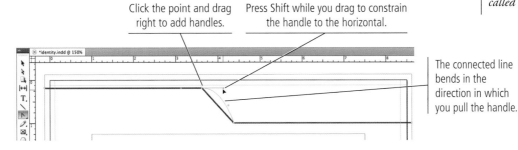

Click the point and drag right to add handles.

Press Shift while you drag to constrain the handle to the horizontal.

The connected line bends in the direction in which you pull the handle.

Note:

The lines that connect anchor points based on the angle and length of the control handles are called Bézier curves.

4. **Click the third point, press Shift, and drag right until the ruler shows that the cursor is at 4.875″.**

   As we just explained, the affected curve gets larger as you drag farther away from the point. Because you're dragging exactly horizontally, the horizontal segment on the right is not curving.

   On the left side of the point, however, you can see the effect of converting Point 3 to a symmetrical point. Dragging to the right side of the point adds direction handles on *both sides* of the point; the length and position of the left handle defines the shape of the curve on the left side of the point — which is the one you want to affect in this step.

Note:

When you drag direction handles, the blue lines preview the effects of your changes.

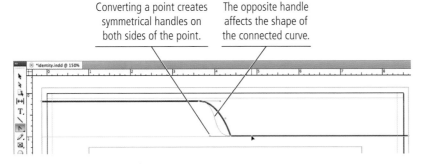

Converting a point creates symmetrical handles on both sides of the point.

The opposite handle affects the shape of the connected curve.

Note:

If you move an anchor point that has direction handles, the handles don't change angle or length. The related curves change shape based on the new position of the point.

5. **Choose the Pen tool in the Tools panel. (It is now nested under the Convert Direction Point tool.)**

   When you choose a nested tool variation, the nested tool becomes the default option in that position on the Tools panel.

6. **Move the cursor over the left endpoint of the line. When you see a diagonal line in the cursor icon, click to connect to the existing endpoint.**

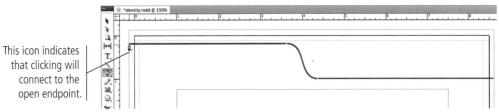

This icon indicates that clicking will connect to the open endpoint.

7. **Press Shift, then click at the top-left bleed guide.**

Shift-click to create a vertical line between the previous point and the point where you click.

8. **Press Shift, then click the top-right bleed guide.**

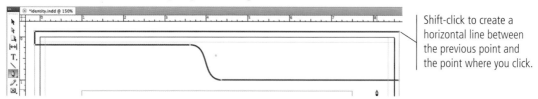

Shift-click to create a horizontal line between the previous point and the point where you click.

9. **Move the cursor over the open endpoint at the right end of the original line. When you see a small circle in the cursor icon, click to close the shape.**

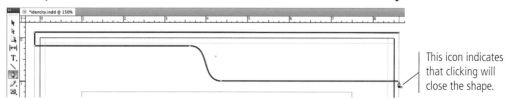

This icon indicates that clicking will close the shape.

You could have created this shape as a regular rectangle and then modified the bottom line with the Pen tool. However, our goal was to teach you how to create a basic line, and then how to perform some basic tasks with the Pen tool and its nested variations.

It's important to realize that there is almost always more than one way to accomplish a specific goal in InDesign. As you gain experience, you will develop personal preferences for the most effective and efficient methods of doing what you need to do.

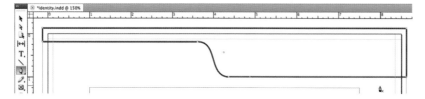

10. **Save the file and continue to the next exercise.**

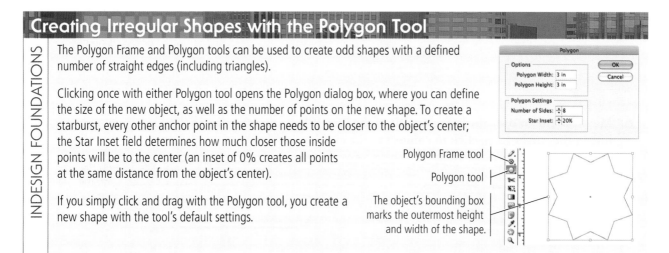

Creating Irregular Shapes with the Polygon Tool

The Polygon Frame and Polygon tools can be used to create odd shapes with a defined number of straight edges (including triangles).

Clicking once with either Polygon tool opens the Polygon dialog box, where you can define the size of the new object, as well as the number of points on the new shape. To create a starburst, every other anchor point in the shape needs to be closer to the object's center; the Star Inset field determines how much closer those inside points will be to the center (an inset of 0% creates all points at the same distance from the object's center).

If you simply click and drag with the Polygon tool, you create a new shape with the tool's default settings.

Polygon Frame tool

Polygon tool

The object's bounding box marks the outermost height and width of the shape.

An anchor point marks the end of a line segment, and the point handles determine the shape of that segment. That's the basic definition of a vector, but there is a bit more to it than that. You can draw Bézier shapes from scratch using the Pen tool, or you can edit the curves that are created as part of another shape (such as a circle).

Each segment in a path has two anchor points and two associated handles. We first clicked to create Point A and dragged (without releasing the mouse button) to create Handle A1. We then clicked and dragged to create Point B and Handle B1; Handle B2 was automatically created as a reflection of B1 (Point B is a **symmetrical point**).

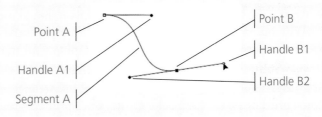

This image shows the result of dragging Handle B1 to the left instead of to the right when creating the initial curve. Notice the difference in the curve here, compared to the curve above. When you drag the handle, the connecting segment arcs away from the direction of the handle you drag.

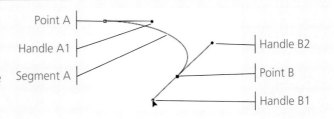

It's important to understand that every line segment is connected to two handles. In this example, Handle A1 and Handle B2 determine the shape of Segment A. Dragging either handle affects the shape of the connected segment.

Clicking and dragging a point creates a symmetrical (smooth) point; both handles start out at equal length, directly opposite one another. Changing the angle of one handle of a symmetrical point also changes the opposing handle of that point. In the example here, repositioning Handle B1 also moves Handle B2, which affects the shape of Segment A. (You can, however, change the length of one handle without affecting the length of the other handle.)

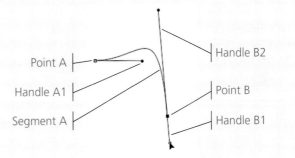

You can create corner points by simply clicking with the Pen tool instead of clicking and dragging. Corner points do not have their own handles; the connected segments are controlled by the handles of the other associated points.

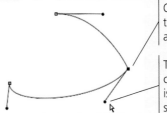

Handle of other connected point controls the segment shape.

Corner point has no handles.

You can convert a smooth point into a corner point by clicking the point with the Convert Direction Point tool [ ] (nested under the Pen tool). You can also add a handle to only one side of an anchor point by Option/Alt-clicking a point with the Convert Direction Point tool and dragging.

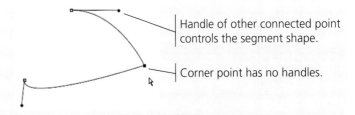

Option/Alt-click this point with the Convert Direction Point tool and drag to create only one handle.

This handle controls the connected segment; the handle is not reflected on the other side of the point.

Although there are several default color choices built into the Swatches panel of every InDesign file, you are not limited to these few options. You can define virtually any color based on specific values of component colors.

When you are building a page to be printed, you should use CMYK colors. The CMYK color model, also called **process color**, uses subtractive color theory to reproduce the range of printable colors by overlapping semi-transparent layers of cyan, magenta, yellow, and black inks in varying percentages from 0–100.

In process-color printing, these four colors of ink are imaged (or separated) onto individual printing plates. Each color separation is printed with a separate unit of a printing press. When printed on top of each other in varying percentages, the semi-transparent inks produce the CMYK **gamut**, or the range of possible colors. Special (spot) colors can also be included in a job by using specifically formulated inks as additional color separations.

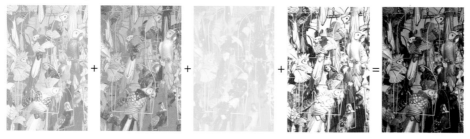

Using theoretically pure pigments, a mixture of equal parts of cyan, magenta, and yellow should produce black. Real pigments, however, are not pure; the actual result of mixing these three colors usually appears as a muddy brown. In the image to the right, the left block is printed with 100% black ink. The right block is a combination of 100% cyan, 100% magenta, and 100% yellow inks.

The fourth color, black (K), is added to the three subtractive primaries to extend the range of printable colors and to allow much purer blacks to be printed than is possible with only the three primaries. Black is abbreviated as "K" because it is the "key" color to which others are aligned on the printing press. Using K for black also avoids confusion with blue in the RGB color model, which is used for jobs that will be distributed digitally (Web sites, some PDF files, etc.).

1. **With identity.indd open, use the Selection tool to make sure the shape at the top of the page is selected.**

2. **At the bottom of the Tools panel, click the Swap Fill and Stroke button.**

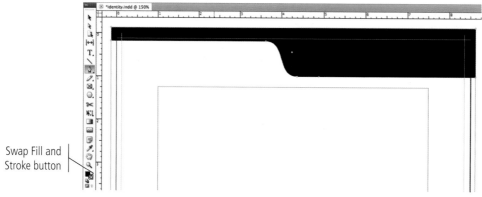

Swap Fill and
Stroke button

3. Open the Color panel.

Remember, all panels can be accessed in the Window menu. Because workspace arrangement is a matter of personal preference, we won't tell you where to place or keep panels. If the Color panel is not in your panel dock, simply choose Window>Color>Color to display that panel.

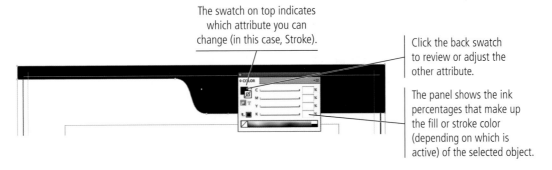

The swatch on top indicates which attribute you can change (in this case, Stroke).

Click the back swatch to review or adjust the other attribute.

The panel shows the ink percentages that make up the fill or stroke color (depending on which is active) of the selected object.

4. Click the Fill swatch to bring it to the front (if it isn't already).

When you apply color from any of the Swatches panels (including the ones in the Control panel), the Color panel shows a swatch of that color as a single slider. You can use this slider to easily apply a percentage of the selected swatch. (You'll work more with color swatches in Project 2.)

The black fill is a saved (default) swatch; it appears in the panel as a single slider.

5. Click the Options button in the top-right corner of the panel and choose CMYK from the Options menu.

This option converts the single swatch slider to the four process-color sliders. You can change any ink percentage to change the object's fill color.

Click here to open the panel Options menu.

> **Note:**
>
> *You can change the color by typing a specific value or by dragging the slider below the color gradient.*

6. Click the M slider and drag until the field shows 40%.

This color, 100% black with some percentage of another ink, is called a **rich black** or **super black**. By itself, plain black ink often lacks density. Rich blacks are commonly used to add density or "temperature" to flat black; adding magenta results in "warmer" blacks, and adding cyan results in "cooler" blacks.

Click and drag the slider to change the ink percentage.

7. Save the file and continue to the next stage of the project.

Stage 3 **Placing External Images**

As you saw in the first stage of this project, InDesign incorporates a number of tools for building graphics directly in a layout. Of course, most page-layout projects will include files from other sources — logos created in Adobe Illustrator, raster-based images created in Adobe Photoshop, digital photographs and scans, stock images and illustrations, and many other types of files can be incorporated into a larger project.

PLACE AN EXTERNAL GRAPHICS FILE

Every image in a layout exists in a frame. You can either create the frame first and place a file into it, or you can simply place an image and create the containing frame at the same time. In this exercise, you are going to place the client's logo, and transform the file to fit into the space to the left of the curved line at the top of the layout.

1. **With identity.indd open, make sure nothing is selected in the layout.**

   To deselect objects, you can choose Edit>Deselect All, or simply click an empty area of the workspace. If you do click the workspace, though, be careful that you don't accidentally click a white-filled object instead of the empty page or pasteboard area.

2. **Choose File>Place. Navigate to the WIP>Crowe folder and select crowe.ai. At the bottom of the dialog box, make sure none of the options are checked.**

   You will learn about these options in later projects. For now, you simply want to place the logo file into the letterhead.

3. **Click Open to load the cursor with the placed file.**

   You still have to place the loaded image into the document.

By default, the loaded Place cursor shows a small thumbnail of the file you're placing.

4. **Click near the top-left corner of the page to place the image.**

   Every image in an InDesign layout exists in a frame. When you click an empty area of the page to place an image, the containing frame is automatically created for you.

Note:

You can turn off the thumbnail preview feature by unchecking the Show Thumbnails on Place option in the Interface pane of the Preferences dialog box.

5. **Click the placed image with the Selection tool to select the frame. Using the Control panel, choose the top-left reference point and then change the frame position to X: 0.25″, Y: 0.3″.**

When the frame is selected, the Control panel defines the frame parameters.

The blue handles show the edge of the graphics frame that contains the logo.

6. **With the frame selected, check the Auto-Fit option in the Control panel.**

By default, the image contained within the frame remains unaffected when you edit the dimensions of a graphics frame. When the Auto-Fit option is checked, however, resizing the frame automatically resizes the contained image to fit the new frame size.

7. **Click the bottom-right handle of the frame. Drag up and left until the cursor feedback shows W: 3.6″. Don't release the mouse button.**

Drag the bottom-right handle to resize the frame.

This option should be checked.

The Selection tool is active.

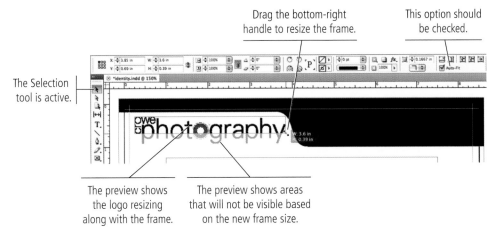

The preview shows the logo resizing along with the frame.

The preview shows areas that will not be visible based on the new frame size.

8. **Press Shift to constrain the proportions of the resized frame.**

Pressing Shift maintains the original height-to-width aspect ratio in the resized frame. This means the resized frame will be large enough to show the entire (resized) logo.

Note:

When the Auto-Fit option is not selected, you can press the Command key while resizing a frame to scale the content at the same time.

9. **With the Selection tool active, move the cursor inside the resized frame.**

This reveals the Content Indicator icon, which you can use to access and manipulate the frame's content without the need to switch tools.

Note:

Unlike raster images, vector graphics can be resized without losing quality.

The Selection tool is active.

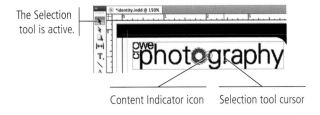

Content Indicator icon   Selection tool cursor

10. Click the Content Indicator icon in the logo frame.

When the frame's content is selected, options in the Control panel relate to the placed object and not the containing frame. The X+ and Y+ fields define the position of the image *within the frame*. As you can see, InDesign remembers the placed file's original size; the Scale X and Scale Y fields show the file's current size as a percentage of the original.

Note:

You can also use the Direct Selection tool to access and edit the content inside a graphics frame.

The Selection tool is active.

The Control panel now show the parameters of the content in the frame.

The red frame indicates that you are now editing the frame's content instead of the containing frame.

11. Press Esc to return to the frame of the selected object.

The graphics frame is again selected, and the Selection tool is still active.

12. Save the file and continue to the next exercise.

 PLACE IMAGES INTO EXISTING FRAMES

In many cases, you will need to place an image or graphic into an existing frame and then manipulate the placed file to suit the available space. In the previous stage of this project, you created eight empty graphics frames across the filmstrip graphic; in this exercise, you will place the client's thumbnail photos into those frames.

1. With identity.indd open, make the filmstrip graphic at the bottom of the page visible in your document window.

2. Using the Selection tool, click one of the empty graphics frames.

When objects are grouped, the Selection tool selects the entire group.

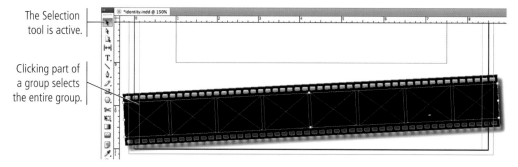

The Selection tool is active.

Clicking part of a group selects the entire group.

3. Open the Layers panel (Window>Layers), then click the arrow to the left of Layer 1 to expand the layer.

Every file has a default layer named "Layer 1", where any objects that you create exist by default. (You will use multiple layers in a later project to create multiple versions of a document.)

The Layers panel in InDesign CS5 also serves another purpose. Every object on a layer is listed in the panel, nested under the appropriate layer name. Groups, which you created in an earlier exercise, can be expanded so you can access and manage the individual components of the group.

Solid-color squares in this column indicate which items are selected.

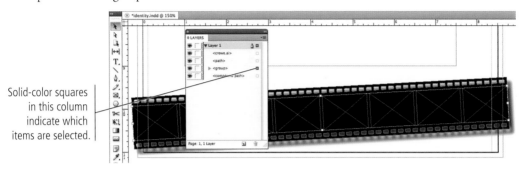

4. Click the arrow to the left of the <group> item to expand the group.

5. Click the Select Item button for the first <rectangle> item in the group.

This method makes it easy to work with individual items in a group, without first breaking apart the group.

Click this icon to select a specific item within the group.

The smaller square indicates that one or more objects in the group is selected.

While still part of the group, only one frame is selected.

Click the arrows to expand or collapse a layer or group.

Click a square to select a specific item.

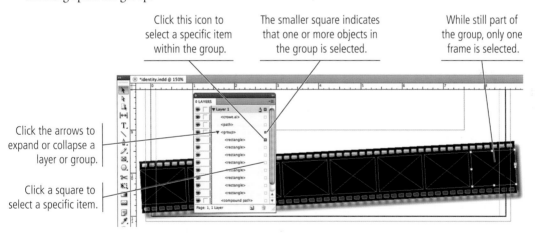

6. In the Control panel, check the Auto-Fit option.

When this option is checked, the image you place into the frame will automatically be scaled proportionally to fit the available space in the frame.

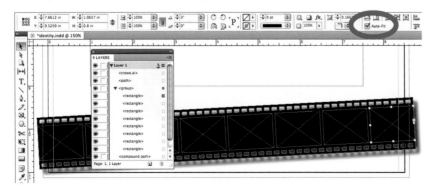

Note:

You can also use the Direct Selection tool to select individual objects within a group.

7. **Repeat Steps 5–6 for the remaining seven placeholder frames.**

8. **Choose File>Place. If necessary, navigate to the WIP>Crowe folder.**

9. **In the Place dialog box, click thumb1.tif to select it. Press Shift and click thumb8.tif to select it and all in-between files.**

   In many cases, you will need to place more than one image from the same location into an InDesign layout. Rather than placing images one at a time, you can streamline the process by loading multiple images into the cursor at once, and then clicking to place each image in the correct location.

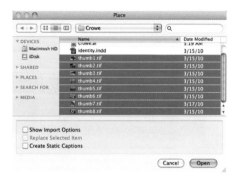

10. **Click Open to load the selected files into the Place cursor.**

    When you select multiple files in the Place dialog box, the cursor is loaded with all of the selected pictures; a number in the cursor shows the number of files that are loaded.

    You can use the Left Arrow and Right Arrow keys to navigate through the loaded images, watching the cursor thumbnails to find the one you want to place.

Eight images are currently loaded in the Place cursor.

This thumbnail shows the content of the first file in the cursor.

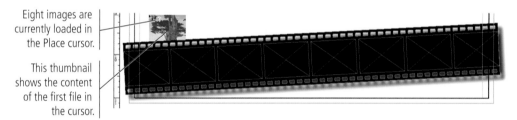

11. **Click inside the left placeholder frame to place the first image.**

    As soon as you place the first file, the next loaded image appears as the cursor thumbnail.

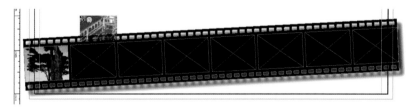

12. **Click inside each empty frame to place the remaining loaded images.**

13. Choose the Direct Selection tool, and then click the fifth image thumbnail.

As already mentioned, the Direct Selection tool can be used to access and manipulate the contents inside a frame. This tool does not require ungrouping. (You could also double-click a grouped item with the Selection tool to aceess only one item in a group, and then use the Content Indicator icon to access the frame content.)

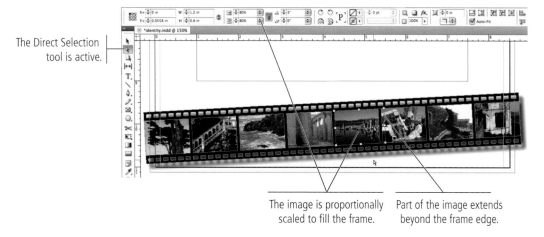

The Direct Selection tool is active.

The image is proportionally scaled to fill the frame.

Part of the image extends beyond the frame edge.

14. In the Control panel, make sure the link icon for the scaling fields is active (unbroken links). Type 100 in the Scale X field and press Return/Enter to apply the change.

Because you used the Auto-Fit option, these thumbnail images have all been placed at 80% proportionally. The images are already small, and reducing the percentage makes the detail in the fifth image *too* small. You can always change the image scaling after it has been scaled by the Auto-Fit option.

Note:

Even though you can't see the entire image, InDesign still has to process the hidden data when you output the file. Whenever possible, it's a good idea to crop the image in Photoshop, and then place the cropped version into your InDesign layout.

15. Click inside the frame area and drag until the right edge of the image is approximately aligned to the right edge of the frame.

When you drag an image within the frame, the entire image becomes visible; this makes it easy to find the area of the image that you want to be visible.

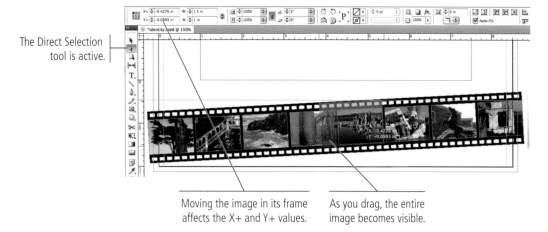

The Direct Selection tool is active.

Moving the image in its frame affects the X+ and Y+ values.

As you drag, the entire image becomes visible.

16. Save the file and continue to the next stage of the project.

Stage 4 Creating and Formatting Basic Text

InDesign is ultimately a page-layout application, not an illustration program. **Page layout** means combining text and graphic elements in a meaningful way to convey a message. Text can be a single word (as in the logo used in this project) or thousands of pages of consecutive copy (as in a dictionary). Virtually every project you build in InDesign will involve text in one way or another; this letterhead is no exception.

CREATE A SIMPLE TEXT FRAME

Adding text to a page is a relatively simple process: draw a frame, and then type. In this exercise, you'll create a new text frame and add the client's tag line, then apply some basic formatting options to style the text.

Keep in mind that this project is an introduction to creating elements on a layout page; there is far more to professional typesetting than the few options you use here. InDesign provides extremely precise control over virtually every aspect of every letter and word on the page. In the following projects, you will learn about the vast number of options that are available for setting and controlling type, from formatting a single paragraph to an entire multi-page booklet.

Note:

Remember from the Getting Started section at the beginning of this book: to complete the projects in this book, you should install and activate the ATC fonts that are provided with the book resource files.

1. **With identity.indd open, select the Type tool in the Tools panel.**

2. **Click in the empty space below the placed logo and drag to create a frame.**

   To type text into a layout, you must first create a frame with the Type tool; when you release the mouse button, you see a flashing bar (called the **insertion point**) where you first clicked to create the text frame.

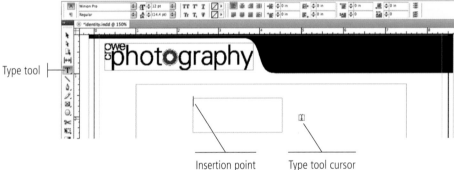

Type tool

Insertion point   Type tool cursor

The tag line for the letterhead is supposed to appear in the black area to the right of the logo. However, if you click inside that area with the Type tool, it will convert the existing shape to a type area. In this case you want a simple rectangular text frame, so you are creating it in an empty area, and then moving it into place.

3. **Review the options in the Control panel.**

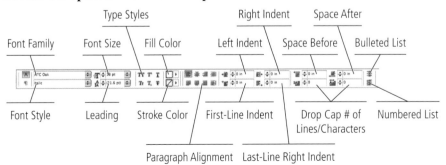

Font Family   Type Styles   Font Size   Fill Color   Left Indent   Right Indent   Space Before   Space After   Bulleted List

Font Style   Leading   Stroke Color   First-Line Indent   Drop Cap # of Lines/Characters   Numbered List

Paragraph Alignment   Last-Line Right Indent

4. **Type** **urban architecture & natural landscapes.**

   The text appears, beginning at the flashing insertion point. Depending on the size of your frame, the text might automatically wrap to a second line within the frame.

   New text in InDesign is automatically set in black 12-pt Minion Pro. This font is installed along with the application, so it should be available on your computer unless someone has modified your system fonts. Don't worry if your type appears in some other font; you will change it shortly.

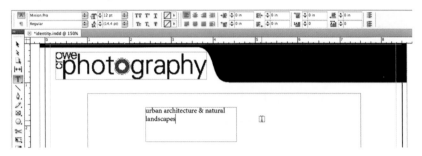

5. **Choose the Selection tool in the Tools panel.**

   You must use the Selection tool to change the position and size of a text frame. You can either drag the handles to manually change the frame, or use the Control panel options to define specific parameters.

6. **In the Control panel, choose the bottom-right reference point and then change the frame's dimensions to:**

X: 8.25″	**W: 4.1″**
Y: 0.8″	**H: 0.25″**

   Some attributes of a type frame are no different than a graphics frame. You can change the position and size (based on the selected reference point) using the fields on the left end of the Control panel.

Most Control panel options for a type frame are the same as for any other frame.

When the frame is selected, these options define the color attributes of the frame.

Because type is black by default, it is not visible over the black shape.

The Selection tool is active.

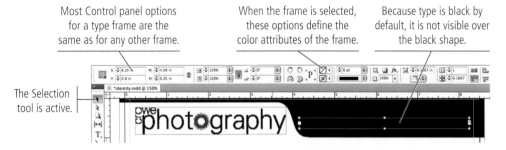

7. **Choose the Type tool, and click inside the repositioned text frame to place the insertion point.**

   Because the default type format is black, you can't see the characters on the black background. Because you know they are there, you can still select them.

The insertion point is placed even though you can't see the black text.

The Type tool is active.

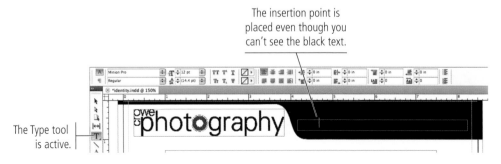

8. **Choose Edit>Select All to select all of the text in the frame.**

   Character formatting such as the font, style, and size apply only to selected characters. You will learn about all of the available character formatting options in Project 2.

9. **In the Control panel, open the Fill swatch panel and click the Paper color.**

   The white-filled text now appears over the black background. (It is still highlighted, so it currently appears in reverse.)

Click here to change the type fill color.   Highlighted text

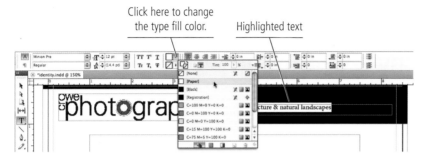

10. **Macintosh: With the text still selected, open the Font menu in the Control panel and choose ATC Oak>Italic.**

    Different styles of the same font appear as submenus to the main font list; the primary font is listed in the menu, and variations are listed in the attached submenu.

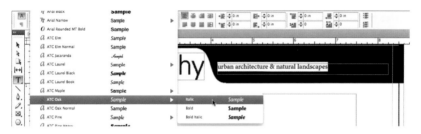

Windows: Open the Font Family menu and choose ATC Oak, and then open the Font Style menu and choose Italic.

Windows does not display different font styles in submenus. You have to choose the font first, and then use the secondary menu to choose the appropriate style.

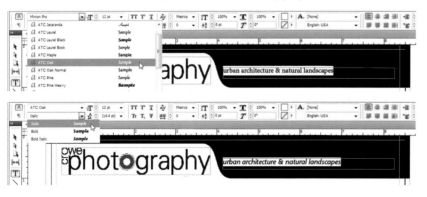

Note:

Type defaults to a 100% black fill with no stroke. (You can apply a stroke to type, but you should be very careful when you do to avoid destroying the letter shapes.)

Note:

There are three primary types of fonts:

***PostScript (Type 1) fonts** have two file components (outline and printer) that must both be available for output.*

***TrueType fonts** have a single file, but (until recently) were primarily used on the Windows platform.*

***OpenType fonts** are contained in a single file that can include more than 60,000 glyphs (characters) in a single font. OpenType fonts are cross-platform; the same font file can be used on both Macintosh and Windows systems.*

InDesign identifies the font types with different icons in the Font menu.

TT   TrueType font

O   OpenType font

a   PostScript font

There are other types of fonts, including PostScript Type 3 and Multiple Master, but these should generally be avoided.

11. Click the Up-Arrow button for the Font Size field until you see a red icon on the right edge of the frame.

Each time you click, you increase the type size by one point. The red X is the **overset text icon**; it indicates that more text exists than will fit into the frame.

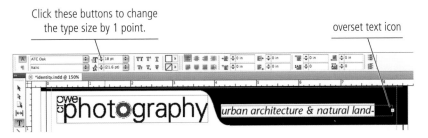

When you see an overset text icon, you can:

- Edit the text to fit the available space, which is usually not allowable for a graphic designer.

- Make the frame larger to fit the text, which is not always possible.

- Add more frames to the story and thread the text into the extra frames, which is also not always possible.

- Reduce the type size or adjust other formatting options to make the type fit into the available space, which can make text unreadable (depending on how small you have to make it).

12. Click the Down-Arrow button once to reduce the type size by 1 point.

This allows all the type to fit in the frame.

13. Click anywhere in the selected text to place the insertion point.

This removes the highlight, indicating that the characters are now deselected.

14. In the Control panel, click the [Paragraph] Align Right option.

Paragraph formatting — including alignment — applies to the entire paragraph where the insertion point is placed. You don't have to first select the entire paragraph. (You will learn about the available paragraph formatting options in Project 2.)

Click here to apply right paragraph alignment.

Insertion point

15. Save the file and continue to the next exercise.

Note:

You can also choose from the common preset type sizes in the menu, or type a specific size in the field.

If you type in the Font Size field, you don't need to type the unit "pt" for the type size; InDesign automatically applies the measurement for you.

Note:

Press Command/Control-Shift-> to increase the type size by 2 points, or Command/Control-Shift-< to decrease the type size by 2 points.

You have a number of options for selecting type characters in a frame.

- Select specific characters by clicking with the Type tool and dragging.
- Double-click a word to select the entire word.
- Triple-click a word to select the entire line that contains the word.
- Quadruple-click a word to select the entire paragraph that contains the word.
- Place the insertion point and press Shift-Right Arrow or Shift-Left Arrow to select the character to the immediate right or left of the insertion point, respectively.
- Place the insertion point and press Shift-Up Arrow or Shift-Down Arrow to select all characters up to the same position as the insertion point in the previous or next line, respectively.
- Place the insertion point and press Command/Control-Shift-Right Arrow or Command/Control-Shift-Left Arrow to select the entire word immediately to the right or left of the insertion point, respectively.
- Place the insertion point and press Command/Control-Shift-Up Arrow or Command/Control-Shift-Down Arrow to select the rest of paragraph immediately before or after the insertion point, respectively.

PLACE AN EXTERNAL TEXT FILE

You just learned how to create a text frame and create new text. You can also import text that was created in an external word-processing application, which is a common situation when creating page-layout jobs (more common, perhaps, than manually typing text in a frame). In this exercise, you import text that was saved in a rich-text format (RTF) file, which can store type-formatting options as well as the actual text.

1. **With identity.indd open, make sure nothing is selected in the layout and then choose File>Place.**

   Remember, you can choose Edit>Deselect All, or simply click in an empty area of the workspace to deselect any selected objects.

2. **Navigate to contact.rtf in the WIP>Crowe folder. Make sure none of the options are checked at the bottom of the dialog box and click Open.**

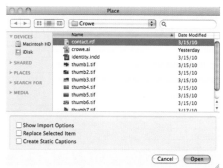

The loaded Place cursor shows a preview of the text you're importing.

3. **Click the loaded Place cursor near the bottom of the page, above the filmstrip graphic but within the margin guides.**

   The resulting text frame is automatically created as wide as the defined margin guides, and extending down to the bottom margin guide on the page.

Placing text from a file automatically creates a text frame to contain the text.

4. **Using the Selection tool, click the bottom-right handle of the frame and drag until the frame is just large enough to contain the text.**

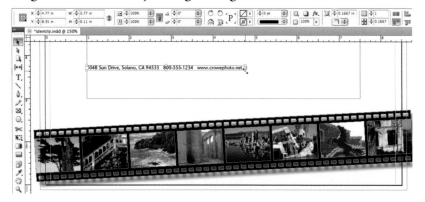

5. **Click the bottom-right bounding box handle of the frame. Press Command/Control-Shift, and then drag to the right.**

   As you drag the frame handle, pressing Command/Control allows you to resize the type along with the frame. Pressing Shift constrains the scaling to maintain the original height-to-width ratio.

6. **When the Scale X and Scale Y fields in the Control panel show approximately 125%, release the mouse button.**

   The Control panel shows the percentage to which the frame and its content are being scaled.

   Click the handle, press Command/Control-Shift, and then drag the handle to resize the frame and the text inside it.

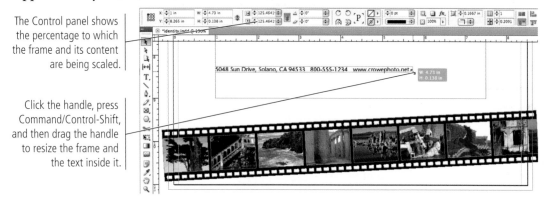

7. **With the Selection tool active, double-click inside the text frame.**

   This automatically switches to the Type tool and places the insertion point in the text in the frame where you double-clicked.

   Double-clicking with the Selection tool places the insertion point into the frame.

   Type options are available in the Control panel.

   The Type tool is automatically selected.

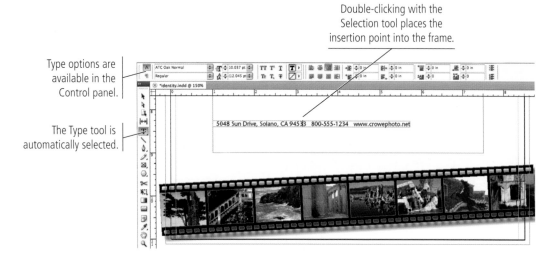

8. **Click the Selection tool to activate it again. Move the cursor outside the top-right corner handle until you see the rotation cursor. Click and drag up until you have rotated the frame by 3°.**

   This is the same angle that you used for the filmstrip graphic.

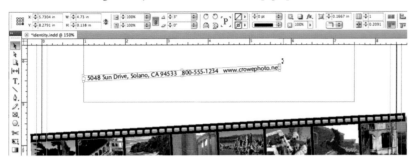

Note:

You can also use the Free Transform tool to rotate an object, but changing tools is not necessary since the same rotation functionality can be accessed with the Selection tool.

9. **Using the Selection tool, move the rotated text frame into place just above the filmstrip, with the right edge at 8.25″.**

   Use the following image as a guide for placing the frame.

10. **Choose View>Extras>Hide Frame Edges.**

    This command turns off the blue borders that surround every frame. Frame edges can be very valuable when you're working with some objects, but they can be distracting in other cases. Always remember that you can toggle the frame edges on and off in the View>Extras submenu.

Note:

If a menu command is not visible, choose Show All Menu Items at the bottom of the menu.

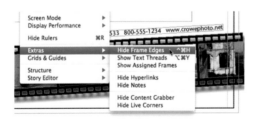

    When frame edges are hidden, moving the Selection tool cursor over a frame reveals its edges. This frame highlighting can make it easier to find exactly the object you want, especially when working in an area with a number of overlapping or nearby objects.

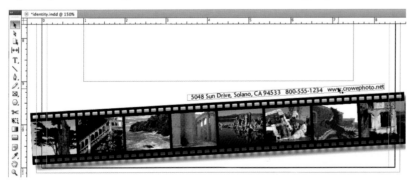

11. **Save the file and continue to the final stage of the project.**

Copying and Pasting

The standard Cut, Copy, and Paste options are available in InDesign, just as they are in most applications. Whatever you have selected will be copied or cut to the Clipboard, and whatever is in the Clipboard will be pasted. InDesign has a number of special pasting options in the Edit menu:

Paste. If you are pasting an object (frame, etc.), the object will be pasted in the center of the document window. If you are pasting text, it will be pasted at the location of the current insertion point; if the insertion point is not currently placed, the text is placed in a new basic text frame in the middle of the document window.

Paste without Formatting. This command is available when text is in the Clipboard; the text is pasted using the default type formatting options (12-pt black Minion Pro, if it hasn't been changed on your system).

Paste Into. This command is available when an object is in the Clipboard and another object is selected. The pasted object becomes the contents of the object that is selected when you choose this command.

Paste in Place. This command pastes an object at the exact position as the original. If you paste on the same page as the original, you create a second object exactly on top of the first. You can also use this command to place a copy in the exact position as the original, but on a different page in the layout.

Managing Stacking Order

The top-to-bottom order of objects is called **stacking order**; each object you create is stacked on top of existing objects. When you have multiple stacked objects — especially ones that are closely spaced — it can be difficult to select exactly what you want. Fortunately, the application provides a number of options to make it easier.

When you move the Selection tool cursor over an object, the edges of the object are highlighted. This lets you know what will be selected if you click.

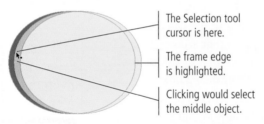

The Selection tool cursor is here.

The frame edge is highlighted.

Clicking would select the middle object.

When an object is already selected, InDesign CS5 favors the already selected object. This prevents you from accidentally selecting an object higher in the stacking order (for example, if you want to drag only the middle object); but this also means you have to be careful if you do want to select a different object.

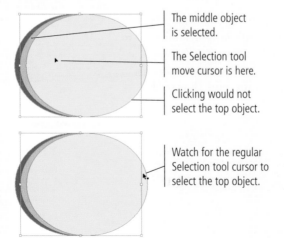

The middle object is selected.

The Selection tool move cursor is here.

Clicking would not select the top object.

Watch for the regular Selection tool cursor to select the top object.

You can use the Object>Select submenu commands (or their related keyboard shortcuts) to access objects relative to their order in the stack.

You can use the Object>Arrange submenu commands (or their related keyboard shortcuts) to change the stacking-order position of objects.

Finally, you can use the individual item listings in the Layers panel to select exactly the object you want, or to rearrange objects in the layer stack.

Drag an item in the panel to a new position in the stacking order.

Click this icon to select a specific object.

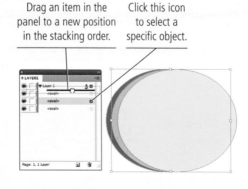

Stage 5 Printing InDesign Files

For a printer to output high-quality pages from Adobe InDesign, some method of defining the page and its elements is required. These definitions are provided by Page Description Languages (PDLs), the most widely used of which is Adobe PostScript 3.

When a file is output to a PostScript-enabled device, the raster image processor (RIP) creates a file that includes mathematical descriptions detailing the construction and placement of the various page elements; the print file precisely maps the location of each pixel on the page. In the printer, the RIP then interprets the description of each element into a matrix of ones (black) and zeros (white). The output device uses this matrix to reconstruct the element as a series of individual dots or spots that form a high-resolution bitmap image on film or paper.

Not every printer on the market is capable of interpreting PostScript information. Low-cost, consumer-level inkjet printers, common in the modern graphic design market, are generally not PostScript compatible. (Some desktop printers can handle PostScript, at least with an additional purchase; consult the technical documentation that came with your printer to make certain it can print PostScript information.) If your printer is non-PostScript compatible, some features in the InDesign Print dialog box will be unavailable and some page elements (particularly EPS files) might not output as expected.

Note:

If you do not have a PostScript output device, you can work around the problem by first exporting your InDesign files to PDF (see Project 2) and then opening the PDFs in Acrobat to print a proof. This is a common workflow solution in the current graphic design industry.

PRINT A SAMPLE PROOF

Not too long ago, every job sent to a commercial printer required a hardcopy proof to accompany the disk as an example of the layout content. As digital file submission continues to gain ground, however, physical printer proofs are becoming less common.

In general, every job you create will be printed at some point in the workflow — whether for your own review, as a client comp, or as a final proof that accompanies a file to the commercial printer. So, whether you need a basic proof or a final job proof, you should still understand what is possible in the InDesign Print dialog box.

Composite proofs print all colors on the same sheet, which allows you to judge page geometry and the overall positioning of elements. Final composite proofs that are provided to the printer should include **registration marks** (special printer's marks used to check the alignment of individual inks when the job is printed), and they should always be output at 100% size.

Note:

It is also important to realize that desktop inkjet and laser printers typically do not accurately represent color.

1. **With identity.indd open, choose File>Print.**

   The Print dialog box includes dozens of options in eight different categories.

   The most important options you'll select are the Printer and PPD (PostScript printer description) at the top of the dialog box. InDesign reads the information in the PPD to determine which of the specific print options are available for the current output.

2. **Choose the printer you want to use in the Printer menu, and choose the PPD for that printer in the PPD menu (if possible).**

3. Review the options in the General pane.

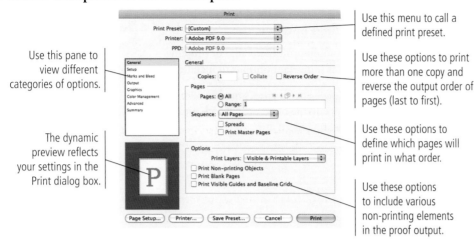

Use this pane to view different categories of options.

Use this menu to call a defined print preset.

Use these options to print more than one copy and reverse the output order of pages (last to first).

The dynamic preview reflects your settings in the Print dialog box.

Use these options to define which pages will print in what order.

Use these options to include various non-printing elements in the proof output.

If you frequently use the same options for printing proofs, simply click the Save Preset button at the bottom of the dialog box after defining those settings. You can then call all of those same settings by choosing the saved preset in the Print Preset menu.

4. Click the Setup option in the list of categories.

These options determine the paper size that will be used for the output (not to be confused with the page size), the paper orientation, and page scaling and positioning options relative to the paper size.

5. If your printer can print to tabloid-size paper, choose Tabloid in the Paper Size menu.

If you can only print to letter-size paper, choose the landscape paper orientation option, and then activate the Tile check box.

To output a letter-size page at 100% on letter-size paper, you have to tile to multiple sheets of paper; using the landscape paper orientation allows you to tile to two sheets instead of four (as shown in the preview area).

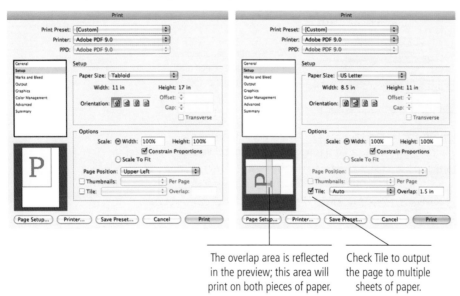

The overlap area is reflected in the preview; this area will print on both pieces of paper.

Check Tile to output the page to multiple sheets of paper.

The Offset and Gap fields should only be used when a job is output to an imagesetter or high-end proofing device. They define page placement on a piece of oversized film or on a printing plate.

6. **Click the Marks and Bleed option in the list of categories.**
Activate the All Printer's Marks option and change the Offset field to 0.125".
Make sure the Use Document Bleed Settings option is checked.

You can specify individual printer's marks, or simply print them all. For proofing purposes, the crop and bleed marks are the most important options to include.

The Offset value determines how far from the page edge printer's marks will be placed; some printers require printer's marks to stay outside the bleed area, which means the offset should be at least the same as than the defined bleed area.

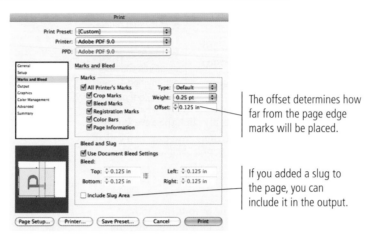

The offset determines how far from the page edge marks will be placed.

If you added a slug to the page, you can include it in the output.

7. **Click the Output option in the list of categories.**
If you can print color, choose Composite CMYK or Composite RGB in the Color menu; otherwise, choose Composite Gray.

In the Color menu, you can choose the color model you want to use. (If you only have a black-and-white printer, this menu will default to Composite Gray.) The composite options output all colors to a single page, which is appropriate for a desktop proof. If you choose either Separations option in the menu, the Inks list shows which inks (separations) will be included in the output.

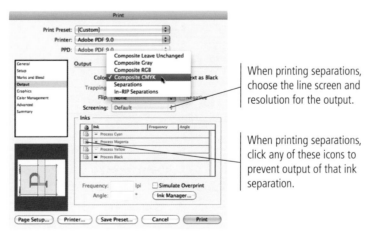

When printing separations, choose the line screen and resolution for the output.

When printing separations, click any of these icons to prevent output of that ink separation.

The Trapping, Flip, Negative, Screening, Frequency, and Angle options should only be used by the output service provider; these options relate to the way separations are imaged on a printing plate for commercial print output.

8. **Click Graphics in the list of categories.**

9. **Choose Optimized Subsampling in the Images Send Data menu.**

   This menu determines how much data is sent to the output device for placed images.

   - All, the default option, sends full-resolution image data.

   - Optimized Subsampling sends only the necessary data to output the best possible resolution on the printer you are using.

   - Proxy outputs low-resolution screen previews, which reduces the time required for output.

   - None outputs all placed images as gray frames with crossed diagonal lines. This is useful for reviewing overall placement when developing an initial layout comp.

10. **Choose Subset in the Fonts Download menu.**

    This menu determines how much font data is downloaded to the printer. (Font data is required by the output device to print the job correctly.)

    - None sends no font information to the printer. (This can cause output problems, especially if you use TrueType fonts.)

    - Complete sends the entire font file for every font that is used in the document.

    - Subset sends font information only for the characters that are used in the document.

11. **Check the Download PPD Fonts option.**

    Professional-quality output devices include a number of resident fonts, from just a few to the entire Adobe type library. If this option is checked, InDesign sends data for all fonts in the document, even if those fonts are installed on the output device. (This can be important because different fonts of the same name might have different font metrics, which can cause text to reflow and appear different in the print than in the file that you created.)

12. **Leave the PostScript and Data Format menus at their default values.**

    The PostScript menu defines which level of PostScript to use. Some older devices cannot process PostScript 3. You should generally leave this menu at the default value.

    The Data Format menu defines how image data is transferred. ASCII is compatible with older devices, and is useful for cross-platform applications. Binary is smaller than ASCII, but might not work on all platforms.

13. **Click Print to output the page.**

14. **When the document comes back into focus, save and close it.**

15. **Close the layout files when you're finished.**

Note:

We're intentionally skipping the Color Management and Advanced panes in the Print dialog box. We explain them in later projects when they are relevant to the project content.

1. _____ is the area of an object that extends past the edge of a page to compensate for variations in the output process.

2. _____ is a special kind of raster image that has only two possible color values, black or white.

3. The _____ defines the outermost dimensions of an object; it is always a rectangle, regardless of the object's specific shape.

4. _____ are based on the concept of anchor points and their defining control handles.

5. _____ are the four primary colors used in process-color printing.

6. The _____ tool is used to select entire frames or other objects.

7. The _____ tool can be used to select the image contained within a specific frame when the frame is part of a group.

8. The _____ panel can be used to create complex shapes by combining multiple objects.

9. The _____ can be used to access a frame's content when the Selection tool is active.

10. The _____ is context sensitive, reflecting different options depending on what is selected in the document.

1. Briefly explain the difference between a vector graphic and a raster image.

2. Briefly explain how resolution affects a page laid out in InDesign.

3. Briefly explain the concept of process color.

Portfolio Builder Project

Use what you learned in this project to complete the following freeform exercise.
Carefully read the art director and client comments, then create your own design to meet the needs of the project.
Use the space below to sketch ideas; when finished, write a brief explanation of your reasoning behind your final design.

art director comments

The owner of your agency is pleased with your work on behalf of your client. She has decided to create more formal branding for your design agency, and wants you to create a new logo and the accompanying collateral pieces with the new logo.

To complete this project, you should:

❏ Develop a compelling logo that suggests the agency's purpose (graphic design). Incorporate the agency's name — Creative Concepts — in the logo.

❏ Build a letterhead using the same specifications that you used to design the Crowe letterhead.

❏ Build a business card that is 3.5″ wide by 2″ high, with 1/8″ bleeds.

❏ Build an envelope layout for #10 business-size envelopes (9.5″ × 4.125″).

client comments

For the logo, I want something that really says 'graphic design' — how can we convince clients that we can design their logos if we don't have a good design for our own? Find or create some kind of imagery that people will immediately recognize as graphics- or art-related.

The letterhead should have the company's mailing address, phone number, and Web site. The business card needs to include a name, title, mailing address, email, and phone number. The envelope should only have the mailing address and the Web site. Use your own contact information as placeholder text for everything.

For the envelope, we're going to print pre-folded envelopes so you can't use bleeds. In fact, you need to keep all objects at least 0.25″ from the edges.

Keep in mind that you're building a complete identity package, so all pieces should have a consistent look. Whatever you do on the letterhead, you should use similar visual elements on all three pieces.

project justification

We designed this project to introduce you to the basics of page layout with InDesign; you will expand on these skills throughout this book. Creating a new document to meet specific project needs — including page size, margins, and the printer's stated bleed requirements — is one of the most important tasks you will complete in InDesign.

After the page structure is created, InDesign has many tools for creating objects — basic shapes, lines and Bézier curves, placeholder frames, and text frames. The built-in drawing tools can create sophisticated artwork directly on the page, such as the filmstrip in this letterhead layout (although InDesign should not be considered an alternative to Adobe Illustrator for creating all vector artwork). You can also place external image and text files, and then transform those files to meet the specific needs of a given project.

There are many different methods for managing objects and their content. The Selection and Direct Selection tools, the Content Indicator icon, frame edge highlighting, and the Layers panel all provide ways to access only — and exactly — what you want to edit.

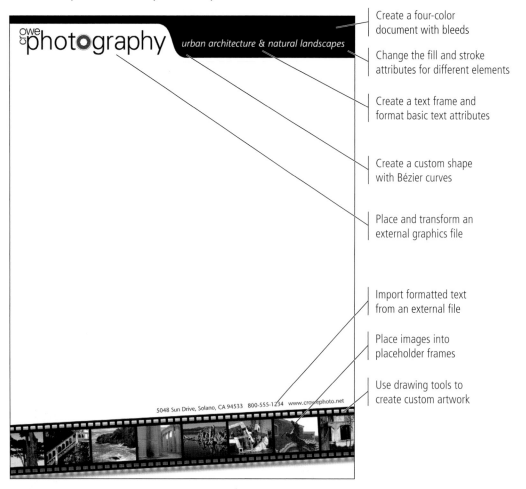

Create a four-color document with bleeds

Change the fill and stroke attributes for different elements

Create a text frame and format basic text attributes

Create a custom shape with Bézier curves

Place and transform an external graphics file

Import formatted text from an external file

Place images into placeholder frames

Use drawing tools to create custom artwork

Festival Poster

Your client is the promoter for the Miami Beach Jazz Festival, which is held annually at several locations throughout the South Beach area. The client wants to create posters that will be plastered all over the city, from local restaurants and clubs to bus stops and construction sites that don't say "Post No Bills." This type of poster should use very little text set in a large, easy-to-read font, and it needs to be eye-catching from a distance, with large, vivid graphics.

This project incorporates the following skills:

❏ Creating a file with the appropriate settings for a four-color, commercially printed poster

❏ Using gradients, graphics, and image effects to attract the viewer's attention

❏ Adding text elements and applying formatting as appropriate for a poster

❏ Threading a single text story across multiple text frames

❏ Understanding the various options for formatting characters and paragraphs

❏ Using inline graphics to highlight important text elements

❏ Creating a PDF file that meets the printer's requirements

Project Meeting

client comments

The poster to promote this festival is basically the "play bill," and we will plaster it all over the city. We want the poster to be very attractive, colorful, and vivid, so the main focus — and most of the poster real estate — should be on the graphics. But the text also has to be readable; I emailed the text I want you to place at the bottom of the poster this morning. Our posters for past years' festivals have always been 11 × 17″, and we want to stick with that size.

This year's festival tag line is "Move Your Feet to the Beat." I found an excellent illustration of a saxophone player that we'd like to use as the main image, and we hope you can make the tag line look like it's coming out of the end of the sax. I also found some nice beach images that might make good backgrounds, so we emailed those to you as well.

art director comments

The client has provided all the pieces you need, so you can get started composing the layout. Most of this job is going to involve compositing multiple images and formatting text, but I want you to go beyond basic image placement. InDesign includes many tools for manipulating images; use some of those to make sure this poster consists of more than just plain pictures.

Finally, I want you to use a special metallic ink for the festival's tag line. That should give the poster just a bit more visual impact than regular flat colors. I think the gold 8660 in Pantone's metallic collection will work well with the other visual elements.

You already know the page size, and according to the printer the poster needs a 1/4″ bleed allowance just to be safe. The final poster should be saved as a PDF using the printer's specs, which I'll email to you.

project objectives

To complete this project, you will:

- ❏ Create a print layout using a master text frame
- ❏ Convert the content type of frames
- ❏ Create a custom gradient to add visual impact
- ❏ Create a custom frame using an image clipping path
- ❏ Apply visual effects to unify various graphic elements
- ❏ Thread the flow of text through multiple text frames
- ❏ Format text characters and paragraphs to effectively convey a message
- ❏ Place inline graphics to highlight important textual elements
- ❏ Place text on a path
- ❏ Apply a spot color
- ❏ Create a PDF file for commercial output

Stage 1 Building Graphic Interest

In Project 1, you learned the basics of placing graphics into a layout and drawing shapes using the built-in InDesign tools. You know that graphics and text are contained in frames, and that objects (including graphics frames) can have stroke and fill attributes. You can use those foundational skills to build virtually any InDesign layout.

InDesign also includes a number of options for extending your artistic options beyond simply compositing text and graphics that were finalized in other applications. The first stage of this project incorporates a number of these creative tools to accomplish your client's stated goal of grabbing the viewer's attention with vivid, attractive graphics.

SET UP THE WORKSPACE

1. **Download ID5_RF_Project2.zip from the Student Files Web page.**

2. **Expand the ZIP archive in your WIP folder (Macintosh) or copy the archive contents into your WIP folder (Windows).**

   This results in a folder named **Jazz**, which contains the files you need for this project. You should also use this folder to save the files you create in this project.

3. **With no file open in InDesign, open the Units & Increments pane of the Preferences dialog box (in the InDesign menu on Macintosh or the Edit menu on Windows).**

4. **Change both Ruler Units menus to Inches and click OK.**

   In Project 1 you changed the default units of measurement for an open file. By changing the preferences with no file open, you're changing the application default preferences; the settings that you define will be applied in any new file you create, but not to already-existing files.

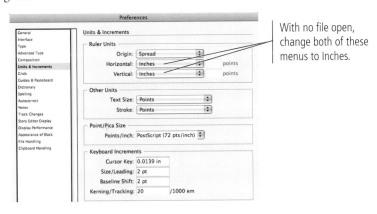

With no file open, change both of these menus to Inches.

5. **Choose File>New>Document.**

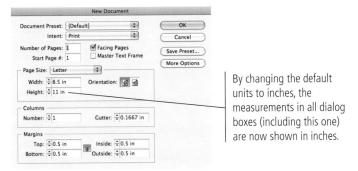

By changing the default units to inches, the measurements in all dialog boxes (including this one) are now shown in inches.

6. **Create a new one-page print document that is 11″ wide by 17″ high (Tabloid-size) with 1″ margins and 0.25″ bleeds on all four sides. Create the file with no master text frame and without facing pages.**

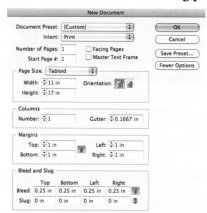

Note:

Industry standards typically call for a 0.125″ bleed, but in this case the printer specifically requested 0.25″ bleed allowance.

7. **Save the file as `poster.indd` in your WIP>Jazz folder and then continue to the next exercise.**

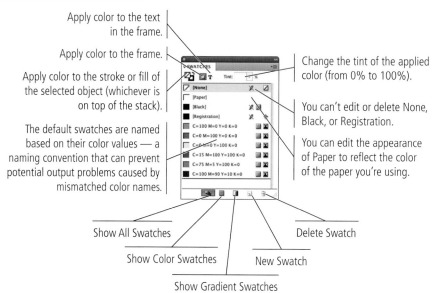

DEFINE COLOR SWATCHES

The Swatches panel is used to apply predefined colors to any element in a layout. Six CMYK color swatches are included in the default set for print documents, as well as three special colors (Paper, Black, and Registration) and a None swatch that removes color from the selected attribute.

Note:

Using the Fill and Stroke swatches at the top of the Swatches panel, you can apply different colors to the fill and stroke of selected text.

Apply color to the text in the frame.

Apply color to the frame.

Apply color to the stroke or fill of the selected object (whichever is on top of the stack).

The default swatches are named based on their color values — a naming convention that can prevent potential output problems caused by mismatched color names.

Change the tint of the applied color (from 0% to 100%).

You can't edit or delete None, Black, or Registration.

You can edit the appearance of Paper to reflect the color of the paper you're using.

Show All Swatches

Show Color Swatches

Show Gradient Swatches

Delete Swatch

New Swatch

Note:

Editing the appearance of the Paper swatch only affects the on-screen preview. It does not appear in the print output.

You can define colors based on one of three color models (CMYK, RGB, or LAB), or you can call spot colors from built-in libraries of special inks. Each different mode and type of color has an identifying icon in the Swatches panel.

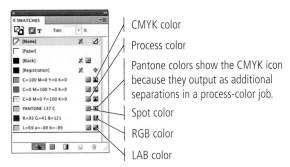

CMYK color

Process color

Pantone colors show the CMYK icon because they output as additional separations in a process-color job.

Spot color

RGB color

LAB color

1. **With `poster.indd` open, open the Swatches panel (Window>Color>Swatches).**

2. **Open the Swatches panel Options menu.**

   This menu has options for creating four types of color swatches: Color, Tint, Gradient, and Mixed Ink.

   - **Color** swatches store specific colors based on defined percentages of each component ink.

   - **Gradient** swatches store specific transitions from one color to another.

   - A **Tint** swatch is a specific stored percentage of another swatch, which is useful if you frequently use (for example) a 30% tint of C=100 M=42 Y=0 K=73. You can apply that tint with a single click instead of applying the color, and then changing the tint of the applied color. Every click you save is a boost in productivity, especially if you're building layouts with multiple elements.

   - **Mixed Ink** swatches allow you to combine percentages of spot and process colors, or of multiple spot colors; this option is only available when at least one spot color exists in the file. The **Mixed Ink Group** option allows you to build multiple swatches at once, based on specific incremental percentages of inks. Be very careful if you use mixed ink swatches; they can be a source of unpredictable color reproduction and potential output problems.

Click here to open the panel Options menu.

This option allows you to import swatches from another InDesign file.

This option finds and adds colors that were applied in the layout without using a defined swatch (e.g., using the Colors panel).

3. **Choose New Color Swatch in the panel Options menu.**

4. Leave the Name with Color Value option checked. Make sure the Color Type is set to Process and the Color Mode is set to CMYK.

There is no industry standard for naming colors, but InDesign comes close with the Name with Color Value option. This type of naming convention — basing names on the color components — serves several purposes:

- You know exactly what components the color contains, so you can easily see if you are duplicating colors.

- You can immediately tell that the color should be a process build rather than a special ink or spot color.

- You avoid mismatched color names and duplicated spot colors, which are potential disasters in the commercial printing production process.

Mismatched color names occur when a defined color name has two different values — one defined in the page layout and one defined in an image file that you placed into your layout. When the files are output, the output device might be confused by different definitions for the same color name; the imported value might replace the project's value for that particular color name (or vice versa). The change could be subtle, or it could be drastic.

A similar problem occurs when the same spot color is assigned different names in different applications. For example, you might define a spot color in InDesign as "Border Color"; another designer might define the same spot color in Illustrator as "Spec Blue." When the illustration is placed into the InDesign layout, two different spot-color separations exist, even though the different color names have the same values.

Color by Numbers

If you base your color choices solely on what you see on your monitor, what appears to be a perfect blue sky will probably not look quite right when it's printed with process-color inks. Even if you have calibrated your monitor, no monitor is 100% effective at simulating printed color. As long as monitors display color in RGB, there will always be some discrepancies.

Every designer should have some sort of process-color chart, available from commercial publishers (some printers might provide the charts produced by the exact press on which your job will be printed). These charts contain small squares of process ink builds so you can see, for example, what a process build of C=10 M=70 Y=30 K=20 will look like when printed. These guides usually show samples in steps of 5% or 10%, printed on both coated and uncoated paper (because the type of paper or substrate can dramatically affect the final result).

When you define process colors in an InDesign project, you should enter specific numbers in the CMYK fields to designate your color choices, rather than relying on your screen preview. As you gain experience defining colors, you will become better able to predict the outcome for a given process-ink build. Rely on what you know to be true rather than what you hope will be true.

The same concept also applies when using special ink libraries. You should have — and use — swatch books that show printed samples of the special inks. You cannot rely on the monitor preview to choose a special ink color. Rather, you should find the color in a printed swatch book, and then enter the appropriate number in the Pantone field (for example) below the color swatches.

Total Area Coverage

When defining the ink values of a process-color build, you must usually limit your **total area coverage** (TAC, also called **total ink coverage** or **total ink density**), or the amount of ink used in a given color.

This might sound complex, but it can be easily calculated by adding the percentages of each ink used to create the color. If a color is defined as C=45 M=60 Y=90 K=0, the total area coverage is 195% (45 + 60 + 90 + 0).

Maximum TAC limits are between 240% and 320% for offset lithography, depending on the paper being used. If you exceed the TAC limits for a given paper-ink-press combination, your printed job might end up with excess ink bleed, smearing, smudging, show-through, or a number of other printing errors because the paper cannot absorb all of the ink.

5. **Define the color with 0% Cyan, 70% Magenta, 95% Yellow, and 0% Black, and then click Add.**

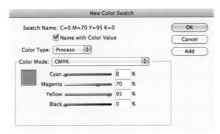

6. **Create two more process-color swatches using the following ink values. Click Done after adding the third color to close the dialog box.**

   Color 1: C=0 M=10 Y=75 K=0

   Color 2: C=0 M=40 Y=0 K=100

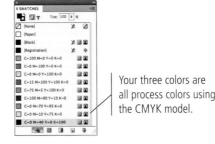

Your three colors are all process colors using the CMYK model.

The third swatch — 100% black and some percent of another color — is called **rich black** or **super black**. Remember, when the inks are printed, adding another ink to solid black enhances the richness of the solid black. Adding magenta typically creates a warmer black, while adding cyan typically creates a cooler black.

7. **Open the Swatches panel Options menu and choose New Color Swatch.**

8. **In the New Color Swatch dialog box, choose Spot in the Color Type menu.**

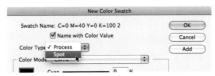

9. **Choose Pantone metallic coated in the Color Mode menu.**

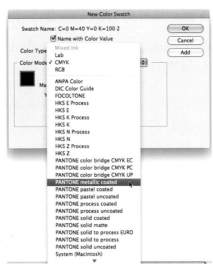

Spot colors are created with special premixed inks to produce a certain color with one ink layer; they are not built from the standard process inks used in CMYK printing. When you output a job with spot colors, each spot color appears on its own separation.

Spot-color inks are commonly used when a special color, such as a corporate color, is required. InDesign includes a number of built-in color libraries, including spot-color systems such as Pantone, Toyo, and DIC. In the United States, the most popular collections of spot colors are the Pantone Matching System (PMS) libraries. TruMatch and Focoltone are also used in the United States; Toyo and DICColor (Dainippon Ink & Chemicals) are used primarily in Japan.

Even though you can choose a color directly from the library on your screen, you should look at a swatch book to verify that you're using the color you intend. Special inks exist because many of the colors cannot be reproduced with process inks, nor can they be accurately represented on a computer monitor. If you specify special colors and then convert them to process colors later, your job probably won't look exactly as you expect.

10. **Place the insertion point in the Pantone field and type 8660.**

You can also scroll through the list and simply click a color to select it.

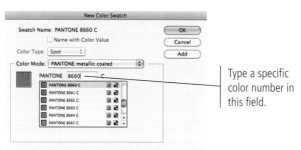

Type a specific color number in this field.

Note:

Spot colors are safely chosen from a swatch book — a book of colors printed with different inks, similar to the paint chip cards used in home decorating.

When choosing spot colors, ask your printer which ink system they support. If you designate TruMatch, but they use Pantone inks, you won't get the colors you expect.

11. **Click OK to return to the document window.**

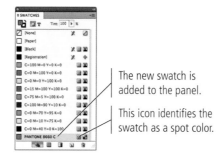

The new swatch is added to the panel.

This icon identifies the swatch as a spot color.

12. **Save the file and continue to the next exercise.**

 CREATE THE POSTER BACKGROUND

The background of this poster is going to be a solid fill of the rich black swatch you defined in the previous exercise. However, an object filling the entire page can cause certain problems. For example, if you try to create a text frame inside the area, you end up converting the frame to a text frame. In this exercise, you use the Layers panel to prevent problems that could be caused by the background shape.

1. **With poster.indd open, choose the Rectangle tool in the Tools panel.**

2. **In the Swatches panel, make sure the Fill swatch is on top and click the C=0 M=40 Y=0 K=100 swatch.**

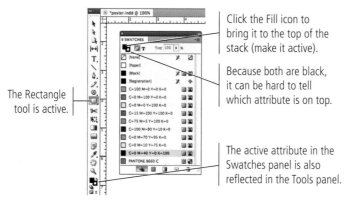

Click the Fill icon to bring it to the top of the stack (make it active).

Because both are black, it can be hard to tell which attribute is on top.

The Rectangle tool is active.

The active attribute in the Swatches panel is also reflected in the Tools panel.

Note:

Remember, all panels (whether docked or not) can be accessed from the Window menu. If you don't see a specific menu command, choose Edit>Show All Menu Items.

3. **Click the Stroke icon at the top of the panel to activate that attribute, then click the None swatch.**

By changing the fill and stroke attributes when no object is selected, you define those attributes for the next object you create.

4. **Using the Rectangle tool, create a rectangle that covers the entire page and extends to the defined bleed guides.**

You can single-click to define the rectangle size, and then drag it into position with the Selection tool. Alternatively, you can simply click and drag with the Rectangle tool, using the Bleed guides to snap the edges of the shape.

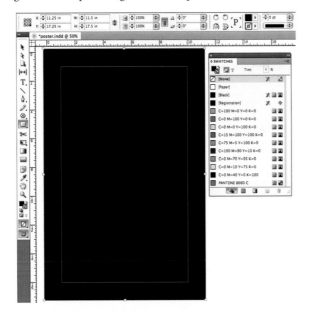

5. **In the Layers panel (Window>Layers), click the arrow to expand Layer 1.**

6. **Click the empty space to the right of the eye icon for the <rectangle> item.**

The second column in the Layers panel can be used to lock individual items or entire layers. (If you lock a whole layer, all items on that layer are automatically locked.)

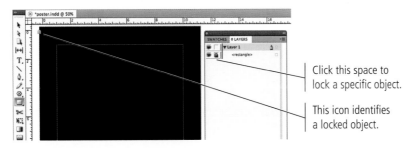

Click this space to lock a specific object.

This icon identifies a locked object.

Note:

You can click an existing lock icon in the Layers panel to unlock an object or layer.

You can also click a lock icon on the page to unlock a specific object.

7. **With the Rectangle tool still selected, change the stroke color to the custom orange swatch. Using the Control panel, change the stroke weight to 6 pt.**

When you locked the rectangle in Step 6, it was automatically deselected. This means that changing the stroke and fill attributes does not affect the existing object.

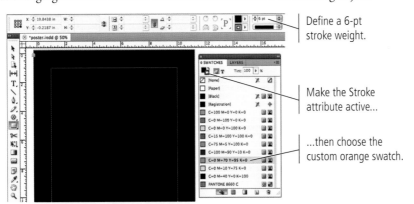

Define a 6-pt stroke weight.

Make the Stroke attribute active...

...then choose the custom orange swatch.

8. **Click and drag to draw a rectangle that fills the area within the defined margin guides.**

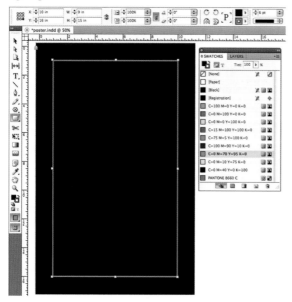

9. **In the Layers panel, click the eye icon to the left of the locked <rectangle>.**

The visible rectangle has the same fill color as the background shape (which is now hidden). To make it easier to see and work with only specific objects, you can use the Layers panel to toggle the visibility of individual objects or entire layers. (If you hide an entire layer, all objects on that layer are hidden.)

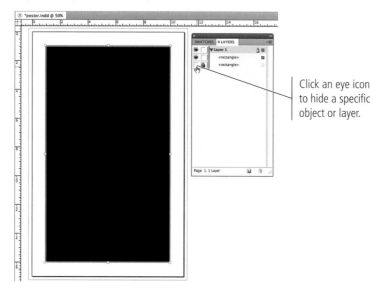

Click an eye icon to hide a specific object or layer.

10. **Save the file and continue to the next exercise.**

DEFINE AND APPLY A GRADIENT

A **gradient**, also called a **blend**, can be used to create a smooth transition from one color to another. You can apply a gradient to any object using the Gradient panel, or you can save a gradient swatch if you plan to use it more than once.

The Gradient panel controls the type and position of applied gradients. You can apply either linear or radial gradients, change the angle of linear gradients, and change the color and location for individual stops along the gradient ramp.

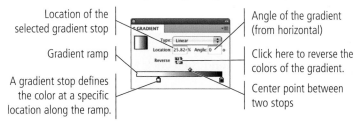

Location of the selected gradient stop

Gradient ramp

A gradient stop defines the color at a specific location along the ramp.

Angle of the gradient (from horizontal)

Click here to reverse the colors of the gradient.

Center point between two stops

1. **With poster.indd open, click outside the area of the visible rectangle to deselect it.**

2. **Choose New Gradient Swatch from the Swatches panel Options menu.**

3. **Click the gradient stop on the left end of the gradient ramp to select it.**

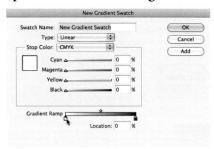

4. **Make sure Linear is selected in the Type menu, and then choose Swatches in the Stop Color menu.**

   You can define gradients using LAB values, CMYK percentages, RGB values, or existing color swatches.

5. **With the first stop selected, click the custom yellow CMYK swatch.**

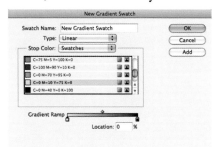

6. **Select the second gradient stop (on the right end of the ramp), and then click the custom orange swatch.**

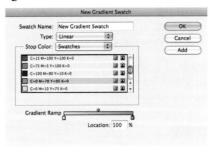

7. **Type Yellow to Orange in the Swatch Name field and then click OK.**

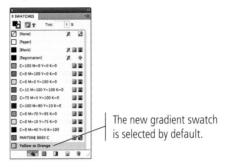

The new gradient swatch is selected by default.

8. **Using the Selection tool, click the visible rectangle on the page to select it.**

9. **Make the Fill icon active in the Swatches panel, and then click the Yellow to Orange gradient swatch.**

It is important to remember but easy to forget: make sure the correct attribute (fill or stroke) is active when you change a color.

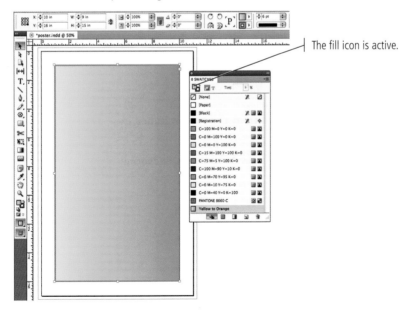

The fill icon is active.

10. **Make the Stroke icon active in the Swatches panel, and then click the Yellow to Orange gradient swatch.**

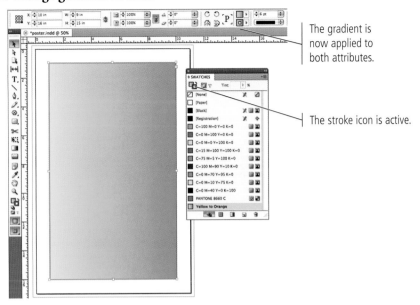

The gradient is now applied to both attributes.

The stroke icon is active.

11. **Save the file and continue to the next exercise.**

MODIFY GRADIENT ATTRIBUTES

As you just saw, it is fairly easy to create and apply a gradient. Once the gradient is in place, you can also modify the specific attributes of a gradient, including its angle and the positioning of specific color stops along its length.

1. **With poster.indd open, make sure the gradient-filled rectangle is selected.**

2. **Using either the Tools or Swatches panel, click to activate the Fill icon.**

3. **Using the Gradient panel (Window>Color>Gradient), change the Angle field to 90° to rotate the gradient.**

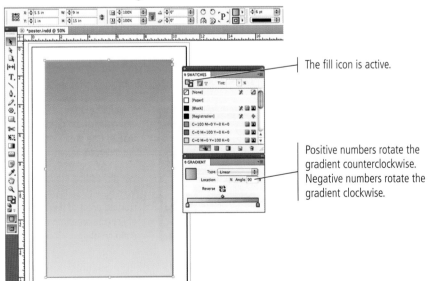

The fill icon is active.

Positive numbers rotate the gradient counterclockwise. Negative numbers rotate the gradient clockwise.

Note:

Remember, all panels can be accessed in the Window menu.

Note:

You can drag a swatch from the Swatches panel to the gradient ramp in the Gradient panel to add a new color stop, or to change the color of an existing stop.

4. **Using the Control panel, change the object height to 10″ based on the top-center reference point.**

   When you change the shape dimensions, the applied gradients are adjusted so the end stops still align to the edges of the object.

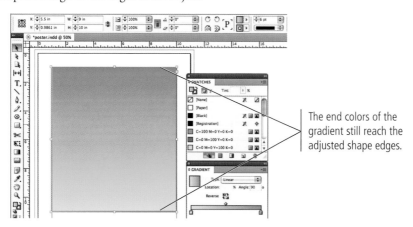

The end colors of the gradient still reach the adjusted shape edges.

5. **With the object still selected, make the Stroke icon active in the Swatches panel.**

   Remember that the attribute on top of the stack is the one you are currently changing. If the wrong attribute is on top of the stack, you will not get the results you are hoping for.

The Gradient Tools

INDESIGN FOUNDATIONS

Clicking a gradient swatch adds a gradient to the selected object, beginning at the left edge and ending at the right edge (for linear gradients), or beginning at the object's center and ending at the object's outermost edge (for radial gradients). When you drag with the Gradient tool, you define the length of the gradient without regard to the object you're filling.

Gradient tool

This box is filled with a gradient that has green at the left end and purple at the right end.

The gradient start and end colors now appear where we first clicked and where we stopped dragging.

We clicked and dragged from here to define the gradient starting point.

Dragging with the Gradient tool changes the length and angle of the gradient.

The Gradient Feather tool has a similar function but produces different results. Rather than creating a specific-colored gradient, the Gradient Feather tool applies a transparency gradient, blending the object from solid to transparent.

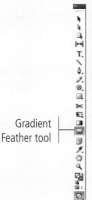

Gradient Feather tool

We placed this image over a blue-filled shape.

The resulting effect blends the image from solid to transparent, allowing the background object to show.

Dragging to here defines the end point of the gradient feather (the area that will be entirely transparent).

We clicked and dragged from here to define the starting point of the feather effect (the area that will be entirely solid).

6. **In the Gradient panel, change the gradient angle to –90° so the stroke goes from yellow at the top to orange at the bottom (the reverse of the fill).**

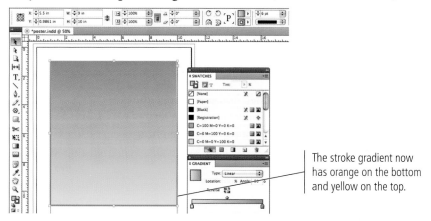

The stroke gradient now has orange on the bottom and yellow on the top.

7. **Click away from the rectangle to deselect it.**

8. **Use the Screen Mode button on the Tools panel or the Application/Menu bar to display the layout in Preview mode.**

   This option hides all guides and frame edges, which makes it easier to see the subtle effect created by the opposing gradients. (We also zoomed in to better show the result.)

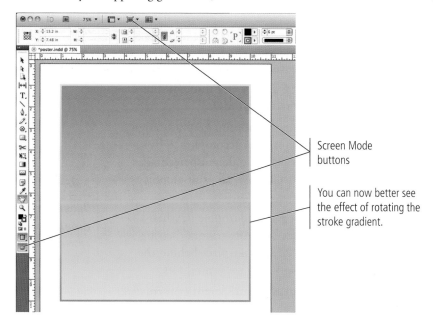

Screen Mode buttons

You can now better see the effect of rotating the stroke gradient.

9. **Choose Normal in the Screen Mode menu to restore the guides and frame edges on screen.**

10. **Save the file and continue to the next exercise.**

The image effects and transparency controls in InDesign provide options for adding dimension and depth, allowing unprecedented creative control directly in the page layout. You can change the transparency of any object (or individual object attributes), apply different blending modes so objects blend smoothly into underlying objects, and apply creative effects such as drop shadows and beveling.

Transparency and effects are controlled in the Effects panel. You can change these options for an entire object (fill and stroke), only the stroke, only the fill, the text (if you're working with a text frame), the graphic (if you're working with a graphics frame), or all objects in a group.

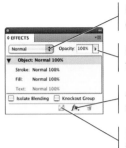

Change the blending mode of the selected attribute.

Change the transparency of the selected attribute.

Apply an effect to the selected attribute.

Remove transparency and effects from the selected attribute.

Note:

The Graphic option is only available when a placed graphic (within a frame) is selected. Group replaces Object in the list only when a group is selected with the Selection tool.

Note:

Effects applied to text apply to all text in the frame; you can't apply effects to individual characters.

Technical Issues of Transparency

Because all of these features and options are related in some way to transparency, you should understand what transparency is and how it affects your output. **Transparency** is the degree to which light passes through an object so objects in the background are visible. In terms of page layout, transparency means being able to "see through" objects in the front of the stacking order to objects lower in the stacking order.

Because of the way printing works, applying transparency in print graphic design is a bit of a contradiction. Commercial printing is, by definition, accomplished by overlapping a mixture of (usually) four semi-transparent inks in different percentages to reproduce a range of colors (the printable gamut). In that sense, all print graphic design requires transparency.

But *design* transparency refers to the objects on the page. The trouble is, when a halftone dot is printed, it's either there or it's not. There is no "50% opaque" setting on a printing press. This means that a transformation needs to take place behind the scenes, translating what we create on screen into what a printing press produces.

When transparent objects are output, overlapping areas of transparent elements are actually broken into individual elements (where necessary) to produce the best possible results. Ink values in the overlap areas are calculated by the application, based on the capabilities of the mechanical printing process; the software converts what we create on screen into the elements that are necessary to print.

When you get to the final stage of this project, you'll learn how to preview and control the output process for transparent objects.

Note:

Transparency is essentially the inverse of opacity. If an object is 20% transparent, it is also 80% opaque.

1. In the open **poster.indd** file, use the Selection tool to select the gradient-filled rectangle.

2. Choose **Object>Content>Graphic.**

Note:

You can also Control/right-click an object and change its content type in the contextual menu.

When you create a frame with one of the basic shape tools, it is considered "unassigned" because it is neither a text frame nor a graphics frame. You can convert any type of frame (graphics, text, or unassigned) to another type using this menu.

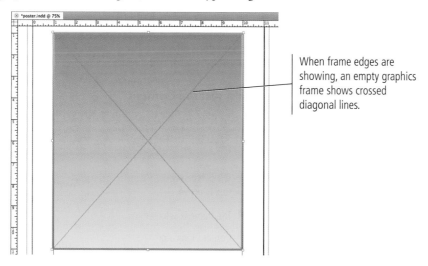

When frame edges are showing, an empty graphics frame shows crossed diagonal lines.

3. With the gradient-filled rectangle still selected on the page, choose **File>Place.** Navigate to the **WIP>Jazz** folder and choose **sunset.jpg.**

4. Check the Replace Selected Item option at the bottom of the dialog box.

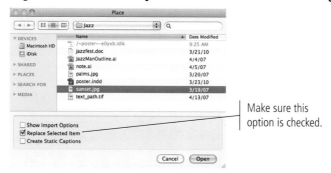

Make sure this option is checked.

5. Click Open to place the image into the frame.

Because you chose the Replace Selected Item option, the image is automatically placed in the selected frame. If another image had already been placed in the frame, the sunset image would replace the existing image (hence the name of the command).

Note:

If Replace Selected Item was not checked in the Place dialog box, the image would be loaded into the cursor.

6. Open the Effects panel (Window>Effects).

When you select an object with the Selection tool, you can apply various effects to the entire object, or to the object fill only, the object stroke only, or any text within the object.

7. Move the Selection tool cursor over the image frame to reveal the Content Indicator.

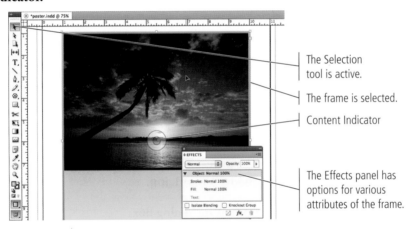

The Selection tool is active.

The frame is selected.

Content Indicator

The Effects panel has options for various attributes of the frame.

Note:

Effects in InDesign are non-destructive, which means they have no effect on the physical file data.

8. Click the Content Indicator icon to access the image in the frame.

When you select only the placed image, you can apply effects to the image itself, independent of the frame.

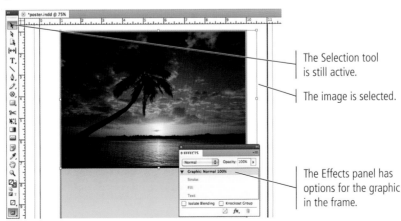

The Selection tool is still active.

The image is selected.

The Effects panel has options for the graphic in the frame.

9. With the Graphic option selected in the Effects panel, choose the Screen option in the Blending Mode menu.

The image now blends into the gradient background, but there is still a hard line marking the bottom edge of the placed image.

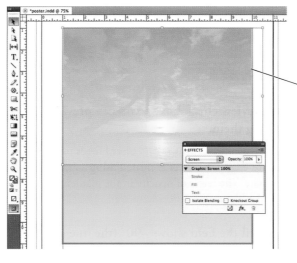

The Screen blending mode merges the image colors into the object's gradient fill.

Blending Modes

Blending modes control how colors in an object interact with colors in underlying objects. Objects are set to Normal by default, which simply overlays the top object's color onto underlying objects. (If the top object is entirely opaque, there is no effect on underlying objects.)

- **Multiply** multiplies (hence the name) the base color by the blend color, resulting in a darker color. Multiplying any color with black produces black; multiplying any color with white leaves the color unchanged.

- **Screen** is basically the inverse of Multiply, always returning a lighter color. Screening with black has no effect; screening with white produces white.

- **Overlay** multiplies or screens the blend color to preserve the original lightness or darkness of the base.

- **Soft Light** darkens or lightens base colors depending on the blend color. Blend colors lighter than 50% lighten the base color (as if dodged); blend colors darker than 50% darken the base color (as if burned).

- **Hard Light** combines the Multiply and Screen modes. Blend colors darker than 50% are multiplied, and blend colors lighter than 50% are screened.

- **Color Dodge** brightens the base color. Blend colors lighter than 50% significantly increase brightness; blending with black has no effect.

- **Color Burn** darkens the base color by increasing the contrast. Blend colors darker than 50% significantly darken the base color by increasing saturation and reducing brightness; blending with white has no effect.

- **Darken** returns the darker of the blend or base color. Base pixels that are lighter than the blend color are replaced; base pixels that are darker than the blend color do not change.

- **Lighten** returns whichever is the lighter color (base or blend). Base pixels that are darker than the blend color are replaced; base pixels that are lighter than the blend color do not change.

- **Difference*** inverts base color values according to the brightness value in the blend layer. Lower brightness values in the blend layer have less of an effect on the result; blending with black has no effect.

- **Exclusion*** is similar to Difference, except that midtone values in the base color are completely desaturated.

- **Hue*** results in a color with the luminance and saturation of the base color and the hue of the blend color.

- **Saturation*** results in a color with the luminance and hue of the base and the saturation of the blend color.

- **Color*** results in a color with the luminance of the base color and the hue and saturation of the blend color.

- **Luminosity*** results in a color with the hue and saturation of the base color and the luminance of the blend color (basically the opposite of the Color mode).

*Avoid applying the Difference, Exclusion, Hue, Saturation, Color, and Luminosity modes to objects with spot colors. It could create unpredictable results (at best) when the file is separated for commercial print requirements.

10. **Click the _fx_ button at the bottom of the Effects panel, and choose Gradient Feather.**

    The Effects dialog box opens to show the Gradient Feather options.

Note:

If you use the Gradient Feather tool, the Gradient Feather effect is automatically applied.

11. **In the Effects dialog box, click the Preview check box so you can preview your results before accepting/applying them.**

    The Gradient Feather effect creates a transparency gradient so an object blends into underlying objects instead of leaving a hard edge. The effect is created using a gradient that shifts from 100% opacity to 0% opacity. The levels of opacity in the gradient determine the opacity of the object to which the feather effect is applied.

12. **Click in the Angle circle and drag until the field shows –90° (the line should point straight down).**

    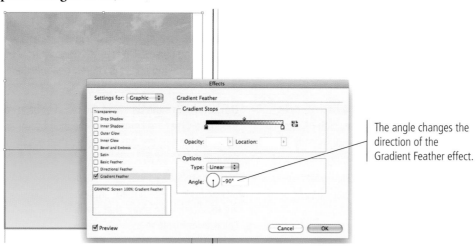

    The angle changes the direction of the Gradient Feather effect.

13. **Drag the left gradient stop until the Location field shows 75%.**

    By extending the solid black part of the gradient to the 75% location, the top three-quarters of the affected image remain entirely visible; only the bottom quarter of the image blends into the background.

    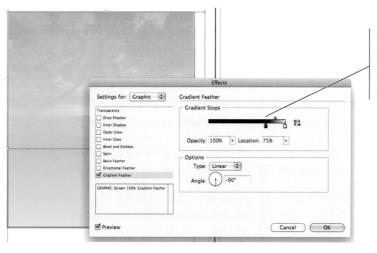

    Moving the first stop extends the black area of the gradient, which extends the part of the image that is entirely opaque.

14. **Click OK to close the Effects dialog box and apply your choices.**

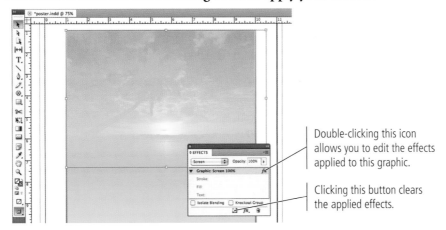

Double-clicking this icon allows you to edit the effects applied to this graphic.

Clicking this button clears the applied effects.

15. **Save the file and continue to the next exercise.**

CREATE AN IRREGULAR GRAPHICS FRAME

You can create basic graphics frames using the Rectangle, Ellipse, and Polygon Frame tools. You can also create a Bézier shape with the Pen tool, and then convert the shape to a graphics frame — which means you can create a frame in virtually any shape. However, it requires a lot of work to trace complex graphics with the Pen tool; fortunately, you can use other options to create complex frames from objects in placed graphics.

1. **In the open poster.indd file, choose File>Place. Navigate to the file JazzManOutline.ai in the WIP>Jazz folder.**

2. **Make sure the Replace Selected Item option is not selected, then click Open.**

If the Replace Selected Item option were turned on, the new image would replace the sunset image from the previous exercise (if the gradient rectangle was still selected) instead of being loaded into the cursor.

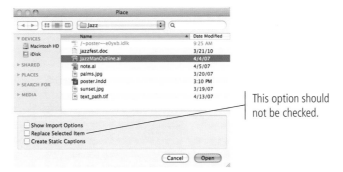

This option should not be checked.

InDesign offers nine different effects options, which you can apply individually or in combinations to create unique flat and dimensional effects for any object. The effects can be applied by clicking the *fx* button at the bottom of the Effects panel, by clicking the *fx* button in the Control panel, or by choosing from the Object>Effects menu.

Drop Shadow and Inner Shadow

Drop Shadow adds a shadow behind the object. **Inner Shadow** adds a shadow inside the edges of the object. For both types, you can define the blending mode, color, opacity, angle, distance, offset, and size of the shadow.

- **Distance** is the overall offset of the shadow, or how far away the shadow will be from the original object. The Offset fields allow you to define different horizontal and vertical distances.

- **Size** is the blur amount applied to the shadow.

- **Spread** (for Drop Shadows) is the percentage that the shadow expands beyond the original object.

- **Choke** (for Inner Shadows) is the percentage that the shadow shrinks into the original object.

- **Noise** controls the amount of random pixels added to the effect.

The **Object Knocks Out Shadow** option for drop shadows allows you to knock out (remove) or maintain the shadow underneath the object area. This option is particularly important if the original object is semi-transparent above its shadow.

The **Use Global Light** check box is available for the Drop Shadow, Inner Shadow, and Bevel and Emboss effects. When this option is checked, the style is linked to the "master" light source angle for the entire file. Changing the global light setting affects any linked shadow or bevel effect applied to any object in the entire file. (If Use Global Light is checked for an effect, changing the angle for that effect also changes the Global Light angle. You can also change the Global Light settings by choosing Object>Effects>Global Light.)

Outer Glow and Inner Glow

Outer Glow and **Inner Glow** add glow effects to the outside and inside edges (respectively) of the original object. For either kind of glow, you can define the blending mode, opacity, noise, and size values.

- For either Outer or Inner glows, you can define the **Technique** as Precise or Softer. **Precise** creates a glow at a specific distance; **Softer** creates a blurred glow and does not preserve detail as well as Precise.

- For Inner Glows, you can also define the **Source** of the glow (Center or Edge). **Center** applies a glow starting from the center of the object; **Edge** applies the glow starting from the inside edges of the object.

- The **Spread** and **Choke** sliders affect the percentages of the glow effects.

Bevel and Emboss

This effect has five variations or styles:

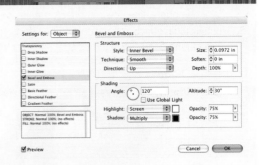

- **Inner Bevel** creates a bevel on the inside edges of the object.
- **Outer Bevel** creates a bevel on the outside edges of the object.
- **Emboss** creates the effect of embossing the object against the underlying layers.
- **Pillow Emboss** creates the effect of stamping the edges of the object into the underlying layers.

Any of these styles can be applied as **Smooth** (blurs the edges of the effect), **Chisel Hard** (creates a distinct edge to the effect), or **Chisel Soft** (creates a distinct, but slightly blurred edge to the effect).

You can change the **Direction** of the bevel effect. **Up** creates the appearance of the layer coming out of the image; **Down** creates the appearance of something stamped into the image. The **Size** field makes the effect smaller or larger, and the **Soften** option blurs the edges of the effect. **Depth** increases or decreases the three-dimensional effect of the bevel.

In the **Shading** area, you can control the light source's **Angle** and **Altitude** (think of how shadows differ as the sun moves across the sky). Finally, you can change the blending mode, opacity, and color of both highlights and shadows created with the Bevel or Emboss effect.

Satin

Satin applies interior shading to create a satiny appearance. You can change the blending mode, color, and opacity of the effect, as well as the angle, distance, and size.

Basic Feather, Directional Feather, and Gradient Feather

These three effects soften the edges of an object:

- **Basic Feather** equally fades all edges of the selected object (or attribute) by a specific width. The **Choke** option determines how much of the softened edge is opaque (high settings increase opacity and low settings decrease opacity). **Corners** can be **Sharp** (following the outer edge of the shape), **Rounded** (corners are rounded according to the Feather Width), or **Diffused** (fades from opaque to transparent). **Noise** adds random pixels to the softened area.

- **Directional Feather** allows you to apply different feather widths to individual edges of an object. The **Shape** option defines the object's original shape (First Edge Only, Leading Edges, or All Edges). The **Angle** field allows you to rotate the feathering effect; if you use any angle other than a 90° increment (i.e., 90, 180, 270, 360), the feathering will be skewed.

- **Gradient Feather** creates a transparency gradient that blends from solid to transparent. This effect underlies the Gradient Feather tool. You can move the start and end stops to different locations along the ramp, or add stops to define specific transparencies at specific locations. You can also choose from a Linear or Radial Gradient Feather effect, and change the angle of a Linear Gradient Feather effect.

3. **Click the loaded cursor anywhere on the page to place the graphic. Using the Control panel, position the bottom-left corner of the resulting frame at X: 1″, Y: 11″.**

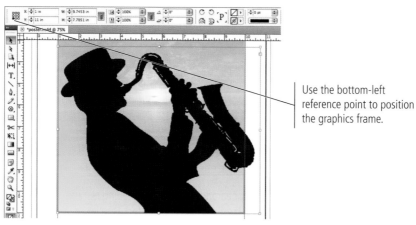

Use the bottom-left reference point to position the graphics frame.

4. **Using the Selection tool, click the Content Indicator icon to access the image inside the frame. Choose Object>Clipping Path>Options.**

A **clipping path** is a hard-edged outline that masks an image. Areas inside the path are visible; areas outside the path are hidden.

5. **In the resulting dialog box, choose Detect Edges in the Type menu.**

InDesign can access Alpha channels and clipping paths that are saved in an image, or you can create a clipping path based on the image content. Because this graphic is a vector graphic with well-defined edges filled with a solid color, InDesign can create a very precise clipping path based on the information in the file.

Clipping Path Options

INDESIGN FOUNDATIONS

Threshold specifies the darkest pixel value that will define the resulting clipping path. In this exercise, the placed image is filled with solid black, so you can set a very high Tolerance value to refine the clipping path. In images with greater tone variation (such as a photograph), increasing the Tolerance value removes lighter areas from the clipped area.

Tolerance specifies how similar a pixel must be to the Threshold value before it is hidden by the clipping path. Increasing the Tolerance value results in fewer points along the clipping path, generating a smoother path. Lowering the Tolerance value results in more anchor points and a potentially rougher path.

Inset Frame shrinks the clipping path by a specific number of pixels. You can also enter a negative value to enlarge the clipping path.

Invert reverses the clipping path, making hidden areas visible and vice versa.

Include Inside Edges creates a compound clipping path, removing inner areas of the object if they are within the Threshold and Tolerance ranges.

Restrict to Frame creates a clipping path that stops at the visible edge of the graphic. You can include the entire object — including areas beyond the frame edges — by unchecking this option.

Use High Resolution Image generates the clipping path based on the actual file data instead of the preview image.

6. **Check the Include Inside Edges option.**

   When this option is not checked, InDesign generates a clipping path based only on the outside edges of the image. The Include Inside Edges option generates a compound clipping path that removes holes in the middle of the outside path.

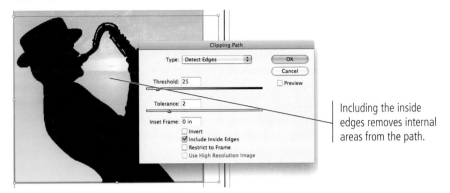

Including the inside edges removes internal areas from the path.

7. **Click OK to close the dialog box and create the clipping path.**

8. **Choose Object>Clipping Path>Convert Clipping Path to Frame.**

9. **With the frame content still selected, press Delete/Backspace to delete the placed file but leave the frame you created.**

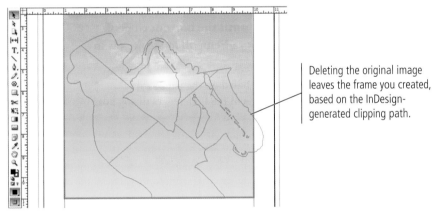

Deleting the original image leaves the frame you created, based on the InDesign-generated clipping path.

10. **Choose File>Place and navigate to palms.jpg in the WIP>Jazz folder. Make sure the Replace Selected Item option is not checked, and click Open. Click inside the empty frame with the loaded cursor to place the image inside the frame.**

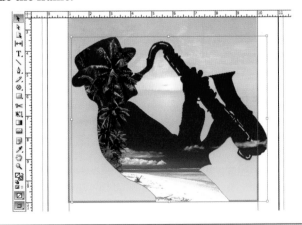

11. **Click the Content Indicator icon to access the placed image inside the frame.**

12. **Using the Control panel, change the top-left corner position of the placed image within the frame to X: –0.25″, Y: –0.25″.**

When you select an image within a frame (using either the Content Indicator or the Direct Selection tool), the Control panel fields define the position of the graphic *relative to* its containing frame. Negative numbers move the graphic up and to the left from the frame edge; positive numbers move the graphic down and to the right.

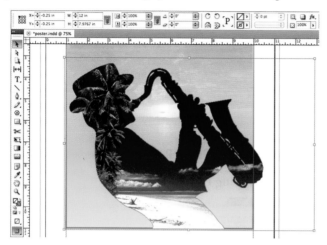

13. **Click the edge of the frame with the Selection tool to re-select the frame (not the placed graphic).**

14. **With the frame selected, press the Up Arrow key until the bottom edge of the frame approximately aligns to the top of the gradient-filled stroke (as in the following image).**

You can use the Arrow keys to nudge the selected object based on the keyboard increment that is defined in the Units & Increments pane of the Preferences dialog box. The default distance is 0.0139″.

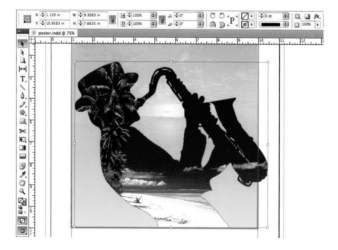

15. **Save the file and continue to the next stage of the project.**

Stage 2 Importing and Formatting Text

Placing text is one of the most critical functions of page-layout software, whether you create the text directly within InDesign or import it from an external file. InDesign provides all the tools you need to format text, from choosing a font to automatically creating hanging punctuation.

 ## CONTROL TEXT THREADING

Some layouts require only a few bits of text, while others include numerous pages. Depending on how much text you have to work with, you might place all the layout text in a single frame, or you might cut and paste different pieces of a single story into separate text frames. In other cases, you might thread text across multiple frames — maintaining the text as a single story but allowing flexibility in frame size and position.

1. **With `poster.indd` open, zoom into the empty area below the placed images.**

2. **Use the Type tool to create a text frame that is 1″ high and 9″ wide (filling the width between the margin guides).**

3. **Select the frame with the Selection tool, and then use the Control panel to make sure the top edge of the text frame is positioned at Y: 11.25″.**

When the Selection tool is active, you can use the Control panel to change the position and dimensions of a text frame.

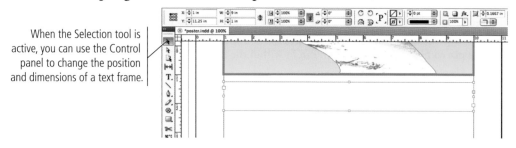

4. **Create three more text frames using the following parameters:**

Frame 2	X: 1″	W: 3.2″
	Y: 12.45″	H: 3.55″
Frame 3	X: 5″	W: 5″
	Y: 12.45″	H: 3.55″
Frame 4	X: 1″	W: 9″
	Y: 16.1″	H: 0.5″

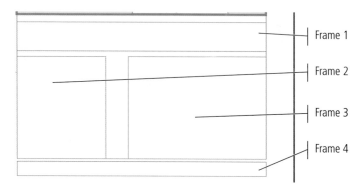

5. **Choose the Type tool, and click inside the first text frame to place the insertion point.**

    When you click in a text frame with the Type tool, you see a flashing insertion point where you click (or in the top-left corner if there is no text in the frame). This insertion point marks the location where text will appear when you type, paste, or import it into the document.

6. **Choose File>Place. Navigate to the file named `jazzfest.doc` in the `WIP>Jazz` folder.**

7. Make sure the Replace Selected Item option is checked and then click Open.

The insertion point is in the first frame.

This option should be checked.

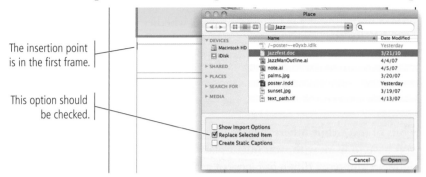

When Replace Selected Item is checked, the imported text file is automatically imported at the location of the insertion point. (If this option is not checked, the text is imported into the cursor.)

Overset text icon

8. Choose the Selection tool in the Tools panel.

When a text frame is selected, you can see the In and Out ports that allow you to link one text frame to another. In this case, the Out port shows the **overset text icon**, indicating that the placed file has more text than can fit within the frame.

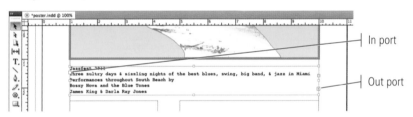

In port

Out port

Note:

The overset text icon is visible even when the In and Out ports are not.

Note:

If you see the overset text icon (the red plus sign), the story does not fit in the current frame (or series of frames). You should always correct overset text.

9. Click the Out port of the first text frame.

Clicking the Out port loads the cursor with the rest of the text in the story. When the loaded cursor is over an existing frame, you can click to place the next part of the story in that frame. When the cursor is not over a frame, you can click and drag to create a frame that will contain the next part of the story. You can do this with the Selection tool (as you just did) or the Direct Selection tool.

This cursor icon indicates that you can click and drag to create a frame to contain the rest of the story.

This cursor icon indicates that you can click to place the rest of the story in the existing frame.

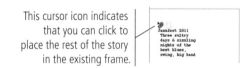

10. Click inside the second frame to link it to the first frame.

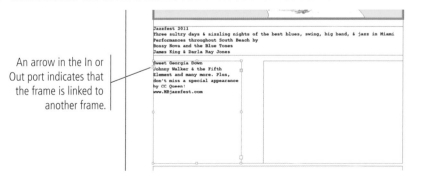

An arrow in the In or Out port indicates that the frame is linked to another frame.

11. **Repeat this process to link from the second frame to the third, and then from the third frame to the fourth.**

You can define the thread of text frames even when there is no text to fill those frames. Simply use the Selection or Direct Selection tool to click the Out port of one frame, and then click anywhere within the next frame you want to add to the thread.

12. **Choose View>Extras>Show Text Threads.**

When this option is toggled on (and you are in Normal viewing mode), you can see all of the threading arrows whenever any of the text frames in the thread is selected.

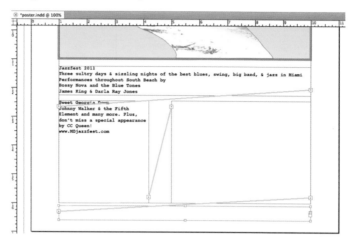

13. **Save the file and continue to the next exercise.**

DEFINE MANUAL FRAME BREAKS

When you thread text from one frame to another (or to multiple columns in the same frame), you often need to control exactly where a story breaks from frame to frame. InDesign includes a number of commands for breaking text in precise locations.

1. **In the open poster.indd file, use the Type tool to click at the end of the first line (after "Jazzfest 2011") to place the insertion point.**

As you complete the following exercises, feel free to zoom in as you think necessary to work with specific areas of your layout.

2. **Choose Type>Insert Break Character>Frame Break.**

InDesign provides several special break characters that allow you to control the flow of text from line to line, from column to column, and from frame to frame. The Frame Break character forces all following text into the next frame in the thread.

The insertion point is at the end of the first paragraph.

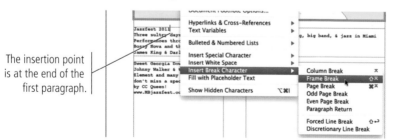

Note:

You can also press Command/Control while the Type tool is active to click a text frame Out port and thread the frames.

Note:

When you load the cursor with overset text, the loaded cursor shows the text from the beginning of the story — even though the beginning is already placed. This is a quirk of the software; when you click with the loaded cursor, the text will flow into the new frame at the proper place in the story.

Note:

*Text that appears as a series of gray bars is called **greeked text**. By default, text smaller than 7 pt (at 100%) is greeked to improve screen redraw time. You can change the greeking threshold in the Display Performance pane of the Preferences dialog box.*

View percentage is part of the determination for greeking text; in other words, if your view percentage is 50%, 12-pt text appears as 6-pt text on screen, so it would be greeked using the default preferences.

3. Choose Type>Show Hidden Characters.

Each paragraph is separated by a paragraph return character (¶). A paragraph can consist of only one or two words or multiple lines. The important thing is to realize that a paragraph is technically any copy between two paragraph returns (or other break characters).

Note:

You can also toggle the visibility of hidden characters using the View Options button in the Application/Menu bar.

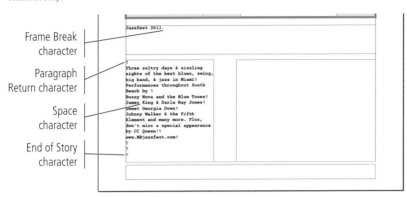

When you placed the Frame Break character in Step 2, everything following the insertion point was pushed to the next frame — including the paragraph return character that had been at the end of the first line. This created an "empty" paragraph that should be deleted.

4. With the insertion point flashing at the beginning of the second frame, press Forward Delete to remove the extra paragraph return.

If you don't have a Forward Delete key (if, for example, you're working on a laptop), move the insertion point to the beginning of the next line and press Delete/Backspace.

5. With hidden characters visible, highlight the paragraph return character at the end of the first sentence in the second frame.

6. Choose Type>Insert Break Character>Frame Break to replace the highlighted paragraph return with a frame break character.

When text is highlighted — including hidden formatting characters — anything you type, paste, or enter using a menu command replaces the highlighted text.

Note:

The Forward Delete key is the one directly below the Help key on most standard keyboards. If you are using a laptop, place the insertion point at the beginning of the first sentence in the second frame ("Three sultry days...") and press Delete/Backspace.

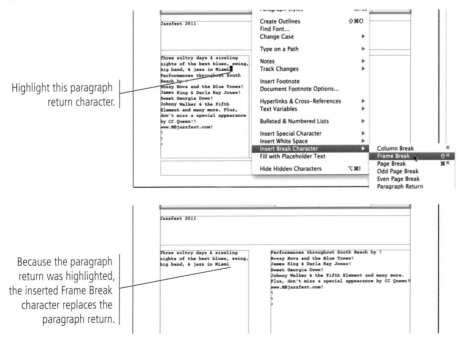

7. **Use the same technique to move only the last paragraph (the Web address) into the fourth text frame.**

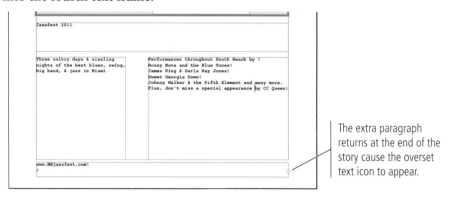

The extra paragraph returns at the end of the story cause the overset text icon to appear.

8. **Delete the extra paragraph return characters from the end of the story (after the Web address).**

It is not uncommon to have multiple extra paragraph returns at the end of imported text. InDesign thinks there is still more text than will fit, even though the extra text is just more empty paragraphs. These serve no purpose and cause an overset text icon (and can cause other problems when master pages are involved), so you should delete them.

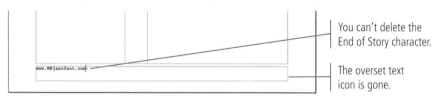

You can't delete the End of Story character.

The overset text icon is gone.

9. **Save the file and continue to the next exercise.**

APPLY CHARACTER FORMATTING

Once text is in a frame, you can use character formatting attributes to determine the appearance of individual letters, such as the font and type size. These attributes can be controlled in the Character panel (Window>Type & Tables>Character) or the Control panel (depending on which options are visible in the Control panel).

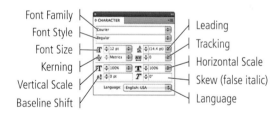

Font Family, Font Style, Font Size, Kerning, Vertical Scale, Baseline Shift, Leading, Tracking, Horizontal Scale, Skew (false italic), Language

- A **font** contains all of the characters (**glyphs**) that make up a typeface, including upper- and lowercase letters, numbers, special characters, etc. (Fonts must be installed and activated on your computer to be accessible in InDesign.) The **font style** is a specific variation of the selected font, such as bold or condensed.

- **Size** is the height of a typeface measured in points.

- **Leading** is the distance from one baseline to the next. InDesign treats leading as a character attribute, even though leading controls the space between lines of an individual paragraph. (Space between paragraphs is controlled using the Space Before/After options in the Paragraph panel.) To change leading for an entire paragraph, you must first select the entire paragraph. This approach means you can change the leading for a single line of a paragraph by selecting any character(s) in that line; however, changing the leading for any character in a line applies the same change to the entire line that contains those characters.

- **Vertical Scale** and **Horizontal Scale** artificially stretch or contract the selected characters. This type of scaling is a quick way of achieving condensed or expanded type if those variations of a font don't exist. Type that has been artificially scaled in this fashion tends to look bad because the scaling destroys the type's metrics; if possible, you should always use a condensed or expanded version of a typeface before resorting to horizontal or vertical scaling.

- **Kerning** increases or decreases the space between pairs of letters. Kerning is used in cases where particular letters in specific fonts need to be manually adjusted to eliminate a too-tight or too-spread-out appearance; manual kerning is usually necessary in headlines or other large type. (Many commercial fonts have built-in kerning pairs, so you won't need to apply too much hands-on intervention with kerning. InDesign defaults to use the kerning values stored in the font metrics.)

- **Tracking**, also known as "range kerning," refers to the overall tightness or looseness across a range of characters.

- **Baseline Shift** moves the selected type above or below the baseline by a specific number of points. Positive numbers move the characters up; negative values move the text down.

- **Skew** artificially slants the selected text, creating a false italic appearance. This option distorts the look of the type and should be used sparingly (if ever).

Note:

*Tracking and kerning are applied in thousandths of an **em** (an em is technically defined as width that equals the type size).*

In addition to the options in the basic Character panel, several styling options are also available in the panel Options menu.

- **All Caps** changes all the characters to capital letters. This option only changes the appearance of the characters; they are not permanently converted to capital letters. To change the case of selected characters to all capital letters — the same as typing with Caps Lock turned on — use the Type>Change Case menu options.

- **Small Caps** artificially reduces the point size of a regular capital letter to a set percentage of that point size. If the font is an Open Type font that contains true small caps, InDesign uses the true small caps.

- **Superscript** and **Subscript** artificially reduce the selected character(s) to a specific percentage of the point size; these options raise (for superscript) or lower (for subscript) the character from the baseline to a position that is a certain percentage of the leading. (The size and position of Superscript, Subscript, and Small Caps are controlled in the Advanced Type Preferences dialog box.)

- **Underline** places a line below the selected characters.

- **Strikethrough** places a line through the middle of selected characters.

- **Ligatures** are substitutes for certain pairs of letters, most commonly fi, fl, ff, ffi, and ffl. (Other pairs such as ct and st are common for historical typesetting, and ae and oe are used in some non-English-language typesetting.)

Note:

Choosing Underline Options or Strikethrough Options in the Character panel Options menu allows you to change the weight, offset, style, and color of the line for those styles.

1. **With `poster.indd` open, choose the Type tool in the Tools panel. Triple-click the first line of text in the story to select it.**

   Character formatting options apply only to selected characters.

2. **In the Character panel (Window>Type & Tables>Character), highlight the existing font name and type ATC M. Press Return/Enter to apply the new font.**

   As you type, InDesign automatically scrolls to the first font that matches what you type. In this case, the software finds the ATC Maple font.

3. **Open the Font Style menu in the Character panel and choose Ultra.**

   You don't need to press Return/Enter when you choose a specific option from the menu.

4. **Open the Font Size menu and choose 72.**

   You can choose one of the built-in font sizes, type a specific value in the field, or click the arrow buttons to change the font size by 1 point.

   Note:

   You can use the Up and Down Arrow keys to nudge paragraph and character style values when the insertion point is in a panel field.

5. **Open the Character panel Options menu and choose the All Caps option.**

   Note:

   Most of these character formatting options are also available in the Control panel.

6. **In the Character panel, type 200 in the Tracking field and press Return/Enter.**

7. **Click four times on the paragraph in the second frame to select the entire paragraph.**

Clicking twice selects an entire *word*, clicking three times selects an entire *line*, and clicking four times selects the entire *paragraph*.

8. **Change the selected text to 34-pt ATC Pine Bold Italic.**

Using these settings, the paragraph doesn't entirely fit within the available space (or at least, not yet). Because the frame is threaded, the paragraph flows into the third frame, and the rest of the text reflows accordingly.

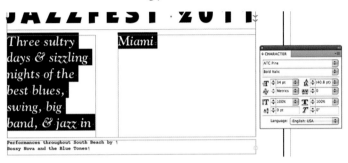

Note:

Leave the Leading value at the automatic setting. By default, InDesign automatically applies leading as 120% of the type size.

9. **With the same text selected, change the Horizontal Scale field to 90%.**

Horizontal and vertical scaling are useful for artificially stretching or contracting fonts that do not have a condensed or extended version. Be careful using these options, though, because the artificial scaling alters the character shapes and can make some fonts very difficult to read (especially at smaller sizes).

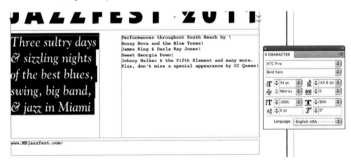

10. **Click three times to select the first line in the third frame, hold down the mouse button, and then drag down to select the other lines in the same frame.**

When you triple-click to select an entire line, dragging up or down selects entire lines above or below the one you first clicked.

11. **With all of the text in the third frame selected, apply 22-pt ATC Pine Bold Italic with 90% horizontal scaling.**

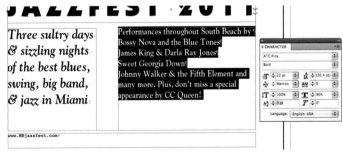

12. **Change the Web address in the fourth text frame to 26-pt ATC Maple Medium.**

13. **Save the file and continue to the next exercise.**

 ## APPLY PARAGRAPH FORMATTING

Character formatting includes any option that affects the appearance of selected characters, such as font, size, horizontal scale, and a host of others. Paragraph formatting options, on the other hand, affect an entire paragraph (everything between two paragraph return characters). Paragraph formatting can control everything from indents to the space between paragraphs to lines above and below paragraphs.

Paragraph formatting can be controlled in the Paragraph panel (Window>Type & Tables>Paragraph) or the Control panel (depending on which options are available).

Note:

In InDesign, a paragraph is defined as all text between two paragraph return characters (¶), even if the paragraph exists on a single line.

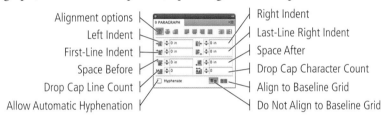

Alignment options
Left Indent
First-Line Indent
Space Before
Drop Cap Line Count
Allow Automatic Hyphenation

Right Indent
Last-Line Right Indent
Space After
Drop Cap Character Count
Align to Baseline Grid
Do Not Align to Baseline Grid

1. **In the open `poster.indd` file, place the cursor anywhere in the paragraph in the second frame.**

2. **In the Paragraph panel, click the Align Right button.**

   Paragraph formatting applies to the entire paragraph where the insertion point is placed, or to any paragraph that is entirely or partially selected. A paragraph does not have to be entirely selected to change its paragraph formatting attributes.

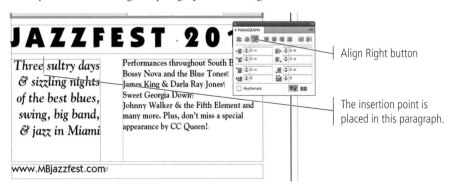

Align Right button

The insertion point is placed in this paragraph.

3. Place the insertion point in the last paragraph of the third frame (Johnny Walker...) and apply centered paragraph alignment.

4. Place the insertion point anywhere in the fourth frame (with the Web address) and apply centered paragraph alignment.

Align Center button

5. Select any part of the first through fifth lines in the third frame.

6. In the Paragraph panel, change the Space Before field to 0.09".

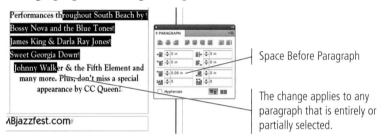

Space Before Paragraph

The change applies to any paragraph that is entirely or partially selected.

Note:

The arrow buttons for paragraph formatting options step through values in increments of 0.0625".

7. Select any part of the second through fifth lines in the same frame and change the Left Indent field to 0.5".

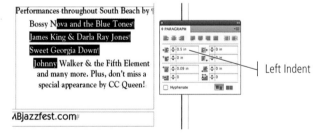

Left Indent

Note:

If you want to apply the same formatting to more than one consecutive paragraph, you can drag to select any part of the target paragraphs. Any paragraph that's even partially selected will be affected.

8. Place the insertion point at the beginning of the sixth line (before the word "and") and press Return/Enter.

When you break an existing paragraph into a new paragraph, the attributes of the original paragraph are applied to the new paragraph.

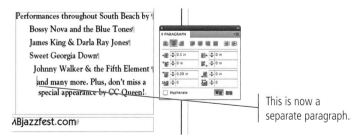

This is now a separate paragraph.

9. **Place the insertion point at the beginning of the fifth line (before "Johnny") and press Delete/Backspace.**

10. **Press Return/Enter to separate the two paragraphs again.**

    This is an easy way to copy paragraph formatting from one paragraph to the next. When you re-separate the two paragraphs, the "Johnny" paragraph adopts the paragraph formatting attributes of the "Sweet Georgia Down" paragraph.

11. **Save the file and continue to the next exercise.**

Copying Type Attributes with the Eyedropper Tool

You can use the Eyedropper tool to copy character and paragraph attributes (including text color), and then apply those attributes to other sections of text.

To copy formatting from one piece of text to another, click with the Eyedropper tool on the formatting you want to copy. If any text is selected when you click the Eyedropper tool, the selected text is automatically re-formatted. If nothing is selected, the Eyedropper tool "loads" with the formatting attributes — the tool icon reverses directions and shows a small i-beam icon in the cursor.

The Eyedropper tool cursor when it is "loaded" with text formatting attributes

You can click the loaded Eyedropper tool on any text to change its formatting, or you can click and drag to format multiple paragraphs at once. As long as the Eyedropper tool remains selected, you can continue to select text to apply

the same formatting. You can also change the formatting in the Eyedropper tool by pressing Option/Alt and clicking text with the new formatting attributes you want to copy.

By default, the Eyedropper tool copies all formatting attributes. You can change that behavior by double-clicking the tool in the Tools panel to access the Eyedropper Options dialog box. Simply uncheck the options you don't want to copy (including individual options in each category), and then click OK.

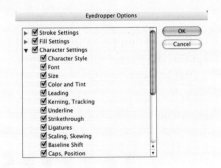

At times, specific arrangements of text can cause a paragraph to appear out of alignment, even though it's technically aligned properly. Punctuation at the beginning or end of a line — such as quotation marks at the beginning of a line or the commas in lines three and four of the second text frame — often cause this kind of optical problem. InDesign includes a feature called **Optical Margin Alignment** to fix this type of problem.

1. **With `poster.indd` open, choose Type>Hide Hidden Characters.**

   Although the paragraph in the second frame is technically correctly right-aligned, the text might appear misaligned because of the commas at the ends of lines three and four.

2. **Place the insertion point anywhere in the second text frame.**

3. **Open the Story panel (Window>Type & Tables>Story) and check the Optical Margin Alignment option. Change the Size field to 34 pt.**

   When Optical Margin Alignment is turned on, punctuation marks move outside the text margins (either to the left for left-aligned text or right for right-aligned text). Moving punctuation outside the margins is often referred to as **hanging punctuation**.

   The field in the Story panel tells InDesign what size type needs to be adjusted. The best effect is usually created by defining the size of the type that needs adjustment.

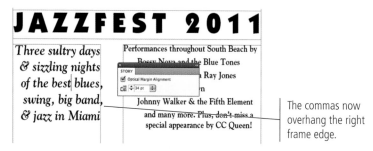

The commas now overhang the right frame edge.

4. **Place the insertion point in the first frame, then choose Ignore Optical Margin in the Paragraph panel Options menu.**

   The Optical Margin Alignment option applies to an entire story (including all text frames in the same thread), not just the selected paragraph. If necessary, you can toggle this option on for individual paragraphs so the selected paragraph is not affected by optical margin alignment that is applied to the overall story.

5. In the Layers panel, click the empty space to the left of the <rectangle> item to make that object visible again.

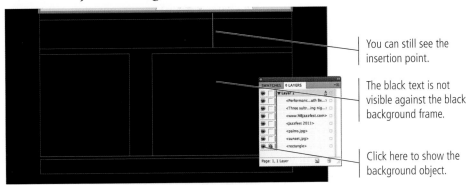

You can still see the insertion point.

The black text is not visible against the black background frame.

Click here to show the background object.

6. With the insertion point still flashing in the now-obscured text, choose Edit>Select All to select all text in the series of linked frames.

The Select All command selects all text in the story, whether that story exists in a single frame or threads across multiple frames. This command also selects overset text that doesn't fit into the current frame (or thread of frames).

7. In the Swatches panel, make sure the Text icon is selected at the top of the panel, and then click the Paper swatch.

In four-color (process) printing, there is no white ink. To achieve white, you have to remove the colors where you want white areas, which is called a **knockout**. By removing or knocking out underlying colors, the paper shows through — regardless of whether it is white or some other color (e.g., if you print on yellow paper, knockout areas will show the yellow color; this is why InDesign refers to this swatch as "Paper" instead of "White").

This "T" icon means you are changing the text color instead of the object color.

8. Click away from the text to deselect it and review the results.

9. Save the file and continue to the next stage of the project.

Stage 3 Graphics as Text and Text as Graphics

Now that you're familiar with the basic options for formatting characters and paragraphs, you can begin to add style to a layout using two techniques — flowing text along a path, and placing graphics inline with text. (There is, of course, much more to learn about working with text than this project covers; you'll learn much more as you complete the rest of the projects in this book.)

PLACE INLINE GRAPHICS

Any graphics frame that you create on a page float over the other elements in the layout. You can position graphics frames over other objects to hide underlying elements, or you can apply a **runaround** so text will wrap around a picture box.

You can also place images as inline graphics, which means they will be anchored to the text in the position in which they are placed. If text reflows, inline objects reflow with the text and maintain their correct positioning. This feature can be very useful for placing custom bullets (which you will do in this exercise), or for a variety of other purposes, such as where sidebar text needs to remain in proximity to the main body copy.

There are two methods for creating inline objects. For simple applications, such as a graphic bullet, you can simply place the graphic and format it as a text character. (An inline graphic is treated as a single text character in the story; it is affected by many of the paragraph-formatting commands, such as space before and after, tab settings, leading, and baseline position.) For more complex applications, you can use the options in the Object>Anchored Object menu.

Understanding the Baseline Grid

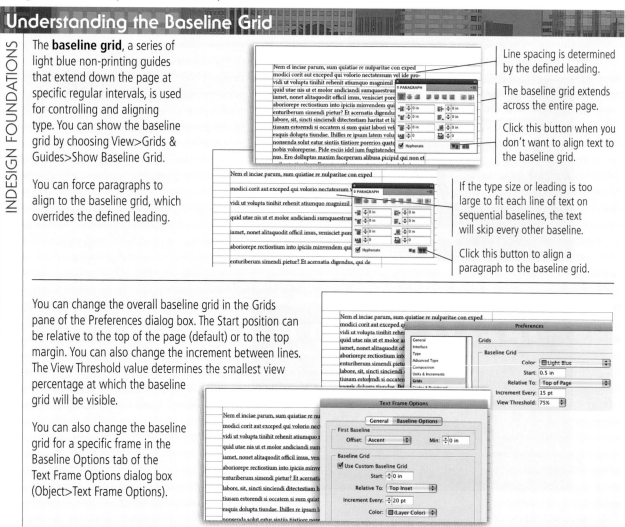

The **baseline grid**, a series of light blue non-printing guides that extend down the page at specific regular intervals, is used for controlling and aligning type. You can show the baseline grid by choosing View>Grids & Guides>Show Baseline Grid.

You can force paragraphs to align to the baseline grid, which overrides the defined leading.

Line spacing is determined by the defined leading.

The baseline grid extends across the entire page.

Click this button when you don't want to align text to the baseline grid.

If the type size or leading is too large to fit each line of text on sequential baselines, the text will skip every other baseline.

Click this button to align a paragraph to the baseline grid.

You can change the overall baseline grid in the Grids pane of the Preferences dialog box. The Start position can be relative to the top of the page (default) or to the top margin. You can also change the increment between lines. The View Threshold value determines the smallest view percentage at which the baseline grid will be visible.

You can also change the baseline grid for a specific frame in the Baseline Options tab of the Text Frame Options dialog box (Object>Text Frame Options).

1. With **poster.indd** open, place the insertion point at the beginning of the second line in the third frame (before the word "Bossy").

2. Choose File>Place and navigate to **note.ai** in the **WIP>Jazz** folder.

The insertion point is at the beginning of this paragraph.

This option should be checked

Note:

You can also select an existing object, cut or copy it, place the insertion point, and then paste the object inline where the insertion point flashes.

3. Make sure the **Replace Selected Item** option is checked, and then click **Open**.

If the insertion point is flashing in a story when you place a graphic using the Replace Selected Item option, the graphic is automatically placed as an inline object.

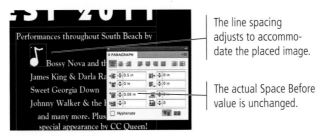

The line spacing adjusts to accommodate the placed image.

The actual Space Before value is unchanged.

Working with Anchored Objects

INDESIGN FOUNDATIONS

The Anchored Object Options dialog box controls the position of an anchored object relative to the frame in which it is placed. Anchored objects can be aligned inline (such as the music-note bullets you created in this project) or above the line.

When an object is anchored using the Above Line option, the object can be anchored to the left, right, or center of the frame. If you're using facing pages, you can also choose Toward Spine or Away from Spine so the anchored object will be placed in the appropriate position relative to the spread center (for example, you might specify that all sidebars have to be on the inside edge, close to the spine).

The Inline option aligns the object with the text baseline, adjusted by the Y Offset value.

The Above Line option moves the object above the line where the object is anchored.

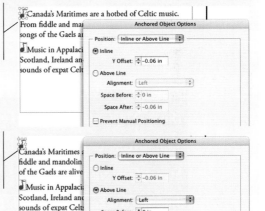

When you use the Above Line option, you can also define the space before and after the anchored object. Space Before defines the position of the object relative to the bottom of the previous line of text. Space After defines the position of the object relative to the first character in the line below the object.

When you work with anchored objects, you can use the Selection tool to drag the object up or down (in other words, change its position relative to the text to which it is anchored). If the Prevent Manual Positioning option is checked, you can't drag the anchored object in the layout.

4. **Select the inline graphic with the Selection tool, and then scale the graphic and frame to 50% horizontally and vertically.**

Although inline graphics are anchored to the text, they are still graphics contained in graphics frames. You can apply the same transformations to inline graphics that you could apply to any other placed graphics.

Use these fields to scale the placed graphic and the containing frame.

After you finalize the scaling, the fields show 100% when the frame is selected with the Selection tool.

Note:

When you select the frame with the Selection tool, resizing the frame also resizes the frame content.

5. **Choose Object>Anchored Object>Options. Check the Preview option at the bottom of the dialog box.**

6. **Make sure the Inline option is selected, and change the Y Offset to −0.07″.**

A negative number moves the anchored object down; a positive number moves it up.

Anchored Object Size and Text Position

When an anchored object is larger than the defined leading for the text in which it is placed, it might appear that changing the Y Offset values moves the text instead of the anchored object. In a way, this is true, because the text will move until it reaches the defined leading value; after that, greater changes will move the object and not the text.

Default text position without the anchored object

Text position after placing the anchored object

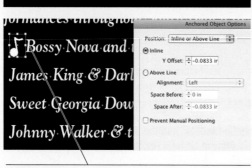

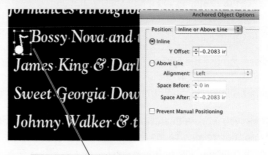

Adjusting the object position allows text to move back to its original place based on defined paragraph formatting.

Further adjustments to the anchored object move the actual object by the specified amount.

7. **Click OK, and then place the insertion point between the anchored object and the letter "B."**

8. **Press Shift-Left Arrow to select the anchored object, and then copy the highlighted object/character.**

   You can select an inline graphic just as you would any other text character. Copying text in InDesign is the same as copying text in other applications: choose Edit>Copy, or press Command/Control-C.

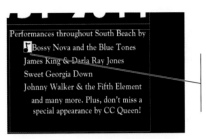

An anchored graphic can be selected just as you would select any other text character.

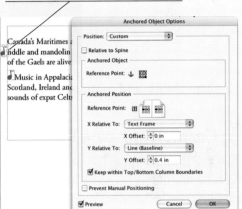

9. **Place the insertion point at the beginning of the next paragraph and paste the copied object.**

As with copying, pasting text — including inline graphics — in InDesign is the same as in other applications: choose Edit>Paste, or press Command/Control-V.

10. **Paste the anchored graphic again at the beginning of the next two paragraphs.**

11. **Apply right paragraph alignment to the last paragraph in the third frame.**

This simply provides better overall balance to the text in the frame.

12. **Save the file and continue to the next exercise.**

 ## CREATE TYPE ON A PATH

Instead of simply flowing text into a frame, you can also create unique typographic effects by flowing text onto a path. A text path can be any shape that you can create in InDesign, whether using one of the basic shape tools, a complex graphic you drew with the Pen tool, or a path created by converting a clipping path to a frame.

1. **With poster.indd open, deselect all objects in the layout.**

As we explained previously, you can choose Edit>Deselect All, or use the Selection tool to click an empty area of the workspace. If you use the click method, make sure you don't click a white-filled object instead of an empty area.

2. **Choose File>Place. Select text_path.tif in the WIP>Jazz folder in the layout and click Open. Position the top-left corner of the placed graphic at X: 0″, Y: 0″.**

When this image is loaded into the cursor, click outside the defined bleed area to place the image and not replace the content in one of the existing frames. Then use the Control panel to position the image correctly. (The image that you are placing is simply a guide that you will use to create the shape of the text path for this exercise.)

3. **Choose the Pen tool. Change the stroke value to 1-pt Magenta (C=0 M=100 Y=0 K=0) and change the fill value to None.**

Because the line in the placed image is black, you're using magenta so you can differentiate your line from the one in the image. The solid white background in the TIF file makes it easy to focus on the line instead of the elements you have already created on the poster.

4. **Using the Pen tool, click once on the left end of the line in the placed image.**

   This first click establishes the first point of the path you're drawing.

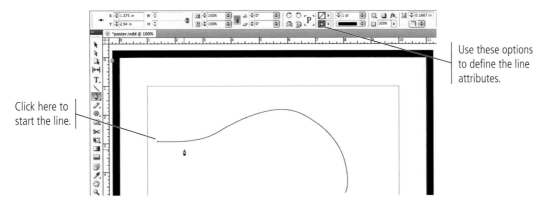

Use these options to define the line attributes.

Click here to start the line.

5. **Click about half way between the point you just set and the topmost arc of the curve, and then drag right to create handles for the second anchor point.**

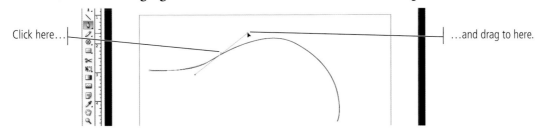

Click here...   ...and drag to here.

6. **Click again near the middle of the arc on the right, and then drag to create handles for the point.**

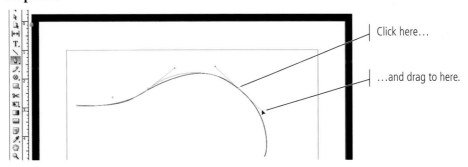

Click here...

...and drag to here.

7. **Click a final time on the right end of the line.**

   Don't worry if your path isn't perfect the first time; you can always edit the anchor points and handles with the Direct Selection tool.

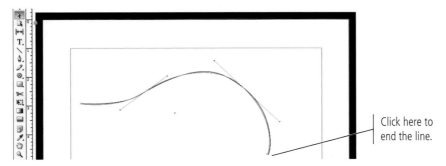

Click here to end the line.

8. **Using the Direct Selection tool, adjust the points and handles until your line closely resembles the one in the placed image.**

9. **Choose the Type on a Path tool. Move the cursor near the path until the cursor shows a small plus sign in the icon, and then click the path.**

This action converts the line from a regular path to a type path.

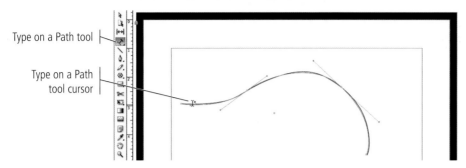

Type on a Path tool

Type on a Path tool cursor

10. **Type** Move your feet to the beat!, **then format the type as 49-pt ATC Maple Ultra.**

Type on a Path Options

You can control the appearance of type on a path by choosing Type>Type on a Path>Options. You can apply one of five effects, change the alignment of the text to the path, flip the text to the other side of the path, and adjust the character spacing around curves (higher Spacing values remove more space around sharp curves).

- The **Rainbow** (default) effect keeps each character's baseline parallel to the path.

- The **Skew** effect maintains the vertical edges of type while skewing horizontal edges around the path.

- The **3D Ribbon** effect maintains the horizontal edges of type while rotating the vertical edges to be perpendicular to the path.

- The **Stair Step** effect aligns the left edge of each character's baseline to the path.

- The **Gravity** effect aligns the center of each character's baseline to the path, keeping vertical edges in line with the path's center.

The **Align options** determine which part of the text (Baseline, Ascender, Descender, or Center) aligns to which part of the path (Top, Bottom, or Center).

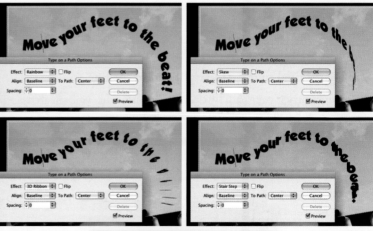

11. **Using the Selection tool, click the text_path.tif image that you used as a guide. Press Delete/Backspace to remove it from the layout.**

12. **Click the text path with the Selection tool to select the actual line. In the Swatches panel, change the object's stroke color to None.**

    A text path can have a fill and stroke value just like any other path.

When the actual path is selected, the Swatches panel defaults to show attributes of the path (not the type).

Note:

When a text path has no stroke color, you can still view the path by choosing View>Extras>Show Frame Edges.

13. **Click the Text Color button at the top of the Swatches panel, and then click the Pantone 8660 C swatch to change the text color.**

    You don't have to select the actual text on a path to change its color. You can use the buttons at the top of the Swatches panel to change the color attributes of either the path or the text.

Click here to change the type fill and stroke colors.

Note:

The screen preview of the metallic ink is not especially pleasing; in this case, you simply have to rely on the printed ink swatch to know what the text will look like when printed.

14. **Click the bar at the left edge of the text path and drag to the right about 1/4″.**

    When you release the mouse button, the left edge of the text moves to the point where you dragged the line. This marks the orientation point of the text on the path.

Drag this line to move the starting point of the text along the path.

15. **Choose Edit>Undo (Command/Control-Z) to return the orientation point to the left end of the line.**

16. **Place the insertion point in the text path and apply right paragraph alignment.**

You can control paragraph formatting on a path just as you can for text in a frame.

17. **Save the file and continue to the final stage of the project.**

Stage 4 **Outputting the File**

If your layout contains transparency or effects, those transparent areas will typically need to be flattened for output. **Flattening** divides transparent artwork into the necessary vector and raster objects. Transparent objects are flattened according to the settings in the selected flattener preset, which you choose in the Advanced options of the Print dialog box (or in the dialog box that appears when you export as PDF, EPS, or another format).

When you work with transparency, InDesign converts affected objects to a common color space (either CMYK or RGB) so transparent objects of different color spaces can blend properly. To avoid color mismatches between different areas of the objects on screen and in print, the blending space is applied for screen and in the flattener. You can define which space to use in the Edit>Transparency Blend Space menu; for print jobs, make sure the CMYK option is selected.

1. **With poster.indd open, choose File>Export.**

2. **In the Export dialog box, navigate to your WIP>Jazz folder as the target destination and choose Adobe PDF (Print) in the Format/Save As Type menu.**

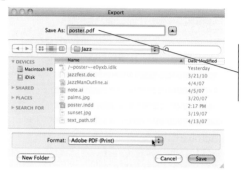

The file name defaults to the existing name, but with the correct extension for the selected format.

3. **Click Save.**

   Before the PDF is saved, you have to define the settings that will be used to generate the PDF file.

4. **Choose High Quality Print in the Adobe PDF Preset menu.**

   The Adobe PDF Preset menu includes six PDF presets that meet common industry output requirements.

   Because there are so many ways to create a PDF — and not all of those ways are optimized for the needs of commercial printing — the potential benefits of the file format are often undermined. The PDF/X specification was created to help solve some of the problems associated with bad PDF files entering the prepress workflow. PDF/X is a subset of PDF that is specifically designed to ensure that files have the information necessary for the digital prepress output process. Ask your output provider whether you should apply a PDF/X standard to your files, and if so, which version to use.

   The Compatibility menu determines which version of the PDF format you will create. This is particularly important if your layout uses transparency. PDF 1.3 does not support transparency, so the file will require flattening. If you save the file to be compatible with PDF 1.4 or later, transparency information will be maintained in the PDF file.

5. **Review the options in the General pane.**

- **Pages** options determine which pages to output, and whether to output facing pages on a single page.

- **Embed Page Thumbnails** creates a thumbnail for each page being exported, or one thumbnail for each spread if the Spreads option is selected.

- **Optimize for Fast Web View** optimizes the PDF file for faster viewing in a Web browser by allowing the file to download one page at a time.

- **Create Tagged PDF** automatically tags elements based on a subset of Acrobat tags (including basic formatting, lists, and more).

- **View PDF after Exporting** opens the PDF file after it has been created.

- **Create Acrobat Layers** saves each InDesign layer as an Acrobat layer within the PDF. Printer's marks are exported to a separate "marks and bleeds" layer. Create Acrobat Layers is available only when Compatibility is set to Acrobat 6 (PDF 1.5) or later.

- **Export Layers** determines whether you are outputting All Layers (including hidden and non-printing layers), Visible Layers (including non-printing layers), or Visible & Printable Layers.

- **Include** options can be used to include specific non-printing elements.

6. **Review the Compression options.**

The compression options determine what and how much data will be included in the PDF file. This set of options is one of the most important when creating PDFs, since too-low resolution results in bad-quality printing, and too-high resolution results in extremely long download times.

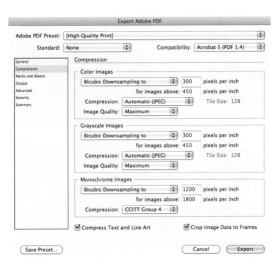

Before you choose compression settings, you need to consider your final goal. If you're creating a file for commercial printing, resolution is more important than file size. If your goal is a PDF that will be posted on the Web, file size is at least equally important as pristine image quality.

You can define a specific compression scheme for color, grayscale, and monochrome images. Different options are available depending on the image type:

- **JPEG compression** options are lossy, which means data is thrown away to create a smaller file. When you use one of the JPEG options, you can also define an Image Quality option (from Low to Maximum).

- **ZIP compression** is lossless, which means all file data is maintained in the compressed file.

- **CCITT compression** was initially developed for fax transmission. Group 3 supports two specific resolution settings (203 × 98 dpi and 203 × 196 dpi). Group 4 supports resolution up to 400 dpi.

- **Run Length Encoding** (RLE) is a lossless compression scheme that abbreviates sequences of adjacent pixels. If four pixels in a row are black, RLE saves that segment as "four black" instead of "black-black-black-black."

Note:

Since you chose the High Quality Print preset, these options default to settings that will produce the best results for most commercial printing applications.

Resolution Options for PDF

When you resize an image in the layout, you are changing its effective resolution. The **effective resolution** of an image is the resolution calculated after any scaling has been taken into account. This number is actually more important than the original image resolution. The effective resolution can be calculated with a fairly simple equation:

$$\text{original resolution} \div \frac{\% \text{ magnification}}{100} = \text{effective resolution}$$

If a 300-ppi image is magnified 150%, the effective resolution is:

$$300 \text{ ppi} / 1.5 = 200 \text{ ppi}$$

If you reduce the same 300-ppi image to 50%, the effective resolution is:

$$300 \text{ ppi} / 0.5 = 600 \text{ ppi}$$

In other words, the more you enlarge a raster image, the lower its effective resolution becomes. Reducing an image results in higher effective resolution, which can result in unnecessarily large PDF files.

When you create a PDF file, you also specify the resolution that will be maintained in the resulting PDF file. The Resolution option is useful if you want to throw away excess resolution for print files, or if you want to create low-resolution files for proofing or Web distribution.

- **Do Not Downsample** maintains all the image data from the linked files in the PDF file.

- **Average Downsampling To** reduces the number of pixels in an area by averaging areas of adjacent pixels. Apply this method to achieve user-defined resolution (72 or 96 dpi for Web-based files or 300 dpi for print).

- **Subsampling To** applies the center pixel value to surrounding pixels. If you think of a 3 × 3-block grid, subsampling enlarges the center pixel — and thus, its value — in place of the surrounding eight blocks.

- **Bicubic Downsampling To** creates the most accurate pixel information for continuous-tone images. This option also takes the longest to process, and it produces a softer image. To understand how this option works, think of a 2 × 2-block grid — bicubic downsampling averages the value of all four of those blocks (pixels) to interpolate the new information.

7. **In the Marks and Bleeds options, check the Crop Marks option and change the Offset field to 0.25″. Check the Use Document Bleed Settings option.**

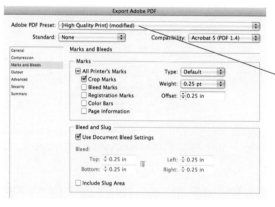

As soon as you choose a setting that is not part of the preset, the preset name shows "(modified)".

Note:

You can manage PDF Presets by choosing File>Adobe PDF Presets>Define. The dialog box that appears lists the built-in presets, as well as any presets you have created. You can also import presets from other users or export presets to send to other users.

8. **In the Compatibility menu, choose Acrobat 4 (PDF 1.3).**

9. **In the Advanced options, choose High Resolution in the Transparency Flattener Preset menu.**

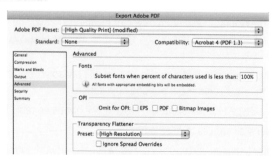

10. Click Export to create your PDF file. If you see a warning message, click OK.

Your PDF file will be flattened, so some features (hyperlinks, bookmarks, etc.) will be unavailable. You didn't use those features in this project, however, so you don't have to worry about this warning.

Note:

The Output options relate to color management, which you will use in Project 6. The Security options allow you to add password protection to a PDF file.

11. Choose Window>Utilities>Background Tasks.

The PDF export process happens in the background. This panel shows how much of the process has been completed (as a percentage), and will list any errors that occur. When the PDF file is finished, the export process is no longer listed in the panel.

The export process is listed in the panel.

12. Save the InDesign file and close it.

Flattener Presets

InDesign includes three default flattener presets:

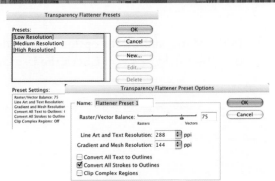

- **Low Resolution** works for desktop proofs that will be printed on low-end black-and-white printers and for documents that will be published on the Web.

- **Medium Resolution** works for desktop proofs and print-on-demand documents that will be printed on PostScript-compatible color printers.

- **High Resolution** works for commercial output on a printing press and for high-quality color proofs.

You can create your own flattener presets by choosing Edit>Transparency Flattener Presets and clicking New in the dialog box. You can also use the Transparency Flattener Presets dialog box to load flattener presets created on another machine — such as one your service provider created for their specific output device and/or workflow.

- The preset **Name** will be listed in the related output menus. You should use names that suggest the preset's use, such as "PDF for XL Printing Company." (Using meaningful names is a good idea for any asset that can have a name — from color swatches to output presets. "My Preset 12" is meaningless, possibly even to you after a few days, while "Preset for HP Indigo" tells you exactly when to use those settings.)

- **Raster/Vector Balance** determines how much vector information will be preserved when artwork is flattened. This slider ranges from 0 (all information is flattened as rasters) to 100 (maintains all vector information).

- **Line Art and Text Resolution** defines the resulting resolution of vector elements that will be rasterized, up to 9600 ppi. For good results in commercial printing applications, this option should be at least 600–1200 ppi (ask your output provider what settings they prefer you to use).

- **Gradient and Mesh Resolution** defines the resolution for gradients that will be rasterized, up to 1200 ppi. This option should typically be set to 300 ppi for most commercial printing applications.

- **Convert All Text to Outlines** converts all type to outline shapes; the text will not be editable in a PDF file.

- **Convert All Strokes to Outlines** converts all strokes to filled paths.

- **Clip Complex Regions** forces boundaries between vector objects and rasterized artwork to fall along object paths, reducing potential problems that can result when only part of an object is rasterized.

INDESIGN FOUNDATIONS

1. The _____ tool can be used to draw the direction and position of a gradient within a frame.

2. The _____ menu command reveals characters such as paragraph returns and tabs.

3. _____ is the space between specific pairs of letters. To change this value, you have to place the insertion point between two characters.

4. The _____ is the theoretical line on which the bottoms of letters rest.

5. The _____ indicates that more text exists in the story than will fit into the available frame (or series of linked frames).

6. The _____ can be used to copy type formatting from one type element to another.

7. The _____ panel is used to apply optical margin alignment.

8. _____ are objects that are attached to specific areas of text.

9. _____ is the resolution of an image after its scaling in the layout has been taken into account.

10. _____ compression for raster images is lossy, which means data is thrown away to reduce the file size.

1. Briefly explain how transparency is applied to objects in an InDesign page layout.

2. Briefly define a clipping path; provide at least two examples of how they might be useful.

3. Briefly explain the difference between character formatting and paragraph formatting.

Portfolio Builder Project

Use what you learned in this project to complete the following freeform exercise.
Carefully read the art director and client comments, then create your own design to meet the needs of the project.
Use the space below to sketch ideas; when finished, write a brief explanation of your reasoning behind your final design.

art director comments

The former marketing director for the Miami Jazz Festival recently moved to California to be the director of the Laguna Beach Sawdust Festival. She was pleased with your work on the jazz festival project, and would like to hire you to create the advertising for next year's art festival event.

To complete this project, you should:

❏ Download the **ID5_PB_Project2.zip** archive from the Student Files Web page to access the client-supplied text file.

❏ Develop some compelling visual element that will be the central focus of the ads.

❏ Create an ad that fits on a tabloid-size newspaper page (9 1/2 × 11 1/2″ with no bleeds).

❏ Create a second version of the same ad to fit a standard magazine trim size (8 1/4 × 10 7/8″ with 1/8″ bleeds).

client comments

The Sawdust Festival is one of the longest running and well-known art shows in California, maybe even the entire United States. We're planning our advertising campaign for the 2010 summer.

You might want to poke around our Web site to get some ideas. There's information about the festival's history, as well as images from previous shows.

We need an ad that will be placed in the pull-out sections of regional newspapers, and another version of the same ad that can go into magazines for travel/tourism audiences (like the WestWays magazine from AAA). Both ads should be four-color, although you should keep in mind the basic color scheme that we use on our Web site.

The ads need to have all the relevant text. But just as important, we want the ad to be art in its own right; the visual element you create will actually be repurposed for festival souvenirs like shirts, posters, and so on.

project justification

This project combined form and function — presenting the client's information in a clear, easy-to-read manner, while using large graphic elements to grab the viewer's attention and reinforce the message of the piece. As the client requested, the main focus is on the graphics in the top two-thirds of the piece while the relevant text is large enough to be visible but isn't the primary visual element.

Completing this poster involved adjusting a number of different text formatting options, including paragraph settings and the flow of text across multiple frames. You should now understand the difference between character and paragraph formatting, and know where to find the different options when you need them.

The graphics options in InDesign give you significant creative control over virtually every element of your layouts. Custom colors and gradients add visual interest to any piece, while more sophisticated tools like non-destructive transparency and other effects allow you to experiment entirely within your page layout until you find exactly the look you want to communicate your intended message.

Apply a spot-color swatch to type

Create and format text on a path

Create custom swatches and gradients for frame fills and strokes

Use blending modes to blend an image into the frame background fill

Use a gradient feather to add soft edges to a placed image

Create a custom graphics frame from an image's clipping path

Place graphics as anchored inline objects

Use optical margin alignment to align punctuation outside the text frame

Control text flow across multiple text frames

HeartSmart Newsletter

Your client is a non-profit foundation that focuses on health education and public awareness. It publishes a monthly newsletter for people on various mailing lists, which are purchased from a list-management vendor. The editor wants to change the existing newsletter template, and wants you to take over the layout once the template has been revised.

This project incorporates the following skills:

❏ Opening and modifying an existing layout template

❏ Managing missing font and link requests

❏ Replacing graphics files to meet specific color output needs

❏ Formatting text with template styles

❏ Controlling text-frame inset, alignment, and wrap attributes

❏ Creating a table with data from a Microsoft Excel worksheet

❏ Preflighting the final layout and creating a job package

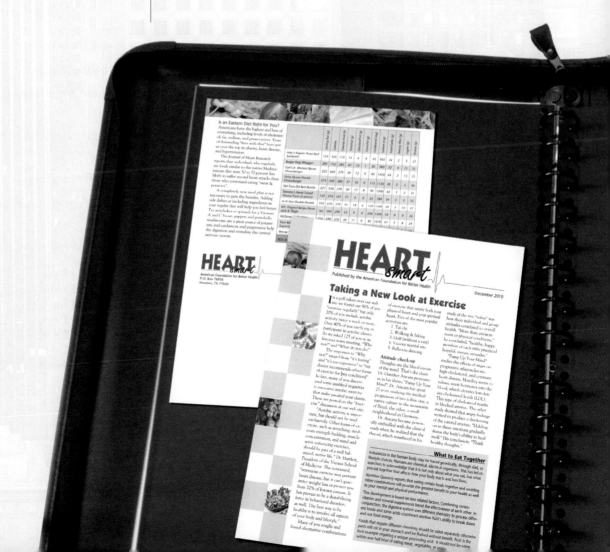

client comments

In the past our newsletter was printed as a two-color job on a duplicator. However, the printer just told us that we can go to four-color printing and pay virtually the same per piece as we used to pay.

We need some other changes too. We want to go from four columns to three on the front, and from three columns to two on the back. The checkerboard area on the front usually has four random pictures, and the bar at the top of the back has a single image. Those all used to be grayscale photos, but now you can use color.

We'd like you to make modifications to the template, and then use the template to create the current issue. We sent you the pictures we want to use for this issue, as well as the three text pieces (the main article, a sidebar for the front, and the story for the back). There's also a table in Microsoft Excel format that we want to include on the back.

art director comments

Whenever you work with a file that someone else created, there is always the potential for problems. When you first open the template, you'll have to check the fonts and images and make whatever adjustments are necessary. Make sure you save the file as a template again before you build the new issue.

Moving from two-color to four-color isn't too big a deal — it's actually easier than going from color to grayscale since color adds possibilities instead of limiting them. You have the opportunity to add color to common design elements (including styles), and you should also use the color version of the nameplate instead of the grayscale one.

The printer said they prefer to work with native application files instead of PDF, so when you're finished implementing the layout, you'll need to check the various elements, and then create a final job package.

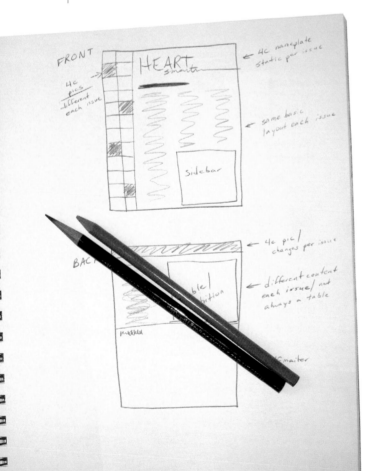

project objectives

To complete this project, you will:

❏ Handle requests for missing fonts and images

❏ Edit master page elements to meet new requirements

❏ Save a layout file as a template

❏ Access master page elements on the layout pages

❏ Format imported text using template styles

❏ Build and format a table using data from a Microsoft Excel spreadsheet

❏ Create a final job package for the output provider

Stage 1 Working with Templates

Templates are commonly used whenever you have a basic layout that will be implemented more than once — for example, the structure of a newsletter remains the same, but the content for each issue changes. InDesign templates are special types of files that store the basic structure of a project. Well-planned templates can store layout elements such as nonprinting guides that mark various areas of the job; placeholder frames that will contain different stories or images in each revision; elements that remain the same in every revision, such as the nameplate; and even formatting information that will be applied to different elements so the elements can be consistent from one issue to the next.

MANAGE MISSING FONTS

When you work with digital page layouts — whether in a template or in a regular layout file — it's important to understand that fonts are external files of data that describe the font for on-screen display and for the output device. The fonts you use in a layout need to be available on any computer that will be used to open the file. InDesign stores a reference to used fonts, but it does not store the actual font data.

1. **Download ID5_RF_Project3.zip from the Student Files Web page.**

2. **Expand the ZIP archive in your WIP folder (Macintosh) or copy the archive contents into your WIP folder (Windows).**

   This creates a folder named **HeartSmart**, which contains the files you need for this project. You should also use this folder to save the files you create in this project.

3. **Select the file heartsmart.indt in the WIP>HeartSmart folder. Choose the Open Original option at the bottom of the dialog box.**

   You have several options when you open an existing template file:

   - If you choose **Open Normal** to open a regular InDesign file (INDD), the selected file appears in a new document window or tab. When you use this option to open a template file (INDT), InDesign creates and opens a new untitled file that is based on the template.

   - When you choose the **Open Original** option, you open the actual InDesign template file so you can make and save changes to the template.

   - You can use the **Open Copy** option to open a regular InDesign file as if it were a template; the result is a new untitled document based on the file you selected.

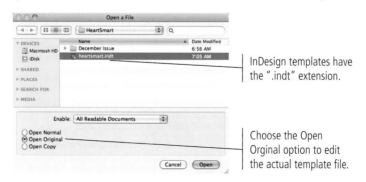

InDesign templates have the ".indt" extension.

Choose the Open Orginal option to edit the actual template file.

4. **Click Open, then review the warning message.**

   InDesign stores links to images placed in a layout; the actual placed-file data is not stored in the InDesign file. If placed files are not available in the same location as when they were originally placed, you'll see a warning message when you open the file. You'll correct this problem in the next exercise.

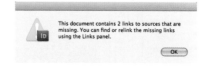

Note:

Missing fonts are one of the most common problems in the digital graphics output process. This is one of the primary advantages of using PDF files for output — PDF can store actual font data so you don't need to include the separate font files in your job package. (However, PDF can't solve the problem of missing fonts used in a layout template.)

5. Click OK in the warning, and then review the information in the resulting Missing Fonts dialog box.

Any time you open a file that calls for fonts that are not installed on your computer system, you see this warning. You could blindly fix the problem now (without knowing what will be affected), but we prefer to review problem areas before making changes.

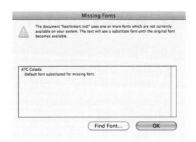

6. Click OK to dismiss the Missing Fonts dialog box.

7. Open the Pages panel (Window>Pages).

The Pages panel is the easiest way to navigate through the pages in a layout, including master pages. You can navigate to any page by simply double-clicking the page's icon, or navigate to a spread by double-clicking the spread page numbers (below the page icons).

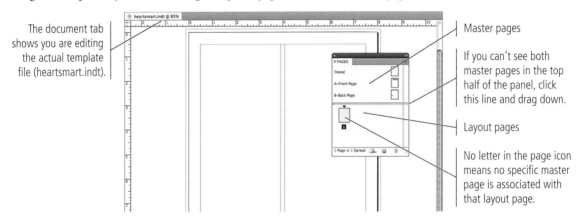

The document tab shows you are editing the actual template file (heartsmart.indt).

Master pages

If you can't see both master pages in the top half of the panel, click this line and drag down.

Layout pages

No letter in the page icon means no specific master page is associated with that layout page.

Think of master pages as templates for different pages in the layout. This file, for example, has two master pages: Front Page and Back Page. The letters preceding each master page name are automatically added and used to identify which layout pages are associated with which master page. (This will become clear as you continue through this project.)

8. Double-click the A-Front Page icon to display that layout.

The top area of the newsletter (the **nameplate** area) includes the newsletter logotype, as well as the "Published by..." line and the issue date. A pink highlight around the type shows that the font used in this area is not available.

9. Using the Type tool, click the frame with the missing font to place the insertion point.

The Control panel shows the missing font name in brackets. Any time you see a font name in brackets, you know you have a potential problem.

Note:

The Missing Font highlighting is only a visual indicator on your screen. It is not included when the job is output.

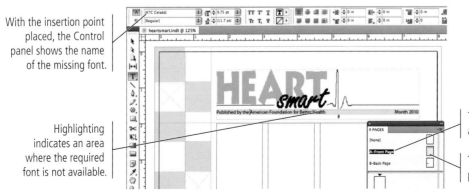

With the insertion point placed, the Control panel shows the name of the missing font.

Highlighting indicates an area where the required font is not available.

The name or number of the active page is highlighted.

The icon of the selected page is highlighted.

10. Choose Type>Find Font.

The Find Font dialog box lists every font used in the layout — including missing ones (with a warning icon). You can use this dialog box to replace any font — including missing ones — with another font that is available on your system.

11. Highlight ATC Colada in the Fonts in Document list and click the More Info button.

The bottom section of the dialog box shows information about the selected font, including the places where it's used (in this case, 66 characters on A-Front Page).

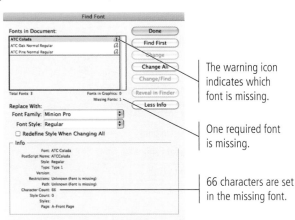

The warning icon indicates which font is missing.

One required font is missing.

66 characters are set in the missing font.

Note:

If the nameplate information is not highlighted, open the Composition pane of the Preferences dialog box and make sure the Highlight Substituted Fonts option is checked.

The highlighting only appears if you are in the Normal viewing mode.

12. In the Replace With area, choose ATC Oak Normal in the Font Family menu.

13. Click Change All to replace all instances of ATC Colada with ATC Oak Normal.

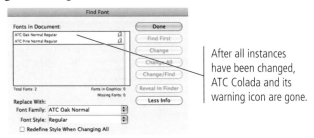

After all instances have been changed, ATC Colada and its warning icon are gone.

Note:

If a font is used in styles, you can apply your font replacement choices to style definitions by checking the Redefine Style When Changing All option.

14. Click Done to close the Find Font dialog box.

Once you have replaced the missing font, the pink highlighting disappears.

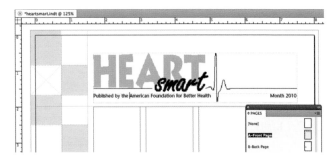

Note:

You can click the Find Next button to review individual instances of a missing font, or you can click the Change or Change/Find button to replace and review individual instances of the selected font.

15. Choose File>Save to save your changes to the template file, and then continue to the next exercise.

Because you used the Open Original option, you are editing the actual template file; this means you can simply use the regular Save command to save your changes to the template. If you used the Open Normal option to open and edit a template file, you would have to use the Save As command and save the edited file with the same name and extension as the original template to overwrite the original.

REPLACE MISSING GRAPHICS

Placed graphics can cause problems if those files aren't where they're supposed to be (or at least where InDesign thinks they should be). Placed graphics files can be either **missing** (they were moved from the location from which they were originally placed in the layout, or the name of the file was changed) or **modified** (they were resaved after being placed into the layout, changing the linked file's "time stamp" but not its location or file name). In either case, you need to correct these problems before the file can be successfully output.

1. **With heartsmart.indt open, display the Links panel (Window>Links).**

   The Links panel lists every file that is placed in your layout. Missing images show a red stop-sign icon; modified images show a yellow yield sign.

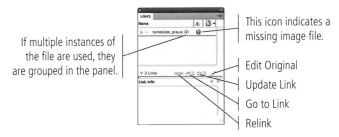

2. **Click the arrow to the left of the nameplate_gray.ai file to show the two instances.**

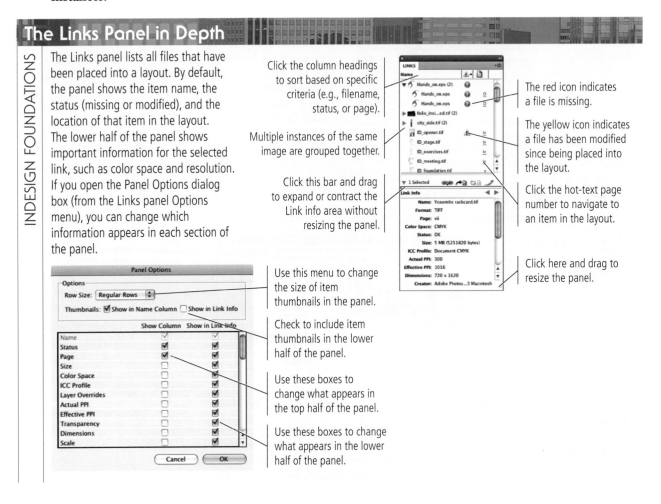

3. **Click the first listed instance to select it, and then click the Go to Link button in the middle of the panel.**

You can also use the hot-text link to the right of an image name to navigate to a specific placed image. The Pages panel shows that the B-Back Page master layout is now active because that is where the selected instance exists.

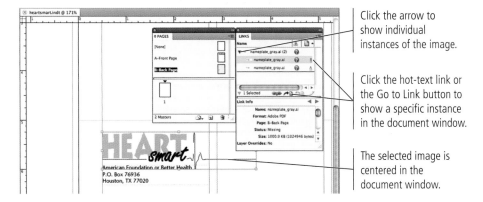

Click the arrow to show individual instances of the image.

Click the hot-text link or the Go to Link button to show a specific instance in the document window.

The selected image is centered in the document window.

4. **With the file still selected in the panel, click the Relink button.**

5. **Navigate to** `nameplate_color.ai` **in the WIP>HeartSmart>December Issue folder and click Open.**

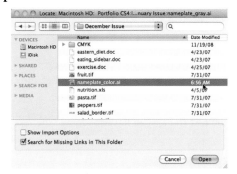

Note:

If the Search for Missing Links option is checked, InDesign will scan the selected folder to find other missing image files.

The selected instance is replaced with the new image. Because this link is a different image than the original, the Links panel now shows two separate items rather than the group of two instances for the same image. The other instance of the original image, listed in the Links panel, is still missing.

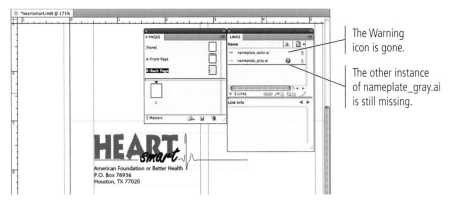

The Warning icon is gone.

The other instance of nameplate_gray.ai is still missing.

6. **Select the remaining missing image in the Links panel and click Go to Link.**

7. **With the file still selected in the panel, click the Relink button.**

8. **Navigate to `nameplate_color.ai` in the WIP>HeartSmart>December Issue folder and click Open.**

The instances are again grouped under the single file name.

The Warning icon is gone.

9. **Save the file and continue to the next exercise.**

EDIT MARGIN AND COLUMN GUIDES

Your client wants to make several changes to the layout, including fewer columns and incorporating color into various elements. These changes will recur from one issue to the next, so you should change the template instead of simply changing the elements in each individual issue.

1. **With `heartsmart.indt` open, double-click the A-Front Page icon to show that layout in the document window.**

2. **Choose Layout>Margins and Columns. In the resulting dialog box, change the Columns field to 3 and the Gutter field to 0.2″, and then click OK.**

   Every layout has a default setup, which you define when you create the file. Master pages have their own margin and column settings that can be different than the default document settings.

   Changing the column guides has no effect on the text frame; you have to change the text frame independently.

Note:

You can change the default margins and columns for a layout by choosing File>Document Setup.

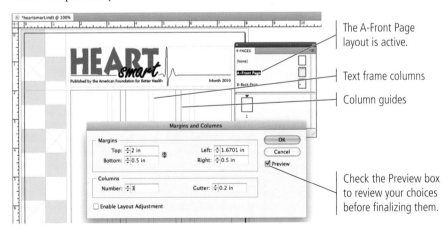

The A-Front Page layout is active.

Text frame columns

Column guides

Check the Preview box to review your choices before finalizing them.

3. **Using the Selection tool, click to select the 4-column text frame, and then Control/right-click the frame and choose Text Frame Options from the contextual menu.**

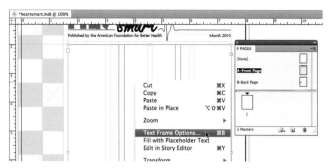

Note:

You can also access the Text Frame Options dialog box from the Object menu.

4. **Change the Number of Columns field to 3 and the Gutter field to 0.2″ to match the changes you made to the column guides. Click OK to close the dialog box.**

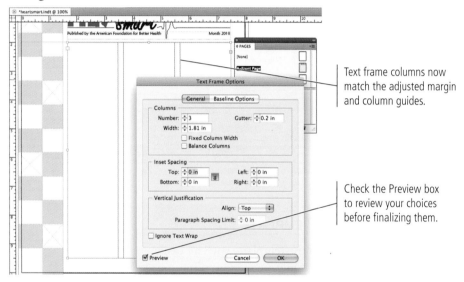

Text frame columns now match the adjusted margin and column guides.

Check the Preview box to review your choices before finalizing them.

5. **In the Pages panel, double-click the B-Back Page icon to display that layout in the document window.**

6. **Choose Layout>Margins and Columns. Change the Bottom Margin setting to 5.25″, change the Columns field to 2, change the Gutter to 0.2″, and then click OK.**

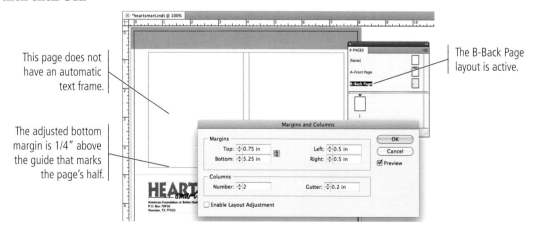

This page does not have an automatic text frame.

The adjusted bottom margin is 1/4″ above the guide that marks the page's half.

The B-Back Page layout is active.

7. **Using the Type tool, create a text frame that fills the adjusted margins on the B-Back Page layout.**

8. **Control/right-click the text frame and choose Text Frame Options from the contextual menu. Change the frame to 2 columns with a 0.2″ gutter, and then click OK.**

   One of the advantages to using a template is eliminating repetitive tasks. Since every issue of the newsletter has a story in this area of the back, it makes sense to create the text frame as part of the master page (and template).

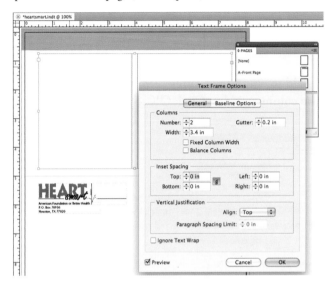

9. **Save the file and close it.**

 CREATE A NEW FILE BASED ON THE TEMPLATE

Once you have made the client's requested changes in the template, you can easily begin each new issue by simply opening the template. Only a few more things need to be addressed before you're ready to work on the current issue of the newsletter.

Every issue of the newsletter has the same structure — one front page and one back page. These layouts are already prepared as master pages, but you have to apply those master pages to the layout pages for individual issues. Since this occurs for every issue, it will remove a few more clicks from the process if you set up the layout pages as part of the template.

1. **Choose File>Open and navigate to your WIP>HeartSmart folder. Select the heartsmart.indt template file and choose the Open Normal option at the bottom of the dialog box.**

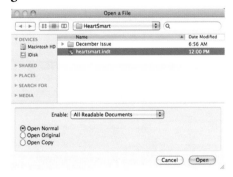

INDESIGN FOUNDATIONS

There are two kinds of pages in InDesign:

- **Layout pages** are the pages on which you place text and images.
- **Master pages** are the pages on which you place recurring information, such as running heads (information at the top of the page) and running footers (information at the bottom of the page).

Master pages are one of the most powerful features in professional layout software. Think of a master page as a template for individual pages; anything on the master appears on the related layout page(s). Changing something on a master layout applies the same changes to the object on related layout pages (unless you already changed the object on the layout page, or detached the object from the master).

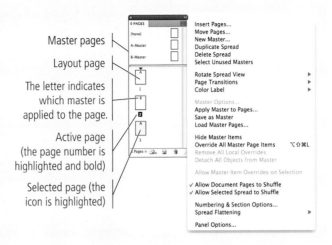

Master pages
Layout page

The letter indicates which master is applied to the page.

Active page (the page number is highlighted and bold)

Selected page (the icon is highlighted)

Master pages are accessed and controlled in the top half of the Pages panel. Layout pages, in the lower half of the panel, show the letter that corresponds to the master applied to that page. The Pages panel Options menu has a number of indispensable options for working with master pages:

- **New Master** opens a dialog box where you can assign a custom prefix, a meaningful name, whether the master will be based on another master page, and the number of pages (from 1 to 10) to include in the master layout.

- **Select Unused Masters** highlights all master pages not associated with at least one layout page (and not used as the basis of another master page). This option can be useful if you want to clean up your layout and remove extraneous elements.

- **Master Options** opens a dialog box with the same options you defined when you created a new master.

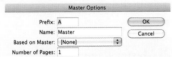

- **Apply Master to Pages** allows you to apply a specific master to selected pages. You can also apply a specific master to a layout by dragging the master icon onto the layout page icon in the lower half of the panel.

- **Save as Master** is useful if you've built a layout on a layout page and want to convert that layout to a master. Instead of copying and pasting the page contents, you can simply activate the page and choose Save as Master.

- **Load Master Pages** allows you to import entire master pages from one InDesign file to another. Assets such as colors and styles used on the imported masters will also be imported into the current InDesign file.

- **Hide/Show Master Items** toggles the visibility of master page items on layout pages.

- **Override All Master Page Items** allows you to access and change master items on a specific layout page. (It's important to realize that this command functions on a page-by-page basis.) You can also override individual objects by pressing Command/Control-Shift and clicking the object you want to override.

- **Remove All Local Overrides** reapplies the settings from the master items to related items on the layout page. (This option toggles to **Remove Selected Local Overrides** if you have a specific object selected on the layout page.)

- **Detach All Objects from Master** breaks the link between objects on a layout page and objects on the related master; in this case, changing items on the master has no effect on related layout page items. (This selection toggles to **Detach Selection from Master** if you have a specific object selected on the layout page.)

- **Allow Master Item Overrides on Selection**, active by default, allows objects to be overridden on layout pages. You can protect specific objects by selecting them on the master layout and toggling this option off.

2. **Click Open to create a new file based on the template.**

Opening a template using the Open Normal option creates a new untitled document that is based on the template.

3. **Double-click the Page 1 icon in the Pages panel.**

4. **In the Pages panel, drag the A-Front Page master icon onto the Page 1 icon in the lower half of the Pages panel.**

   When a master page is applied to a layout page, everything on the master page is placed on the layout page.

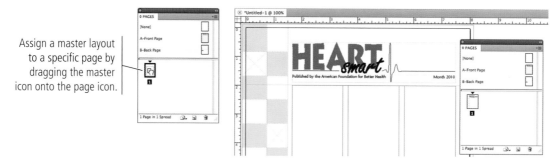

Assign a master layout to a specific page by dragging the master icon onto the page icon.

5. **Using the Selection tool, try to select the empty text frame on the page.**

   This step will have no effect, and nothing will be selected. By default, you can't select master page items on a layout page; changes have to be made on the master page.

   When you change an object on a master page, the same changes reflect on associated layout pages. For example, if you change the red box to blue on A-Front Page, the red box will turn blue on Page 1 as well.

   In many cases, however, you might need to change a master page item for only a single page in the layout — a common occurrence when you use placeholder text or graphics frames on a master page. In this case, you have to override the master page layout for the specific layout page (or for a specific item by Command/Control-Shift-clicking that item), so you can select and change the overridden master page items.

Note:

You can change the size of page icons in the Pages panel by choosing Panel Options at the bottom of the panel's Options menu.

6. **Control/right-click the Page 1 icon and choose Override All Master Page Items from the contextual menu.**

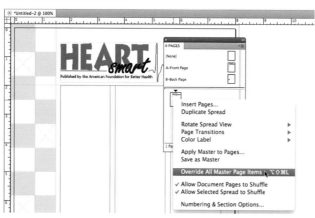

7. Click to select the empty text frame.

By overriding the master page layout for this page, you make it possible to select and change master page items — including the text frame — on the layout page.

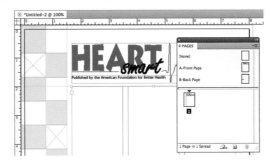

8. Click the B-Back Page icon and drag it into the bottom half of the Pages panel (below the Page 1 icon).

You can add new pages to your layout by dragging any of the master page icons into the lower half of the panel.

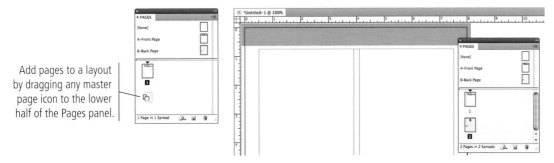

Add pages to a layout by dragging any master page icon to the lower half of the Pages panel.

9. Control/right-click the Page 2 icon and choose Override All Master Page Items from the contextual menu.

You can now select and change the text frame on Page 2, as well as the other objects from the B-Back Page master.

Note:

Command/Control-Shift-click an object to detach individual objects from the master page.

10. Choose File>Save As. Navigate to your WIP>HeartSmart folder as the location for saving the template.

Because you opened the template to create a normal layout file, you have to use the Save As command to overwrite the edited template file.

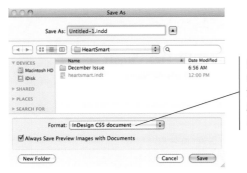

Because you created a new layout file from the template, the Format/Save As Type menu defaults to InDesign CS5 Document.

11. **Change the file name to** `heartsmart`.

12. **In the Format/Save As Type menu, choose InDesign CS5 Template.**

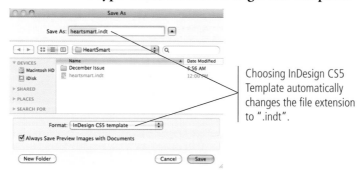

Choosing InDesign CS5 Template automatically changes the file extension to ".indt".

13. **Click Save, then read the resulting message.**

   Because you defined the same name as the original template, you have to confirm that you want to overwrite the template file with the new version.

14. **Click Replace. When the save is complete, close the template file.**

 ## IMPLEMENT THE NEWSLETTER TEMPLATE

By saving your work as a template, you have eliminated a significant amount of repetitive work that would otherwise need to be redone for every issue. There are still some tasks that will need to be done for each issue, such as changing the issue date and adding images to the front and back pages. These elements will change in each issue, so they can't be entirely "templated." But if you review the layout as it is now, you'll see that the template includes placeholders for these elements, so adding these elements is greatly simplified.

1. **Choose File>Open and navigate to your WIP>HeartSmart folder. Select the** `heartsmart.indt` **template file, choose the Open Normal option at the bottom of the dialog box, and click Open.**

   As in the previous exercise, opening the template file creates a new untitled document that is based on the template.

2. **Immediately choose File>Save As and navigate to your WIP>HeartSmart folder. Change the file name to** `newsletter_dec.indd` **and click Save.**

3. **Navigate to Page 1 of the file. Using the Type tool, highlight "Month 2010" in the nameplate area and type** December 2010.

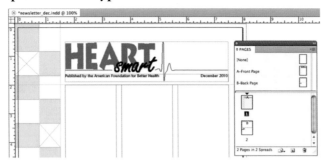

4. **Save the file and continue to the next exercise.**

 ## Use Mini Bridge to Place Images

Adobe Bridge is a stand-alone application that ships and installs along with InDesign. This asset-management tool enables you to navigate, browse, and manage files anywhere on your system. If you have the entire Adobe Creative Suite, Bridge can also help streamline the workflow as you flip from one application to another to complete a project.

Mini Bridge provides access to certain file-management operations of the full Bridge application, directly from a panel within InDesign. Specifically, it makes it very easy to place files into a layout by simply dragging and dropping.

1. **With** newsletter_dec.indd **open, Shift-click the Go to Bridge button in the Application/Menu bar to open the Mini Bridge panel.**

Shift-click this button to open the Mini Bridge panel.

2. **In the Mini Bridge panel, click the Browse Files button.**

3. **Use the panel's Content pod to navigate to the WIP>HeartSmart>December Issue folder.**

   Navigating in the panel is very similar to the basic operating system navigation; simply double-click a folder icon to open it and show the folder's contents. (We can't be sure where your WIP folder is stored; you need to navigate through the correct path on your system.)

Note:

If Bridge is not already running on your computer, it might take a while for the Mini Bridge panel to show anything.

4. **Click the View button at the bottom of the panel and choose As Thumbnails.**

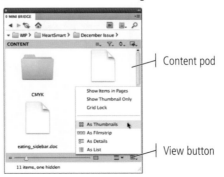

Content pod

View button

INDESIGN FOUNDATIONS

The Mini Bridge panel provides access to a number of file management options, directly within the InDesign interface.

The **Path bar** shows the list of folders that is the "address" of the files currently displayed in the Content pod.

The **Content pod** (which is always visible) shows the files in the selected folder.

The **Navigation pod** shows a standard file navigation structure, which you can use to find a particular location on your computer.

The **Preview pod** shows a larger version of the selected thumbnails (in the Content pod).

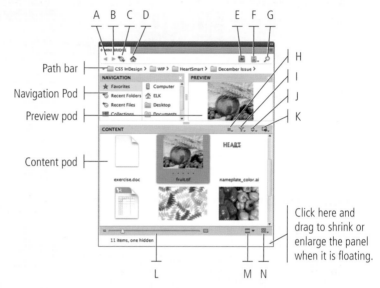

A Use the **Go Back** button to navigate back one step in the panel's history.

B Use the **Go Forward** button to navigate forward one step in the panel's history.

C Use the **Go to Parent, Recent Items, or Favorites** button to access a menu of the relevant folders on your computer.

D Use the **Home Page** button to restore the panel to its default interface, with buttons to browse files and change the panel's settings.

E Use the **Go to Adobe Bridge** button to switch to the full Bridge application.

F Use the **Panel View** button to show or hide the Path bar, Navigation pod, and Preview pod in the panel.

G Use the **Search** button to find specific files anywhere on your computer.

H Use the **Select** button to show or hide rejected files, hidden files, and folders. This menu also includes commands to select all files in the current folder, deselect all selected files, or invert the current selection (select only the unselected files).

I Use the **Filter Items** button to show only certain items in the panel's Content pod, based on user-defined ratings for each file (see below).

J Use the **Sort** button to change the order of files in the panel's Content pod, based on specific criteria such as file name, type, or date created or modified.

K Use the **Tools** button to access options for placing the selected file in InDesign or Photoshop, or to access a number of other Photoshop-specific options (such as loading all selected files into Photoshop layers).

L Use the **Thumbnail Size** slider to change the size of thumbnails in the panel's Content pod.

M Click the **Preview** button to show a larger version of the selected thumbnail. If you click the arrow to the right of the button, you can view selected files as a slideshow, enter Review mode, or view full-screen previews.

N Click the **View** button to change the appearance of items in the panel's Content pod.

Control/right-click a file in Review mode to access specific options for that file.

Use the buttons to navigate from one file to another.

Ratings appear above the file name.

Labels appear around the rating.

Use these buttons to zoom, create a collection, and exit Review mode.

5. **Scroll through the thumbnails to find fruit.tif. Click the fruit.tif thumbnail in the panel, and then drag it to the first empty graphics frame on the left side of Page 1.**

When you release the mouse button, the selected image is automatically placed into the frame where you drag.

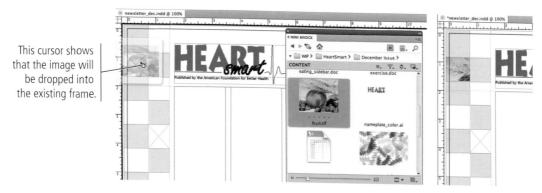

This cursor shows that the image will be dropped into the existing frame.

6. **In the Mini Bridge panel, click the pasta.tif thumbnail to select it. Press Command/Control and then click the peppers.tif and salad_bowl.tif thumbnails to add them to the active selection.**

Press Shift to select multiple contiguous files, or press Command/Control to select multiple non-contiguous files.

7. **Click any of the selected thumbnails, drag into the document window, and then release the mouse button.**

Even if you release the mouse button over an existing frame, InDesign stores all three in the loaded place cursor; nothing is automatically placed in the file.

Note:

If the cursor is not over an existing frame when you release the mouse button, the selected file is loaded into the cursor; you can then click and drag to create a frame that will contain the loaded image.

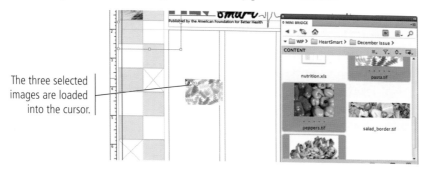

The three selected images are loaded into the cursor.

8. **Click the loaded cursor on the second graphics frame to place the first loaded image.**

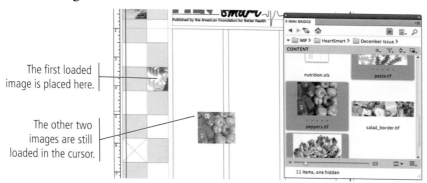

The first loaded image is placed here.

The other two images are still loaded in the cursor.

9. **Click to place the remaining images in the other two empty graphics frames.**

10. Using the Direct Selection tool or the Content Indicator, click to select the image within the top frame. Control/right-click the selected image and choose Fitting>Fill Frame Proportionally from the contextual menu.

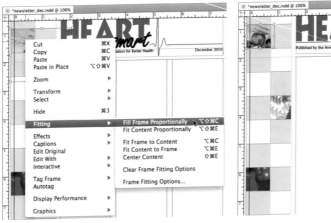

Note:

The same Fitting options are available in the Object>Fitting menu.

Note:

Fitting options are available when either the frame or the frame content are selected. When the content is selected, however, you can see the red bounding box that marks the edge of the placed image (rather than only the frame bounding box).

11. Repeat Step 10 for the other three images on the left side of the page.

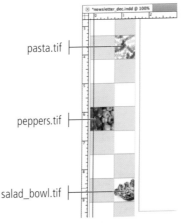

pasta.tif

peppers.tif

salad_bowl.tif

Content Fitting Options

INDESIGN FOUNDATIONS

The Fitting options resize content relative to the containing frame, or resize the containing frame to match the placed content.

- **Fill Frame Proportionally** resizes content to fill the entire frame while preserving the content's proportions.

- **Fit Content Proportionally** resizes content to fit entirely within its containing frame, maintaining the current aspect ratio of the image. Some empty space might result along one dimension of the frame.

- **Fit Frame to Content** resizes the frame to the dimensions of the placed content.

- **Fit Content to Frame** resizes content to fit the dimensions of the containing frame, even if that means scaling the content out of proportion (stretched in one direction or another).

- **Center Content** centers content within its containing frame, but neither the frame nor the content is resized.

Filling proportionally fills the frame; some areas of the image might be cropped.

Fitting proportionally places the entire image into the frame; some areas of the frame might be empty.

12. Control/right-click the fourth image and choose Fitting>Center Content.

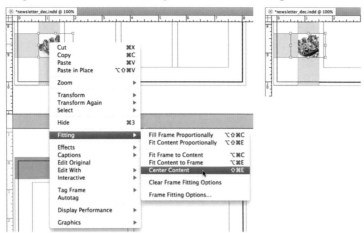

13. Navigate to Page 2 of the layout. Using the Mini Bridge panel, drag the salad_border.tif thumbnail into the graphics frame at the top of the page.

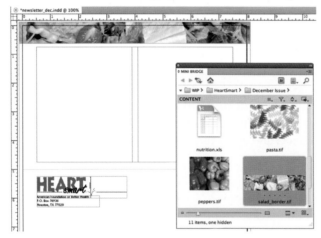

14. Save the file and continue to the next stage of the project.

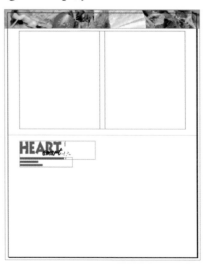

Stage 2 Working with Styles

The principles of good design state that headings, subheadings, body copy, and other editorial elements should generally look the same throughout a single job — in other words, editorial elements should be consistent from one page to another, whether the job is two pages or two hundred.

In Project 2 you learned about the various text formatting options that can be applied in an InDesign layout. For any bit of text, there are dozens of character- and paragraph-formatting options, from the font and type size to the space above and below paragraphs. Whenever you work with longer blocks of copy, you'll apply the same group of formatting options to multiple pieces of text.

If you were to change each editorial element manually, you would have to make hundreds of clicks to create a two-page newsletter. Fortunately, InDesign makes it easy to store groups of text-formatting options as **styles**, which can be applied to any text with a single click.

Note:

Styles ensure consistency in text and paragraph formatting throughout a publication. Rather than trying to remember how you formatted a sidebar 45 pages ago, you can simply apply a predefined Sidebar style.

The major advantages of using styles are ease of use and enhanced efficiency. Changes can be made instantly to all text defined as a particular style. For example, you might easily modify leading in the Body Copy style or change the font in the Subhead style from Helvetica to ATC Oak Bold. When a style definition changes, any text that uses that style automatically changes too.

InDesign supports both character styles and paragraph styles. **Character styles** apply only to selected words; this type of style is useful for setting off a few words in a paragraph without affecting the entire paragraph. **Paragraph styles** apply to the entire body of text between two ¶ symbols; this type of style defines the appearance of the paragraph, combining the character style used in the paragraph with line spacing, indents, tabs, and other paragraph attributes.

Note:

Paragraph styles define character attributes and paragraph attributes; character styles define only the character attributes. In other words, a paragraph style can be used to format text entirely — including font information, line spacing, tabs, and so on.

In this project, the client's original INDT template included a number of styles for formatting the text in each issue. Because the text frames already exist in the template layout, you only need to import the client's text and apply the existing styles.

APPLY TEMPLATE STYLES

Most InDesign jobs incorporate some amount of client-supplied text, which might be sent to you in the body of an email or saved in any number of text file formats. Many text files will be supplied from Microsoft Word, the most popular word-processing application in the United States market.

Microsoft Word includes fairly extensive options for formatting text (although not quite as robust or sophisticated as what you can do with InDesign). Many Microsoft Word users apply **local formatting** (selecting specific text and applying character and/or paragraph attributes); more sophisticated Microsoft Word users build text formatting styles similar to those used in InDesign.

Styles are most advantageous when working with text-intensive documents that have recurring editorial elements, such as headlines, subheads, and captions; when working with several people concurrently on the same project; and when creating projects with specific style requirements, such as catalogs or magazines.

1. With Page 1 of `newsletter_dec.indd` active in the document window, choose File>Place and navigate to the file `exercise.doc`.

   All text files for this project are in the WIP> HeartSmart>December Issue folder.

2. **Check the Show Import Options box at the bottom of the dialog box, and make sure Replace Selected Item is not checked.**

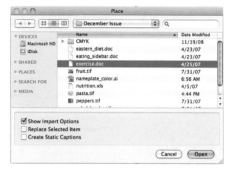

3. **Click Open. In the resulting dialog box, review the options in the Formatting section.**

   When you import a Microsoft Word file into InDesign, you can either preserve or remove formatting saved in the Microsoft Word file (including styles defined in Microsoft Word).

4. **Make sure the Preserve Styles and Formatting option is selected and the Import Styles Automatically radio button is selected. Choose Auto Rename in both conflict menus, and then click OK.**

5. **If you see a Missing Fonts warning, click OK.**

   You're going to replace the Microsoft Word formatting with InDesign styles, which should correct this problem.

6. **Click the loaded cursor in the empty three-column text frame.**

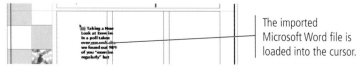

The imported Microsoft Word file is loaded into the cursor.

Microsoft Word files can include a fairly sophisticated level of formatting attributes, from basic text formatting to defined paragraph and character styles to automatically generated tables of contents. When you import a Word file into InDesign, you can determine whether to include these elements in the imported text, as well as how to handle conflicts between imported elements and elements that already exist in your InDesign layout.

If these elements exist in the Microsoft Word file, checking the associated boxes imports those elements into your InDesign file.

Choose this option to convert straight quote marks to typographer's or "curly" quotes.

Choose this option to strip out all formatting applied in the file and import the file as plain text.

Choose this option to import the Microsoft Word file, including formatting.

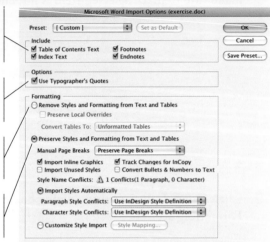

The **Manual Page Breaks** menu determines how page breaks in Word translate to InDesign. You can preserve manual breaks, convert them to column breaks, or ignore them. This option is important because Word users tend to force breaks where appropriate in the file — which rarely translates to a properly formatted InDesign layout. More often than not, you'll end up removing these page breaks, but it might be a good idea to include them in the import and remove them after you've reviewed the imported text.

If graphics have been placed into a Word file, the **Import Inline Graphics** option allows you to include those graphics as anchored objects in the InDesign story. If you choose to include graphics, it is extremely important to understand that the graphics might be embedded into the story instead of linked to the original data file (depending on how the graphic was placed into the Word file).

If you choose **Import Unused Styles**, all styles in the Word file will be imported into the InDesign layout. The most significant issue here is that styles might require fonts that you have not installed.

Word includes a powerful collaboration tool call Track Changes, which allows one person to review another person's changes to a file. (As publishers, we use this feature every day so editors and authors can review each other's changes before permanently changing the text.) If you check the **Track Changes** option, any tracked changes from the Word file will be included in your InDesign layout. This might cause a lot of items to show up in your text that aren't supposed to be there (typos, errors, or, for example, something the general counsel office removed from the original text for a specific legal reason).

Convert Bullets & Numbers to Text allows you to convert automatically generated numbering and bullet characters into actual text characters. This option is extremely useful if the text includes lists; if you don't check this option, you'll have to manually re-enter the bullets or line numbers into the imported text.

The **Style Name Conflicts** area warns you if styles in the Word file conflict with styles in the InDesign file (in other words, they have the same style names but different definitions in the two locations). If you are importing styles from the Word file, you have to determine how to resolve these conflicts.

Import Styles Automatically allows you to choose how to handle conflicts in paragraph and character styles. **Use InDesign Style Definition** preserves the style as you defined it; text in the Word file that uses that style will be reformatted with the InDesign definition of the style. **Redefine InDesign Style** replaces the layout definition with the definition from the Word file. **Auto Rename** adds the Word file to the InDesign file with "_wrd_1" at the end of the style name.

If you choose **Customize Style Import**, the Style Mapping button opens a dialog box where you can review and control specific style conflicts. Click an option in the InDesign Style column to access a menu, where you can choose which InDesign style to use in place of a specific Word style.

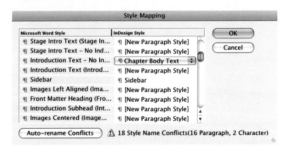

If you always receive Microsoft Word files from the same source, you can save your choices (including Style Mapping options) as a preset, or even click the Set as Default button in the Import Options dialog box.

At this point, the story does not fit into the frame because you haven't yet applied the appropriate styles to the imported text.

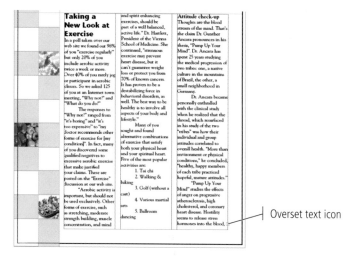

Overset text icon

7. **Open the Paragraph Styles panel (Window>Styles>Paragraph Styles).**

8. **Place the insertion point in the first paragraph of the imported story (the main heading) and look at the Paragraph Styles panel.**

The imported text appears to be preformatted, but the Paragraph Styles panel tells a different story. This paragraph is formatted as "Normal+." When you see a plus sign next to a style name, the selected text includes some formatting other than what is defined in the style.

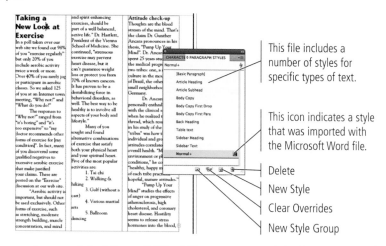

This file includes a number of styles for specific types of text.

This icon indicates a style that was imported with the Microsoft Word file.

Delete

New Style

Clear Overrides

New Style Group

Note:

You should be able to guess the purpose of these styles from their names. It's always a good idea to use indicative names when you create styles or other user-defined assets.

When you imported the Microsoft Word file, you preserved the formatting in the file; this is usually a good idea so you can see what the writer intended. Now that the text is imported into your layout, however, you want to apply the template styles to make the text in this issue consistent with other issues.

When you import text into InDesign, any number of new styles might appear in the Styles panels; the most common imported style is Normal. Text in a Microsoft Word file is typically formatted with the Normal style — even if you don't realize it; user-applied formatting is commonly local (meaning it is applied directly to selected text instead of with a defined style).

9. **With the insertion point still in place, click the Article Heading style in the Paragraph Styles panel.**

Using styles, you can change all formatting attributes of selected text with a single click. Because you are working with paragraph styles, the style definition applies to the entire paragraph where the insertion point is placed.

Note:

You can reapply the basic style definition to selected text by clicking the Clear Overrides button at the bottom of the Paragraph Styles panel, or by Option/Alt clicking the applied style name.

Note:

Paragraph styles can include character attributes as well as paragraph attributes; character styles can only define character-formatting attributes.

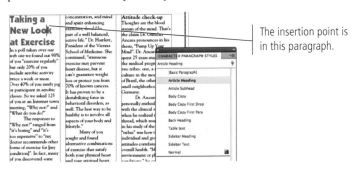

The insertion point is in this paragraph.

10. **Click and drag to select any part of the remaining paragraphs in the story, and then click the Body Copy style in the Paragraph Styles panel.**

Paragraph styles apply to any paragraph that is partially or entirely selected. You don't have to select an entire paragraph before applying a paragraph style.

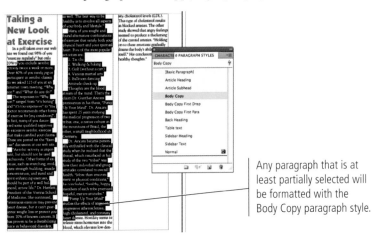

Any paragraph that is at least partially selected will be formatted with the Body Copy paragraph style.

11. **Format the first paragraph after the heading using the Body Copy First Drop style.**

12. **In the second column, format the subheading ("Attitude Checkup", after the numbered list) with the Article Subhead style.**

13. **Format the next paragraph (after the subhead) with the Body Copy First Para style.**

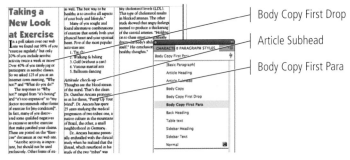

Body Copy First Drop

Article Subhead

Body Copy First Para

14. **Save the file and continue to the next exercise.**

USE MINI BRIDGE TO PLACE TEXT

You already saw that you can use the Mini Bridge panel to easily place images into an InDesign layout. The same concept is true for text files: simply drag a text file from the panel into the layout. If you release the mouse button over an existing empty frame, the text is placed inside that frame. If you release the mouse button over an empty area, or over a frame that already has content, the text is loaded into the cursor.

1. With **newsletter_dec.indd** open, navigate to Page 2 of the layout.

2. Open the Mini Bridge panel (if necessary) and navigate to the WIP>HeartSmart>December Issue folder.

3. Click the **eastern_diet.doc** file and drag it into the two-column frame on the top of Page 2.

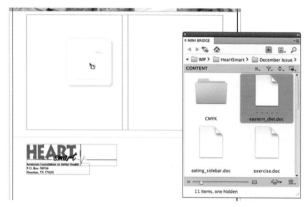

This imports the file using the default import options. In this case, the formatting is maintained, styles are imported, and conflicting styles are automatically renamed — resulting in the new Normal_wrd_1 style, which conflicts with the previously imported Normal style.

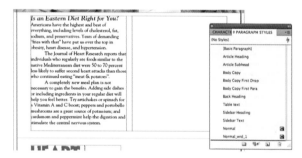

4. Format the first paragraph with the Back Heading style.
   Format the second paragraph with the Body Copy First Para style.
   Format the rest of the story with the Body Copy style.

5. Save the file and continue to the next exercise.

EDIT A PARAGRAPH STYLE TO SPAN COLUMNS

As a general rule, headlines in newsletters and newspapers extend across the top of the entire related story. In previous versions of the software, this required a separate frame that spanned the width of the multi-column body frame. InDesign CS5 includes a paragraph formatting option that makes it easy to span a paragraph across multiple columns *without* the need for a separate frame. This can be applied to individual paragraphs, or defined as part of a paragraph style.

1. **With newsletter_dec.indd open, navigate to Page 1.**

2. **Control/right-click the Article Heading style in the panel and choose Edit "Article Heading" in the contextual menu.**

3. **Click the Preview option in the bottom-left corner of the dialog box.**

   When the Preview option is active, you can see the result of your choices before you finalize them.

4. **Select Span Columns in the list of options on the left side of the dialog box.**

5. **Choose Span Columns in the Paragraph Layout menu.**

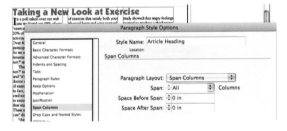

> **Note:**
>
> *The Split Column option can be used to divide a specific paragraph into multiple columns within a frame's defined column.*

6. **Make sure the Span field is set to All.**

   You can use the Span field to extend a paragraph over only a certain number of columns.

7. **Click the Up Arrow button for the Space After Span field.**

   The Space Before and Space After fields determine how much space is placed between the span paragraph and the paragraphs above or below. (This is the same concept used in the Space Above and Space Below options for regular paragraph formatting.)

> **Note:**
>
> *The arrow buttons increase or decrease the related values by 0.0625".*

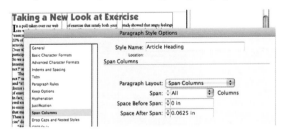

8. **Click OK to finalize the new style definition.**

9. **Save the file and continue to the next exercise.**

 CREATE A SIDEBAR BOX

Many page layouts have a primary story (which might flow across multiple pages), as well as related-but-not-connected stories called **sidebars**. These elements are usually not linked to the main story, and they are often placed in their own boxes with some unique formatting to draw attention to the box. Amateur designers often create three separate elements to achieve this effect — an unnecessary degree of complexity when you can change multiple text frame options to create the effect with a single object.

1. **On Page 1 of `newsletter_dec.indd`, create a text frame with the following dimensions (based on the top-left reference point):**

   X: 3.67″   W: 3.95″
   Y: 6.6″   H: 3″

2. **Fill the text frame with a 20% tint of Pantone 1945 C.**

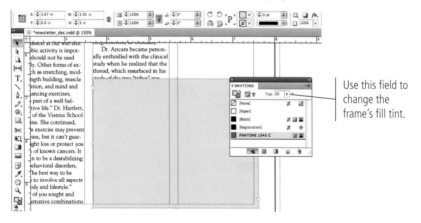

Use this field to change the frame's fill tint.

3. Place the file `eating_sidebar.doc` into the new frame, preserving the formatting in the imported file.

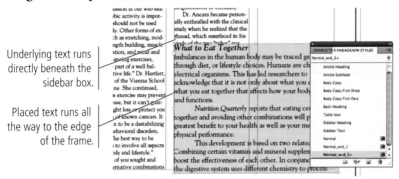

Underlying text runs directly beneath the sidebar box.

Placed text runs all the way to the edge of the frame.

4. Format the first line of the sidebar with the Sidebar Heading style.

5. Format the rest of the text in this frame using the Sidebar Text style.

If a paragraph includes local formatting, simply clicking a new style name might not work perfectly. As you can see in this example, the first two words in the second body paragraph are italicized; in the Paragraph Styles panel, the Sidebar Text style shows a plus sign — indicating that some formatting other than the style definition has been applied.

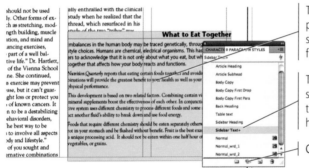

The second through fourth paragraphs don't have the same formatting as the first paragraph.

The plus sign indicates that some formatting other than the style definition has been applied.

Clear Overrides

Note:

Sometimes there is no apparent reason why text imported from Microsoft Word is not properly formatted when you apply a style in InDesign, as in the case on the third and fourth body paragraphs in this sidebar box. This is usually caused by formatting options in Microsoft that are not supported in InDesign. You should simply be aware that you often need to clear overrides in the imported text before the InDesign style is properly applied.

6. Select the three incorrectly formatted paragraphs of body copy in the sidebar box.

You can click and drag to select the paragraphs, or click four times on the first paragraph you want to select and then drag to the last paragraph you want to select.

7. Click the Clear Overrides button at the bottom of the Paragraph Styles panel.

In this case, you do have to select the entire paragraphs; if not, the overrides will be cleared only from the selected characters.

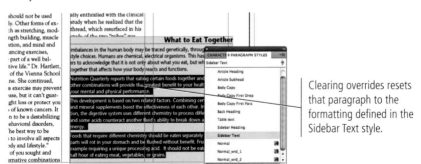

Clearing overrides resets that paragraph to the formatting defined in the Sidebar Text style.

8. **Select the first two words of the second sidebar paragraph. Change the font to ATC Oak and choose Italic in the Font Style menu.**

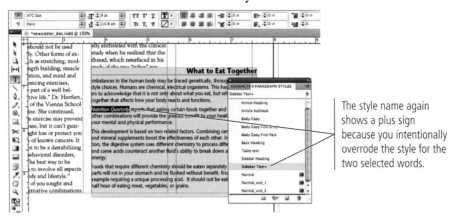

The style name again shows a plus sign because you intentionally overrode the style for the two selected words.

9. **Save the file and continue to the next exercise.**

EDIT TEXT INSET AND WRAP SETTINGS

A number of frame attributes can affect the appearance of text both within and around a text frame. In this exercise, you adjust the text inset and text wrap to force text into the proper position.

1. **With newsletter_dec.indd open, Control/right-click the sidebar box and choose Text Frame Options from the contextual menu.**

2. **In the resulting dialog box, make sure the Preview option is checked.**

3. **Make sure the chain icon for the Inset Spacing fields is active.**

   Like the same chain icon in other dialog boxes, this forces all four inset values to the same value.

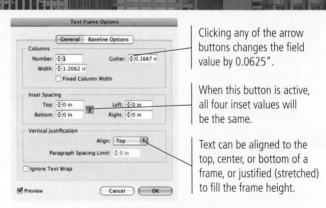

4. **Change the Top Inset field to 0.1″, and then press Tab to move the highlight and apply the new Inset Spacing value to all four fields.**

   Text inset is the distance text is moved from the inside edge of its containing frame.

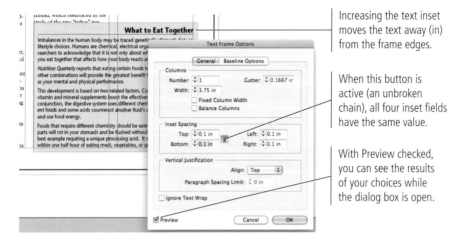

Increasing the text inset moves the text away (in) from the frame edges.

When this button is active (an unbroken chain), all four inset fields have the same value.

With Preview checked, you can see the results of your choices while the dialog box is open.

5. **In the Vertical Justification Align menu, choose Justify.**

   Text can be vertically aligned to the top, bottom, or center of its containing frame, or it can be justified — stretched to extend the entire height of the containing frame.

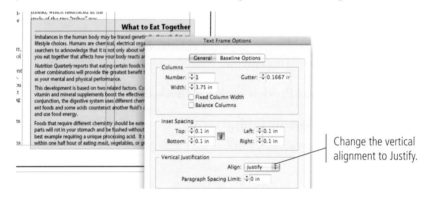

Change the vertical alignment to Justify.

Note:

When you vertically justify type, the Paragraph Spacing Limit field defines the maximum space that can be added between paragraphs to fill the frame.

6. **Click OK to close the dialog box and apply your choices.**

7. **Open the Text Wrap panel (Window>Text Wrap).**

   Text wrap is the distance around the edge of an object where surrounding text will flow.

8. **Click the sidebar frame with the Selection tool, and then click the second button from the left in the Text Wrap panel.**

9. **Make sure the chain icon is active so all four offset values are the same. Change the Top Wrap field to 0.1″ and then press Tab to apply the value to all four fields.**

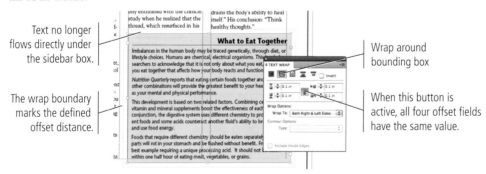

Text no longer flows directly under the sidebar box.

The wrap boundary marks the defined offset distance.

Wrap around bounding box

When this button is active, all four offset fields have the same value.

10. **Select the 3-column text box and open the Text Frame Options dialog box. Choose Justify in the Vertical Justification Align menu and click OK.**

This command aligns the bottom lines in the two right columns.

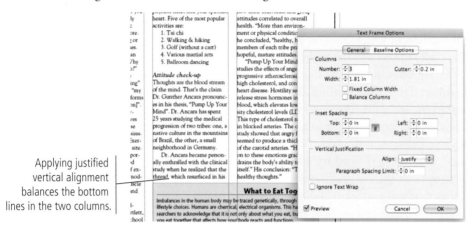

Applying justified vertical alignment balances the bottom lines in the two columns.

11. **Save the file and continue to the next stage of the project.**

Text Wrap Options

By default, text wrap attributes affect all overlapping objects, regardless of stacking order; you can turn this behavior off by checking the Text Wrap Only Affects Text Beneath option in the Composition pane of the Preferences dialog box. InDesign provides five options for wrapping text around an object; specific wrap attributes are controlled in the Text Wrap panel (Window>Text Wrap)

- **No Text Wrap** allows text to run directly under the object.

- **Wrap Around Bounding Box** creates a straight-edged wrap around all four sides of the object's bounding box.

- **Wrap Around Object Shape** creates a wrap in the shape of the object. In this case, you can also define which contour to use:

  - **Bounding Box** creates the boundary based on the object's bounding box.

  - **Detect Edges** creates the boundary using the same detection options you use to create a clipping path.

  - **Alpha Channel** creates the boundary from an Alpha channel saved in the placed image.

  - **Photoshop Path** creates the boundary from a path saved in the placed image.

  - **Graphic Frame** creates the boundary from the containing frame.

  - **Same as Clipping** creates the boundary from a clipping path saved in the placed image.

  - **User-Modified Path** appears by default if you drag the anchor points of the text wrap boundary.

- **Jump Object** keeps text from appearing to the right or left of the frame.

- **Jump to Next Column** forces surrounding text to the top of the next column or frame.

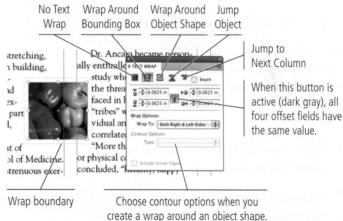

No Text Wrap · Wrap Around Bounding Box · Wrap Around Object Shape · Jump Object

Jump to Next Column

When this button is active (dark gray), all four offset fields have the same value.

Wrap boundary

Choose contour options when you create a wrap around an object shape.

Regardless of which wrap you apply, you can define the offset value, the distance that any surrounding text will remain away from the object. (If you use the Object Shape wrap option, you can define only a single offset value; for the other types, you can define a different offset value for each edge.

If you use the Bounding Box or Object Shape wrap option, you can also define the Wrap To options — whether the wrap is applied to a specific side (right, left, right and left, or the largest side), or toward or away from the spine.

Stage 3 Working with Tables

Many page layouts incorporate tables of information, from basic tables with a few rows and columns to multi-page catalog spreadsheets with thousands of product numbers and prices. InDesign includes a number of options for building tables, each having advantages and disadvantages depending on what you need to accomplish. Regardless of which method you use to create a table, the same options are available for formatting the table, the cells in the table, and the content in the cells.

When you place an insertion point in an existing text frame, you can create a new table from scratch by choosing Table>Insert Table. This method allows you to define your own table parameters, including the number of rows and columns, the number of header and footer rows (top and bottom rows that appear in every instance of the table if the table breaks across multiple columns or frames), and even a defined style for the new table (table styles store formatting options such as gridline weight and color, cell inset, and other attributes that will you learn about in this stage of the project).

You can also create a table by selecting a series of tab-delimited text in the layout and choosing Table>Convert Text to Table. (Tab-delimited means that the content of each column is separated by a tab character.) Using this method, the new table becomes an inline object in the text frame that contained the original tabbed text.

Finally, you can create a new table in InDesign by placing a Microsoft Excel file (Microsoft Excel is the most common application for creating spreadsheets). You'll use this method to complete this stage of the HeartSmart newsletter project.

PLACE A MICROSOFT EXCEL TABLE

Microsoft Excel spreadsheets can be short tables of text or complex, multi-page spreadsheets of data. In either case, Microsoft Excel users tend to spend hours formatting their spreadsheets for business applications. Those formatting options are typically not appropriate for commercial printing applications, but they give you a better starting point in your InDesign file than working from plain tabbed text.

1. With **newsletter_dec.indd** open, navigate to Page 2. Click the Pasteboard area to make sure nothing is selected.

2. Choose File>Place and navigate to the file **nutrition.xls** in the WIP>HeartSmart>December Issue folder.

3. Uncheck the Replace Selected Item option, make sure Show Import Options is checked, and click Open.

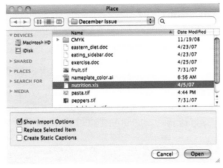

4. Review the options in the resulting dialog box. Make sure your options match what is shown in the following image, and then click OK.

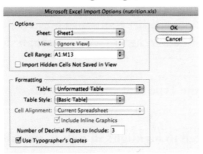

Note:

If you see a warning about missing fonts, click OK; you're going to reformat the table text in the next exercise, so missing fonts won't be a problem.

5. With the table loaded into the cursor, click in the empty area of the right column (in the top half of the page).

The new table is placed into the layout; a text frame is automatically created to contain the table. (The table currently extends beyond the right edge of the text frame, and the overset text icon in the frame's Out port indicates that the frame is not high enough to fit all the rows of the table).

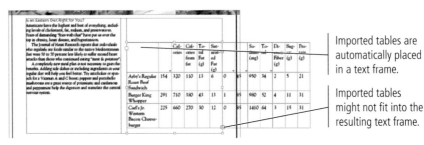

Imported tables are automatically placed in a text frame.

Imported tables might not fit into the resulting text frame.

Obviously this table still needs some significant modification to make it a cohesive part of the newsletter layout. Some placed tables require more work than others, but be prepared to do at least some clean-up work whenever you place a spreadsheet/table.

6. Drag the text frame with the table to the top edge of the right column.

7. Control/right-click the table and choose Fitting>Fit Frame to Content.

This is the same command you can use to resize a graphics frame; in this case, you're making the text frame big enough to show the entire table width. You should now be able to see the bottom row of the table.

8. Save the file and continue to the next exercise.

FORMAT CELL CONTENTS

When you work with tables in InDesign, think of the table cells as a series of text frames. Text in a table cell is no different than text in any other text frame; it can be formatted using the same options you've already learned, including with paragraph and character styles.

1. **With** `newsletter_dec.indd` **open, select the Type tool and click in the top-left cell of the table.**

2. **Click and drag to the bottom-right table cell to highlight all cells in the table.**

3. **Click Table Text in the Paragraph Styles panel to format all the text in the selected table cells.**

4. **If a plus sign appears next to the Table Text style name (in the Paragraph Styles panel), click the Clear Overrides button at the bottom of the panel to apply only the base style definition to the text.**

   As with files from Microsoft Word, some options in Microsoft Excel spreadsheets might require this two-step process to apply your style definitions to the selected text.

Note:

When working with tables in InDesign, pressing Tab moves the insertion point from one table cell to the next (from left to right, top to bottom). This means you can't press Tab to insert a tab character into text in an InDesign table; you have to choose Type>Insert Special Character>Other>Tab.

	Serving Size (g)	Calo-ries	Calories from fat	Total Fat (g)	Satu-rated Fat (g)	Trans Fat (g)	Cho-lesterol (mg)	Sodium (mg)	Total Carbs (g)	Dietary Fiber (g)	Sugars (g)	Protein (g)
Arby's Regular Roast Beef Sandwich	154	320	110	13	6	0	45	950	34			
Burger King Whopper	291	710	380	43	13	1	85	980	52			
Carl's Jr. Western Bacon Cheeseburger	225	660	270	30	12	0	85	1410	64			
Dairy Queen Double Cheeseburger	219	540	280	31	16	0	115	1130	30			
Del Taco Del Beef Burrito	227	550	270	30	17	0	90	1090	42			
Domino's Hand-Tossed Cheese Pizza (2 pieces)	159	374	101	11	5	0	23	784	54			
In-N-Out Double-Double	330	670	370	41	18	0	120	1440	39			
KFC Original Recipe Drumstick & Thigh	185	500	290	33	9	0	240	1500	16			
McDonald's Big Mac	216	590	310	34	11	0	85	1070	47	3	8	24
Taco Bell Beef Burrito Supreme	247	440	160	18	7	0	35	1220	52	6	5	17
Wendy's Big Bacon Classic	282	570	260	29	12	0	100	1460	46	3	11	34
RDA (based on a 2000-calorie diet)			65	20			300	2400	300	25		

PARAGRAPH STYLES

Table text
[Basic Paragraph]
Article Heading
Article Subhead
Body Copy
Body Copy First Drop
Body Copy First Para
Back Heading
Table text
Sidebar Heading
Sidebar Text

Styles can be used to format table text just as you would format any other text in the layout.

Note:

You have to use the Type tool to select table cells, either individually, or as entire rows/columns.

5. **Click in any cell to deselect all table cells.**

6. **Place the cursor over the top edge of the first column of the table. When you see a down-pointing arrow, click to select the entire column.**

   You can also select rows by placing the cursor immediately to the left of a row and clicking when the cursor changes to a right-facing arrow.

The down-pointing arrow means you can click to select the entire column.

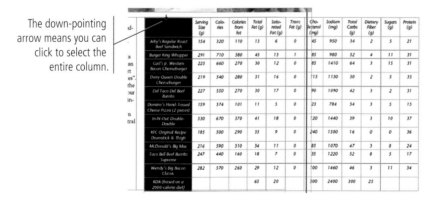

	Serving Size (g)	Calo-ries	Calories from fat	Total Fat (g)	Satu-rated Fat (g)	Trans Fat (g)	Cho-lesterol (mg)	Sodium (mg)	Total Carbs (g)	Dietary Fiber (g)	Sugars (g)	Protein (g)
Arby's Regular Roast Beef Sandwich	154	320	110	13	6	0	45	950	34	2	5	21
Burger King Whopper	291	710	380	43	13	1	85	980	52	4	11	31
Carl's Jr. Western Bacon Cheeseburger	225	660	270	30	12	0	85	1410	64	3	15	31
Dairy Queen Double Cheeseburger	219	540	280	31	16	0	115	1130	30	2	5	35
Del Taco Del Beef Burrito	227	550	270	30	17	0	90	1090	42	3	2	31
Domino's Hand-Tossed Cheese Pizza (2 pieces)	159	374	101	11	5	0	23	784	54	3	5	15
In-N-Out Double-Double	330	670	370	41	18	0	120	1440	39	3	10	37
KFC Original Recipe Drumstick & Thigh	185	500	290	33	9	0	240	1500	16	0	0	36
McDonald's Big Mac	216	590	310	34	11	0	85	1070	47	3	8	24
Taco Bell Beef Burrito Supreme	247	440	160	18	7	0	35	1220	52	8	5	17
Wendy's Big Bacon Classic	282	570	260	29	12	0	100	1460	46	3	11	34
RDA (based on a 2000-calorie diet)			65	20			300	2400	300	25		

7. Change the selected column to left paragraph alignment.

You can use the Control panel or Paragraph panel, or simply press Command/Control-L to change the alignment of the text within the table cell.

	Serving Size (g)	Calories	Calories from fat	Total Fat (g)	Saturated Fat (g)	Trans Fat (g)	Cholesterol (mg)	Sodium (mg)	Total Carbs (g)	Dietary Fiber (g)	Sugars (g)	Protein (g)
Arby's Regular Roast Beef Sandwich	154	320	110	13	6	0	45	950	34	2	5	21
Burger King Whopper	291	710	380	43	13	1	85	980	52	4	11	31
Carl's Jr. Western Bacon Cheeseburger	225	660	270	30	12	0	85	1410	64	3	15	31
Dairy Queen Double Cheeseburger	219	540	280	31	16	0	115	1130	30	2	5	35
Del Taco Del Beef Burrito	227	550	270	30	17	0	90	1090	42	3	2	31
Domino's Hand-Tossed Cheese Pizza (2 pieces)	159	374	101	11	5	0	23	784	54	3	5	15
In-N-Out Double-Double	330	670	370	41	18	0	120	1440	39	3	10	37
KFC Original Recipe Drumstick & Thigh	185	500	290	33	9	0	240	1500	16	0	0	36
McDonald's Big Mac	216	590	310	34	11	0	85	1070	47	3	8	24
Taco Bell Beef Burrito Supreme	247	440	160	18	7	0	35	1220	52	8	5	17
Wendy's Big Bacon Classic	282	570	260	29	12	0	100	1460	46	3	11	34
RDA (based on a 2000-calorie diet)				65	20		300	2400	300	25		

8. Save the file and continue to the next exercise.

FORMAT CELL ATTRIBUTES

As we mentioned in the previous exercise, table cells are very similar to regular text frames. Individual cells can have different attributes such as height and width, text inset, vertical positioning, and text orientation. These options can be controlled in the Table panel, the Control panel, and the Cell Options dialog box.

1. With newsletter_dec.indd open, click in the second cell of the first row, and then drag right to select all cells in the row except the first cell.

2. In the Table panel (Window>Type & Tables>Table), choose Exactly in the Row Height menu, and then change the field to 0.875″.

3. Change the Column Width field to 0.2785″.

4. Click the Rotate Text 270° button so the left edge of the text aligns to the bottom edge of the cell.

5. Click the Align Center button so the text in each cell is centered vertically.

Because the text is rotated, this button actually aligns the text between the left and right cell edges. It's important to remember that the vertical align options are based on the orientation of the text.

6. Apply left paragraph alignment to the selected text.

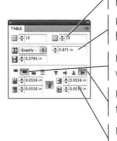

Use these fields to change the number of rows and columns.

Use these fields to control the height and width of cells.

Use these buttons to change the vertical alignment of text within cells.

Use these buttons to rotate text within the cells.

Use these fields to define inset values for cells.

Note:

Text is still text, even though it's placed inside a table cell. You can apply all of the same text-formatting options to table text that you can apply to text in a regular text frame.

7. **Click the second cell in the second row, and drag down and right to select all the cells that contain numeric data.**

8. **Apply centered vertical alignment to the selected cells.**

9. **Make sure the chain icon for the cell inset fields is active. Change the Top Cell Inset field to 0 and then press Tab to apply the same value to all four fields.**

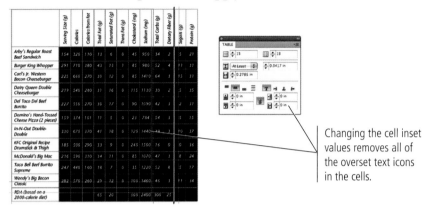

Changing the cell inset values removes all of the overset text icons in the cells.

10. **Select the first four cells in the last row and choose Table>Merge Cells.**

   This function extends the contents of a single cell across multiple cells. (You can also open the Table panel Options menu and choose Merge Cells.)

11. **Select the entire first column of the table and change only the Left Cell Inset value to 0.0625".**

   To change only one value, you have to make sure the chain icon is not active.

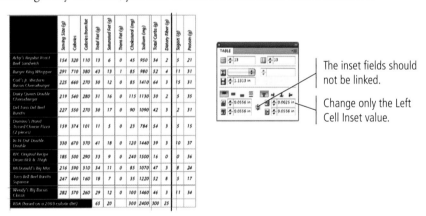

The inset fields should not be linked.

Change only the Left Cell Inset value.

12. **Place the cursor over the right edge of the first column until the cursor becomes a two-headed arrow.**

   When you see this cursor, you can drag the gridline to resize a column or row.

13. Click and drag right until the column is wide enough to allow the Wendy's Big Bacon Classic to fit on one line.

The two-headed arrow means you can drag to resize a row or column.

14. Place the insertion point in the cell with the Wendy's product name.

When you make the column wide enough to fit the text, the row automatically shrinks to one row. In the Table panel, you can see that the Row Height menu is set to At Least; this option allows cells to shrink to fit the height of cell contents, down to the defined minimum height.

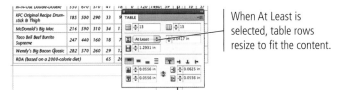

When At Least is selected, table rows resize to fit the content.

15. Save the file and continue to the next exercise.

 DEFINE TABLE FILLS AND STROKES

Like text frames, table cells can also have fill and stroke attributes. InDesign includes a number of options for adding color to tables, from changing the stroke and fill of an individual cell to defining patterns that repeat every certain number of rows and/or columns.

1. With newsletter_dec.indd open, make sure the table on Page 2 is selected. Open the Table panel Options menu and choose Table Options>Table Setup.

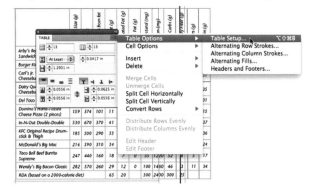

Note:

Resizing the width of a cell resizes the entire column; resizing the height of a cell resizes the entire row.

You can press the Shift key while dragging a gridline to resize a row or column without affecting the overall table size; only the rows or columns next to the gridline you drag are resized.

Note:

You can also choose Table>Table Options>Table Setup to access the dialog box.

2. **In the Table Setup tab, apply a 0.5-pt solid border of 100% Pantone 1945 C.**

Note:

In the Table Options dialog box, you can use the Row Strokes and Column Strokes tabs to define patterns based on a sequence you choose in the Alternating Pattern menus. Alternating rows can have different stroke styles, weights, colors, and tints; you can also skip a specific number of rows at the top and bottom of a table.

3. **In the Fills tab, choose Every Other Row in the Alternating Pattern menu. Set the First field to 1 row and apply 20% Pantone 1945 C. Set the Next field to 1 row and apply None as the color.**

When frame edges are visible, it's difficult (if not impossible) to see the table border and cell strokes.

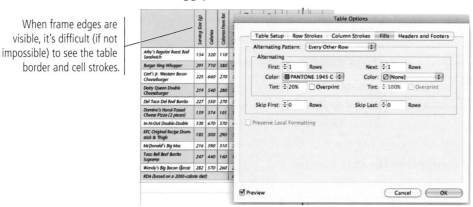

4. **Click OK to apply your choices.**

Managing Table Setup

INDESIGN FOUNDATIONS

The Table Setup tab of the Table Options dialog box defines the table dimensions, table border, spacing above and below the table, and how strokes are applied to the table.

The **Stroke Drawing Order** allows you to control the appearance where gridlines of different styles or colors meet. If Best Joins is selected, styled strokes such as double lines result in joined strokes and gaps.

Change the border attributes of the table; this value is also the value of individual cell edges for cells around the outside of the table.

Change the space above and below the table relative to other text in the same containing frame.

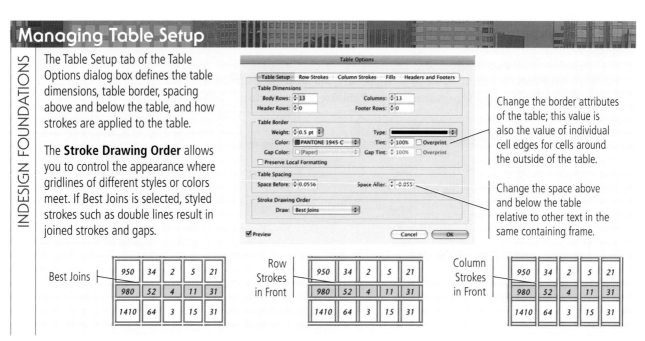

5. **Select the last row in the table. Using the Swatches panel, change the cell fill tint to 50%.**

Remember, table cells are very similar to individual text frames. You can change the color of cell fills and strokes using the Swatches panel, and you can change the cell stroke attributes using the Stroke panel.

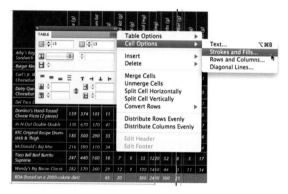

Cell fills can be changed in the Swatches panel, just as you would change the fill of a text frame.

Note:

When the insertion point is placed in a table cell, press the Escape key to select the active cell.

6. **Select all cells in the table. Open the Table panel Options menu and choose Cell Options>Strokes and Fills.**

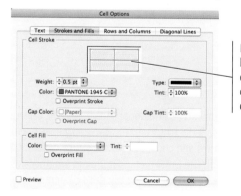

Note:

If you place the cursor at the top-left corner of the table, it changes to a diagonal arrow icon. Clicking with this cursor selects all cells in the table.

7. **In the preview area of the dialog box, click all three horizontal lines to remove the strokes from the tops and bottoms of the cells.**

8. **Apply a 0.5-pt, 100% Pantone 1945 C stroke value, using the Solid stroke type.**

These settings change the attributes of the vertical gridlines for all selected cells.

By deselecting the horizontal lines before defining the stroke, you can change the appearance of only the vertical gridlines.

Note:

You can apply different stroke values to every cell in a table (although you probably wouldn't want to).

9. **Click OK to apply the stroke values to your table.**

10. **Click away from the table to deselect it, and then choose View>Extras> Hide Frame Edges to review the table formatting.**

	Serving Size (g)	Calories	Calories from fat	Total Fat (g)	Saturated fat (g)	Trans Fat (g)	Cholesterol (mg)	Sodium (mg)	Total Carbs (g)	Dietary Fiber (g)	Sugars (g)	Protein (g)
Arby's Regular Roast Beef Sandwich	154	320	110	13	6	0	45	950	34	2	5	21
Burger King Whopper	291	710	380	43	13	1	85	980	52	4	11	31
Carl's Jr. Western Bacon Cheeseburger	225	660	270	30	12	0	85	1410	64	3	15	31
Dairy Queen Double Cheeseburger	219	540	280	31	16	0	115	1130	30	2	5	35
Del Taco Del Beef Burrito	227	550	270	30	17	0	90	1090	42	3	2	31
Domino's Hand-Tossed Cheese Pizza (2 pieces)	159	374	101	11	5	0	23	784	54	3	5	15
In-N-Out Double-Double	330	670	370	41	18	0	120	1440	39	3	10	37
KFC Original Recipe Drumstick & Thigh	185	500	290	33	9	0	240	1530	16	0	0	36
McDonald's Big Mac	216	590	310	34	11	0	85	1070	47	3	8	24
Taco Bell Beef Burrito Supreme	247	440	160	18	7	0	35	1220	52	8	5	17
Wendy's Big Bacon Classic	282	570	260	29	12	0	100	1460	46	3	11	34
RDA (based on a 2000-calorie diet)				65	20		300	2400	300	25		

Note:

If you can't see the borders and strokes, try hiding frame edges (View>Extras>Hide Frame Edges) while you experiment with these options.

11. **Using the Selection tool, Control/right-click the table and choose Fitting>Fit Frame to Content from the contextual menu.**

Controlling Cell Attributes

INDESIGN FOUNDATIONS

Basic attributes of table cells can be defined in the Text tab of the Cell Options dialog box (Table>Cell Options). Most table cell options are exactly the same as for regular text frames; the only choice unique to tables is **Clip Contents to Cell**. If you set a fixed row height that's too small for the cell content, an overset text icon appears in the lower-right corner of the cell. (You can't flow text from one table cell to another.) If you check the Clip Contents to Cell option, any content that doesn't fit in the cell will be clipped.

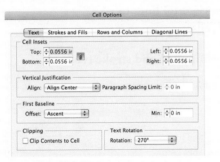

As with any text frame, a table cell can have its own fill and stroke attributes. These attributes can be defined in the Strokes and Fills tab (or using the Swatches and Stroke panels). You can turn individual cell edges (strokes) on or off by clicking specific lines in the preview.

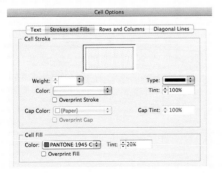

The Rows and Columns tab controls row height and column width. If **At Least** is selected in the Row Height menu, you can define the minimum and maximum possible row height; rows change height if you add or remove text, or if you change the text formatting in a way that requires more or less space. If **Exactly** is selected, you can define the exact height of the cell.

If you're working with an extremely long table, you can break the table across multiple frames by threading (as you would for any long block of text). The **Keep Options** can be used to keep specific (selected) rows together after a break, and they determine where those rows will go, based on your choice in the Start Row menu.

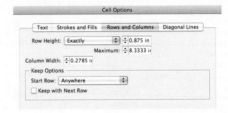

You can add diagonal lines to specific cells using the Diagonal Lines tab. You can apply lines in either direction (or both) and choose a specific stroke weight, color, style, and tint. The Draw menu determines whether the line is created in front of or behind the cell's contents.

12. Drag the table until the top-right corner of the frame snaps to the top-right margin guide on Page 2.

Text runs right under the table, and is visible where cells have a fill of None.

13. With the frame still selected, click the second button in the Text Wrap panel (Window>Text Wrap) so the Eastern Diet story wraps around the frame that contains the table. Change the Left Wrap field to 0.125″.

A table is always contained inside a text frame. To control the wrap around a table, you have to actually apply the wrap attributes to the frame that contains the table.

The table's text wrap keeps the copy away from the table edge.

Note:

Remember, you can turn off the Link button in the Text Wrap panel to apply different wrap values to each side of the frame.

14. Save the file and continue to the final stage of the project.

Understanding Table Styles

INDESIGN FOUNDATIONS

If you've spent any amount of time refining the appearance of a table, and you think you might want to use the same format again, you can save your formatting choices as a style. InDesign supports both table styles and cell styles, which are controlled in the Table Styles panel and Cell Styles panel.

Table and cell styles use the same concept as text-formatting styles. You can apply a cell style by selecting the cells and clicking the style name in the Cell Styles panel. Clicking a style in the Table Styles panel applies the style to the entire selected table.

The Clear Overrides button clears text-formatting options; the Clear Attributes button clears cell attributes.

Table styles store all options that can be defined in the Table Setup dialog box (except the options for header and footer rows). You can also define cell styles (called **nesting styles**) for specific types of rows, as well as the left and right columns in the table.

Cell styles store all options that can be defined in the Cell Options dialog box, including the paragraph style that is applied to cells where that style is applied.

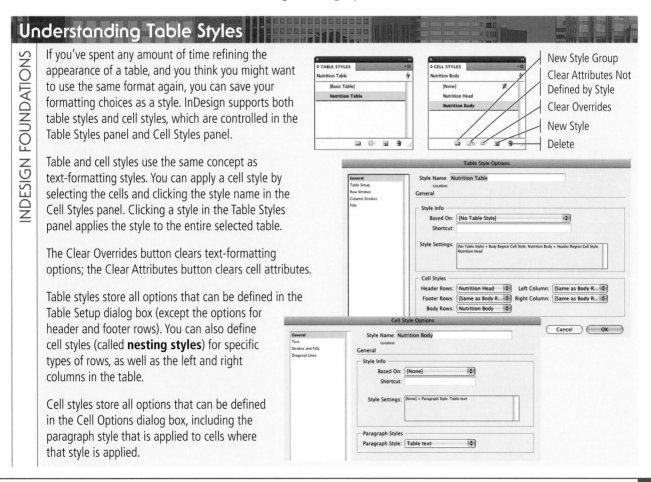

Long tables of data often require more than one text frame (or column, depending on the table). In this case, you can break a table across multiple frames and use repeating headers and footers for information that needs to be part of each instance of the table (for example, column headings). Repeating headers and footers eliminate the need to manually insert the repeating information in each instance of the table.

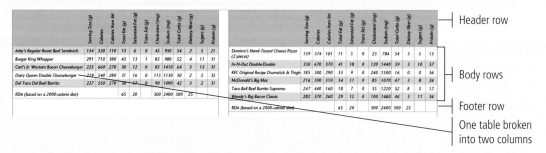

Header row

Body rows

Footer row

One table broken into two columns

Repeating header and footer rows are dynamically linked; this means that changing one instance of a header or footer changes all instances of the same header or footer.

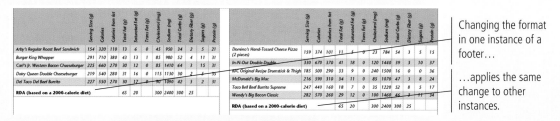

Changing the format in one instance of a footer…

…applies the same change to other instances.

Finally, this capability also means the headers and footers remain at the top and bottom of each instance, even if other body rows move to a different instance.

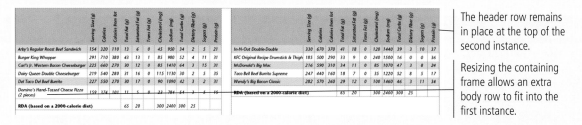

The header row remains in place at the top of the second instance.

Resizing the containing frame allows an extra body row to fit into the first instance.

You can add new header and footer rows to a table when you create the table, or by changing the options in the Headers and Footers tab of the Table Options dialog box. You can also convert existing rows to headers or footers by selecting one or more rows and choosing Table>Convert Rows>To Header or To Footer. You can also control these elements in the Headers and Footers dialog box.

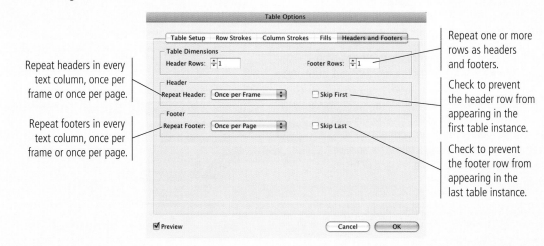

Repeat headers in every text column, once per frame or once per page.

Repeat footers in every text column, once per frame or once per page.

Repeat one or more rows as headers and footers.

Check to prevent the header row from appearing in the first table instance.

Check to prevent the footer row from appearing in the last table instance.

Stage 4 Preflighting and Packaging the Job

When you submit an InDesign layout to a commercial output provider, you need to send all of the necessary pieces of the job — the layout file, any placed (linked) graphics or other files, and the fonts used in the layout. Before you copy everything to a disk and send it out, however, you should check your work to make sure the file is ready for commercial printing.

When you opened the original template at the beginning of this project, you replaced missing fonts and graphics — two of the most common problems with digital layout files. However, successful output on a commercial press has a number of other technical requirements that, if you ignore them, can cause a file to output incorrectly or not at all. InDesign includes a preflighting utility that makes it easy to check for potential errors, as well as a packaging utility that gathers all of the necessary bits for the printer.

DEFINE A PREFLIGHT PROFILE

InDesign includes a dynamic, built-in preflighting utility that can check for common errors as you build a file. If you introduce a problem while building a file, the bottom-left corner of the document window shows a red light and the number of potential errors. In the following exercise, you define a profile to check for errors based on the information you have. This is certainly not an exhaustive check for all possible output problems. You should always work closely with your output provider to build responsible files that will cause no problems in the output workflow.

Note:

Ask your output provider if they have defined an InDesign preflight profile that you can load into your application to check for the problems that will interrupt their specific workflows.

1. **With newsletter_dec.indd open, look at the bottom-left corner of the document window.**

2. **Click the arrow to the right of the No Errors message and choose Preflight Panel from the menu.**

   The message currently shows no errors, but at this point you don't know exactly what is being checked. The Preflight panel provides an interface for defining preflight profiles, as well as reviewing the specific issues identified as errors.

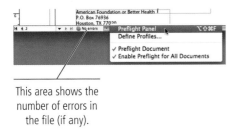

This area shows the number of errors in the file (if any).

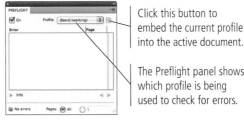

Click this button to embed the current profile into the active document.

The Preflight panel shows which profile is being used to check for errors.

3. **Open the Preflight panel Options menu and choose Define Profiles.**

4. **In the Preflight Profiles dialog box, click the "+" button in the left side of the dialog box to create a new profile.**

   Rather than relying on generic built-in profiles, you should be aware of and able to control exactly what is (and is not) flagged as an error.

5. Type `HeartSmart Check` in the Profile Name field, then click the empty area below the list of profiles to finalize the new name.

Click to load external profiles, export profiles for other users, or embed a profile into a document.

Use this field to name the new profile.

Click in this area to show the new profile name in the list.

Click to delete the selected profile.

Click to create a new profile.

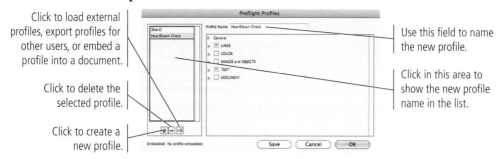

6. With the HeartSmart Check profile selected on the left side of the dialog box, expand the General category on the right. Highlight the existing text in the Description field, and then type `Verify newsletter for 4c press`.

Use these arrows to expand the various categories.

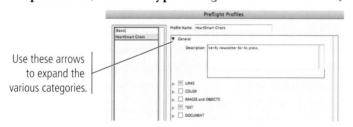

Note:

This description is simply a reminder of the profile's intent.

7. Collapse the General category and expand the Links category. Check the Links Missing or Modified option.

Image files placed in a layout need to be available when the job is output. By checking this option, you are warned if any placed image has been moved or modified since it was placed into the layout.

8. Collapse the Links category and expand the Color category. Check and expand the Color Spaces and Modes Not Allowed option, and then check the RGB and Spot Color options.

You know this newsletter is going to be output as a 4-color job. Spot colors will create an extra separation, which can be a very costly error. By setting these options, you will receive a warning if you create a spot color in a job that should be output as 4-color.

To achieve the best-quality, predictable output, it's a good idea to check for RGB images and control the conversion process in an image-editing application (i.e., Photoshop).

Note:

Some output processes use a method called in-RIP separation to convert RGB images to CMYK during the output process. However, the conversion process can cause significant color shift if it is not controlled.

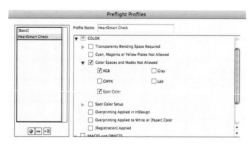

9. **Collapse the Color category and expand the Images and Objects category. Check and expand the Image Resolution option. Check the three Minimum Resolution options. Change the Color and Grayscale minimums to 300 and change the 1-bit option to 1200.**

   As you learned in Project 1, commercial output devices typically require at least 300 ppi to output raster images at good quality. By setting these minimum restrictions, you will receive a warning if your (or your client's) images do not have enough resolution to output at good quality using most commercial printing processes.

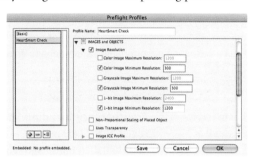

Note:

Remember: required resolution is actually two times the line screen (lpi) used for a specific job. If possible, always ask your service provider what resolution to use for your job. If you don't know the lpi (and can't find out in advance), 300 ppi resolution is a safe choice for most printing.

10. **Collapse the Images and Objects category and expand the Text category. Check the Overset Text and Font Missing options.**

    Overset text could simply be the result of extra paragraph returns at the end of a story. However, you should always check these issues to be sure that some of the client's text has not been accidentally overset.

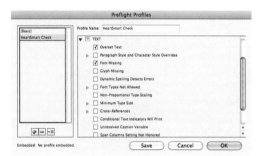

11. **Collapse the Text category and expand the Document category. Check the Number of Pages Required option. Expand that option, choose Exactly in the menu, and type 2 in the field.**

    You know that every issue of the newsletter should be exactly 2 pages. If your file has more or less than 2 pages, you will receive an error message.

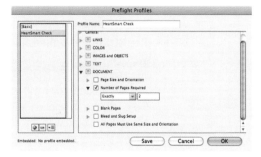

12. **Click OK to save the profile and close the dialog box.**

13. **Continue to the next exercise.**

The Preflight Profiles dialog box includes a number of options for identifying potential errors. If you are going to build responsible files, you should have a basic understanding of what these options mean.

This is by no means an exhaustive list of all potential problems in digital page-layout files; it's a list of the problems Adobe included in the Preflight Profile dialog box. Other problems are beyond the scope of most graphic designers and are better left to prepress professionals to correct, given the specific equipment conditions in their workflows.

It should also be noted that some of these issues are not necessarily errors, but nonetheless should be reviewed before a job is output. For example, blank pages might be intentionally placed into a document to force a chapter opener onto a right-facing page; in this case, the blank page is not an error. In other cases, a blank page might be left over after text is edited; in this case, the blank page would be an error. You can use the Preflight panel to find definite errors, but also use it to verify that what you have is exactly what you want.

Links

- **Links Missing or Modified.** Use this option to receive a warning if a placed file has been moved (missing) or changed (modified) since it was placed into a layout. If a placed file is missing, the output will use only the low-resolution preview that you see on screen. If a placed file has been modified, the output will reflect the most up-to-date version of the placed file — which could be drastically different than the original, potentially destroying your overall layout.

- **Inaccessible URL Links.** Use this option to find hyperlinks that might cause problems if you are creating an interactive PDF document.

- **OPI Links.** OPI is a workflow tool that allows designers to use low-resolution FPO (for placement only) files during the design stage. When the job is processed for output, the high-resolution versions are swapped out in place of the FPO images. Although not terribly common anymore, some larger agencies still use OPI workflows.

Document

- **Page Size and Orientation.** Use this option to cause an error if the document size is not a specific size; you can also cause an error if the current document is oriented other than the defined page size (i.e., portrait instead of landscape or vice versa).

- **Number of Pages Required.** Use this option to define a specific number of pages, the smallest number of pages that can be in the document, or whether the document must have pages in multiples of a specific number (for example, multiples of 16 for 16-page signature output).

- **Blank Pages.** Use this option to find blank pages in the document.

- **Bleed and Slug Setup.** Use this option to verify the document's bleed and slug sizes against values required by a specific output process.

- **All Pages Must Use Same Size and Orientation.** Because InDesign CS5 supports multiple page sizes in the same document, you can check this option to verify that all pages in the file have the same size.

Color

- **Transparency Blending Space Required.** Use this option to define whether CMYK or RGB should be used to flatten transparent objects for output. (Refer to Project 2 for more on transparency flattening.)

- **Cyan, Magenta, or Yellow Plates Not Allowed.** Use this option to verify layouts that will be output with only spot colors, or with black and spot colors.

- **Color Spaces and Modes Not Allowed.** Use this option to create errors if the layout uses RGB, CMYK, Spot Color, Gray, or LAB color models. (Different jobs have different defined color spaces. The option to flag CMYK as an error can be useful, for example, if you are building a layout that will be output in black only.)

- **Spot Color Setup.** Use this option to define the number of spot colors a job should include, as well as the specific color model that should be used (LAB or CMYK) when converting unwanted spot colors for process printing.

- **Overprinting Applied in InDesign.** Use this option to create an error if an element is set to overprint instead of trap. (These issues are explained in Project 6.)

- **Overprinting Applied to White or [Paper] Color.** By definition, White or [Paper] is technically the absence of other inks. Unless you are printing white toner or opaque spot ink, white cannot, by definition, overprint. Use this option to produce an error if White or [Paper] elements are set to overprint.

- **[Registration] Applied.** The [Registration] color swatch is a special swatch used for elements such as crop and registration marks. Any element that uses the [Registration] color will output on all separations in the job. Use this option to find elements that are incorrectly colored with the [Registration] color instead of (probably) black.

INDESIGN FOUNDATIONS

Images and Objects

- **Image Resolution.** Use this option to identify placed files with too little or too much resolution. As you know, commercial output devices typically require 300 ppi to output properly. The maximum resolution options can be used to find objects that, typically through scaling, result in unnecessarily high resolutions that might take considerable time for the output device to process.

- **Non-Proportional Scaling of Placed Object.** Use this option to find placed files that have been scaled with different X and Y percentages.

- **Uses Transparency.** Use this option to find any element affected by transparency. As you learned in Project 2, you should carefully preview transparency flattening before outputting the job.

- **Image ICC Profile.** Use this option to find placed images that have embedded ICC profiles. Typically used in color-managed workflows, placed images often store information — in the form of profiles — about the way a particular device captured or created the color in that image. You can cause errors if the image profile results in CMYK conversion, or if the embedded image profile has been overridden in the layout.

- **Layer Visibility Overrides.** Use this option to find layered Photoshop files in which the visibility of specific layers has been changed within InDesign.

- **Minimum Stroke Weight.** There is a limit to the smallest visible line that can be produced by any given output device. Use this option to find objects with a stroke weight smaller than a specific point size.

- **Interactive Elements.** Use this option to find elements with interactive properties (more on this in Project 7).

- **Bleed/Trim Hazard.** Use this option to find elements that fall within a defined distance of the page edge, or spine for facing-page layouts (i.e., outside the live area).

- **Hidden Page Items.** Use this option to create an error if any objects on a page are not currently visible.

Text

- **Overset Text.** Use this option to find any frames with overset text.

- **Paragraph Style and Character Style Overrides.** Use this option to find instances where an applied style has been overridden with local formatting.

- **Font Missing.** Use this option to create an error if any required font is not available on the computer.

- **Glyph Missing.** Use this option to identify glyphs that aren't available (more on glyphs in Project 4).

- **Dynamic Spelling Detects Errors.** Use this option to cause an error if InDesign's dynamic spelling utility identifies any errors in the document.

- **Font Types Not Allowed.** Use this option to prohibit specific font types that can cause problems in modern output workflows.

- **Non-Proportional Type Scaling.** Use this option to identify type that has been artificially stretched or compressed in one direction (i.e., where horizontal or vertical scaling has been applied).

- **Minimum Type Size.** Use this option to identify any type set smaller than a defined point size. You can also identify small type that requires more than one ink to reproduce (a potential registration problem on commercial output devices).

- **Cross-References.** Use this option to identify dynamic links from one location in a file to another. You can cause errors if a cross reference is out of date or unresolved.

- **Conditional Text Indicators Will Print.** Use this option to create an error if certain visual indicators will appear in the final output. (You explore conditional text in Project 6.)

- **Unresolved Caption Variable.** Use this option to find dynamic caption variables for which there is no defined metadata. (You will learn about creating captions in Project 5.)

- **Span Columns Setting Not Honored.** Use this option to find paragraphs with a defined column-span setting that is prevented by other objects on the page.

- **Tracked Change.** Use this option to find instances of text that have been changed but not accepted when Track Changes is enabled. (You will explore this utility in Project 6.)

Now that you have defined the issues that you know are errors, you can check your file for those issues and make the necessary corrections.

1. **With `newsletter_dec.indd` open, click the Profile menu in the Preflight panel and choose HeartSmart Check as the profile to use.**

2. **In the bottom of the panel, make sure the All radio button is checked.**

   When the All option is active, the entire document is checked. You can use the other radio button to define a specific page or range of pages to preflight.

   As soon as you call the HeartSmart Check profile, the panel reports 8 errors.

Note:

Preflight profiles become part of the application, but are not linked to or saved in a specific document unless you intentionally embed the profile.

This pane lists the problem categories that caused the errors.

The now-active profile results in 8 errors.

Use this menu to call a specific profile.

Use this option to check only certain pages.

3. **Expand the Info section of the Preflight panel.**

   This area offers information about a specific error, and offers suggestions for fixing the problem.

4. **Click the arrow to expand the Color list, and then click the arrow to expand the Color Space Not Allowed list.**

5. **Click the rectangle listing to select it, and then click the hot-text page number for that item.**

   The hot-text link on the right side of the Preflight panel changes the document window to show the specific item that caused the error.

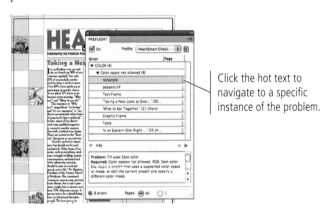

Click the hot text to navigate to a specific instance of the problem.

6. **In the Swatches panel, Control/right-click the Pantone 1945 C swatch and choose Swatch Options from the contextual menu.**

7. **In the Swatch Options dialog box, change the Color Mode menu to CMYK, change the Color Type menu to Process, and check the Name with Color Value option.**

You have to change the mode before you can change the type or naming convention.

By changing the color name, you can tell by a quick glance at the Swatches panel that the color is now a CMYK build.

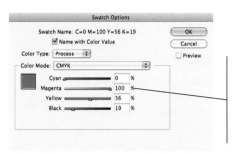

When you change the Color Mode menu, the software automatically finds the nearest possible CMYK values to the spot-color ink.

Note:

Spot colors are not always errors. Check the project's specifications carefully before you convert spot colors to process. Also, be aware that spot colors are often outside the CMYK gamut; converting a spot color to process can result in drastic color shift.

8. **Click OK to apply the new swatch options.**

The former spot color now shows the process-color icon.

Seven of the errors have been corrected by fixing this single issue.

9. **Select the remaining problem instance in the Preflight panel and click the hot-text link to show that element in the layout.**

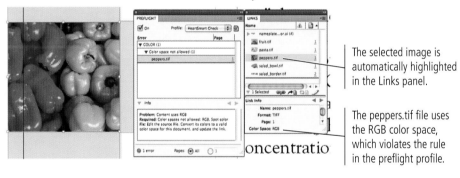

The selected image is automatically highlighted in the Links panel.

The peppers.tif file uses the RGB color space, which violates the rule in the preflight profile.

10. **In the Links panel, click the Relink button. Navigate to `peppers_cmyk.tif` in the WIP>HeartSmart>December Issue>CMYK folder and click Open. If you see the Image Import Options dialog box, click OK to accept the default options.**

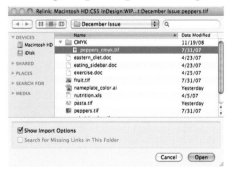

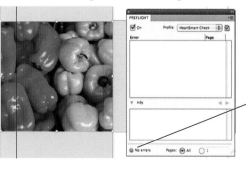

After linking to the CMYK version of the image, the file shows no errors (based on the profile you defined).

11. **Save the file and continue to the next exercise.**

Now that your file is error-free, you can package it for the output provider. As we have already stated, the images and fonts used in a layout must be available on the computer used to output the job. When you send the layout file to the printer, you must also send the necessary components. InDesign includes a Package utility that makes this process very easy.

1. **With newsletter_dec.indd open, choose File>Package.**

2. **Review the information in the Package dialog box, and then click Package.**

   If you had not preflighted the file before opening the Package dialog box, you would see warning icons identifying problems with image color space or missing fonts. Because you completed the previous exercise, however, potential errors have been fixed, so this dialog box simply shows a summary list of information about the file you are packaging.

   Use these options to review various categories of information.

   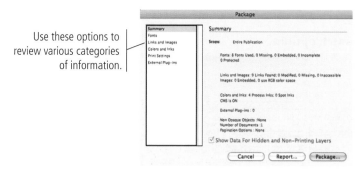

3. **If you see a message asking you to save, click Save.**

4. **In the Printing Instructions dialog box, add your contact information, and then click Continue.**

   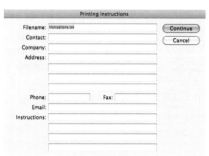

5. **Navigate to your WIP>HeartSmart folder as the target location. Make sure the Copy Fonts, Copy Linked Graphics, and Update Graphic Links options are checked, and then click Package.**

   When you create a job package, InDesign automatically creates a new folder for the job.

   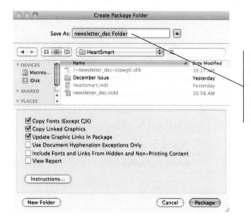

   This field defines the name of the folder that will be created. All files for the job will be placed in this folder.

6. **Read the resulting warning and click OK.**

   As with any software, you purchase a license to use a font — you do not own the actual font. It is illegal to distribute fonts freely, as it is illegal to distribute copies of your software. Most (but not all) font licenses allow you to send your copy of a font to a service provider, as long as the service provider also owns a copy of the font. Always verify that you are not violating font copyright before submitting a job.

   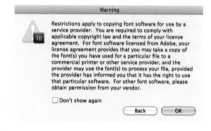

   When the process is complete, the necessary job elements appear in the job folder (in your WIP>HeartSmart folder).

   If you hand off the job package folder to another user (or if someone sends you a job package), the fonts in the collected Document Fonts folder will be available in InDesign when you open the packaged INDD file — even if those fonts are not installed at the computer's system level.

   Document-installed fonts are installed when the related document is opened and uninstalled when you close that file. These fonts supersede any existing font of the same PostScript name within the document. Document-installed fonts are not available to other documents, or in other applications.

7. **Close the InDesign file.**

1. An image file that has been renamed since it was placed into an InDesign layout shows the status of _____.

2. The _____ is used to monitor the status of images that are placed into a layout.

3. _____ is the distance between the edge of a frame and the text contained within that frame.

4. _____ is the distance between the edge of an object and text in other overlapping frames.

5. _____ apply only to selected text characters; this is useful for setting off a few words in a paragraph without affecting the entire paragraph.

6. _____ apply to the entire body of text between two ¶ symbols.

7. While working in a table, the _____ key has a special function; pressing it does not insert the associated character.

8. When the _____ row height method is selected, table rows change height if you add or remove text from the table cells, or if you change the text formatting in a way that requires more or less space.

9. A(n) _____ is a special kind of table row that repeats at the top of every instance of the same table.

10. _____ is the process of checking a layout for errors before it goes to print.

1. Briefly explain the significance of a Missing Font warning.

2. List three advantages of using templates.

3. Briefly define "styles" in relation to text formatting.

Use what you learned in this project to complete the following freeform exercise.

Carefully read the art director and client comments, then create your own design to meet the needs of the project.

Use the space below to sketch ideas; when finished, write a brief explanation of your reasoning behind your final design.

art director comments

The Humane Society wants to create a wall calendar to give away as a part of its annual fundraising drive. Each month will be on one sheet, which can be flipped when the month is over.

To complete this project, you should:

❏ Design a layout that incorporates the month grid, as well as space for an image and four coupons.

❏ Use whatever page size you think is most appropriate for the job.

❏ Use the master page to build the basic structure of each page (month) in the calendar.

❏ Find images or illustrations for each month; make sure you choose ones that don't require a licensing fee.

client comments

As a not-for-profit organization, we try to dedicate most of our finances to caring for our furry (and feathery, and leathery) friends. The printer has donated the resources to print the job, and your agency has donated your time as well — for which we're extremely grateful.

We want each month to have a different picture of cute, cuddly, happy pets with their people; we want to encourage adoption. Make sure you include different kinds of animals; the Humane Society isn't just for dogs and cats. Can you find images that won't cost anything to use?

Each month will also include a set of three coupons for local pet-related businesses. When you build the layout, plan space for those; when the layout's done, we'll let our donor companies know how much space they have for the coupons.

One final thing: we thought it might be fun to include a monthly 'fun fact' about animals. Can you find some little text snippets to include each month?

project justification

_____

_____

_____

_____

_____

_____

_____

_____

_____

_____

_____

_____

_____

_____

_____

This project introduced a number of concepts and tools that will be very important as you work on more complex page-layout jobs. Importing text content from other applications — specifically, Microsoft Word and Microsoft Excel — is a foundational skill that you will use in most projects; this newsletter showed you how to control that content on import, and then re-format it as appropriate in the InDesign layout.

Templates, master pages, and styles are all designed to let you do the majority of work once and then apply it as many times as necessary; virtually any InDesign project can benefit from these tools, and you will use them extensively in your career as a graphic designer. This project provided a basic introduction to these productivity tools; you will build on these foundations as you complete the remaining five projects of this book.

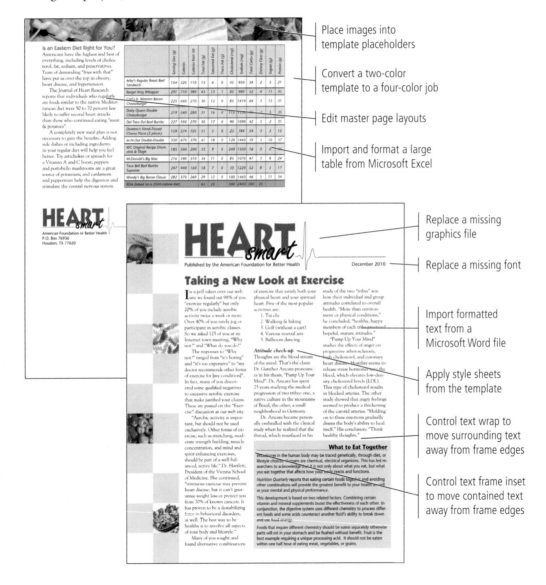

Place images into template placeholders

Convert a two-color template to a four-color job

Edit master page layouts

Import and format a large table from Microsoft Excel

Replace a missing graphics file

Replace a missing font

Import formatted text from a Microsoft Word file

Apply style sheets from the template

Control text wrap to move surrounding text away from frame edges

Control text frame inset to move contained text away from frame edges

Realtor Collateral Booklet

Your client is the Southern California Realtors Association, which provides support materials for member realtors. They hired you to create a booklet with tips for sellers who want to make their homes more attractive to buyers. The booklet will be printed in very large quantities and distributed to agents' offices, so the individual realtors can use it as a tool when they are contacted about listing a home for sale. The ultimate consumer for this piece is the home seller (not the agent), so it needs to be visually inviting and easy to read.

This project incorporates the following skills:

- ❏ Understanding and controlling facing-page layouts
- ❏ Converting regular layout pages to master pages
- ❏ Using master pages to apply repetitive layout elements
- ❏ Using special characters and markers
- ❏ Automatically flowing text across multiple pages
- ❏ Basing style sheets on other style sheets to improve consistency
- ❏ Applying bulleted list formatting
- ❏ Controlling page breaks with paragraph Keep options
- ❏ Controlling automatic hyphenation
- ❏ Printing a booklet using built-in imposition options
- ❏ Exporting a PDF file with animated page transitions

Project Meeting

The idea behind this booklet is to give realtors something they can hand to potential sellers — kind of a tactful way to point out what homeowners need to do to prepare their house for sale. This way the agents don't have to blatantly say things like "scrub the mold off your bathtub before showing it." So really, the booklet is a tool for the agents to hand out, but ultimately it's for the sellers to use as a checklist of things to do before an open house.

The text was created in Microsoft Word, using a custom template with all the text formats we use in a number of similar collateral pieces. We're also sending you some images from our agents' files; we have permission to use them in marketing materials without paying a specific licensing fee. Our research shows that a 5.5 × 8.5″ booklet is well received by most consumers, so we want the finished booklet to be that size.

This booklet was originally specified as 16 pages with a separate cover, but the client decided that a self-cover will work just as well. We had already designed the front and back covers for the initial pitch, so you can import the cover layouts into the main booklet file.

People don't like to read long blocks of body copy, and this project has a large amount of text. A lot of it will work well as lists, however, so you'll use bullets to break up most of the body text. Each spread will also have a large picture and a callout box to add visual interest.

This project — like most documents with a lot of text — will also require tighter control over the text flow than when you work with smaller bits of text. Long documents like this one require special attention to detail to prevent problems such as bad line and page breaks.

Consistency is important for any document with more than a few pages; the same basic grid should be used for most internal pages in the booklet. Completing this project will be much easier if you take the time to build the basic layout on master pages.

To complete this project, you will:

❑ Convert layout pages to master pages and import them into the main booklet file

❑ Build master pages with placeholders for the different elements of the layout

❑ Define styles based on other styles to improve consistency and facilitate changing multiple styles at once

❑ Format paragraphs as bulleted lists to improve readability

❑ Control paragraph positioning using Keep options in applied styles

❑ Control automatic hyphenation to prevent bad line breaks

❑ Print a sample booklet for client approval

❑ Export a PDF version with page transitions

Stage 1 Working with Master Pages

In Project 3, you worked with the existing master pages in a newsletter template. To complete this booklet project, you will dig deeper into the capabilities and advantages of master pages. As a general rule, you should use facing pages any time a design will be read like a book — left to right, Page 2 printed on the back of Page 1 and facing Page 3, and so on. For facing-page layouts, the left page mirrors the right page of each **spread**. The side margins are referred to as "inside" (near the spine) and "outside" (away from the spine) instead of "left" and "right."

CREATE THE BOOKLET FILE

Multi-page documents, such as the booklet you build in this project, typically require special layout considerations so the pages will appear in the correct arrangement when the job is finished. You'll deal with output considerations in Stage 3. For now, however, you need to understand two issues related to setting up this type of file:

- Books and booklets usually have facing pages, which means opposing left and right pages of a spread mirror each other.

- Files with facing pages can have different margin values on the inside (near the spread center) and outside (away from the spread center) edges.

Note:

*Layout pages can be viewed as individual pages, or they can be viewed as two or more pages at a time, which is called a **spread**.*

1. **Download ID5_RF_Project4.zip from the Student Files Web page.**

2. **Expand the ZIP archive in your WIP folder (Macintosh) or copy the archive contents into your WIP folder (Windows).**

   This creates a folder named **Realtors**, which contains the files you need for this project. You should also use this folder to save the files you create in this project.

3. **In InDesign, choose File>New. In the New Document dialog box, set the document to have 1 page that starts with page number 1.**

4. **Choose Letter – Half in the Page Size menu, using portrait orientation.**

   The 5.5 × 8.5″ size is common enough to be included in the list of built-in page sizes.

5. **Make sure the Facing Pages and Master Text Frame options are checked.**

   The Master Text Frame option creates an automatic text frame that snaps to the defined margins, using the number of columns and gutter width defined in the Columns area of the dialog box. This frame is placed on the default master page layout, so it will also appear on every layout page associated with the default master page layout.

6. **In the Columns area, define 2 columns with a 0.2″ gutter.**

7. **In the Margins area, apply a 0.5″ margin to all four sides of the page.**

8. **Define a 0.125″ bleed on all four sides.**

   If you can't see the Bleed and Slug options, click the More Options button below the Save Preset button.

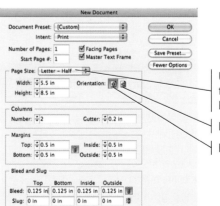

Use this menu to choose the predefined Letter – Half preset.

Landscape orientation

Portrait orientation

9. Click OK to create the new document.

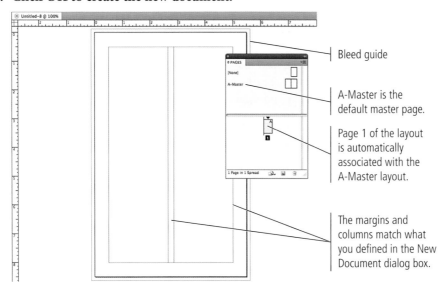

Bleed guide

A-Master is the default master page.

Page 1 of the layout is automatically associated with the A-Master layout.

The margins and columns match what you defined in the New Document dialog box.

10. Save the file as `booklet_working.indd` in your WIP>Realtors folder and continue to the next exercise.

Understanding Master Page Icons

When you work with facing pages, the default master page is actually a spread. In the Pages panel, the A-Master layout icon shows two pages, representing the two pages in the master page spread. Depending on your needs, you can also create master pages with a single page instead of a spread.

Change this field to "1" if you want a master layout with only a single page.

If you double-click the name of a master page in the Pages panel, you select the entire page or spread that makes up that master layout. You can select only one page of a master page spread by clicking the left or right page icon for that master.

In a facing-page document, the default A-Master has two pages (a spread).

You can add a single-page master layout to a facing-page document.

Double-clicking the master page name selects all pages in the master layout.

If an entire master page spread is already selected (both page icons are highlighted), you have to first deselect the spread before you can select only one page of the spread. You can do this by simply clicking any other page icon — master page or regular page — in the panel.

Single-click either page icon in a master page spread to select only that page, rather than the entire spread.

When you add pages to the layout by dragging a master page, the selected page icons determine what will be added. If both pages of a master spread are highlighted, dragging the selected icons into the lower half of the panel will add the entire master page spread. If only one page of the master spread is selected, you can add a single page to the layout.

Both pages of the spread are selected.

When you drag the selected master into the layout, two pages will be added.

One page of the spread is selected.

When you drag the selected master into the layout, one page will be added.

This project was originally defined by the client as a 16-page booklet "plus cover." In other words, the main booklet file would have 16 pages, but the cover would be created and printed as a separate file. Once printed, the two pieces would be combined and bound together into a single finished piece.

Based on the amount of text they created, your clients have decided to create the booklet as 16 pages "including self cover," which means the first and last pages of the main booklet file will be the front and back covers (respectively). The first step in completing this project is to bring the cover pages into the main layout.

1. **Open the file cover.indd from the WIP>Realtors folder.**

   This layout includes two pages — the front cover and the back cover. Like many projects, however, these pages were not created using master pages.

   Although you could simply copy the page contents from this file into your main file, it is a better idea to work with master pages whenever possible. Doing so gives you the most flexibility and control over the various layouts. Once you develop master pages, you can easily import the layouts into other files and apply the layouts to specific layout pages as necessary.

   Fortunately, it is very easy to create a master page layout from a regular page layout.

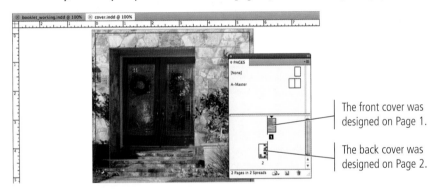

The front cover was designed on Page 1.

The back cover was designed on Page 2.

2. **In the Pages panel, Control/right-click the Page 1 icon and choose Save as Master from the contextual menu.**

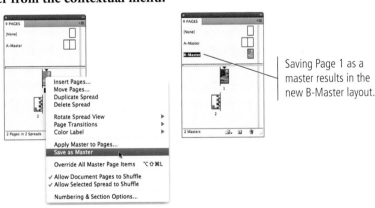

Saving Page 1 as a master results in the new B-Master layout.

3. **Control/right-click the new B-Master icon (in the top section of the Pages panel) and choose Master Options for "B-Master" from the contextual menu.**

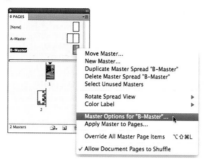

4. **In the resulting Master Options dialog box, change the name to Front Cover and click OK.**

5. **Repeat this process to convert the Page 2 layout to a master page layout named Back Cover.**

6. **In the top section of the Pages panel, Control/right-click the A-Master layout name and choose Delete Master Spread "A-Master" from the contextual menu.**

The default master layout in this file was never used, so you can simply delete it.

7. **Save the file as cover_masters.indd in your WIP>Realtors folder, and then close the file.**

8. **Continue to the next exercise.**

IMPORT MASTER PAGES

Now that the front and back covers are saved as master pages, you can easily import and apply them in the booklet file.

1. **With `booklet_working.indd` open, choose Load Master Pages from the Pages panel Options menu.**

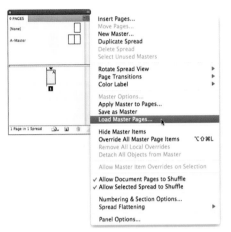

2. **In the resulting dialog box, navigate to the file `cover_masters.indd` in your WIP>Realtors folder and click Open.**

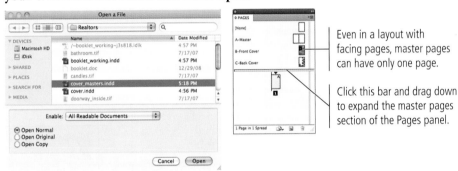

Even in a layout with facing pages, master pages can have only one page.

Click this bar and drag down to expand the master pages section of the Pages panel.

3. **Open the Swatches and Paragraph Styles panels.**

Loading master pages from one file to another is an all-or-nothing process. Both master pages from the cover_masters.indd file are now part of the new file.

When you load a master page from one file to another, all required assets (styles, swatches, etc.) are also imported. One color swatch has been added to the Swatches panel (in addition to the default swatches); two paragraph styles have been added to the Paragraph Styles panel.

Note:

There is no dynamic link between the master pages now in the booklet file and the master pages in the original cover file. Changing one version of the front cover master (for example) will not affect the other version.

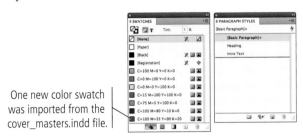

One new color swatch was imported from the cover_masters.indd file.

4. **In the Pages panel, drag the B-Front Cover icon onto the Page 1 icon.**

By default, Page 1 of any new file is associated with the A-Master layout. You can change this by simply dragging a different master onto the page icon.

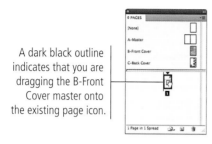

A dark black outline indicates that you are dragging the B-Front Cover master onto the existing page icon.

After releasing the mouse button, Page 1 is associated with the B-Front Cover master.

5. **In the Pages panel, select only the left page of the A-Master spread and drag it below the Page 1 icon.**

Using facing pages, new pages are added to the left and right of the spread center. When you release the mouse button, the new Page 2 is automatically added on the left side of the spread center.

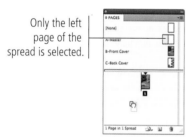

Only the left page of the spread is selected.

Page 2 is automatically added to the left side of the spread.

6. **Double-click the Page 2 icon in the Pages panel to show that page in the document window.**

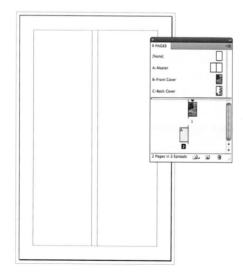

Note:

You can also Control/ right-click a page icon in the lower section of the Pages panel and choose Apply Master to Page from the contextual menu.

Note:

*Pages on the left side of the spread center are called **left-facing** or **verso** pages.*

*Pages on the right side of the spread center are called **right-facing** or **recto** pages.*

Note:

By convention, odd-numbered pages are right-facing and even-numbered pages are left-facing.

7. **Drag the C-Back Cover icon onto the Page 2 icon to change the associated master.**

8. **Make sure guides (View>Grids & Guides>Show Guides) and frame edges (View>Extras>Show Frame Edges) are visible.**

Two objects now appear on Page 2 — a text frame and a graphics frame. The frame edges appear as dotted lines instead of solid lines. This indicates that the objects are from the associated master page; you can't select them on the layout page unless you override the master page items for that layout page.

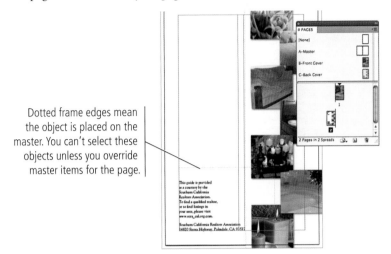

Dotted frame edges mean the object is placed on the master. You can't select these objects unless you override master items for the page.

9. **In the Pages panel, drag the left page of the A-Master spread to the left of the Page 2 icon.**

Before you release the mouse button, a vertical black bar indicates the potential position of the new page.

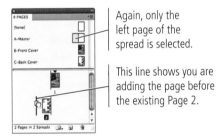

Again, only the left page of the spread is selected.

This line shows you are adding the page before the existing Page 2.

After you release the mouse button, the new page is automatically added before Page 2. Because this is a facing-page layout, the new Page 2 becomes the left-facing page, and the old Page 2 — now Page 3 — moves to the right side of the spread.

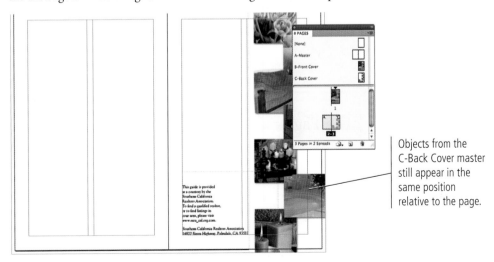

Objects from the C-Back Cover master still appear in the same position relative to the page.

10. **Save the file and continue to the next exercise.**

You need to understand the differences between spread master pages and single-page master pages, especially when working with facing pages. In the booklet file you're building now, you have both kinds of master pages — the covers are single-page masters and the A-Master layout is a spread of two facing pages.

When you work with a spread master page, the objects on the master page layout are positioned relative to the entire spread. Objects on regular layout pages, however, are positioned relative to the page on which they are created.

This concept is particularly important if you work with objects that bleed off the left or right side of a page, or if you override the master page items on a specific page.

When you move a page from one side of a spread to the other (e.g., from left to right), any bleed object will continue to bleed past the same edge of its new page position — possibly interfering with the other page of the spread.

A related problem occurs when you override and change master page items on regular layout pages. When you override master page items, they become regular layout page items. Adding pages to the middle of a layout moves those items relative to their new page position; the original master page objects are added directly behind the overridden objects. (If necessary, you can eliminate the overridden objects by choosing Remove All Local Overrides from the Pages panel Options menu, or you can select specific objects and choose Remove Selected Local Overrides.)

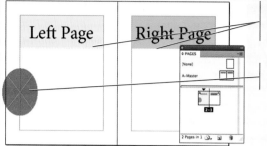

Dotted frame edges indicate that these objects are master page objects.

This shape was created on Page 2 of the layout.

After adding a new A-Master page in front of Page 2...

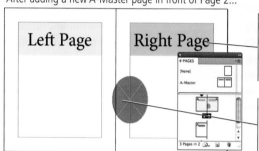

On the new Page 3, the object from the right side of the master spread replaces the object from the left side of the master spread.

The object from Page 2 is in the same position relative to the page where it was created, which is now Page 3.

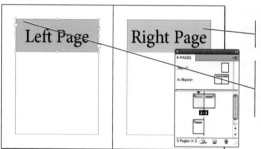

This frame is still a master page object.

We overrode master page items for Page 2, then changed the object fill color from yellow to magenta.

After adding a new A-Master page in front of Page 2...

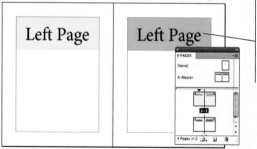

Because overriding master page items converts them into regular page items, the overridden object moves relative to the page on which it is placed (the moved Page 2).

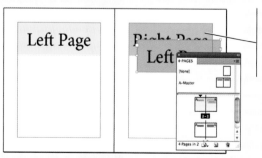

Moving the overriden object shows that the correct master page object has been added to the page, directly behind the overridden object.

EDIT THE DEFAULT MASTER PAGE

The main body of the booklet will be 14 pages in 7 spreads; each spread will have the same basic layout:

- A large image fills the background of each left-facing page.

- A heading and introductory paragraph sits at the bottom of each left-facing page.

- The right-facing page of each spread has two columns of body copy.

- Each right-facing page has a callout box of related checklist items.

- The right-facing page of each spread includes the page number and the words "Home Enhancement Guide."

Because these elements are common to most pages in the layout, it makes sense to create them on a master page layout. You could either create a new master page for the body spread or simply edit the existing default master page.

1. **With booklet_working.indd open, double-click the words "A-Master" in the top section of the Pages panel.**

   Double-clicking a master page navigates to that master layout in the document window. Each page of the A-Master spread has the margin and column settings you defined in the New Document dialog box.

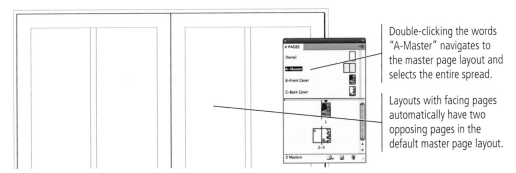

Double-clicking the words "A-Master" navigates to the master page layout and selects the entire spread.

Layouts with facing pages automatically have two opposing pages in the default master page layout.

   Based on the specified elements of the interior pages, each page in this spread has different margin and column requirements. Fortunately, InDesign allows you to modify those settings for individual pages in the spread.

2. **Click once on any page other than the A-Master spread in the Pages panel.**

   When you double-click the master page name in the Pages panel, the entire spread is selected (highlighted) in the panel. To change a setting for only one page of the spread, you first have to deselect the spread (by selecting some other page), and then select only the specific page you want to modify.

Note:

You can click a regular page or a master page icon; the important point is to deselect the A-Master spread.

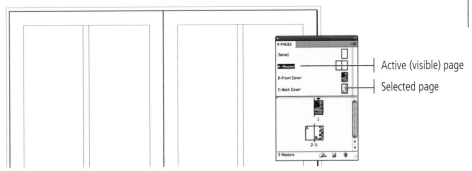

Active (visible) page

Selected page

3. **In the Pages panel, click once on the left page icon of the A-Master spread.**

4. **With the left page of the A-Master layout selected, choose Layout>Margins and Columns.**

Note:

Clicking a page icon once selects that page without changing the visible page in the document window.

5. **With the Preview option checked, make sure the four margin fields are not linked. Change the top margin to 5″, change the outside margin to 2″, and change the number of columns to 1.**

   Make sure you see the broken chain links between the margin fields; you want all four margins to be constrained to the same value.

   Unfortunately, changing the margins and columns does not automatically change the settings of the master text frame. You have to change those separately.

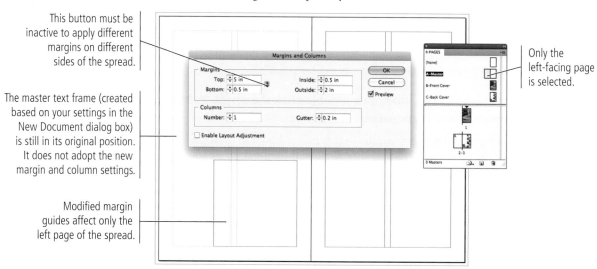

This button must be inactive to apply different margins on different sides of the spread.

The master text frame (created based on your settings in the New Document dialog box) is still in its original position. It does not adopt the new margin and column settings.

Modified margin guides affect only the left page of the spread.

Only the left-facing page is selected.

6. **Click OK to apply the changes.**

7. **In the document window, choose the Gap tool in the Tools panel. Place the cursor in the top margin area of the left-facing page.**

   The Gap tool allows you to actively manipulate white space on a page, rather than manipulating only specific objects. When you place the cursor between existing objects, or between an object and the page edge, the gray highlight shows which space you are editing; the arrow indicator behind the cursor icon shows what can be moved by clicking and dragging.

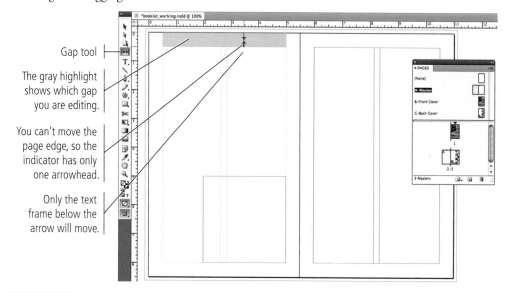

Gap tool

The gray highlight shows which gap you are editing.

You can't move the page edge, so the indicator has only one arrowhead.

Only the text frame below the arrow will move.

8. **Click in the margin area above the left page of the spread. Drag down until the cursor feedback shows a height of 5″.**

When you edit the gap between a page edge and an object, you resize the object in the direction you drag. When you drag near the adjusted margin guide, the frame edge snaps to align with the guide.

Note:

If you press Option/ Alt while dragging the margin, you can increase the margin without affecting the object's size; the existing object edge simply moves based on the new margin gap.

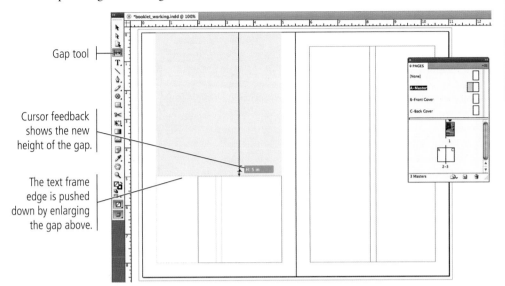

Gap tool

Cursor feedback shows the new height of the gap.

The text frame edge is pushed down by enlarging the gap above.

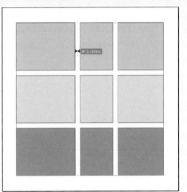

Understanding the Gap Tool

INDESIGN FOUNDATIONS

The Gap tool is designed to let you actively manipulate the white space on a page. Using one or more modifier keys, the Gap tool can also resize or move objects that touch the gap you edit.

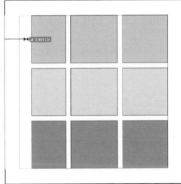

Click and drag a margin to change the space between the page edge and nearby objects, and affect the size of objects that touch the margin.

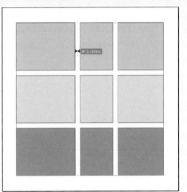

Click and drag a gap between objects to move the gap and affect the size of adjacent objects.

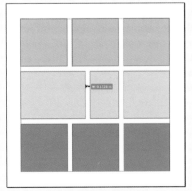

Shift-click and drag to move the gap only between immediately adjacent objects.

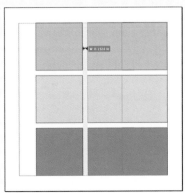

Option/Alt-click and drag to move the white space and adjacent objects, without affecting the objects' size.

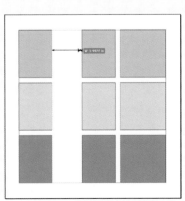

Command/Control-click and drag to resize the gap and change the size of adjacent objects.

9. **Click in the margin area on the left side of the page. Drag right until the cursor feedback shows a width of 2″.**

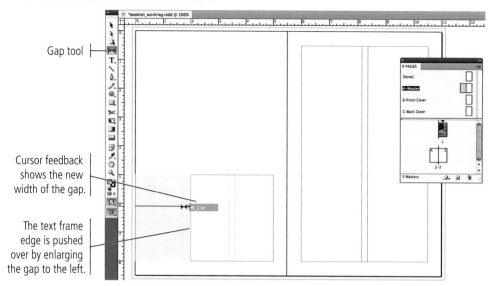

Gap tool

Cursor feedback shows the new width of the gap.

The text frame edge is pushed over by enlarging the gap to the left.

10. **Using the Selection tool, click the reduced text frame to select it. Control/right-click the frame and choose Text Frame Options from the contextual menu.**

11. **In the Text Frame Options dialog box, change the number of columns to 1, change all four Inset Spacing values to 0.125″, and choose Center in the Vertical Justification Align menu. Click OK to apply the changes.**

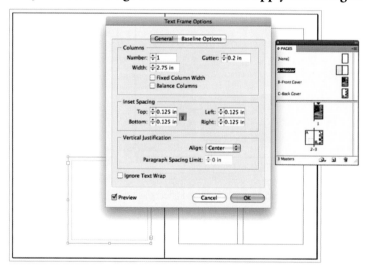

12. **In the Pages panel, select only the right page of the A-Master spread. Choose Layout>Margins and Columns and change the bottom margin to 3.25". Click OK.**

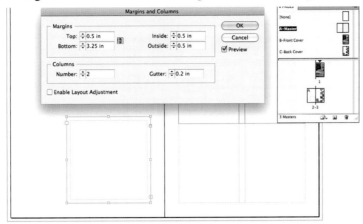

13. **Using the Gap tool, click and drag to change the white space at the bottom of the right-facing page to 3.25".**

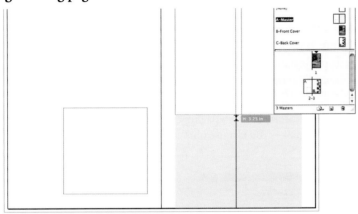

14. **Save the file and continue to the next exercise.**

 ## ADD COMMON ELEMENTS TO A MASTER PAGE LAYOUT

In addition to the master text frame, you need several other elements to appear on every spread in the body of the document: the graphics frame on the left page of the spread, as well as the callout box and page footer on the right page of the spread. Again, it makes sense to create master page placeholders for these objects rather than recreating the objects on every individual layout page. Doing so reduces the number of repetitive tasks as much as possible to enhance your productivity.

1. **With booklet_working.indd open, make sure the A-Master layout is showing in the document window.**

2. **Create a new text frame with the following dimensions (based on the top-left reference point):**

> X: 7.375"   W: 3.75"
> Y: 5.65"   H: 2.35"

> By default, InDesign measurements reflect an object's position relative to the entire spread; the X: 7.375" position is actually 1.875" from the left edge of the right page. You can change this behavior by changing the Ruler Units origin in the Units & Increments pane of the Preferences dialog box.

3. **Using the Swatches panel, fill the new text frame with the C=100 M=35 Y=90 K=20 swatch.**

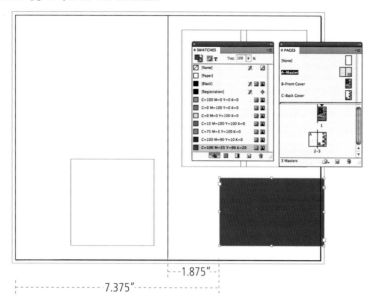

4. **Control/right-click the new frame and choose Text Frame Options from the contextual menu. Change the Top, Bottom, and Left Inset Spacing fields to 0.125″, and change the Right Inset Spacing field to 0.625″. Click OK.**

Because the frame bleeds off the page edge, you need to adjust the frame inset on only the bleed side to match the rest of the layout. Instead of overlaying two frames — one with the green fill and one with the text frame — you can use uneven inset spacing to achieve the same goal.

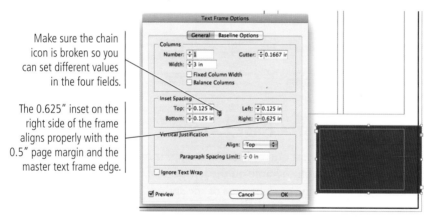

5. **Using the Selection tool, click the master text frame on the right page of the spread. Click the Out port of the master text frame, and then immediately click the green text frame to link the two frames.**

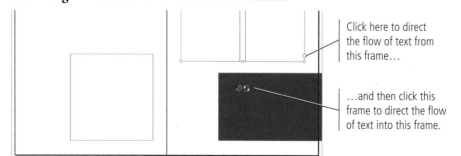

Note:

The client's content is supplied in a single file, and the callout text for each spread appears within the main body of the text. The text includes the heading "Through the Buyer's Eyes," so you can identify the appropriate text.

6. **Choose View>Extras>Show Text Threads.**

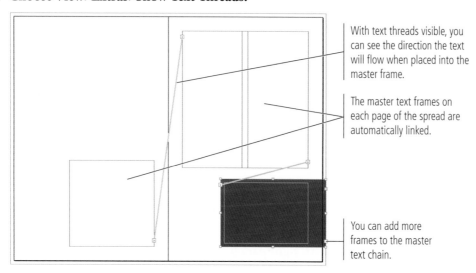

With text threads visible, you can see the direction the text will flow when placed into the master frame.

The master text frames on each page of the spread are automatically linked.

You can add more frames to the master text chain.

7. **Turn off the text threads (View>Extras>Hide Text Threads).**

8. **Using the Rectangle Frame tool, create an empty graphics frame that fills the entire left page of the spread (including the bleed area). Fill the frame with a 20% tint of the dark green swatch.**

9. **Choose Object>Arrange>Send to Back to move the graphics frame behind the text frame.**

   Each spread in the booklet will include a large image on the left side of the spread. Placing it on the master layout eliminates the need to manually draw the frame on each spread. You added the fill color simply as a visual reference for placing the image.

10. **Select the master text frame on the left page of the spread. Change its fill color to Paper and change its Opacity value to 85%.**

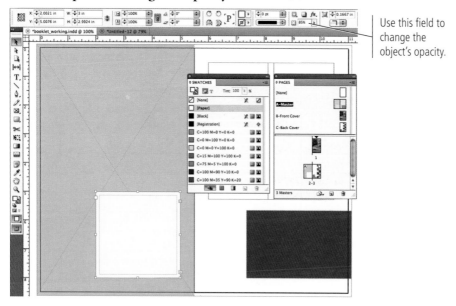

Use this field to change the object's opacity.

11. **Save the file and continue to the next exercise.**

PLACE AUTOMATIC PAGE NUMBER MARKERS

The next item to add to the master page layout is the page footer information — the page number and the name of the booklet. Rather than manually numbering each page in the booklet, which can be time consuming and invites human error, you can use special characters to automatically number the pages in any layout.

1. With **booklet_working.indd** open, make sure the A-Master layout is showing.

2. Create a new text frame with the following dimensions (based on the top-left reference point):

   X: 6″   W: 4.5″
   Y: 8.125″   H: 0.25″

3. Inside the new frame, type Home Enhancement Guide, and then change the formatting to 12-pt ATC Laurel Bold with right paragraph alignment.

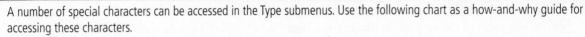 ## Special Characters and White Space

A number of special characters can be accessed in the Type submenus. Use the following chart as a how-and-why guide for accessing these characters.

Menu			What it's used for
Insert Special Character	Markers	Current Page Number	Places the current page number
		Next Page Number	Places the page number of the next frame in the same story
		Previous Page Number	Places the page number of the previous frame in the same story
		Section Marker	Places a user-defined text variable that is specific to the current layout section. (You'll work with section numbering in Project 8.)
		Footnote Number	Inserts a number character based on the options defined in the Footnote Options dialog box
	Hyphens and Dashes	Em Dash	Places a dash that has the same width as the applied type size
		En Dash	Places a dash equivalent to one-half of an em dash
		Discretionary Hyphen	Allows you to hyphenate a word in a location other than what is defined by the currect dictionary, or hyphenate a word when automatic hyphenation is turned off; the discretionary hyphen only appears if the word is hyphenated at the end of a line
		Nonbreaking Hyphen	Places a hyphen character that will not break at the end of a line; used to keep both parts of a phrase on the same line of the paragraph
	Quotation Marks	Double Left Quotation Marks	"
		Double Right Quotation Marks	"
		Single Left Quotation Mark	'
		Single Right Quotation Mark	'
		Straight Double Quotation Marks	"
		Straight Single Quotation Mark	'
	Other	Tab	Forces following text to begin at the next defined or default tab stop
		Right Indent Tab	Forces following text to align at the right indent of the column or frame
		Indent to Here	Creates a hanging indent by forcing all following lines in the paragraph to indent to the location of the character
		End Nested Style Here	Interrupts nested style formatting before the defined character limit
		Non-joiner	Prevents adjacent characters from being joined in a ligature or other alternate character connection

4. **Place the insertion point immediately after the word "Guide" and press the Spacebar once.**

Because the text is right-aligned, the Space character is not visible; a space at the end of a line is not considered in the line length or type position when InDesign aligns paragraphs.

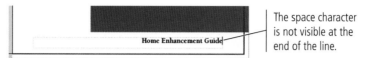

Home Enhancement Guide

The space character is not visible at the end of the line.

5. **With the insertion point flashing after the space character (which you can't see), choose Type>Insert Special Character>Markers>Current Page Number.**

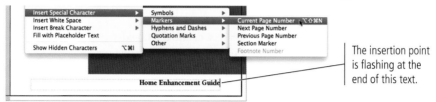

The insertion point is flashing at the end of this text.

Special Characters and White Space (continued)

Menu		What it's used for
Insert White Space	Em Space	Space equivalent to applied type size
	En Space	One-half of an em space
	Nonbreaking Space	Places a space character the same width as pressing the Spacebar; this character prevents a line break from occurring, which allows you to keep related words together on the same line.
	Nonbreaking Space (Fixed Width)	Same as the regular nonbreaking space, but does not change size when a paragraph uses justified alignment.
	Hair Space	One-twenty-fourth of an em space
	Sixth Space	One-sixth of an em space
	Thin Space	One-eighth of an em space
	Quarter Space	One-fourth of an em space
	Third Space	One-third of an em space
	Punctuation Space	Same width as a period in the applied font
	Figure Space	Same width as a number in the applied font
	Flush Space	Variable space in a justified paragraph placed between the last character of the paragraph and a decorative character (a "bug") used to indicate the end of a story
Insert Break Character	Column Break	Forces text into the next available column (or frame, if used in a one-column frame or the last column of a multi-column frame)
	Frame Break	Forces text into the next available frame
	Page Break	Forces text into the first available frame on the next page, skipping any available frames or columns on the same page
	Odd Page Break	Forces text into the first available frame on the next odd-numbered page
	Even Page Break	Forces text into the first available frame on the next even-numbered page
	Paragraph Return	Creates a new paragraph (same as pressing Return/Enter)
	Forced Line Break	Creates a new line without starting a new paragraph (called a "soft return")
	Discretionary Line Break	Creates a new line if the character falls at the end of the line; if the character falls in the middle of the column, the line is not broken

6. If the hidden characters are not visible, choose Type>Show Hidden Characters.

The Current Page Number command inserts a special character that reflects the correct page number of any page where it appears. Because you placed this character on the A-Master page, the character shows as "A" in the text box.

Now that the Space character is no longer the last character in the line, you can see it — as long as hidden characters are showing.

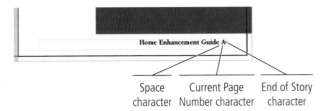

Home Enhancement Guide A

Space character | Current Page Number character | End of Story character

In this case, the single, regular Space character is not enough to separate the booklet name from the page number. InDesign provides a number of options for increasing (and decreasing) white space without simply pressing the Spacebar numerous times.

7. Highlight the Space character before the Page Number character.

Keyboard Shortcuts for Special Characters

Character	Keyboard Shortcut	
	Macintosh	**Windows**
Current page number	Command-Option-Shift-N	Control-Alt-Shift-N
Em dash	Option-Shift-Hyphen (-)	Alt-Shift-Hyphen (-)
En dash	Option-Hyphen	Alt-Hyphen
Discretionary hyphen	Command-Shift-Hyphen	Control-Shift-Hyphen
Nonbreaking hyphen	Command-Option-Hyphen	Control-Alt-Hyphen
Double left quotation marks	Option-[	Alt-[
Double right quotation marks	Option-Shift-[	Alt-Shift-[
Single left quotation mark	Option-]	Alt-]
Single right quotation mark	Option-Shift-]	Alt-Shift-]
Straight double quotation marks	Control-Shift-'	Alt-Shift-'
Straight single quotation mark	Control-'	Alt-'
Tab	Tab	Tab
Right indent tab	Shift-Tab	Shift-Tab
Indent to here	Command-\	Control-\
Em space	Command-Shift-M	Control-Shift-M
En space	Command-Shift-N	Control-Shift-N
Nonbreaking space	Command-Option-X	Control-Alt-X
Thin space	Command-Option-Shift-M	Control-Alt-Shift-M
Column break	Enter (numeric keypad)	Enter (numeric keypad)
Frame break	Shift-Enter (numeric keypad)	Shift-Enter (numeric keypad)
Page break	Command-Enter (numeric keypad)	Control-Enter (numeric keypad)
Paragraph return	Return	Enter
Forced line break	Shift-Return	Shift-Enter

8. **Choose Type>Insert White Space>Em Space.**

   An **em** is a typographic measure equivalent to the applied type size. An em space is white space equal to one em.

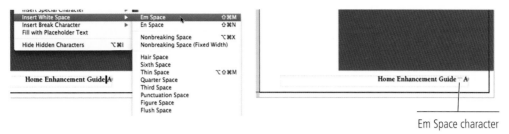

Em Space character

9. **Add a second Em Space character immediately after the first.**

10. **Select all text in the footer and change the type size to 10 pt.**

    Special and hidden characters are still characters; changing the type formatting affects these characters in the same way as regular characters.

11. **Save the file and continue to the next stage of the project.**

Stage 2 Controlling the Flow of Text

Because you imported the covers as master pages and built a spread layout to hold the various body elements, all the necessary pieces are now in place to import the client's provided text and graphics. The time you spent building effective master pages will enable you to quickly place the layout content and create a multi-page document; you significantly reduce overall development time because you don't have to manually create these elements on each page.

You are building a document with 16 facing pages. You could manually insert the necessary pages, and then manually link the text from one page to the next. But anytime you see the word "manually," you should look for ways to automate some or all of the process. The ability to automate work is one of the defining characteristics of professional page-layout software such as InDesign.

 ## IMPORT AND AUTO-FLOW CLIENT TEXT

In Project 3, you used styles in an InDesign template to format the text imported from a Microsoft Word file. You learned that by applying styles, you can apply multiple formatting attributes — both character and paragraph — with a single click. InDesign is not the only software that supports text-formatting styles; Microsoft Word does as well.

Many clients will submit text with local formatting — they might have highlighted some text and changed the font, size, spacing, etc. — that you will strip out and replace with the proper InDesign translations. More sophisticated users, however, will send files that are formatted with Microsoft Word styles. In this case, you can import the styles from Microsoft Word directly into your InDesign layout to use as the basis for your work.

1. **With `booklet_working.indd` open, open the Type pane of the Preferences dialog box.**

   Remember, preferences are accessed in the InDesign menu on Macintosh and the Edit menu on Windows.

2. **Make sure the Smart Text Reflow option is checked, choose End of Story in the Add Pages To menu, and check the Delete Empty Pages option. Click OK.**

   When Smart Text Reflow is active, InDesign automatically adds pages to accommodate an entire story that is placed in a master text frame. This option applies to adding text within a story, and to changing formatting in a way that affects the number of required pages — which you will do in a later exercise.

   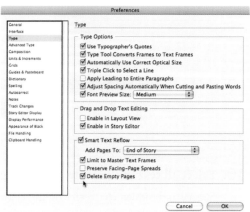

   - You can use the **Add Pages To** menu to determine where pages are added to the file (at the end of the current story, the current section, or the current document).

   - If **Limit To Master Text Frames** is not checked, you can add or remove pages when editing text in frames other than a master text frame. This option only applies if the existing frame is already part of a text thread with at least one other frame. (New pages added when the text frame is not a master text frame have a single-column text frame that matches the default page margins for the file.)

   - If **Preserve Facing-Page Spreads** is active, pages added to the middle of a document are added as document spreads based on the applied master layout. When unchecked, only the necessary pages will be added; subsequent existing pages are reshuffled (left-facing to right-facing) if necessary.

   - If **Delete Empty Pages** is active, unnecessary pages are removed from the layout if you delete text (or format text to require less space).

3. **Navigate to Page 2 of the layout and then choose File>Place. Navigate to the file `booklet.doc` in the WIP>Realtors folder. Make sure the Show Import Options box is checked and click Open.**

4. **In the Import Options dialog box, make sure the Preserve Styles and Formatting from Text and Tables option is selected.**

5. **In the Manual Page Breaks menu, choose No Breaks.**

   This command removes any page and section breaks that exist in the client's Microsoft Word file.

Note:

If Smart Text Reflow is not active, you can press Shift and click the loaded text cursor in a master text frame (on a layout page) to automatically flow the entire story; InDesign adds pages as necessary to accommodate the entire story. (In this case, new pages are always added at the end of the document, regardless of the position of the text box where you first click to place the text. The Smart Text Reflow preference is not activated.)

6. **Select the Import Styles Automatically option, choose Auto Rename in both conflict menus, then click OK.**

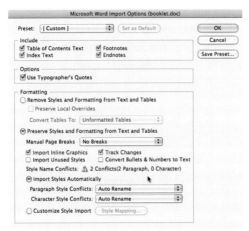

7. **Review the resulting warning, then click OK to import the text.**

When you import Microsoft Word files with their formatting, you frequently see the Missing Fonts warning.

Many actions in Microsoft Word — such as using the B or I buttons to apply **faux bold** or **faux italic** type styles — can cause problems in InDesign because InDesign tries to translate those faux formatting options to the best-possible "real" font variants required for commercial printing applications.

The good news is that in many cases, you can replace the fonts used in the Microsoft Word file with something more appropriate for your overall design. It would be a waste of time to correct these font problems until you know that it's necessary. In this case, you're eventually going to replace the style that calls for the missing fonts, so there's no point in spending time resolving the missing-font problem.

This is a common workflow issue when you work with client-supplied files. Every situation is different, but we find it best to import client formatting so we can review the editorial priority, and then edit or define styles as necessary to complete the page layout.

8. **Click the loaded text cursor inside the margin guides on Page 2.**

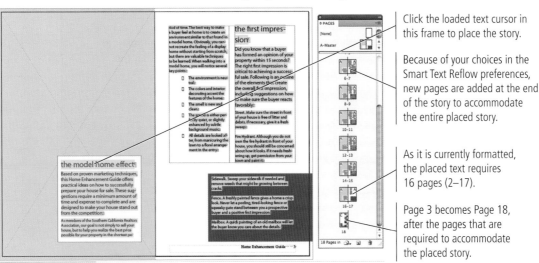

Click the loaded text cursor in this frame to place the story.

Because of your choices in the Smart Text Reflow preferences, new pages are added at the end of the story to accommodate the entire placed story.

As it is currently formatted, the placed text requires 16 pages (2–17).

Page 3 becomes Page 18, after the pages that are required to accommodate the placed story.

9. **Save the file and continue to the next exercise.**

As you can see in the current booklet file, the text is just a long block with little to identify the editorial priority (e.g., headings, subheadings, and so on). Fonts used in the client's file aren't available, as indicated by the pink "missing font" highlight.

This type of situation occurs frequently. When it does, you should begin by reviewing the text to see if applied styles can provide any clues about which elements belong where and at what editorial priority.

1. **With Page 2 of booklet_working.indd showing, click the Type tool in the first paragraph (the model home effect).**

2. **Look at the Paragraph Styles panel (Window>Styles>Paragraph Styles).**

   The first paragraph is formatted with the Section Head style. You can assume that other text with the same basic appearance is also a section head.

Insertion point

The highlighted style is applied to the selected text (insertion point).

The Heading and Intro Text styles were imported when you loaded the cover master page layouts into the booklet file.

The disk icon identifies styles that were imported with the text file.

3. **In the Paragraph Styles panel, Control/right-click the Section Head style and choose Delete Style from the contextual menu.**

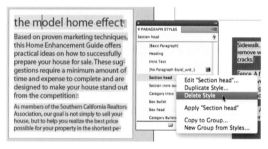

4. **In the Delete Paragraph Style dialog box, choose Heading in the Replace With menu and click OK.**

   If you delete a style sheet that's being used, you have to determine what to do with text that uses the style you want to delete. If you want to maintain the formatting of that text without applying a different style, you can choose [No Paragraph Style].

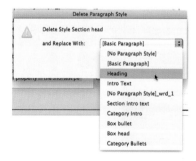

After the Section Head style has been replaced with the Heading style, the associated headings in the layout change in appearance to match the new style definition.

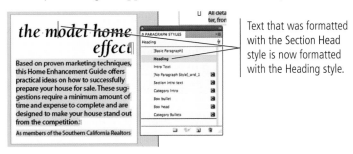

Text that was formatted with the Section Head style is now formatted with the Heading style.

5. **Move the insertion point to the next paragraph.**

The second paragraph is formatted with the Section Intro Text style. Again, you can assume that other text with the same appearance is also introductory text for a section.

6. **Using the same process as in Steps 3–4, replace the Section Intro Text style with the Intro Text style.**

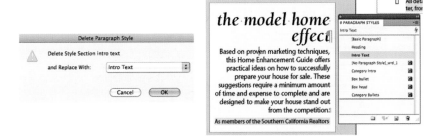

7. **In the Paragraph Styles panel, drag [No Paragraph Style]_wrd_1 to the panel's Delete button.**

It's a good idea to remove unnecessary styles from the InDesign document.

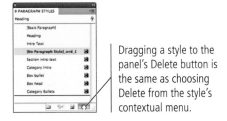

Dragging a style to the panel's Delete button is the same as choosing Delete from the style's contextual menu.

8. **In the resulting dialog box, choose [No Paragraph Style] in the Replace With menu. Make sure the Preserve Formatting option is selected.**

InDesign's default [No Paragraph Style] is not a style — in fact, it is the express lack of a defined style. The imported [No Paragraph Style]_wrd_1 is considered a style, so you have to decide what to do with the formatting that was applied to any text associated with that style.

Note:

Any time you choose [No Paragraph Style] in the Replace With menu, the Preserve Formatting option becomes available in the Delete Paragraph Style dialog box.

9. **Save the file and continue to the next exercise**

In most cases, styles that are imported with a text file will need at least some modification — if for no other reason than InDesign has more sophisticated options that are relevant to commercial printing. In addition, your clients are not designers, so their formatting choices are most likely not up to par with professional-quality graphic design.

1. **With Page 2 of `booklet_working.indd` visible in the document window, zoom out so you can see the entire spread.**

2. **Place the insertion point in the third paragraph of imported copy.**

   This paragraph is formatted with the Category Intro style.

3. **Control/right-click the Category Intro style and choose Edit "Category Intro" in the contextual menu.**

Note:

You can edit the default type settings for a layout by editing the [Basic Paragraph] style. You can edit the default type settings for all new InDesign layouts by editing the [Basic Paragraph] style when no file is open.

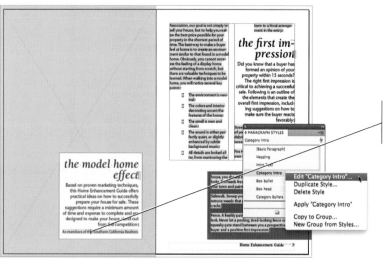

This paragraph is formatted with the Category Intro style.

Editing styles is both easy and efficient. When you change the options in a style definition, any text formatted with that style reformats with the changed definition.

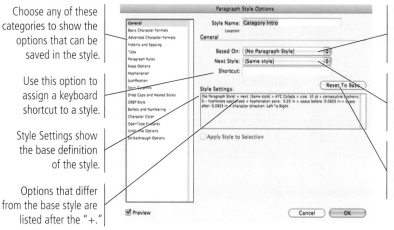

Choose any of these categories to show the options that can be saved in the style.

Use this option to assign a keyboard shortcut to a style.

Style Settings show the base definition of the style.

Options that differ from the base style are listed after the "+."

Styles can be based on existing styles, adopting the formatting in the Based On style.

Next Style determines which style will be applied when you press Return/Enter while typing.

Click to restore the base settings, removing all other options from the style definition.

4. **In the Basic Character Formats options, change the formatting to 9.5-pt ATC Pine Normal.**

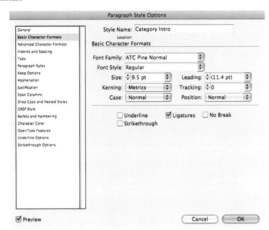

Note:

You can also edit a style by double-clicking the style in the panel. However, double-clicking a style in the panel applies the style to the current text, and then opens the Paragraph Style Options dialog box.

By Control/right-clicking the style in the panel, you can edit the style without applying it to the currently selected text.

5. **In the Indents and Spacing options, change the Space Before field to 0.1″ and change the Space After field to 0″.**

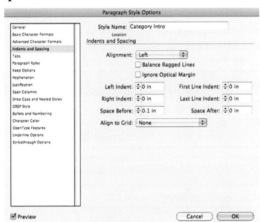

Note:

If you check the Preview box in the Paragraph Style Options dialog box, you can see the effect of your changes before you click OK.

6. **Click OK to change the style definition.**

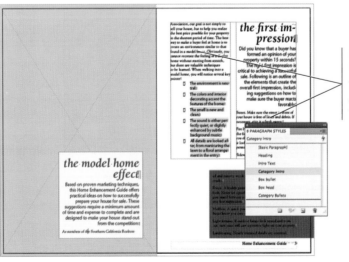

Much of the text in this layout is formatted with the Category Intro style. All of that text now reflects the updated definition.

Note:

Any Space Before value is ignored when a paragraph begins at the top of a frame or column.

7. **Save the file and continue to the next exercise.**

INDESIGN FOUNDATIONS

By completing the first three projects, you've already learned about a considerable number of options for formatting text — both character and paragraph attributes — but there's still more to learn. tyles can store a very large number of settings, which you'll see when you complete the next exercise. Use the following chart as a reminder of exactly what can be stored in a paragraph style definition, as well as where to find the equivalent in the application interface for selected text. (Character styles include a subset of these same options: General, Basic Character Formats, Advanced Character Formats, Character Color, OpenType Features, Underline Options, and Strikethrough Options.)

Category	Options			Application Equivalent
General	Based On Style Settings	Next Style Reset to Base	Shortcut Apply Style to Selection	N/A
Basic Character Formats	Font Family Leading	Style Kerning	Size Tracking	Character panel
	Case	Position	Styles	Character panel Options menu
Advanced Character Formats	Horizontal Scale Skew	Vertical Scale Language	Baseline Shift	Character panel
Indents and Spacing	Alignment Left & Right Indent Space Before	Balance Ragged Lines First Line Indent Space After	Ignore Optical Margin Last Line Indent Align to Grid	Paragraph panel
Tabs	X position	Leader	Align On	Tabs panel
Paragraph Rules	Rule Above On Width Rule attributes (Weight, Type, Color, etc.)	Rule Below On Offset	Left & Right Indents Gap attributes	Paragraph panel Options menu
Keep Options	Keep with Next [N] Lines Start Paragraph		Keep Lines Together	Paragraph panel Options menu
Hyphenation	Hyphenate On/Off (and all related options)			Paragraph panel Options menu
Justification	Word Spacing Auto Leading	Letter Spacing Single Word Justification	Glyph Scaling Composer	Paragraph panel Options menu
Span Columns	Paragraph Layout Single Column	Span Columns	Split Column	Paragraph panel Options menu
Drop Caps and Nested Styles	Number of Lines	Number of Characters		Paragraph panel
	Character Style for Drop Characters Scale for Descenders	Nested Styles	Align Left Edge Nested Line Styles	Paragraph panel Options menu
GREP Style	New GREP Style	Apply [Style]	To Text Pattern	Paragraph panel Options menu
Bullets and Numbering	List Type Text After Bullet	List Style Character Style	Bullet Character Bullet/Number Position	Paragraph panel Options menu
Character Color	Fill Color, Tint, Overprint attributes Stroke Color, Tint, Weight, Overprint attributes			Swatches panel/ Control panel
OpenType Features	Titling, Contextual, & Swash Alternates Ordinals, Fractions, Discretionary Ligatures, Slashed Zero, Figure Style, Positional Form Stylistic Sets			Character panel Options menu
Underline Options	Underline On	Stroke attributes	Gap attributes	Character panel Options menu
Strikethrough Options	Strikethrough On	Stroke attributes	Gap attributes	Character panel Options menu

There are two important points to remember about designing long documents. First, changing the definition of a style changes all text formatted with that style. Second, text should be consistently formatted from one page to the next; body copy (for example) should use the same basic font throughout the entire layout.

If you think of these two points together, consider what happens if you decide to change the font for the main body copy (for example, changing from Times New Roman to Adobe Garamond). Changing the main body font means you should also change any related styles that are variations of the main body text, such as bulleted or numbered lists.

The best way to manage this type of situation is to create secondary styles that are based on the main style. This way, changes to the main style (called the **parent style**) are reflected in styles that are based on that style (the **child styles**).

1. **With Pages 2–3 of `booklet_working.indd` visible, place the insertion point in the first bulleted paragraph where the font is still missing.**

   This text is formatted with the Category Bullets style. The plus sign to the right of the style name indicates that some formatting other than the style definition has been applied to the selected paragraph — called a **local formatting override**.

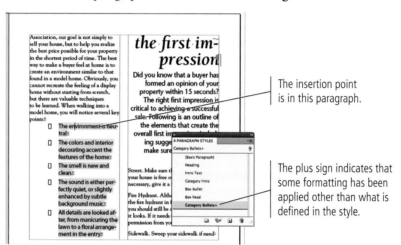

The insertion point is in this paragraph.

The plus sign indicates that some formatting has been applied other than what is defined in the style.

Note:

Local formatting overrides are common when you import text from a client-supplied Microsoft Word file.

2. **Control/right-click the Category Bullets style in the Paragraph Styles panel and choose Edit "Category Bullets" from the contextual menu.**

3. **In the General options pane, choose Category Intro in the Based On menu.**

   When you redefine an existing style to be based on another style, InDesign tries to maintain the original formatting of the style that you are editing instead of the one it is being based on. In the Style Settings area, you can see the style will be Category Intro +. Everything after the plus sign is different than the style defined in the Based On menu.

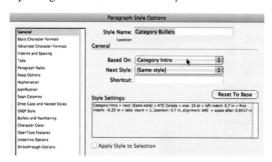

4. **Click the Reset To Base button above the Style Settings area.**

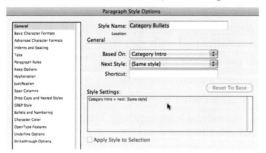

5. **In the Indents and Spacing options, change the Space Before field to 0.05″ and click OK.**

The missing-font problem is solved because the Category Bullet style now calls for the same font as its parent (ATC Pine Normal).

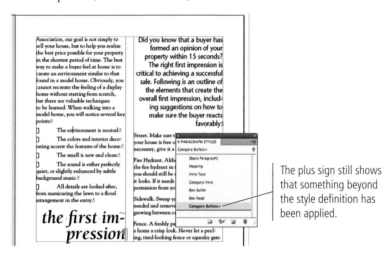

The plus sign still shows that something beyond the style definition has been applied.

6. **With the insertion point anywhere in the selected text, choose Edit>Select All to select the entire story.**

You can clear overrides for any selected text, whether for a single character or an entire story. In this case, all overrides were created in the original Microsoft Word file; rather than manually clearing overrides in each paragraph, you can simply select the entire story and clear all overrides at once.

7. **At the bottom of the Paragraph Styles panel, click the Clear Overrides button.**

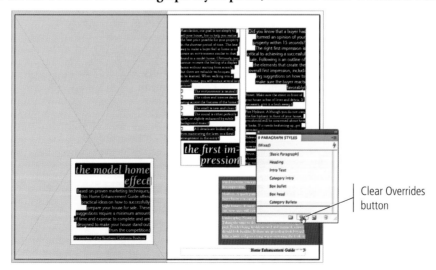

Clear Overrides button

By clearing overrides, the bullet characters are removed from the Category Bullets style. You will add these back in later when you edit the style definition again.

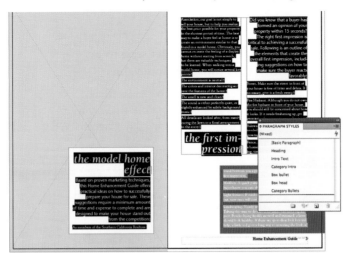

8. **Deselect all text, navigate to Page 5, and place the insertion point in the first paragraph with the missing font highlight.**

   This text is formatted with the Box Head style.

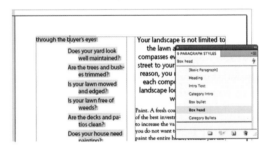

9. **Using the same method as in Steps 2–5, edit the Box Head style to be based on the Heading style with the following modifications:**

Basic Character Formats	**Size: 15 pt**
	Leading: Auto
Indents and Spacing	**Paragraph Alignment: Left**

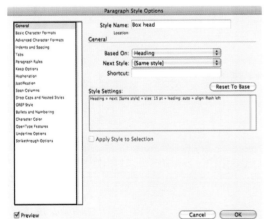

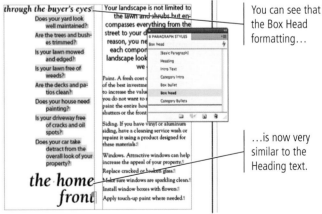

You can see that the Box Head formatting…

…is now very similar to the Heading text.

10. **Place the insertion point in the first bulleted paragraph with the missing font highlight.**

    This text is formatted with the Box Bullet style.

11. **Using the same method from Steps 2–5, change the Box Bullet style to be based on the Category Intro text style with a 0.05″ Space Before value.**

    You could actually base this style on the Category Bullet style, but we try to avoid too many levels of nested styles. More levels of nesting means greater complexity when you need to make changes.

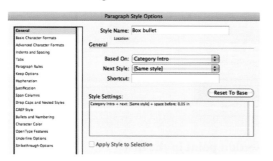

12. **Save the file and continue to the next exercise.**

 ## Define Bullets and Numbering Options

By changing the style definitions in the previous exercise, you removed the bullets from two different types of lists (the category bulleted lists and the box bulleted lists); these bullets need to be replaced. You also need to convert the Category Intro text paragraphs to bullets to create improved visual separation.

You could manually type the bullet characters at the beginning of each line, but it's much easier and more efficient to use the Bullets and Numbering formatting options.

1. **With booklet_working.indd open, Control/right-click the Category Intro style in the Paragraph Styles panel and choose Edit "Category Intro" from the contextual menu.**

2. **In the Paragraph Style Options dialog box, display the Bullets and Numbering pane.**

3. **In the List Type menu, choose Bullets.**

    By default, you can apply the Bullets or Numbers type of list.

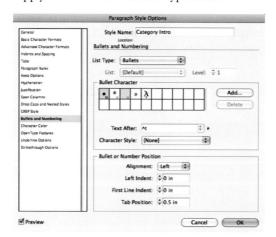

Note:

You can also define custom lists by choosing Type>Bulleted & Numbered Lists>Define Lists. If you've defined a custom list type, it will be available in the List Type menu of the Paragraph Style Options dialog box.

4. Click the Add button to the right of the Bullet Character list.

The Add Bullets dialog box allows you to choose a character for the bullet. This character defaults to the same font used in the style, but you can choose any font and font style from the menus at the bottom of the dialog box.

5. In the Add Bullets dialog box, find and select the tilde (~) character.

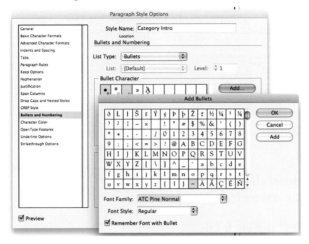

6. Make sure the Remember Font with Bullet option is checked, and then click OK to return to the Paragraph Style Options dialog box.

The selected bullet character is added to the list of available bullet characters. If you don't check the Remember Font with Bullet option, the character will be applied in whatever font is used for the style.

7. Click the tilde character in the grid of available characters to select it.

8. Leave the Text After field at the default (^t, which is the code for a Tab character).

9. In the Bullet or Number Position area, change the Left Indent value to 0.125", and change the First Line Indent value to –0.125". Leave the Tab Position value at its default.

This negative first-line indent is called a **hanging indent**.

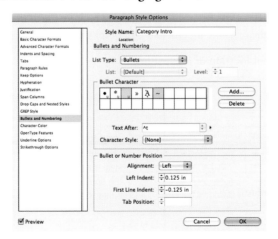

Note:

The Remember Font with Bullet option can be important if you use extended characters or decorative or dingbat fonts as bullet characters. If you select the solid square character (■) in the Zapf Dingbats font, for example, changing to a different font would show the letter "n" as the bullet character.

Note:

Changing these fields also changes the same fields in the Indents and Spacing options.

10. **Click OK to change the style definition and return to the layout.**

Because the two bullet styles are based on the Category Intro style, virtually all text in the layout (except the heading and intro text) now has the initial tilde character and the hanging indent you just defined.

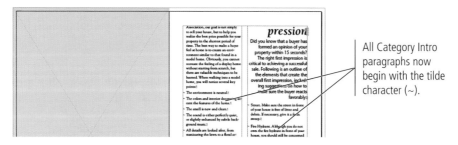

All Category Intro paragraphs now begin with the tilde character (~).

11. **Control/right-click the Category Bullets style and choose Edit "Category Bullets" in the contextual menu.**

12. **In the Bullets and Numbering options, click the Double-Chevron (») character from the default Bullet Character list.**

13. **Change the Left Indent field to 0.25″ and click OK.**

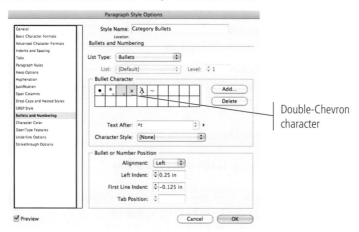

Double-Chevron character

14. **Navigate through the layout to review the effect of changing the character and indent options for the secondary bulleted list.**

The Category Bullet paragraphs are indented 0.125″ from the column edge because the negative first-line indent was not equal to the first-line indent value. In other words:

Left Indent + First-Line Indent = Indent location of the first line

$0.25 + (-0.125) = 0.125$

Text formatted with the Category Bullet style now starts with the double-chevron bullet character.

15. Edit the Box Bullet style to use a check box-like character as the bullet character, with a 0.2″ left indent and –0.2″ first-line indent.

For the bullet character, try the "o" character from the Zapf Dingbats (Macintosh) or Wingdings (Windows) fonts. If you don't have one of these fonts, use any character from any font that you think works well as a bullet character.

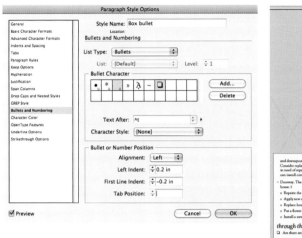

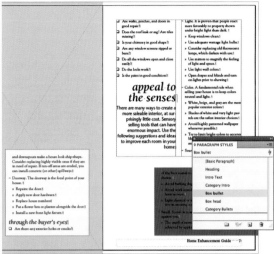

16. Save the file and continue to the next exercise.

The Glyphs Panel in Depth

INDESIGN FOUNDATIONS

ASCII is a text-based code that defines characters with a numeric value between 001 and 256. The standard alphabet and punctuation characters are mapped from 001 to 128. **Extended ASCII characters** are those with ASCII numbers higher than 128; these include symbols (bullets, copyright symbols, etc.) and some special characters (en dashes, accent marks, etc.). Some of the more common extended characters can be accessed in the Type>Insert submenus.

OpenType fonts can store more than 65,000 **glyphs** (characters) in a single font — far beyond what you could access with a keyboard (even including combinations of the different modifier keys). The large glyph storage capacity means that a single OpenType font can replace the multiple separate "Expert" fonts that contain variations of fonts (Minion Swash, for example, is no longer necessary when you can access the Swashes subset of the Minion Pro font).

Unicode fonts include two-bit characters that are common in some foreign language typesetting (e.g., Cyrillic, Japanese, and other non-Roman or pictographic fonts).

The Glyphs panel (Window>Type & Tables>Glyphs or Type>Glyphs) provides access to individual glyphs in a font, including basic characters in regular fonts, extended ASCII and OpenType character sets, and even pictographic characters in Unicode fonts.

Using the Glyphs panel is simple: make sure the insertion point is flashing where you want a character to appear, and then double-click the character you want to place. You can view the character set for any font by simply changing the menu at the bottom of the panel. By default, the panel shows the entire font, but you can show only specific character sets using the Show menu.

Access recently used glyphs from different fonts

Show all characters of a font or display only specific types of characters

Show the characters of a different font

Change to a different variation of the selected font

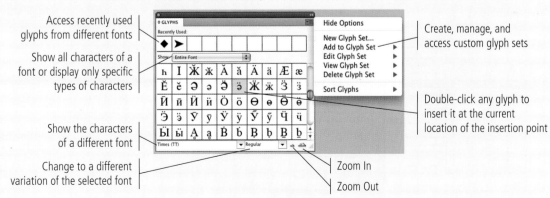

Create, manage, and access custom glyph sets

Double-click any glyph to insert it at the current location of the insertion point

Zoom In

Zoom Out

In the completed booklet, each spread will have a single section heading followed by a section intro on the left page. The main and secondary bullet points will all appear on the right side, and the "through the buyer's eyes" bullets will appear in the colored frame. Rather than manually placing page and frame breaks, you can use styles and paragraph formatting options to automatically place text in the correct frames on the correct sides of the spread.

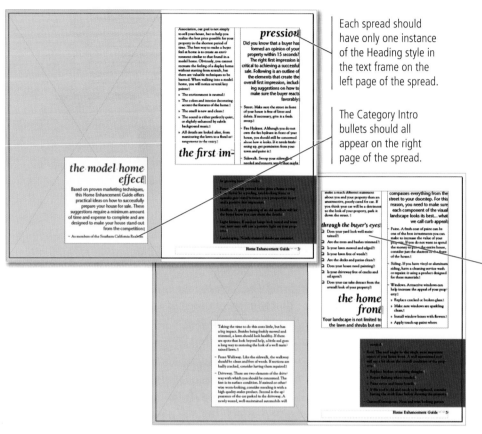

Each spread should have only one instance of the Heading style in the text frame on the left page of the spread.

The Category Intro bullets should all appear on the right page of the spread.

The callout heading and bullets should be placed within the colored frame on the right page of the spread.

1. **With the Page 2–3 spread of booklet_working.indd visible, Control/right-click Heading in the Paragraph Styles panel and choose Edit "Heading" from the contextual menu.**

2. **Display the Keep Options pane. In the Start Paragraph menu, choose On Next Even Page. Click OK to change the style definition.**

   Each section heading should appear on the left page of a spread, and left-facing pages are even-numbered.

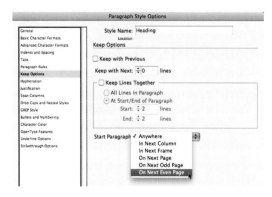

3. Navigate through the layout and review the results.

When you get to Page 6, you might notice a problem — the "through the buyer's eyes" heading has moved to the wrong place. Because the Box Head style is based on the Heading style, it adopts the Start Paragraph option that requires this heading to appear on the next even-numbered page. It should move to the green frame on the right side of the spread, which requires a different Start Paragraph option.

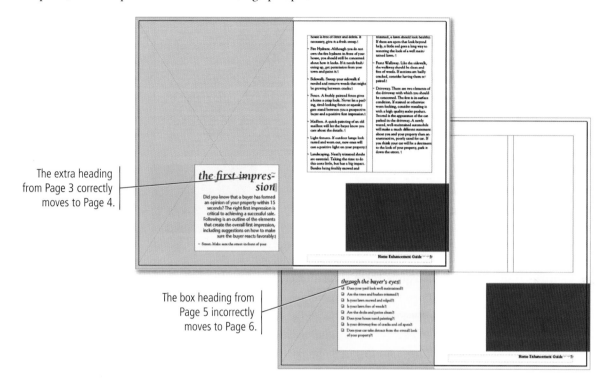

The extra heading from Page 3 correctly moves to Page 4.

The box heading from Page 5 incorrectly moves to Page 6.

4. Control/right-click the Box Head style and choose Edit "Box Head" from the contextual menu. In the Keep Options pane, choose In Next Frame in the Start Paragraph menu and click OK to redefine the style.

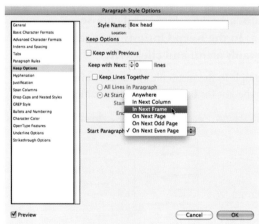

5. **Navigate through the layout and review the results.**

   The even-numbered pages show another problem with the current formatting. The left page of the spread should contain only the heading and the intro text; you need to force all remaining text onto the right side of the spread. You could do this manually, but a new style can handle the formatting for you.

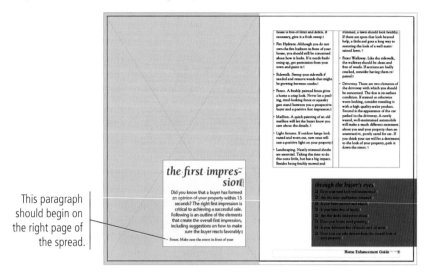

This paragraph should begin on the right page of the spread.

6. **Control/right-click the Category Intro style and choose Duplicate Style from the contextual menu.**

7. **Change the Style Name field to Category Intro - First and choose Category Intro in the Based On menu. In the Keep Options pane, choose In Next Column from the Start Paragraph menu and click OK.**

   The In Next Column option moves a paragraph to the next column in the same frame or to the next frame if the text is already in the last (or only) column of a frame.

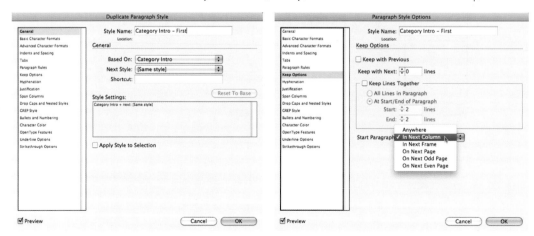

8. **Place the insertion point in the first Category Intro paragraph on Page 4 (the first paragraph with a tilde character as the bullet character), and then click the Category Intro – First style in the Paragraph Styles panel.**

As soon as you apply the style, the paragraph automatically moves to the next available frame in the text chain.

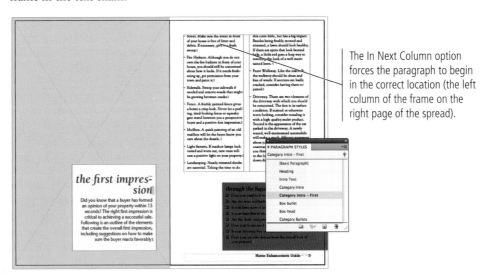

The In Next Column option forces the paragraph to begin in the correct location (the left column of the frame on the right page of the spread).

9. **Navigate through the layout and apply the Category Intro – First style to the third paragraph on each spread.**

10. **Navigate through the layout and review your work.**

Page 7 highlights another potential issue with the position of text in the layout. Despite all the available automation and productivity options, some things simply must be resolved manually. There is no way to tell InDesign, for example, "If only one secondary bullet fits in the first column, move the preceding primary bullet to the next column." Resolutions to issues such as these, which add polish to a professional layout, must be determined and applied manually.

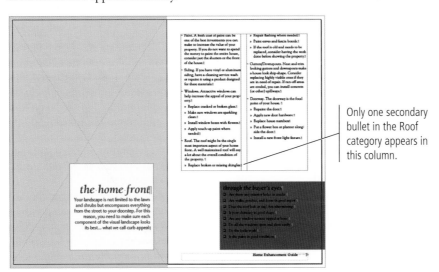

Only one secondary bullet in the Roof category appears in this column.

11. **On Page 7, place the insertion point in the intro paragraph of the Roof category, and then apply the Category Intro – First style.**

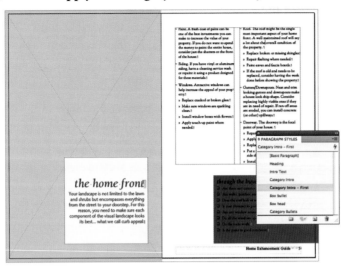

12. **Navigate through the layout and apply the same change as necessary.**

   We applied the formatting on Pages 11 and 15.

13. **Navigate through the layout and review your work.**

   Page 4 shows a problem with unbalanced columns, in this case resulting from a few lines of one paragraph remaining at the bottom of the left column.

   In addition to determining where a paragraph can start, the Keep options are also used to control **orphans** (single lines of a paragraph at the end of a column) and **widows** (single lines of a paragraph at the top of a column, or a very short last line of a paragraph). Typography conventions suggest that at least two lines of a paragraph should be kept together at the beginning and end of a column or frame. (Headings at the end of a frame or column are also sometimes considered orphans.)

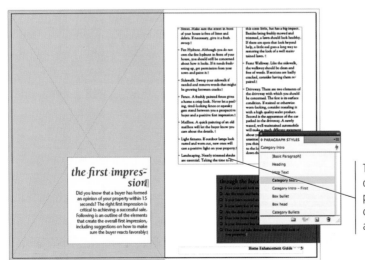

Two lines is not technically an orphan, but breaking this paragraph across the columns creates an unbalanced appearance on the page.

Note:

These same options can be applied to any specific paragraph by choosing Keep Options from the Paragraph panel Options menu.

14. **Control/right click Category Intro in the Paragraph Styles panel and choose Edit "Category Intro" from the contextual menu. In the Keep Options pane, activate the Keep Lines Together check box and choose the All Lines in Paragraph option. Click OK to change the style definition.**

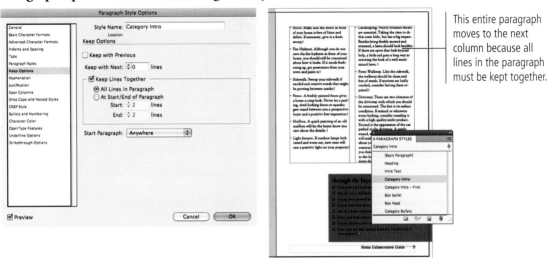

This entire paragraph moves to the next column because all lines in the paragraph must be kept together.

15. **Save the file and continue to the next exercise.**

 ## CONTROL AUTOMATIC HYPHENATION

Automatic hyphenation is another key to professional page layout. Typographic conventions recommend no hyphenation in headings, no more than three hyphens in a row, and at least three characters before or after a hyphen. Some designers follow stricter rules, such as not hyphenating proper nouns; others prefer no hyphenation at all. Whatever your requirements, you can control the hyphenation of any paragraph either locally or in a style definition.

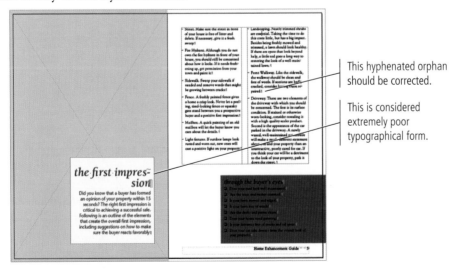

This hyphenated orphan should be corrected.

This is considered extremely poor typographical form.

1. **With the Page 4–5 spread of booklet_working.indd visible, Control/right-click the Heading style and choose Edit "Heading" from the contextual menu.**

2. **In the Paragraph Style Options dialog box, show the Hyphenation options.**

3. **Uncheck the Hyphenate option and click OK.**

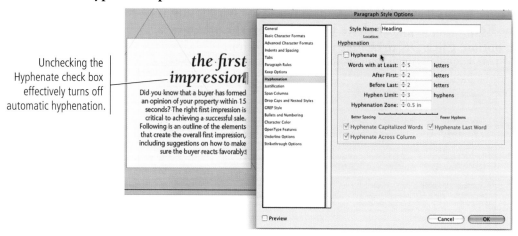

Unchecking the Hyphenate check box effectively turns off automatic hyphenation.

4. **Control/right-click the Category Intro style and choose Edit "Category Intro" from the contextual menu.**

Remember, most of the other styles are based on the Category Intro style; by changing the hyphenation options for this style, you also change the options for all styles based on it.

5. **In the Hyphenation options, change the After First and Before Last fields to 3. Click OK to change the style definition.**

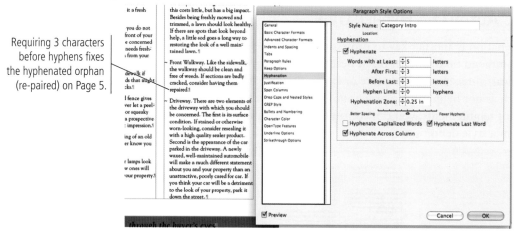

Requiring 3 characters before hyphens fixes the hyphenated orphan (re-paired) on Page 5.

The Hyphenation options allow you to control the way InDesign hyphenates text. (If the Hyphenate box is unchecked, InDesign will not hyphenate text in the paragraph.)

- **Words With At Least _ Letters** defines the minimum number of characters that must exist in a hyphenated word.

- **After First _ Letters** and **Before Last _ Letters** define the minimum number of characters that must appear before and after a hyphen.

- **Hyphen Limit** defines the maximum number of hyphens that can appear on consecutive lines. (Remember, you are defining the limit here, so zero means there is no limit — allowing unlimited hyphens.)

- **Hyphenation Zone** defines the amount of white space allowed at the end of a line of unjustified text before hyphenation begins.

- If **Hyphenate Capitalized Words** is checked, capitalized words (proper nouns) can be hyphenated.

- If **Hyphenate Last Word** is checked, the last word in a paragraph can be hyphenated.

- If **Hyphenate Across Column** is checked, the last word in a column or frame can be hyphenated.

Note:

These options can be applied to any specific paragraph by choosing Hyphenation from the Paragraph panel Options menu.

6. **Navigate to Page 2. Place the insertion point before the word "home" in the heading and press Shift-Return/Enter.**

This character, called a **soft return**, forces a new line without starting a new paragraph.

As with balancing columns, there is some subjective element to balancing lines of copy — especially headlines.

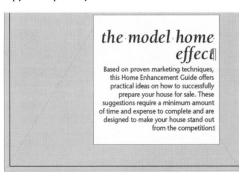
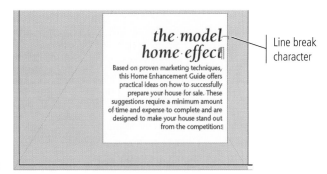

Line break character

7. **Navigate through the layout and add soft returns as necessary to balance the two-line headings.**

We adjusted the headings on Pages 8, 10, and 14.

8. **Save the file and continue to the next exercise.**

Paragraph Composition Options

INDESIGN FOUNDATIONS

InDesign offers two options for controlling the overall flow of text (called **composition**) within a paragraph: **Adobe Paragraph Composer** (the default) and **Adobe Single-line Composer**. Both methods create breaks based on the applied hyphenation and justification options for a paragraph.

You can change the composition method for an individual paragraph in the Paragraph panel Options menu or the Justification dialog box; or you can change the composition method for a paragraph style in the Justification pane of the Paragraph Style Options dialog box.

The Adobe Paragraph Composer evaluates the entire paragraph as a unit; changing one line of a paragraph might alter other lines in the paragraph (including earlier lines) to create what the software defines as the "best" overall paragraph composition. For example, adding a manual line break on Line 6 to eliminate a hyphen might also cause Lines 2 through 5 to reflow if InDesign determines the shift will create a better overall paragraph. (Although primarily a matter of personal preference, Adobe Paragraph Composer can be annoying for anyone who wants tight or exact control over the text in a layout.)

The Adobe Single-line Composer is a better choice if you prefer to control your own text flow. Using Single-line Composer, adding a manual line break on Line 6 (for example) will not affect preceding lines in the paragraph.

Change the composer for a paragraph style in the Justification options for that style.

Change the composer for selected paragraphs in the Paragraph panel Options menu.

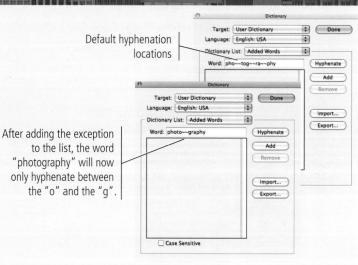

INDESIGN FOUNDATIONS

InDesign applies automatic hyphenation based on the defined language dictionary. You can override the hyphenation as defined in the dictionary by choosing Edit>Spelling>Dictionary.

Default hyphenation locations

If you highlight a word before opening the dictionary, it automatically appears in the Word field. Clicking the Hyphenate button shows the possible hyphenation locations as defined in the dictionary. You can override the automatic hyphenation by adding or deleting the consecutive tilde characters in the Word field. When you change the hyphenation of a word, you have to click the Add button to add the new hyphenation scheme to the dictionary.

After adding the exception to the list, the word "photography" will now only hyphenate between the "o" and the "g".

REDEFINE STYLES BASED ON LOCAL FORMATTING OVERRIDES

You might have noticed one final formatting problem when you reviewed the current layout: the black text in the callout boxes (on the right-facing pages) is very difficult to read because the boxes have a dark fill color. Although you are going to change the box color on each spread, you are going to use other dark colors that still make the black text difficult to read.

Rather than simply changing the style definitions for text in the colored boxes, you are going to experiment with different options within the layout. When you're satisfied with the results, you're going to use local formatting to redefine the applied styles.

1. **With booklet_working.indd open, navigate to the green box on Page 5.**

2. **Select the entire first paragraph in the green box (through the buyer's eyes).**

3. **Using the Swatches panel, change the text color to 10% of the dark green swatch.**

4. **Move the insertion point to the end of the paragraph and review the results.**

   The light tint of the green swatch makes the text far more readable. However, in the next exercise you're going to change the box colors to match the respective images on the left-facing page of each spread. Rather than using a light green tint — which won't match the end result on every spread — you can use the Paper swatch to knock out the text from any background color.

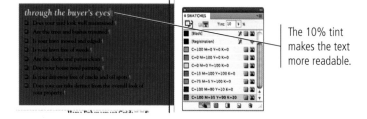

The 10% tint makes the text more readable.

5. **Select the paragraph again and change the text color to Paper, then move the insertion point to any location within the reformatted heading.**

6. **Open the Paragraph Styles panel Options menu and choose Redefine Style.**

This option makes it easy to experiment with formatting within the context of the layout, and then change a style definition to match what you created with local formatting.

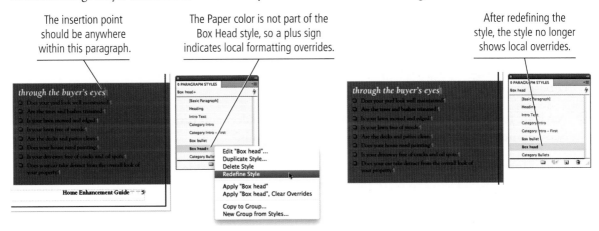

The insertion point should be anywhere within this paragraph.

The Paper color is not part of the Box Head style, so a plus sign indicates local formatting overrides.

After redefining the style, the style no longer shows local overrides.

7. **Select one of the bulleted paragraphs (below the heading) and change the text color to Paper.**

By default, changing the color of text in the paragraph also changes the color of the applied bullet.

8. **With the same paragraph selected, open the Paragraph Styles panel Options menu and choose Redefine Style.**

Because more than one Box Bullet paragraph appears on this page, you can see how redefining the style based on local formatting affects all text where that style is applied.

Redefining the style changes all text formatted with that style.

9. **With the same paragraph selected, change the font to ATC Oak Normal, then redefine the Box Bullet style to match the local formatting override.**

White text on a colored background is called **knockout text**. Anything "white" is actually removed from the colored areas because you typically don't print white ink. Knocking out small text — especially a serif font, such as this 9.5-pt ATC Pine Normal text — can cause output problems. To help minimize potential problems on press, you are changing the formatting for the small knockout text to a sans-serif font.

Changing the font doesn't affect the bullet character; that character is defined only in the style's Bullets and Numbering options.

10. **Save the file and continue to the next exercise.**

PLACE IMAGES INTO MASTER FRAMES

For all intents and purposes the booklet text is finished. The next task is to place the images. Because you placed the graphics frame on the master page layout, you can simply place most of these images into the existing frames without any additional intervention.

1. **With booklet_working.indd open, navigate to Page 2 of the layout and choose File>Place.**

2. **Navigate to the file front.tif (in your WIP>Realtors folder) and turn off the Show Import Options and Replace Selected Item options.**

3. **Click Open to load the image into the cursor, and then click inside the graphics frame on Page 2 to place the image.**

   As with placing text into the master text frame, you don't have to override the master page to place the image into the graphics frame. InDesign assumes that clicking inside an existing frame — even one from the master page — means you want to place the image inside that frame. Once you place the image, the frame is automatically detached from the master page.

4. **Place the remaining images on the left page of each layout spread:**

Page 4	**doorway_outside.tif**
Page 6	**doorway_inside.tif**
Page 8	**candles.tif**
Page 10	**flowers.tif**
Page 12	**bathroom.tif**
Page 14	**storage.tif**

   Use whatever method you prefer to place these images. If you use the Mini Bridge panel, simply click and drag an image into the layout and then click the frame where you want to place the image. Because the frames are not technically on the layout pages until you place the images, you can't simply release the mouse button over the frame to place the images; you have to intentionally click to place the images and detach the frames from the master layout.

5. **Navigate to Page 3 of the layout. Using the Selection tool, select and delete the green-filled text frame.**

6. **Place the file `squares.tif` (in the WIP>Realtors folder) onto Page 3 and position the file as shown in the following image.**

7. **Deselect the squares.tif image.**

The page number is
obscured by the white
area of the placed image.

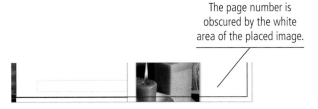

8. **Command/Control-Shift-click the text frame at the bottom of the page.**

Command/Control-Shift-clicking a master page object allows you to detach a single master page item without detaching the entire page from the master page.

Command/Control-Shift-
click to detach the object
from the master layout.

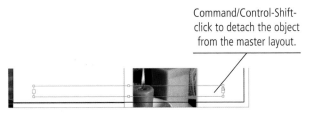

9. **With the text frame selected, choose Object>Arrange>Bring to Front. Delete the words "Home Enhancement Guide" from the text frame, leaving only the page number.**

10. **Save the file and continue to the next exercise.**

Using similar or complementary colors on each page of a spread is one way to help unify a design. When you created the master pages, you applied a dark green fill to the sidebar text box. Now that the images are in place, it would be better to use colors from each spread's image on the associated sidebar box. The Eyedropper tool, which you can use to pull or **sample** colors from existing objects, makes it easy to apply image colors to native object fills.

1. **With `booklet_working.indd` open, navigate to the Page 4–5 spread.**

2. **Click the pasteboard area with the Selection tool to make sure nothing is selected in the file.**

3. **Choose the Eyedropper tool. Using whatever method you prefer, change the Stroke color to None and then make sure the Fill color is the active attribute.**

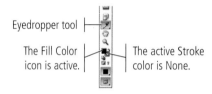

Eyedropper tool

The Fill Color icon is active.

The active Stroke color is None.

4. **Click a dark green area in the image on the left side of the spread.**

Empty Eyedropper tool cursor

We sampled this color from the image.

5. **Move the filled Eyedropper cursor over the green-filled text frame and click to change the frame's fill color to the sampled color from Step 4.**

Filled Eyedropper tool cursor

Click inside the frame to fill it with the sampled color.

6. **Navigate to the Page 6–7 spread. Press Option/Alt to clear the Eyedropper tool, and then click a dark brown area in the image on the left side of the spread.**

As long as the Eyedropper tool remains selected, it retains the last-sampled color so you can continuously apply the sampled attributes to multiple objects. Pressing Option/Alt allows you to sample a new color.

Press Option/Alt to sample a new color.

7. **Click the green-filled text frame on Page 7 to fill it with the new sampled color.**

Click inside the frame to fill it with the new sampled color.

8. **Repeat the process from Steps 6–7 to change the box color on each spread of the layout.**

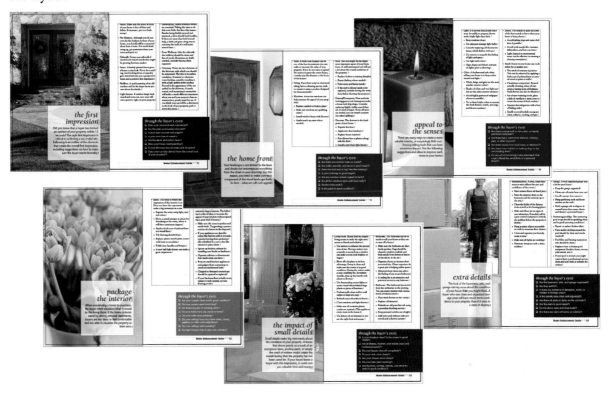

9. **Save the file as `booklet_final.indd`, and then continue to the final stage of the project.**

Stage 3 Outputting Variations of Files

The final stage of this project requires creating two versions of final output:

- A desktop proof for your client, showing the spreads as they will appear in the final bound booklet

- A low-resolution PDF file that prospective clients can download from the organization's Web site

InDesign includes a number of tools that make it easy to create both versions without destroying the integrity of the original layout file.

CREATE A FOLDING DUMMY

When a page is printed, it is typically output on a sheet larger than the job's trim size. Multiple pages are often **imposed** (arranged) on a single press sheet, and the printed pieces are later cut from the press sheet and trimmed to their final size. In some cases, entirely different jobs can be **ganged** (combined) together to make the best use of available space on the press sheet.

Multi-page documents that use facing pages have special output requirements; understanding these requirements means you will also be able to see how your design might be affected by output processes after the file leaves your desk. When multiple-page books and booklets are produced, they are not printed as individual pages. Instead, they are printed in signatures of eight, sixteen, or more pages at a time. A **signature** consists of multiple pages of a document, all printed on the same press sheet, which is later folded and cut to the final trim size. Each signature is composed of

Note:

*A **reader's spread** is a set of two pages that appear next to each other in a printed document — Page 2 faces Page 3, and so on.*

*A **printer's spread** refers to the way pages align on a press sheet so, after a document is folded and cut, the reader's spreads will be in the correct locations.*

Understanding Imposition

INDESIGN FOUNDATIONS

If you fold a piece of paper in half twice, number the pages, and then unfold the paper, you will see the basic imposition for an eight-page signature.

If you look at your folded piece of paper, you can see that the tops of all the pages are folded together. If elements bleed to the top of a page, given the inaccuracy of folding machines (±0.03125″), that ink would appear on the edge of the page it abutted on the signature (for example, see Pages 12 and 13 in the following illustration).

The pages of a signature must be cut apart at the top, which requires at least 1/8″ at the top of the page for the trim. The outside edge of half the pages also must be cut apart (this is called a **face trim**) so the pages of the finished piece can be turned. This face trim also requires 1/8″ around the page edge. That trim would shorten an 8.5 × 11″ book to 8.375 × 10.875″. This shorter size might be fine, but it could also ruin a design and layout. There's a better solution.

On the press-sheet layout, space is added between the tops of the printer's spreads to allow room for bleed and cutting apart the pages. This separation is probably all that's required for a 16-page saddle-stitched booklet printed on a 70# text-weight paper. If you use a heavier paper (for example, a 100# coated sheet for an annual report), or if

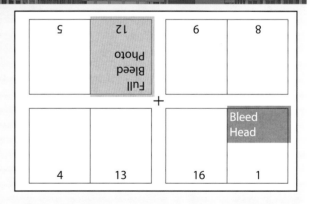

you have more than one 16-page signature, you need to allow room for **creep**, which is the progressive extension of interior pages of the folded signature beyond the trim edge of the outside pages.

If you have questions about folds or imposition, you should always call your service provider. Somebody there will be able to advise you on the best course to take. In most cases, these issues will be handled entirely by the service provider, often using software specifically designed for the prepress workflow. If you try to do too much, you might cause them extra work (and yourself extra expense).

two flats. (The term **flat** is a relic of the days when film was manually stripped together on a light table; it is still sometimes used to describe one side of one signature.)

Layouts are designed in reader's spreads, but arranged into printer's spreads on the printing plate. (**Imposition** refers to the arrangement of a document's pages on a printing plate to produce the final product.)

1. **Fold a piece of paper in half lengthwise, and then in half widthwise.**

2. **While the paper is still folded, write the sequential page numbers 1 through 8 on the folded sections.**

3. **Unfold it and you will see the printer's spreads for an eight-page document.**

   The dummy unfolds to show how an eight-page signature is laid out. Page 8 and Page 1 create a single printer's spread.

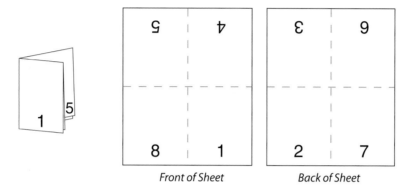

Front of Sheet   Back of Sheet

 PRINT A BOOKLET PROOF

You probably don't want to (and really, you shouldn't have to) think about creating full impositions for a press. At times, however, you might want to print proofs in printer's spreads to show clients. You could work through a complicated manual process of rearranging pages, but the InDesign Print Booklet command is far easier — and it's non-destructive.

1. **With `booklet_final.indd` open, choose File>Print Booklet.**

   This dialog box shows only the output options related to printing printer's spreads. These options are set; you can't directly change the printer that will be used for output.

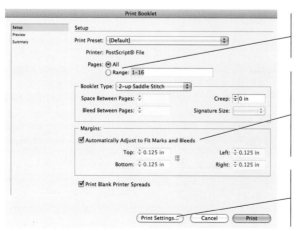

Use these options to output the entire file as a booklet, or output only a specific range of pages.

Check this box to allow InDesign to automatically calculate the margins to accommodate bleeds (as defined in the Document Setup dialog box) and printer's marks (as applied in the Print dialog box).

Click this button to access the Print dialog box, change the printer-specific settings, and define printer's marks.

Note:

In printer's spreads, the sum of pairs of page numbers always totals the number of pages in the signature, plus 1. For example, in a 16-page signature, Page 4 faces Page 13, Page 16 faces Page 1, and so on.

If a saddle-stitched (stapled) book is made up of multiple signatures, the page numbers on printer's spreads equal the total number of pages in the publication, plus 1. For example, a saddle-stitched booklet is 32 pages, made up of two 16-page signatures. The page numbers on each printer's spread total 33: Page 16 faces Page 17, Page 22 faces Page 11, and so on.

2. **In the Setup pane of the dialog box, make sure 2-up Saddle Stitch is selected in the Booklet Type menu.**

   In the Booklet Type menu, you can choose what kind of imposition to create.

   - **2-up Saddle Stitch** creates two-page printer's spreads from the entire layout or selected page range. If the layout doesn't contain enough pages to create the necessary printer's spreads, InDesign automatically adds blank pages at the end of the layout.

   - **2-up Perfect Bound** creates two-page printer's spreads that fit within the specified signature size (4, 8, 12, 16, or 32 pages). If the number of layout pages to be imposed is not divisible by the selected signature size, InDesign adds blank pages as needed at the end of the finished document.

   - **Consecutive** creates a two-, three-, or four-page imposition appropriate for a foldout brochure.

   You can also define settings to adjust for imposition issues related to printer's spreads versus reader's spreads.

   - **Space Between Pages** defines the gap between pages in the printer's spread. This option is available for all but saddle-stitched booklet types.

   - **Bleed Between Pages** defines the amount that page elements can bleed into the space between pages in a printer's spread (from 0 to half the defined space between the pages) for perfect-bound impositions.

   - **Creep** defines the amount of space necessary to accommodate paper thickness and folding on each signature.

   - **Signature Size** defines the number of pages in each signature for perfect-bound impositions.

   - **Print Blank Printer Spreads** determines whether any blank pages added to a signature will be printed.

3. **Click the Print Settings button.**

4. **In the resulting Print dialog box, choose the printer and PPD you will use to output the booklet.**

5. **In the Setup options, choose US Letter in the Paper Size menu and choose landscape orientation.**

6. **In the Marks and Bleed options, uncheck the All Printer's Marks and Use Document Bleed Settings options, and change all four Bleed values to 0".**

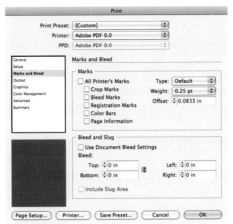

Note:

If you have a printer with tabloid-paper capability, you could output the file with marks and bleeds, and then trim the proof to size. Doing so would eliminate any issue with the margins required by some desktop printers, which would prevent the pages from printing the outer edges of the layout.

7. **Click OK to return to the Print Booklet dialog box.**

8. **In the Print Booklet dialog box, uncheck the Automatically Adjust to Fit Marks and Bleeds option. With the Chain icon checked, change all four Margin fields to 0".**

   You're only printing a client proof on letter-size paper, so you do not need bleeds or printer's marks.

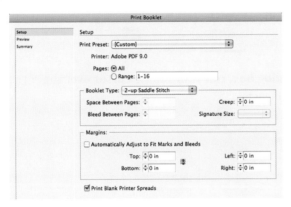

9. **Click Preview in the list of options.**

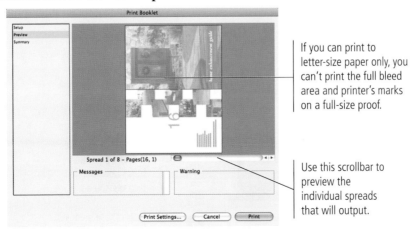

If you can print to letter-size paper only, you can't print the full bleed area and printer's marks on a full-size proof.

Use this scrollbar to preview the individual spreads that will output.

10. **Click Print.**

11. **When the file is finished spooling to the printer, continue to the next exercise.**

CREATE A PDF WITH PAGE TRANSITIONS

In addition to the printed job, your client requested a low-resolution PDF file that can be posted on the organization's Web site. To add interest to the digital version, you are going to add interactive page transitions that affect the way new pages appear when users navigate through the PDF file.

1. **With booklet_final.indd open, open the Page Transitions panel (Window>Interactive>Page Transitions).**

2. **In the Pages panel, double-click the Page 2-3 spread numbers (below the page icons) to select the entire spread.**

   Remember, there can be a difference between the active and selected pages. Double-clicking the targeted page or spread ensures that the spread you want is the one selected.

3. **Open the Page Transitions panel Options menu and select Choose.**

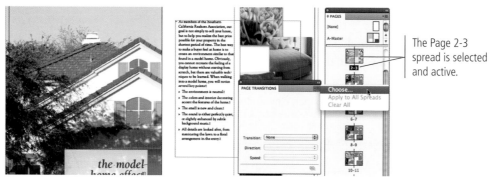

The Page 2-3 spread is selected and active.

4. **In the resulting Page Transitions dialog box, roll your mouse cursor over the icons to preview the general effect of each.**

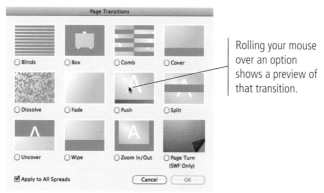

Rolling your mouse over an option shows a preview of that transition.

5. **Make sure the Apply to All Spreads option is unchecked, then activate the Comb radio button and click OK.**

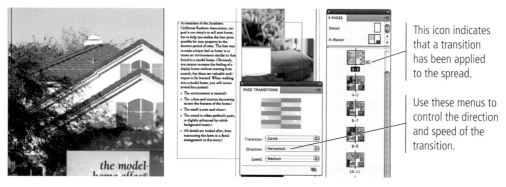

This icon indicates that a transition has been applied to the spread.

Use these menus to control the direction and speed of the transition.

6. **Double-click the Page 4-5 spread numbers in the Pages panel. In the Page Transitions panel, choose Wipe in the Transition menu.**

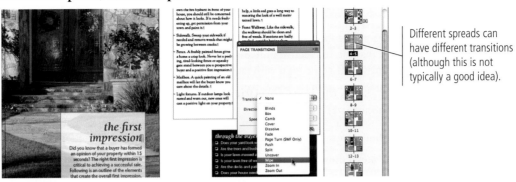

Different spreads can have different transitions (although this is not typically a good idea).

7. **With the Page 4-5 spread selected, click the Apply to All Spreads button at the bottom of the Page Transitions panel.**

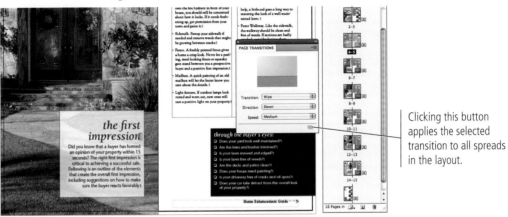

Clicking this button applies the selected transition to all spreads in the layout.

8. **Choose File>Export. Choose Adobe PDF (Interactive) in the Format/Save As Type menu and then click Save.**

9. **Review the options in the resulting Export to Interactive PDF dialog box.**

The Adobe PDF (Interactive) option opens a simplified dialog box with only the settings that are relevant to PDF files intended for digital distribution.

- **Pages** determines which pages will be included in the resulting PDF file. It is important to understand that the Interactive PDF export treats every *spread* as a page in the resulting file. If you design with facing pages, as in this document, every facing-page spread in the Pages panel will result in a single page in the PDF file.

- **View After Exporting**, when active, automatically opens the file in your system's default PDF application.

- **Embed Page Thumbnails** creates a thumbnail preview for every page that is exported.

- **Create Acrobat Layers** maintains any InDesign layers as Acrobat layers in the resulting PDF file. (If you have Acrobat 6.0 or later, you can access those layers to create multiple versions from the same PDF file.)

- **Create Tagged PDF** automatically tags elements in the story based on a subset of the Acrobat tags that InDesign supports (basic text formatting, lists, tables, etc.).

- **View** determines the default view percentage of the exported PDF file. You can cause the file to open at actual size, fit the page into the Acrobat window based on a number of dimensions, or choose a specific percentage (25, 50, 75, or 100).

- **Layout** determines how spreads appear in the resulting PDF file.
    - The **Single Page** options export each spread separately.
    - The **Continuous** options export files so that users can scroll through the document and view parts of successive pages at the same time. Using the non-continuous options, scrolling has the same effect as turning a page; you can't view successive spreads at once.
    - The **Two-Up Facing** options exports two spreads side-by-side.
    - The **Two-Up Cover Page** options export the first spread as a single page, and then the remaining spreads two at a time side-by-side. This allows the pages to appear as they would in a book, with even-numbered pages on the left and odd-numbered pages on the right.

- **Presentation Opens In Full Screen Mode** opens the resulting PDF without showing Acrobat's menus or panels. You can then use the Flip Pages Every field to automatically change pages after a defined interval.

- **Page Transitions** defaults to the From Document option, which maintains the settings that you define in the Transitions panel. You can choose None to export the PDF without page transitions, or choose one of the available methods in the attached menu to override any settings that exist in the document.

- **Buttons and Media** options can be used to include movies, sounds, and buttons that are created or placed in the InDesign file. If you choose Appearance Only, the PDF will show only the static version of those interactive objects.

- **Compression** determines how images in the resulting PDF are managed to reduce file size for digital distribution. JPEG (Lossy) removes data, and can result in poor image quality. JPEG 2000 (Lossless) reduces file size without discarding image data, but can result in larger file size than JPEG (Lossy). Automatic allows the software to determine the best quality for images.

- **JPEG Quality** defines how much compression is applied if you choose JPEG (Lossy) or Automatic compression. Higher quality settings result in larger files.

- **Resolution** defines the resolution of raster images in the exported PDF. High resolution is important if you want users to be able to zoom in close to an image, but higher resolution settings mean larger file sizes.

Note:

The default view and layout options open the file based on the reader application's default options.

10. Define the following settings:

- Make sure the All [Pages] radio button is selected.
- Check the View After Exporting option
- Choose Fit Height in the View menu
- Choose Single Page in the Layout menu.
- Check the Open in Full Screen Mode option.
- Leave the Flip Pages Every option unchecked.
- Choose From Document in the Page Transitions menu.
- Choose JPEG 2000 (Lossless) in the Compression menu.
- Define the target Resolution as 72 ppi.

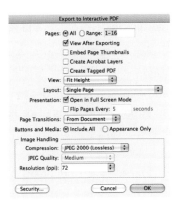

11. Click OK to create the PDF file.

12. Read the resulting warning message, and then click OK.

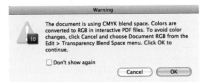

If you get a Full Screen warning message when Acrobat opens, click Yes to allow the file to switch to Full Screen mode.

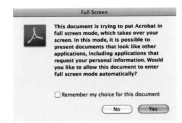

13. When the PDF file opens, press the Down Arrow button to see the interactive page transitions.

You have to view the file in Full-Screen mode to see the page transitions.

14. Press the Escape key to exit Full-Screen mode, then close the PDF file. Return to InDesign and then close the InDesign file.

1. _____ have inside and outside margins instead of left and right margins.

2. When _____ is active, InDesign automatically adds pages to accommodate an entire story that is placed in a master text frame.

3. A local formatting override is indicated by _____ next to the style name in the Paragraph Styles panel.

4. A negative first-line indent is called a(n) _____.

5. A(n) _____ is a single line of a paragraph at the end of a column.

6. A(n) _____ is a single line of a paragraph at the top of a column, or a very short (one-word) last line of a paragraph.

7. _____ in the Paragraph Style Options dialog box can used to force a paragraph to begin in the next linked frame.

8. _____ fonts can store more than 65,000 glyphs (characters) in a single font file; the same font file works on both Macintosh and Windows.

9. You can use the _____ option to create a parent/child relationship between two styles, in which changes made to the parent style reflect in the child style as well.

10. _____ is the process of arranging pages on a press sheet so, when folded and trimmed, the pages of a job appear in the correct order.

1. Briefly explain the difference between facing pages and non-facing pages.

2. Briefly explain the difference between reader's spreads and printer's spreads.

3. Briefly explain the advantages and disadvantages of nesting text-formatting styles.

Use what you learned in this project to complete the following freeform exercise.
Carefully read the art director and client comments, then create your own design to meet the needs of the project.
Use the space below to sketch ideas; when finished, write a brief explanation of your reasoning behind your final design.

art director comments

Your clients are very happy with the finished Home Enhancement Guide. They would like you to create another collateral booklet that they can provide to prospective home buyers, providing contact information for agents in specific geographic areas.

To complete this project, you should:

❏ Download the **ID5_PB_Project4.zip** archive from the Student Files Web page to access the client-supplied text.

❏ Create a 16-page booklet using the same document size as the Home Enhancement Guide.

❏ Design a facing-page layout that is aesthetically pleasing, which clearly presents the necessary information.

❏ Find or create supportive images for each spread that match the overall theme of the project.

client comments

This booklet will list each member agent by general location, including their name and photo, contact information, and their types of property specialties. We sent you a text file with a short blurb for the inside front page, as well as the realtor information from our database. We don't have the agents' photos yet; we'll forward them as soon as possible. Just make sure you leave space for them in the layout.

For the covers, use the same layout as the Home Enhancement Guide. On the front cover, use a different picture and change the title to "Buyer's Resource Guide". On the back, replace the checkerboard image with the same pictures that you use in the Buyer's Guide booklet.

We want the first spread to include only the introductory blurb and some kind of graphics — maybe a montage of different home styles.

One last thing: for now, leave the center spread open. We might want to add something different there, but we haven't figured out what yet.

project justification

_____
_____
_____
_____
_____
_____
_____
_____
_____
_____
_____
_____
_____
_____
_____
_____

Controlling the flow of text in a document — especially for documents with more than one or two pages — is just as important as controlling the appearance of the different type elements. InDesign provides powerful tools that let you control virtually every aspect of document design, from the exact position of individual paragraphs to entire blocks of text to automatic page numbers based on the location of special characters in the layout.

Changing the master page settings for this booklet allowed you to automatically flow a single story across multiple pages. Using the Keep options for the applied styles, you were able to position each element in the appropriate frame on the appropriate spread, which significantly reduced the amount of manual evaluation and adjustment that would have been required without these features.

Using effective master pages also allowed you to place repeating elements to appear on every spread in the layout. Combining that functionality with special characters, you also eliminated a number of unnecessarily repetitive tasks, such as manually numbering the pages.

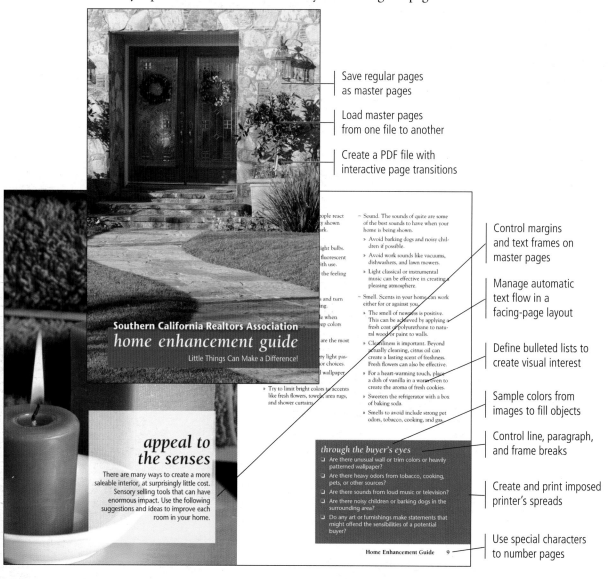

Save regular pages as master pages

Load master pages from one file to another

Create a PDF file with interactive page transitions

Control margins and text frames on master pages

Manage automatic text flow in a facing-page layout

Define bulleted lists to create visual interest

Sample colors from images to fill objects

Control line, paragraph, and frame breaks

Create and print imposed printer's spreads

Use special characters to number pages

Ireland Travel Brochure

Your client is a travel agency that is creating a set of brochures to promote a series of travel packages to various countries in Europe. The client wants to create a letterfold rack brochure for Ireland tourism. The job includes a relatively small amount of copy, a number of images, and a basic form that people can fill out and enter to win a free trip — a common technique for gathering potential clients' contact information.

This project incorporates the following skills:

❑ Building a template for specific folding requirements

❑ Defining slug information using static and variable text

❑ Converting text to complex frames

❑ Using a library to access frequently used objects

❑ Using object styles to reduce repetitive tasks

❑ Working with embedded clipping paths and Alpha channels

❑ Controlling irregular text wraps

❑ Importing text from a Microsoft Word file

❑ Importing styles from existing InDesign files

❑ Creating captions using stored image metadata

❑ Controlling tabs to format columns of text

client comments

We are planning a new series of brochures to promote our European vacation packages. These need to fit into our standard rack holders, which means the finished size should be 4″ wide by 9″ high. A letterfold will give us three panels on each side, which should be plenty for the information we want to include.

The brochures will mostly be hand-outs for people who walk into our office or visit our booth at trade shows, but some will be mailed so we want the brochure to be a self-mailer.

These brochures will be mostly visual, with a little bit of descriptive copy. We're sending you the text and images for the Ireland brochure first, because that's the only one that's been finalized so far.

We went back and forth for weeks over the styles for our other collateral, and we were all finally happy with the results on other pieces your agency designed. We want to use the same formatting in these brochures that you used in all our other jobs.

art director comments

A lot of people design folding documents incorrectly. Some use a six-page layout with each page the size of the final folded job; others use two pages, each divided into three equal "columns." In both cases, all panels on the job are the exact same width — which is wrong.

For a letterfold, the job needs to have one panel narrower than the others. Plus, each side of the brochure has to mirror the other so the narrow panel is in the correct location when the job is printed, trimmed, and folded.

The last item to remember is that the brochure will be a self-mailer; the back panel needs to be left blank, with only the return address in the upper-left corner.

project objectives

To complete this project, you will:

- ❏ Create a folding layout template on master page spreads
- ❏ Use the slug area to mark folding panels
- ❏ Define a custom text variable to track file status
- ❏ Use InDesign library files to store and access frequently used objects and groups
- ❏ Use object styles to apply consistent formatting to multiple frames
- ❏ Apply an Alpha channel that is embedded in a Photoshop file
- ❏ Control text wraps around basic frames and irregular shapes
- ❏ Import text and styles from a Microsoft Word file
- ❏ Create new styles based on existing formatting in the layout
- ❏ Add dynamic captions based on image metadata

Stage 1 **Building a Folding Template**

There are several common types of folds:

Letterfolds have two folds and three panels to a side. (These are often incorrectly called "trifold" because they result in three panels.) The panel that folds in should be 1/16″ to 1/8″ narrower than the two outside panels; ask your service provider how much allowance is required for the paper you're using.

Accordion folds can have as many panels as you prefer. When it has six panels (three on each side), it's often referred to as a **Z-fold** because it looks like the letter Z. Because the panels don't fold into one another, an accordion-fold document has panels of consistent width.

Double-parallel folds are commonly used for eight-panel rack brochures (such as those you often find in a hotel or travel agency). Again, the panels on the inside are narrower than the outside panels. This type of fold uses facing pages because the margins need to line up on the front and back sides of the sheet.

Barrel folds (also called **roll folds**) are perhaps the most common fold for 14 × 8.5″ brochures. The two outside panels are full size, and each successive panel is narrower than the previous one. You can theoretically have as many panels as you want, but at some point the number of fold-in panels will become unwieldy.

Gate folds result in a four-panel document; the paper is folded in half, and then each half is folded in half toward the center so the two ends of the paper meet at the center fold. The panels that fold in are narrower than the two outside panels. This type of brochure allows two different spreads: the first revealed when you open the outer panels, and the second revealed when you open the inner flaps.

It's important to consider the output process when planning a job with documents that are not just a single sheet of standard-size paper — documents with multiple pages folded one or more times, or other non-standard page sizes. The mechanics of commercial printing require specific allowances for cutting, folding, and other finishing processes. There are two basic principles to remember when designing documents that fold:

- Folding machines are mechanical devices, and paper sometimes shifts as it flows through the machine's paper path. Most are accurate to about 0.0125 ″.

- Paper has thickness; thicker paper requires more allowance for the fold.

Because of these two principles, any panel that folds into the other panels needs to be smaller than the other panels. You should note that the issues presented here have little to do with the subjective elements of design. Layout and page geometry are governed by specific variables, including mechanical limitations in the production process. These principles are rules, not suggestions. If you don't leave adequate margins, for example, design elements will be cut off or won't align properly from one page to the next.

When working with folding documents, the trim size of a folded document is actually the size of the flat sheet *before* it's folded. Once you know the flat trim size of a job, you have to calculate the size of individual panels before you set up the layout.

For example, imagine that you're printing a letterfold brochure on a laser printer that can only print to letter-sized paper. The flat trim size, then, is 11″ wide by 8.5″ high. The first required calculation is the base size of each panel:

11″ ÷ 3 = 3.6667″

But remember, the fold-in panel has to be narrower than the other two panels; you also have to factor the required folding variance (which your service provider can tell you) into the panel size. Half of the difference is removed from the fold-in panel, and one-fourth of the difference is added to each outer panel. Assuming a folding variance of 1/8″ (0.125):

Fold-in panel = 3.6667 – 1/16 = 3.6042″

Outer panel 1 = 3.6667 + 1/32 = 3.698″

Outer panel 2 = 3.6667 + 1/32 = 3.698″

You can safely round these values to 3.6″ and 3.7″, resulting in a panel variance of 0.1″, which is enough for most papers that can be run through a desktop laser printer. This seems like a complicated series of calculations, and it is only relevant when printing to a defined flat trim size.

In other cases, however, you might know the finished size of your folding brochure. For example, a rack card or brochure is commonly 4″ × 9″, which fits into standard display racks (hence the name). If you know the final target size, it is easy to calculate the size of individual panels used to build the folding document. Using the 4″ × 9″ rack card with a required 1/8″ panel variance as an example:

Outer Panel 1 = 4″

Outer Panel 2 = 4″

Fold-in Panel = 4″ – 0.125″ = 3.875″

Because the different panels in a folding document are different sizes, earlier versions of the software required you to define each side of a folding document as a separate page. You had to use page guides to define the folds and margins of individual panels. In InDesign CS5, however, the application now supports multiple page sizes in a single document — which makes it far easier to set up the basic document layout for items such as folding brochures.

1. **Download ID5_RF_Project5.zip from the Student Files Web page.**

2. **Expand the ZIP archive in your WIP folder (Macintosh) or copy the archive contents into your WIP folder (Windows).**

   This results in a folder named **Ireland**, which contains the files you need for this project. You should also use this folder to save the files you create in this project.

3. **Choose File>New. In the New Document dialog box, define the following parameters, then click OK to create the new file:**

Intent	Print
Number of Pages	1
Start Page #	1
Facing Pages	Not Checked
Master Text Frame	Checked
Page Size	Width: 4″
	Height: 9″
Columns	1
Margins	0.25″ on all four sides
Bleed	0.125″ on all four sides
Slug	0.5″ on the top and bottom
	0″ on the left and right

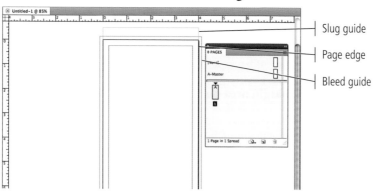

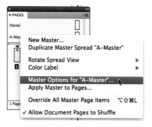

Slug guide

Page edge

Bleed guide

4. **In the Pages panel, Control/right-click the A-Master page name and choose Master Options for "A-Master" in the contextual menu.**

5. **In the resulting dialog box, type `Outside` in the Name field and type `3` in the Number of Pages field. Click OK to return to the layout.**

The outside of the brochure has three panels, so you are defining three pages in the master page spread — one page for each panel.

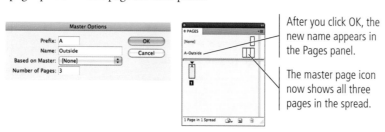

After you click OK, the new name appears in the Pages panel.

The master page icon now shows all three pages in the spread.

Note:

It's always a good idea to use a meaningful name for any element you define in InDesign, including a master page.

6. Double-click the A-Outside layout to display the master page in the document window.

The master page spread now has three pages, as you defined in Step 5. All three pages have the 0.25″ margins, as you defined when you created the file. The bleed area surrounds the entire spread because each page automatically abuts the other pages in the spread.

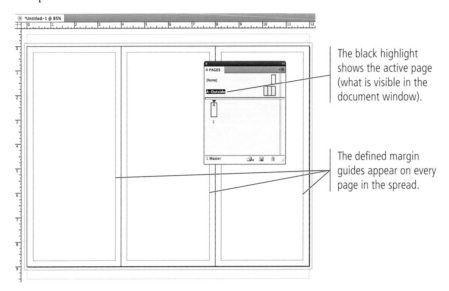

The black highlight shows the active page (what is visible in the document window).

The defined margin guides appear on every page in the spread.

7. Using the Selection tool, click inside the margin area on the left page of the spread to select the master text frame.

Unfortunately, adding pages to a master page does not automatically place a master frame on each new page. You have to manually create the frames on the two new pages.

8. Option/Alt-click the master text frame and drag right to clone it. Drag until the cloned frame snaps to the margins on the center page.

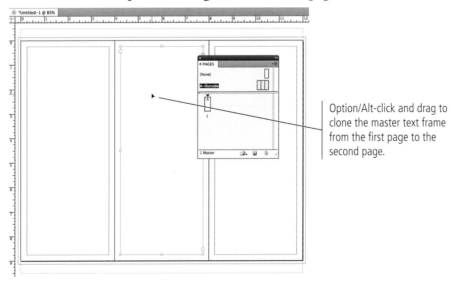

Option/Alt-click and drag to clone the master text frame from the first page to the second page.

9. Repeat Step 8 to add a text frame to the right page in the spread.

10. **Choose the Page tool in the Tools panel, and then click the left page in the spread to select it.**

The Page tool makes it possible to change the dimensions of a single (selected) page in the document.

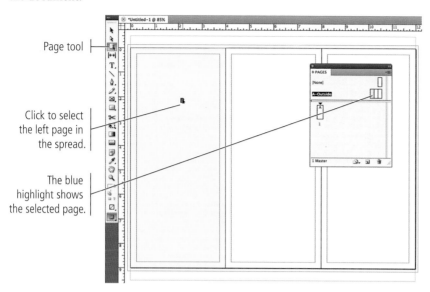

Page tool

Click to select the left page in the spread.

The blue highlight shows the selected page.

11. **In the Control panel, check the Enable Layout Adjustment and Objects Move with Page options.**

12. **Choose the right-center reference point. Click in the W field after the existing value, then type -.125 and press Return/Enter to apply the change.**

InDesign understands mathematical operators in most dialog box and panel fields. Because you know you need to remove 1/8″ from the fold-in panel width, it is very easy to simply subtract that amount from the existing value.

Choose the right-center reference point as the point that will remain fixed when you change the page width.

Type after the existing value.

Check this option to resize the master text frame along with the page.

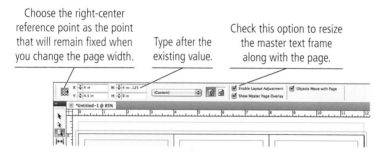

The margins on the selected page are still 0.25″ from the adjusted page edges. Because you activated the Enable Layout Adjustment option, the text frame on the page adjusted and remains snapped to the adjusted margins. If you had not checked this option, the text frame would have retained its original size.

After pressing Return/Enter, the selected page is 1/8″ narrower than the other two pages in the spread.

The margins on the adjusted page are still 1/4″ from each edge.

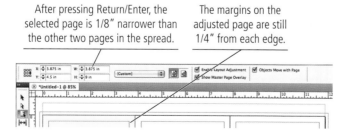

13. **Save the file as letterfold.indd in your WIP>Ireland folder, and then continue to the next exercise.**

Until CS5, a multi-piece job with different page sizes required separate documents for each layout. Now, you can create various page sizes in the same InDesign file so the different pieces of a job — for example, the letterhead and business card in an identity package — always stay together. This means you have only one file to manage, and it also means that assets such as styles or swatches can be created once and used in multiple pieces without extra steps.

You can change the selected page to another preset using the menu at the bottom of the Pages panel, or by selecting the page with the Page tool and then using the Control panel to redefine the page size (as you did in the previous exercise).

The currently active size (if any) is checked.

Click here to change the page size of the selected page to a different preset size.

Using the Page tool, you can check the **Enable Layout Adjustment** option to resize objects on the page along with the page. The options for this setting can be defined by choosing Layout>Layout Adjustment.

When checked, the objects on the page are also resized to fit the new page size.

When more than one page exists in a spread (master or layout), you can use the Page tool to move the pages on the spread independently (for example, adding a gap between the pages in the spread). If **Objects Move with Page** is checked in the Control panel, objects on the page will be repositioned along with the page you drag.

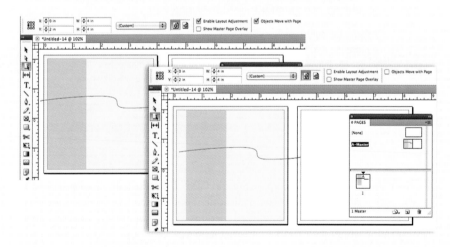

The **Show Master Page Overlay** displays the related master page in relation to an adjusted page size. This option makes it easier to position defined master content relative to the resized page.

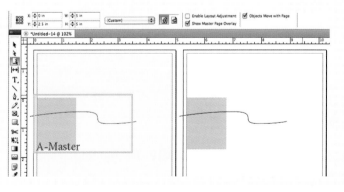

When you work with folding grids, it's easy to forget which panel goes where. You can use the layout slug area to add nonprinting elements as self-reminders, as well as to place folding marks that the output provider can use for reference. These elements should be placed on the master page layout.

1. **With `letterfold.indd` open, make sure the A-Outside master page layout is showing in the document window.**

2. **Select the Type tool and create a text frame above the left panel of the left-facing page, between the bleed and slug guides.**

3. **Type `Outside Left Panel – Fold In` in the frame, and then apply centered paragraph alignment.**

Placing these objects outside the bleed but inside the slug area prevents them from interfering with the layout elements.

4. **Choose Window>Output>Attributes to open the Attributes panel.**

5. **Select the text frame in the slug area with the Selection tool, and then check the Nonprinting box in the Attributes panel.**

   These objects are for your information only; they should not be included in the output.

Note:

If you want to print these frames, you can override this setting using the Print Nonprinting Objects option in the General print settings.

6. **Control/right-click the text frame and choose Allow Master Item Overrides to deactivate the option and protect this object on associated layout pages.**

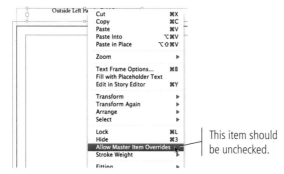

This item should be unchecked.

7. **Using the Selection tool, press Option/Alt, then click and drag to clone the text frame to the right.**

8. **Position the clone above the center page in the spread, and then change the text in the frame to Outside Center Panel – Mailing Area.**

Note:

Like the original frame from which they are cloned, these text frames are also set as nonprinting objects.

9. **Repeat Steps 7–8 to place a text frame over the right page of the spread, with the text Outside Right Panel – Front.**

10. **Using the Line tool, click the slug guide above the line that separates the left and center pages in the spread. Press Shift and drag down to the bleed guide.**

    Pressing Shift constrains the line to a multiple of 45° angle.

11. **Using the Control panel, position the line at X=3.875″ (the same as the left page's width).**

12. **In the Stroke panel (Window>Stroke), change the line Weight to 0.5-pt and choose Dashed in the Type menu. After applying the Dashed line type, type 3 pt in the first Dash field at the bottom of the panel.**

    If you don't see the Type menu in the Stroke panel, open the panel Options menu and choose Show Options.

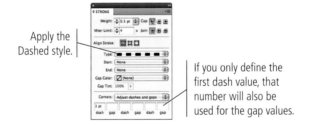

Apply the Dashed style.

If you only define the first dash value, that number will also be used for the gap values.

13. **Control/right-click the dashed line and toggle off the Allow Master Item Overrides option.**

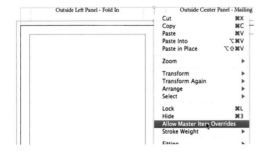

14. Clone the line and place the copy above the line that separates the center and right pages in the spread (X: 7.875").

15. Select the two lines and clone them down, placing the cloned lines in the bottom slug area.

16. Save the file and continue to the next exercise.

 PLACE TEXT VARIABLES

The final item to add on the master page is a custom slug, which is file information that will be printed outside the trim and bleed areas. You already defined the slug area in the first exercise of this project; you can now use text variables to place the same information on each of the three master pages in the layout.

1. With **letterfold.indd** open, make sure the **A-Outside layout is showing.**

2. Create a new text frame in the slug area below the left page of the spread.

3. With the insertion point flashing in the new text frame, choose Type>Text Variables>Insert Variable>File Name.

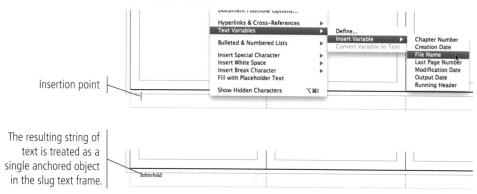

Insertion point

The resulting string of text is treated as a single anchored object in the slug text frame.

4. With the insertion point after the File Name variable, press the spacebar, type / `Modified:`, then press the Spacebar again.

5. Choose Type>Text Variables>Insert Variable>Modification Date.

6. If necessary, adjust the frame width so the entire footer slug fits on one line, but remains only under the left page of the spread.

7. Save the file and continue to the next exercise.

Note:

Even though you can't select the actual characters within the text variable instance, you can still change the formatting of variables by highlighting the instance in the layout and making whatever changes you want.

In addition to the built-in text variables, you can also define your own variables to meet the specific needs of a project. In this exercise, you will add a custom variable to track the current status of the project as you build it.

This information should appear on both spreads, which means it needs to be placed on both master page layouts. (You will create the second spread in the next exercise.) You could accomplish the same result by simply typing the status in the slug of each master page; however, you would have to make the same change on each of the master pages in each stage of the project.

By defining a text variable that you will place on both master pages, you can simply change the variable definition as you progress through each stage of the project, and then all instances of the placed variable will automatically reflect that change.

1. **With `letterfold.indd` open, choose Type>Text Variables>Define.**

2. **In the Text Variables dialog box, click the New button.**

3. **In the Name field of the New Text Variable dialog box, type `Project Status`.**

4. **In the Type menu, choose Custom Text.**

   Eight of these options are the same as those that already appear in the Text Variables>Insert Variables submenu. You can, however, define more than one variable for a single type. For example, you can define two different modification date variables — one that shows the day, month, year, and time; and one that shows only the day and month.

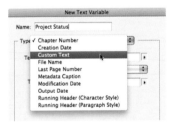

5. **Click the menu to the right of the Text field.**

   Using the Custom Text option, you can determine what text appears in the variable. The menu provides access to common special characters (these are the same characters you can access in the Type>Insert Special Character submenus).

6. **Choose Ellipsis from the menu.**

7. **With the insertion point after the code for the Ellipsis character, press the Spacebar and then type Work In Progress.**

8. **Click OK to close the New Text Variable dialog box.**

   The new Project Status variable now appears in the list.

Note:

If you delete a variable that is used in the layout, you can choose to replace placed instances with a different variable, convert the instances to regular text, or simply remove the placed instances.

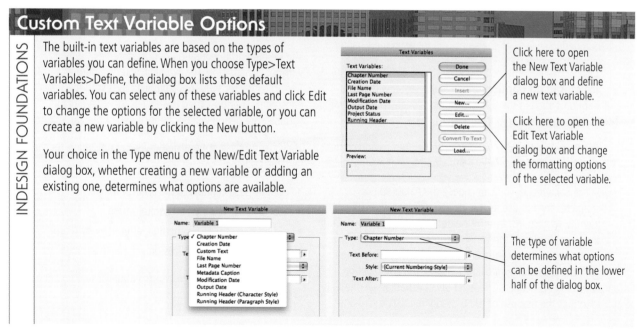

Custom Text Variable Options

INDESIGN FOUNDATIONS

The built-in text variables are based on the types of variables you can define. When you choose Type>Text Variables>Define, the dialog box lists those default variables. You can select any of these variables and click Edit to change the options for the selected variable, or you can create a new variable by clicking the New button.

Your choice in the Type menu of the New/Edit Text Variable dialog box, whether creating a new variable or adding an existing one, determines what options are available.

Click here to open the New Text Variable dialog box and define a new text variable.

Click here to open the Edit Text Variable dialog box and change the formatting options of the selected variable.

The type of variable determines what options can be defined in the lower half of the dialog box.

For all but the Custom Text variable, you can define the characters that precede (Text Before field) or follow (Text After field) the variable information. You can type specific information in either of these fields, or you can use the associated menus to place symbols, em or en dashes, white-space characters, or typographer's quotation marks.

The **Chapter Number** variable inserts the chapter number based on the file's position in a book document (you will work with InDesign books in Project 8). You can use the Style menu to format the chapter number as lowercase or uppercase letters, lowercase or uppercase Roman numerals, or Arabic numbers.

The **Creation Date** variable inserts the time the document is first saved. The **Modification Date** variable inserts the time the document was last saved. The **Output Date** variable inserts the date the document was last printed, exported to PDF, or packaged. You can use the **Date Format** menu to modify the date format for all three of these variables. You can either type a format directly into the field, or you can use the associated menu to choose the options you want to include. If you want to simply type the format into the field, you have to use the correct abbreviations.

The **File Name** variable inserts the name of the open file. You can use the check box options to include the entire folder path and the file extension. (The path and extension will not appear until you save the file at least once.)

Abbreviation	Description	Example
M	Month number	1
MM	Month number (two digits)*	01
MMM	Month name (abbreviated)	Jan
MMMM	Month name (full)	January
d	Day number	3
dd	Day number (two digits)*	03
E	Weekday name (abbreviated)	Wed
EEEE	Weekday name (full)	Wednesday
yy	Year number (last two digits)	09
yyyy	Year number (four digits)	2009
G	Era (abbreviated)	AD
GGGG	Era (full)	Anno Domini
h	Hour	1
hh	Hour (two digits)*	01
H	Hour (24-hour format)	16
HH	Hour (two digits, 24-hour format)*	16
m	Minute	9
mm	Minute (two digits)*	09
s	Second	2
ss	Second (two digits)*	02
a	AM or PM	AM
z	Time zone (abbreviated)	PST
zzzz	Time zone (full)	Pacific Standard Time

*The two-digit formats force a leading zero in front of numbers lower than 10 (for example, 9/25/09 would appear as 09/25/09 if you use the two-digit Month format).

The **Last Page Number** variable can be used to create a "Page x of y" notation. This variable can indicate the last page number of the entire document or the current section (in the Scope menu). You can also determine the numbering style (with the same options as in the Chapter Number variable).

The **Metadata Caption** option is the same as the Live Caption option in the Object>Captions submenu. (You will use this option later in this project.)

The **Running Header** variables can be used to find content on the page based on applied paragraph or character styles.

In the Style menu, you can choose the paragraph or character style to use as the variable content. The Use menu identifies which instance of the defined style (first or last on the page) to use as the variable content. For example, say you have a glossary page and all the terms are formatted with the Glossary Term character style. You could define two Running Header (Character Style) variables — one that identifies the first use of the Glossary Term style and one

that identifies the last use of the Glossary Term style on the current page. You can then place the two variables in a text frame to create a running header that shows the first and last terms on the page — e.g., [First Term] – [Last Term].

The Delete End Punctuation option identifies the text without punctuation. For example, you can identify a Bold Run-In character style that is applied to text that always ends with a period. When the style is identified as the variable, the period will not be included in the variable text.

The Change Case options determine capitalization for the variable text:

- Upper Case capitalizes the entire variable.
- Lower Case removes all capitalization.
- Title Case capitalizes the first letter in every word.
- Sentence Case capitalizes only the first word.

The **Custom Text** variable inserts whatever text you define in the associated field.

9. **Click Done to close the Text Variables dialog box.**

10. **Create a new text frame in the slug area under the right page of the spread.**

11. **With the insertion point flashing in the new frame, type Project Status, press the Spacebar, and then choose Type>Text Variables>Insert Variable>Project Status.**

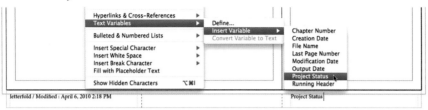

The variable text you defined is placed immediately after the space. Because it is a variable instance, it is surrounded by a gray border.

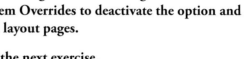

Note:

You can convert a particular instance of a text variable to regular text by selecting an instance in the layout and choosing Type>Text Variables>Convert Variable to Text. You can convert all instances of a specific variable to regular text by opening the Text Variables dialog box, selecting a specific variable, and clicking the Convert to Text button.

12. **Select both text frames in the bottom slug area. Control/right-click either frame and choose Allow Master Item Overrides to deactivate the option and protect both objects on associated layout pages.**

13. **Save the file and then continue to the next exercise.**

 ## CREATE THE INSIDE MASTER PAGES

When you plan a folding document layout, it is also important to understand how the two sides of the document relate to one another. Fold marks on the front and back should line up; this means that if one panel is a different size than the others, the back side of the sheet must be laid out as a mirror image of the front side.

In the illustration to the right, a document has one fold — a smaller panel that folds over to cover half of the inside of the brochure. Fold marks on the outside layout must mirror the inside of the brochure so that, when folded, the two sides line up properly.

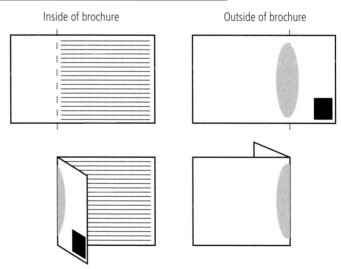

Inside of brochure   Outside of brochure

1. **With letterfold.indd open, Control/right-click the A-Outside master page name and choose Duplicate Master Spread "A-Outside" in the contextual menu.**

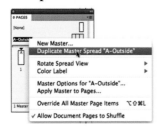

2. **Control/right-click the resulting B-Master layout name and choose Master Options for "B-Master" in the contextual menu.**

3. **Type Inside in the Name field and then click OK to apply the new name to the B master page layout.**

The new B-Inside master page spread is automatically displayed in the document window. All of the elements that you created on the A-Inside master are in place because you duplicated the existing master page.

The highlight shows the new B-Inside master spread is now active in the document window.

4. **Choose the Page tool in the Tools panel. In the Control panel, make sure the Objects Move with Page option is checked.**

Because the inside of the brochure needs to be a mirror image of the outside of the brochure, you need to move the shorter panel to the other side of the spread.

5. **Click the left page in the spread to select it, and then drag right until the reduced panel snaps to the right edge of the spread.**

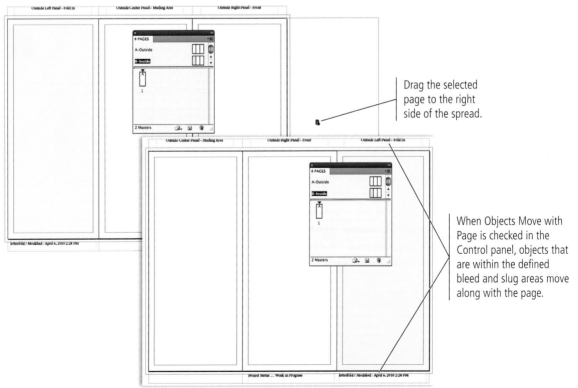

Drag the selected page to the right side of the spread.

When Objects Move with Page is checked in the Control panel, objects that are within the defined bleed and slug areas move along with the page.

6. In the text frames in the top slug area, change the text to:

   Left page   Inside Left Panel

   Center page: Inside Center Panel

   Right page: Inside Right Panel - Fold In

7. **Click the slug guide over the right edge of the right page.**

   The folding guide that was over the page edge is still over the page edge — which is incorrect. You need to move this guide into place over the line between the center and right pages of the spread.

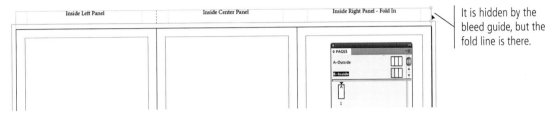

It is hidden by the bleed guide, but the fold line is there.

8. **Drag the fold line left until it is over the line between the center and right pages of the spread (X: 8″).**

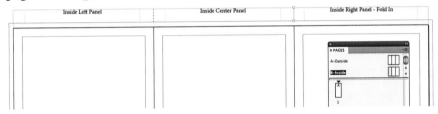

9. **In the bottom slug area, drag the text frame with the file name and modification date to be below the left page of the spread.**

10. **Drag the frame with the file status to be below the right page of the spread.**

11. **Click the slug guide below the right edge of the right page to select the moved folding line, then drag the fold line left until it is below the line between the center and right pages of the spread (X: 8″).**

12. **Save the file and continue to the next exercise.**

SAVE A TEMPLATE

As the previous exercises demonstrated, setting up a brochure properly can be time-consuming. Once you have set up a folding layout, it's a good idea to save the layout as a template so the same structure can be applied to any similar type of layout. Every time you want to create a rack card with the same folded size, you can open this template and begin with an empty file that contains the correct guides and marks.

Note:

You can Shift-click to select multiple pages in the Pages panel and override master page items for all selected pages at one time.

1. **With letterfold.indd open, click the A-Outside master page layout name to select the entire spread.**

   Clicking a master page name selects all pages in that spread. If you wanted to select actual layout pages (instead of master pages), you could click the page number sequence below a spread (in the lower half of the panel) to select all pages in that spread.

Pages Panel Options

In Projects 3 and 4, you learned about some of the options for working with master pages. The Pages panel Options menu also has a number of other choices for working with document pages.

- **Insert Pages** allows you to insert from 1 to 9999 pages before or after a specific page, or at the start or end of the document. You can also determine which master page to base the new pages on.

- **Move Pages** allows you to reposition specific pages anywhere in the current document or in another open document.

- **Duplicate Master Page/Spread** allows you to replicate the selected page (or spread), including all elements on that page or spread.

- **Delete Master Page/Spread** removes the page (or spread) from the document.

- **Rotate Spread View** changes the appearance of the page within the document window. This option does not affect the physical dimensions of the page, but is useful for working with a page that's oriented differently than the overall document.

- **Page Transitions** are visual effects that apply when a document is exported as a PDF or SWF file that will be distributed digitally.

- **Color Label** applies a colored bar below the selected page icon(s), which provides an additional visual indicator of a specific, user-defined status.

- **Allow Document Pages to Shuffle** is checked by default. You can toggle off this option if you want to create spreads of more than two pages (called an **island spread**) in a facing-page layout.

- **Allow Selected Spread to Shuffle** is checked by default. If you toggle this option off, adding pages before an island spread maintains the island spread pages as you created them.

- **Numbering & Section Options** give you control over the manner in which pages and chapters are numbered, where page or chapter numbers begin, and what format is used for page numbers.

- **Spread Flattening** allows you to apply flattener settings to individual spreads in a document, overriding the document flattener settings. Default uses the document settings. None (Ignore Transparency) eliminates any function that requires transparency. Custom opens the Custom Spread Flattener settings.

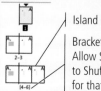

Island spread

Brackets indicate that Allow Selected Spread to Shuffle is turned off for that spread.

2. **Click and drag the master page layout into the lower half of the Pages panel, below the existing Page 1.**

Because all three pages in the master layout are selected, releasing the mouse button adds a three-page spread below the existing Page 1.

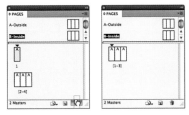

Note:

You can also use the Layout>Pages>Insert Pages option to add multiple pages to a layout.

3. **Click the Page 1 icon in the Pages panel, and drag it to the panel's Delete button.**

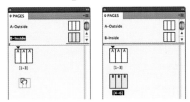

4. **Click the B-Inside master page layout name to select the entire spread.**

5. **Click and drag the B-Inside layout into the lower half of the Pages panel, below the spread you added in Step 2.**

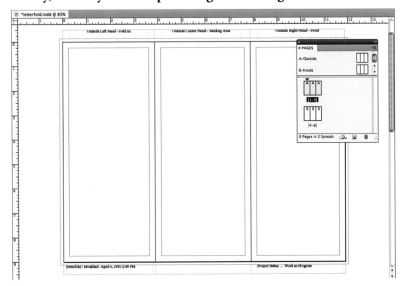

6. **In the lower half of the Pages panel, double-click the [1-3] page numbers below the first spread to navigate to that spread.**

7. **Choose View>Fit Spread in Window.**

This command shows the entire spread of Pages 1–3, including the defined bleed areas. The slug areas, however, are not entirely visible.

8. **If necessary, reduce your view percentage so the slug areas are visible.**

9. **Control/right-click the selected spread and choose Override All Master Page Items in the contextual menu.**

This command allows you to access the text frames you created on the master layout. You won't be able to access the fold marks or nonprinting slug items, which you protected by toggling off the Allow Master Item Overrides option.

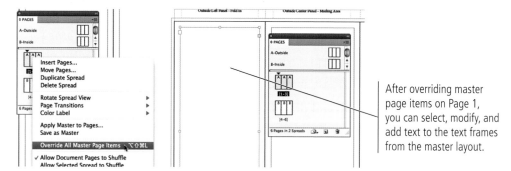

After overriding master page items on Page 1, you can select, modify, and add text to the text frames from the master layout.

10. **Repeat Step 9 for the Pages 4-6 spread.**

11. **Open the Type pane of the Preferences dialog box. Uncheck the Smart Text Reflow option and then click OK.**

Because you know this type of brochure will always have only the specific number of pages that you already defined, you don't want the software to automatically add pages to fit long blocks of text.

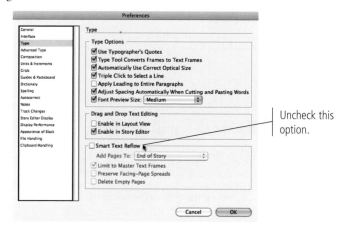

Uncheck this option.

Note:

If this option is already unchecked, simply click Cancel to close the Preferences dialog box.

12. **Choose File>Save As and navigate to your WIP>Ireland folder. Choose InDesign CS5 Template in the Format/Save As Type menu and click Save.**

These pages and settings will be available whenever you implement the layout. Remember, every click you can save by adding template elements will save that much time later — every time you re-use the same template.

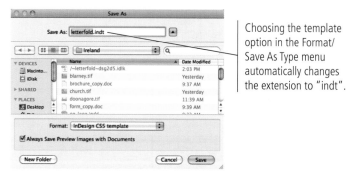

Choosing the template option in the Format/Save As Type menu automatically changes the extension to "indt".

13. **Close the file and continue to the next stage of the project.**

Stage 2 Advanced Frame Options

You've already learned how to place graphics and control them within their frames. InDesign, of course, offers many more functions that provide control over graphics. Some of these (such as libraries and object styles) improve your productivity by automating repetitive tasks; other options (such as creating a custom frame from formatted text) enhance your creative capabilities when designing a page layout.

CONVERT TEXT TO OUTLINES

1. **Create a new file by opening your `letterfold.indt` template (WIP>Ireland).**

   Remember, to create a new file from a template, you have to open the template file using the Open Normal option.

2. **Save the new file as `letterfold_ireland.indd` in your WIP>Ireland folder.**

3. **In the Pages panel, double-click the [1-3] page numbers below the page icons to show that spread in the document window.**

4. **Using the Type tool, click inside the empty text frame on Page 3. Type IRELAND in the frame, and format it as 120-pt ATC Oak Bold.**

5. **Press Command/Control to temporarily access the Selection tool and reveal the frame's handles. Drag the frame handles until the frame is large enough to show the entire word you just typed.**

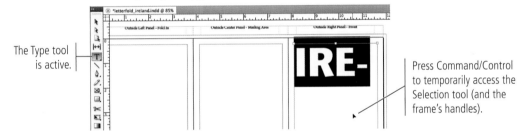

The Type tool is active.

Press Command/Control to temporarily access the Selection tool (and the frame's handles).

When you release the Command/Control key, the Type tool is still active.

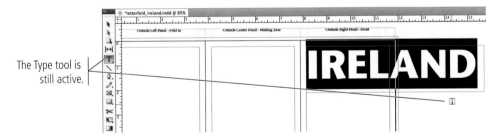

The Type tool is still active.

6. **Click with the Type tool between the I and the R to place the insertion point. Using the Character panel, change the kerning to -70 to reduce the space between these two letters.**

Use this field to adjust kerning.

Place the insertion point between two letters.

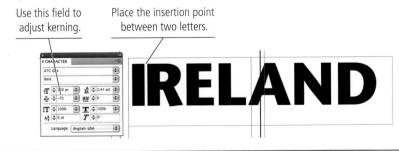

7. Continue adjusting the kerning in this word as necessary.

Kerning is largely a matter of personal preference. Our choices are shown here.

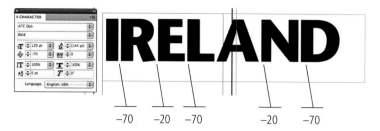

−70   −20   −70   −20   −70

8. Choose the Selection tool in the Tools panel.

9. Click the text frame to select it, and then choose Type>Create Outlines.

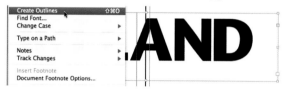

By converting the text to outlines, you eliminate the potential problem of a missing font file. You also create a group of letter-shaped objects that can contain other objects — such as a picture of Ireland's iconic shamrocks.

Note:

You can convert individual characters to inline objects by selecting specific characters before you choose Type>Create Outlines.

After converting the text to outlines, the text frame is gone; it is replaced by a bounding box for the group of letter shapes.

10. With the new frame selected, choose File>Place. Navigate to `shamrocks.tif` in your WIP>Ireland folder, activate the Replace Selected Item option, and then click Open.

The image is placed directly into the shape of the letters.

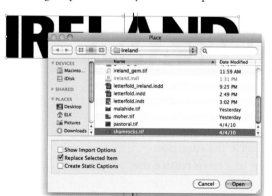

11. Save the file and continue to the next exercise.

In this exercise, you are going to combine the IRELAND graphics frame with another shape. When you create a compound path out of multiple shapes, attributes and contents of the topmost selected shape are applied to the resulting combined shape. Even when objects do not technically overlap, the concept of stacking order still applies. Objects created later are higher in the stacking order than older objects unless you manually rearrange those objects. You can always use the Layers panel subitem listings to monitor and control the stacking order of objects.

1. With **letterfold_ireland.indd** open, click any of the letter-shaped frames with the Selection tool to select the entire group.

2. Use the Control panel to rotate the group counterclockwise by 90°.

3. Drag the rotated group until the top-right corner snaps to the top-right Bleed guide on Page 3.

4. Drag the bottom-center handle until its Y position is 7.625″.

   Because the group is rotated, dragging the bottom handle actually changes the objects' *width* rather than its height.

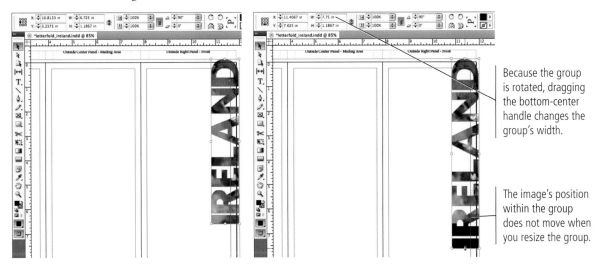

Because the group is rotated, dragging the bottom-center handle changes the group's width.

The image's position within the group does not move when you resize the group.

5. Drag the left-center handle until its X position is 10.125″.

   Because the group is rotated, dragging the left handle changes the group's height.

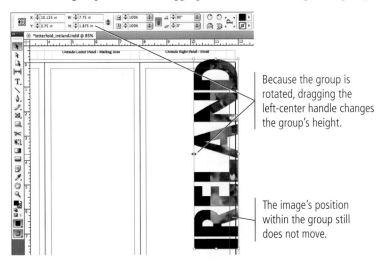

Because the group is rotated, dragging the left-center handle changes the group's height.

The image's position within the group still does not move.

Note:

When you drag a specific handle, the X and Y fields in the Control panel show the position of the handle you drag. The selected reference point is not relevant.

6. **Using the Rectangle tool, click and drag to create a frame on the left half of Page 3, aligning its bottom edge to the left edge of the rotated frame.**

   Use the image after Step 7 as a positioning guide.

7. **Open the Layers panel and expand the Layer 1 listing.**

   As you know, you created the rectangle after the IRELAND group; that means the rectangle is higher in the stacking order than the shamrocks.tif image.

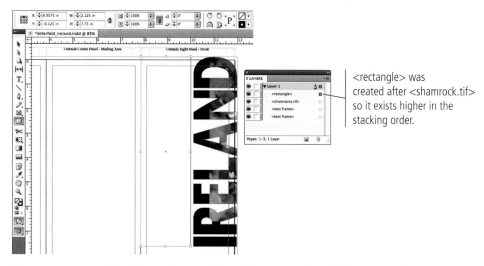

<rectangle> was created after <shamrock.tif> so it exists higher in the stacking order.

You want to extend the shamrock image beyond the letter-shaped frames into the rectangle. You can easily combine the rectangle and letter-shaped frames using the Pathfinder functions. Most Pathfinder operations, however, apply attributes of the topmost object to the entire resulting shape. This means you have to rearrange object stacking order before you can combine the two shapes into a single compound path.

8. **In the Layers panel, click the <rectangle> item and drag it below the <shamrock.tif> item.**

9. **Using the Selection tool, Shift-click the rectangle and the IRELAND frame to select both objects in the layout.**

10. **Choose Object>Pathfinder>Add.**

    This command combines the selected objects into a single compound path. The black fill of the original IRELAND shapes now extends into the rectangle.

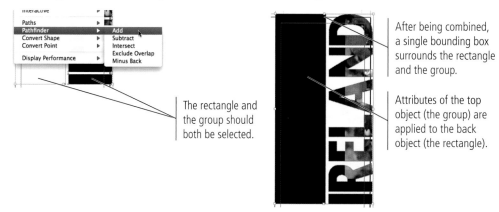

The rectangle and the group should both be selected.

After being combined, a single bounding box surrounds the rectangle and the group.

Attributes of the top object (the group) are applied to the back object (the rectangle).

11. **Place the Selection tool cursor over any part of the combined shape to reveal the Content Indicator icon.**

12. **Click the Content Indicator icon to access the placed image.**

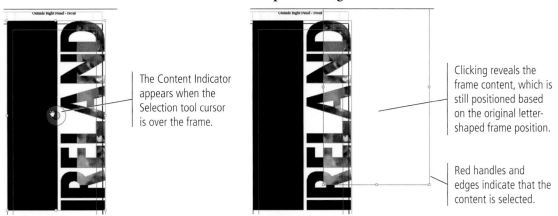

The Content Indicator appears when the Selection tool cursor is over the frame.

Clicking reveals the frame content, which is still positioned based on the original letter-shaped frame position.

Red handles and edges indicate that the content is selected.

13. **Drag the placed image to fill the entire combined frame.**

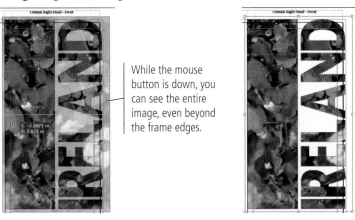

While the mouse button is down, you can see the entire image, even beyond the frame edges.

14. **Save the file and continue to the next exercise.**

 ## CREATE AN INDESIGN LIBRARY

In many cases, you might need to use the same content (such as a logo) or the same group of objects with different content (such as a logo with a grouped text frame containing contact information) on multiple pages throughout a single document, or even in multiple documents. In these situations, you can use an InDesign library to speed the process.

1. **Open the file gg_logo.indd from the WIP>Ireland folder.**

    This file includes a single group, with your client's logo and address information. It has been used with this same alignment in many other projects, and the client wants to maintain consistency from document to document.

    Rather than copying and pasting the group from one document to another, you can use an InDesign Library file to make the group easily accessible in any InDesign file.

2. **Choose File>New>Library. Navigate to your WIP>Ireland folder as the target location. Change the file name to go_global.indl.**

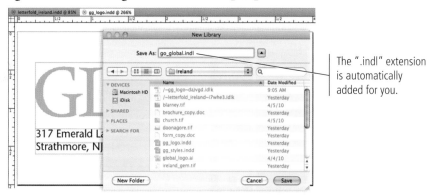

The ".indl" extension is automatically added for you.

3. **Click Save to create the new library.**

A library is a special type of file that stores objects (including the objects' content) for use in any InDesign file. Library files are not linked or specific to any individual layout (.indd) file, so you can open and use items from any existing library in any layout that you subsequently build.

4. **In the gg_logo layout, select the group on the page and drag it into the GO_GLOBAL library panel.**

The Library panel appears as soon as you click Save in the New Library dialog box.

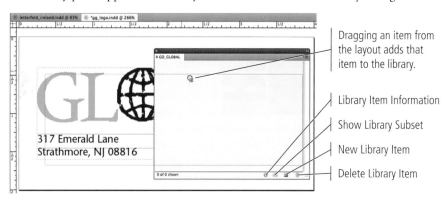

Dragging an item from the layout adds that item to the library.

Library Item Information

Show Library Subset

New Library Item

Delete Library Item

Note:

You can also click the New Library Item button at the bottom of the Library panel to add the selected object as a new library item.

Dragging an object from the layout into the Library panel has no effect on the object that is already placed in the layout. When you release the mouse button, the new library item appears in the panel and the original item in the layout is exactly the same as it was before you dragged it into the library.

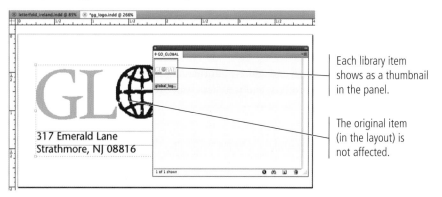

Each library item shows as a thumbnail in the panel.

The original item (in the layout) is not affected.

Note:

Choose Add Items On Page [N] As Separate Objects in the Library panel Options menu to add all objects on the page as separate library items.

Choose Add Items On Page [N] in the panel Options menu to add all objects on the page as a single library item.

5. **With the new library item selected, click the Library Item Information button at the bottom of the panel.**

6. **In the resulting Item Information dialog box, change the Item Name field to Logo With Address.**

7. **In the Description field, type Use this group wherever the logo and address are required, then click OK.**

8. **Close the gg_logo.indd file without saving.**

   Library files are not linked to a specific InDesign file; you can use them to access common styled elements from any InDesign file.

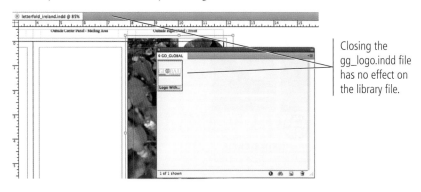

Closing the gg_logo.indd file has no effect on the library file.

9. **With the outside spread of letterfold_ireland.indd visible, drag the Logo With Address item from the Library panel into the layout.**

10. **Rotate the placed group 90° counterclockwise, and align it to the bottom-left margin guide on Page 2 (the center page in the spread).**

Rotating the placed instance has no effect on the library item.

11. **Drag a second copy of the library item into the layout, and position the new instance at the bottom of Page 3. (Use the image after Step 12 as a guide.)**

12. **Using the Selection tool, double-click the text frame at the bottom of Page 3 to select only that frame in the group. Press Delete/Backspace to remove the selected frame.**

Double-click the frame to access only one piece of the group.

There is no dynamic link between items in the library and instances placed in a layout. Changing one placed instance has no effect on the original library item or on other placed instances of the same item.

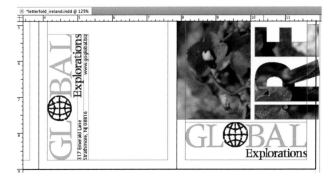

13. **Click the Close button on the Library panel to close the library file.**

This project is only a two-page brochure, and all instances of the library item appear on the same spread. But think of a layout with more than a few pages — a newsletter, a booklet, or even a multi-file multi-chapter book. You can use library items to easily access common graphics such as logos; to maintain consistency between sidebars on Page 1 and Page 42; and even to use the same graphic-and-text-frame structure for graphics with captions on every page of a 240-page book.

14. **Save the InDesign file and continue to the next exercise.**

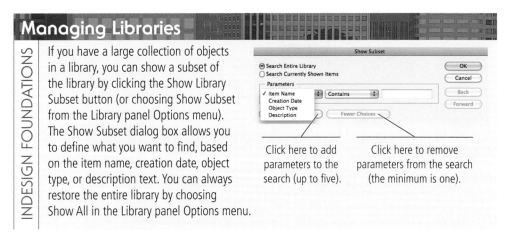

Managing Libraries

INDESIGN FOUNDATIONS

If you have a large collection of objects in a library, you can show a subset of the library by clicking the Show Library Subset button (or choosing Show Subset from the Library panel Options menu). The Show Subset dialog box allows you to define what you want to find, based on the item name, creation date, object type, or description text. You can always restore the entire library by choosing Show All in the Library panel Options menu.

Click here to add parameters to the search (up to five).

Click here to remove parameters from the search (the minimum is one).

A library is simply a type of file that contains and provides access to other objects — text frames, graphics frames, groups, and so on. Library items are subject to the same requirements as objects in a regular InDesign file. If a library item contains text, the fonts used to format that text must be available on any system that uses that library item. Similarly, if a library item contains a placed image or graphic, the placed file must be available in the same location as when it was added to the library.

1. **With letterfold_ireland.indd open, make the inside spread (Pages 4–6) visible in the document window.**

2. **Choose File>Open. Select the ireland.indl library file from your WIP>Ireland folder and click Open.**

   You can open a library file using the same File>Open command (Command/Control-O) that you use to open a regular InDesign file. This library contains two items that will be part of the Ireland tourism brochure.

3. **Move your mouse over the left item in the library panel and read the description.**

   If a library item includes descriptive text, that text appears in the tool tip when you move your mouse over that item. This description provides useful information about what you should do with the item.

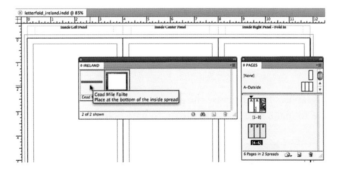

Note:

Céad míle fáilte is Gaelic for "a hundred thousand welcomes."

4. **Click the left item and drag it into the active layout. Position the object at the bottom of the spread (aligned to the bottom bleed guide).**

   Library items do not store fonts. If a library item uses a specific font, that font must be active on whatever system uses the library. You probably don't have the MacLachlan Bold font that is used in this library item, so the text should appear highlighted in pink — the indication of a missing font.

5. **Open the Swatches and Paragraph Styles panels.**

   If a library item uses styles or other assets (including defined swatches), those required assets are placed in any file where you place the library item.

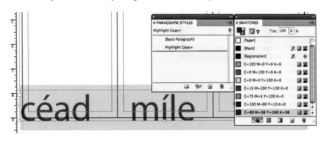

Note:

If a library item uses a style (text or object) that conflicts with a style in the document where you're placing an instance, the style definition from the document overrides the style definition from the library item.

6. **Double-click the Highlight Copy paragraph style to open the Paragraph Style Options dialog box.**

7. **In the Basic Character Formats options, change the font to ATC Oak Bold, then click OK to redefine the style.**

   When the missing-font highlight is gone, you can see the dark green fill color of the text frame that you placed from the library.

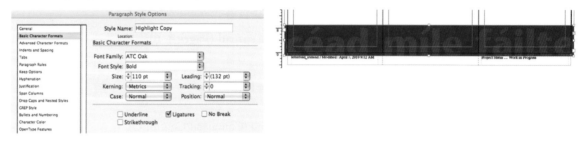

8. **Move your mouse over the Text Frame item in the Library panel and read the description.**

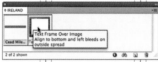

9. **Navigate to the outside spread (Pages 1–3).**

10. **Click the Text Frame item and drag into the open file. Position the placed instance aligned to the bottom-left bleed guide on the spread.**

11. **Open the Links panel.**

    Library items store the links to placed graphics files. Because the graphic is not embedded in the library item, you have to make sure the links are up to date before outputting the file.

Note:

Deleting an object from the library has no effect on placed instances in the layout. Deleting a placed instance has no effect on the item in the library.

12. **Click the missing image in the Links panel and click the Relink button. Navigate to `pastoral.tif` in your WIP>Ireland folder and click Open.**

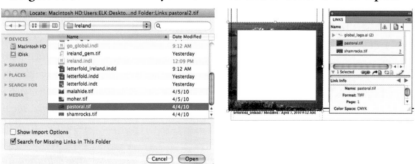

13. **Close the IRELAND Library panel, then save the InDesign file and continue to the next exercise.**

EDIT THE BASIC GRAPHICS FRAME STYLE

An object style stores multiple frame formatting options in a single unit so you can apply all settings with one click. Object styles can include virtually any attribute that can be applied to a frame in the layout. Like text-formatting styles, object styles are dynamic — which means that changing an object style automatically changes the appearance of any object that uses that style.

Object styles are accessed and managed in the Object Styles panel (Window> Styles>Object Styles). Every layout includes a default [Basic Graphics Frame] and a default [Basic Text Frame] style, which are applied to all frames you create in the layout.

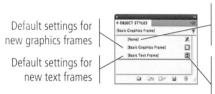

Default settings for new graphics frames

Default settings for new text frames

Click [None] to separate a specific (selected) frame from the [Basic] default.

Drag one of these icons to another style to change the default graphics and text frame settings to a different existing style.

You can edit object styles just as you edit a text-formatting style; changes to the style automatically apply to objects that use the style. In this exercise, you apply and change the Basic Graphics Frame style — which exists by default in every layout — so a number of frames can have the same basic settings (i.e., no stroke value, and a defined text wrap attribute).

Note:

By default, the [Basic Graphics Frame] style has a 1-pt black stroke and no text wrap. You're going to change the default settings so you can apply the same settings to all three graphics on the page.

1. With `letterfold_ireland.indd` open, make the inside spread visible in the document window.

2. Using the Rectangle Frame tool, click the left margin guide on Page 4 and drag to the right margin guide on Page 6.

3. While still holding down the mouse button, press the Right Arrow key three times to split the frame into four equal-sized, evenly spaced frames.

   Remember, the frame tools are "gridified"; pressing the Arrow keys while dragging creates a grid of frames within the area you drag.

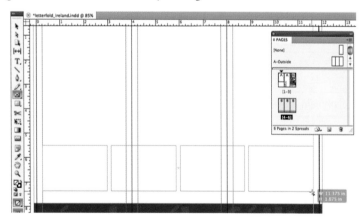

4. Release the mouse button to create the four frames.

5. With the four frames still selected, use the Control panel to change the frames' height to 2.35″ and position the top edge at 5.8″.

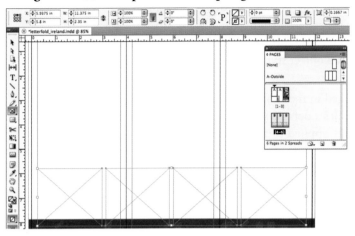

What's in an Object Style?

Use the following chart as a reminder of exactly what can be stored in an object style definition, as well as where to find the equivalent in the application interface for a selected object.

Category	Options		Application Equivalent
General	Based on Reset to base	Shortcut	N/A
Fill	Color	Tint	Swatches panel
Stroke	Color	Tint	Swatches panel
	Weight Gap attributes	Type	Stroke panel
Stroke & Corner Options	Stroke alignment End cap End treatment (arrowheads)	Join Miter limit Corner effects (bevel, etc.)	Stroke panel
Paragraph Styles	Default paragraph style for frame		Paragraph Styles panel
Text Frame General Options	Columns Vertical justification	Inset spacing Ignore text wrap	Text Frame Options dialog box (Object>Text Frame Options)
Text Frame Baseline Options	First baseline	Custom baseline grid options	Text Frame Options dialog box (Object>Text Frame Options)
Story Options	Optical margin alignment		Story panel
Text Wrap & Other	Text wrap type Wrap options	Offset Contour options	Text Wrap panel
	Nonprinting check box		Attributes panel
Anchored Object Options	Position (Inline, Above Line, Custom) Prevent manual positioning		Anchored Object Options dialog box (Object>Anchored Object>Options)
Frame Fitting Options	Crop amount Fitting on empty frame	Alignment reference point	Frame Fitting Options dialog box (Object>Fitting>Frame Fitting Options)
Effects	Effect (including Transparency) for object, fill, stroke, or text		Effects panel

6. Open the Object Styles panel (Window>Styles>Object Styles). With the four frames selected in the layout, click [Basic Graphics Frame] in the Object Styles panel.

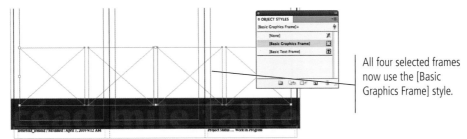

All four selected frames now use the [Basic Graphics Frame] style.

7. In the Object Styles panel, Control/right-click [Basic Graphics Frame] and choose Edit "[Basic Graphics Frame]".

Note:

You can also double-click an object style in the panel to open the Object Style Options dialog box for that style.

8. Click Fill in the Basic Attributes list and choose Paper as the Fill color.

9. Click Stroke in the Basic Attributes list and change the weight to 0.5 pt.

10. Click Text Wrap & Other in the Basic Attributes list and apply a text wrap based on the object bounding box with a 0.0625″ offset on all four sides.

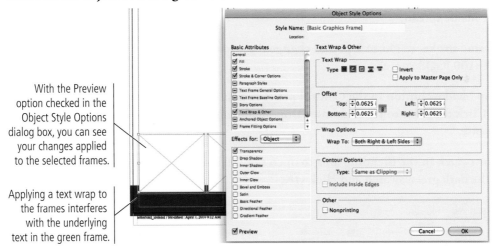

With the Preview option checked in the Object Style Options dialog box, you can see your changes applied to the selected frames.

Applying a text wrap to the frames interferes with the underlying text in the green frame.

11. Click OK to return to the layout.

12. Using the Selection tool, click to select the green text frame under the empty frames. Control/right-click the green frame and choose Text Frame Options from the contextual menu.

13. **In the Text Frame Options dialog box, check the Ignore Text Wrap option and then click OK.**

   This option allows the text to reappear in the frame because the frame is no longer affected by the text wrap attributes of the four overlying empty graphics frames.

Note:

If you want to change the default attributes of new frames, you should edit the [Basic Graphics Frame] or [Basic Text Frame] object style.

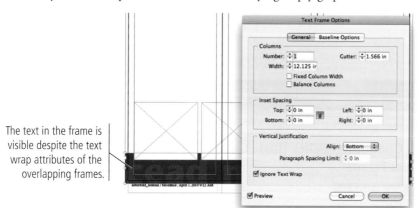

The text in the frame is visible despite the text wrap attributes of the overlapping frames.

14. **Save the file and continue to the next exercise.**

 ## CREATE A NEW OBJECT STYLE

As you saw in the previous exercise, you can edit the default styles for new text and graphics frames. When you need to define the same options for multiple frames, but you don't want to affect every new object that you create, you can create a new object style to minimize repetitive work.

1. **With letterfold_ireland.indd open, select the empty graphics frame on the left side of the inside spread.**

2. **Change the frame stroke weight to 2 pt and change the stroke color to the C=89 M=38 Y=100 K=38 swatch.**

3. **Click the Drop Shadow button in the Control panel to apply a drop shadow to the frame. Click the fx button and choose Drop Shadow to open the Effects dialog box.**

4. **Click the color swatch in the Blending area to open the Effect Color dialog box. Choose the dark green swatch and click OK.**

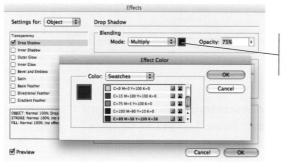

Click this swatch to change the color of the applied effect.

Note:

Object styles do not store the dimensions or position of a frame.

5. **In the Effects dialog box, change the Opacity setting to 45%. Change the X Offset and Y Offset to 0.04″ to reduce the strength of the effect, and then click OK to return to the document.**

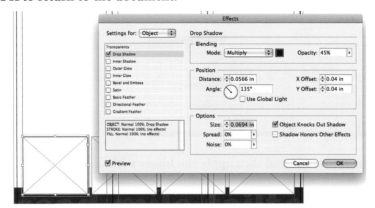

6. **With the frame selected, click the Create New Style button in the Object Styles panel.**

    Object styles follow the same basic principles as text-formatting styles. When you create a new style, it is added with the default name "Object Style [N]" (where "N" is a sequential number); the new style has the same settings as the currently selected object.

Note:

You can also open the Object Styles panel Options menu and choose New Object Style.

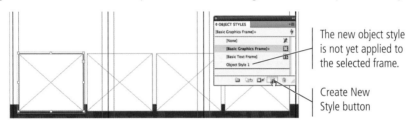

The new object style is not yet applied to the selected frame.

Create New Style button

7. **Control/right-click Object Style 1 in the panel and choose Edit "Object Style 1" in the contextual menu.**

8. **In the Object Style Options dialog box, change the style name to Image With Shadow.**

9. **In the Style Settings window, choose Stroke in the category list to review the related settings.**

10. **Change the Weight field to 0 pt, and then click OK to rename the style and return to the document.**

Select a category to see the options that can be stored in the style.

You can add effects to the object, stroke, fill, and/or text.

Change the stroke weight to 0 pt.

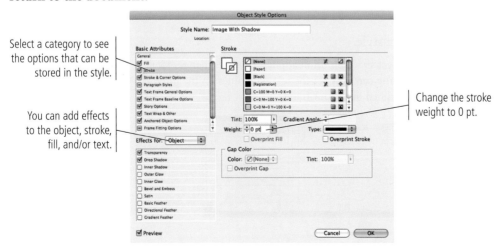

11. **With the original graphics frame still selected in the layout, click Image with Shadow in the Object Styles panel to apply the style to the frame.**

Even though the object style is based on the selected object, you still have to manually apply the new style to the object. It's easy to forget this step.

Applying the style removes the stroke from the frame.

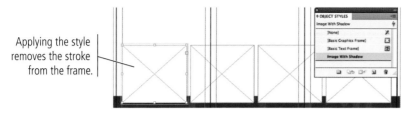

12. **Select the three remaining empty frames, and then apply the Image with Shadow style to those frames.**

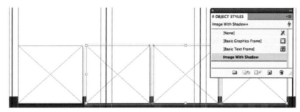

Note:

By defining an object style, you consolidated a number of formatting options into a single click.

13. **Control/right-click Image with Shadow in the Object Styles panel and choose Edit "Image With Shadow".**

14. **Click Text Wrap & Other in the list of Basic Attributes. Change the Top offset value to 0.1875″ and change the Bottom offset value to 0″.**

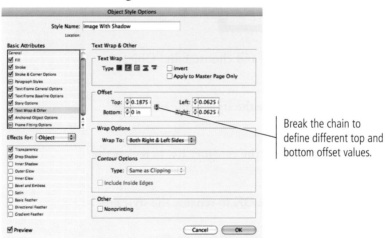

Break the chain to define different top and bottom offset values.

15. **Click OK to redefine the object style.**

As with text styles, changing an object style definition applies the same changes to all objects where the style is applied. (You can only see the text wrap lines on the three selected frames, but it has been modified in all four frames.)

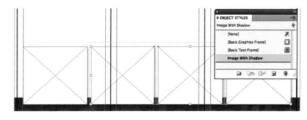

16. **Save the file and continue to the next exercise.**

IMPORT AN OBJECT STYLE

If you have already taken the time to build an element once, why not save time and effort by reusing that same element? Object styles are not limited to the file in which you create them. You can easily import object styles from one InDesign file to another.

1. **With** `letterfold_ireland.indd` **open, make the outside spread visible in the document window.**

2. **Using the Type tool, click to place the insertion point in the white text frame at the bottom of Page 1.**

3. **Choose File>Place. Choose** `form_copy.doc` **in the WIP>Ireland folder. Check the Replace Selected Item option and click Open.**

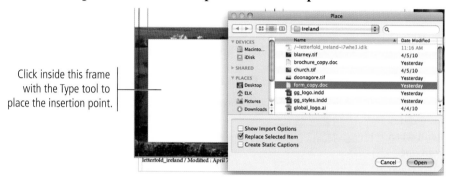

Click inside this frame with the Type tool to place the insertion point.

Text wrap attributes apply to all objects on the same layer, regardless of the stacking order of those objects. Because you edited the [Basic Graphics Frame] object style to include a text wrap, the graphics frame behind the white text frame now has a text wrap that interferes with the overlapping text frame.

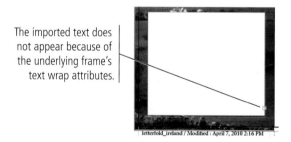

The imported text does not appear because of the underlying frame's text wrap attributes.

4. **Control/right-click the white text frame and choose Text Frame Options in the contextual menu. Check the Ignore Text Wrap option and then click OK.**

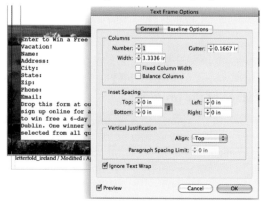

5. **Open the Object Styles panel (Window>Styles>Object Styles), and choose Load Object Styles in the Object Styles panel Options menu.**

6. **Navigate to `gg_styles.indd` (in the WIP>Ireland folder) and click Open.**

7. **Uncheck the two basic frame styles, leaving only the Form Box option checked.**

If you change the [Basic Graphics Frame] style for a file (as you did in an earlier exercise), be careful when importing object styles from one InDesign file to another. You could inadvertently overwrite the changes you already made, meaning you would have to redo your earlier work.

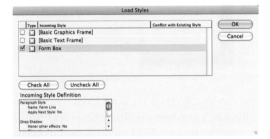

8. **Click OK to import the Form Box object style.**

9. **Click the text frame with the Selection tool, and then click Form Box in the Object Styles panel.**

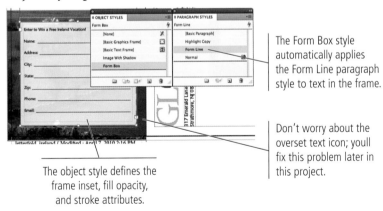

The Form Box style automatically applies the Form Line paragraph style to text in the frame.

Don't worry about the overset text icon; youll fix this problem later in this project.

The object style defines the frame inset, fill opacity, and stroke attributes.

10. **Save the file and continue to the next stage of the project.**

Stage 3 Advanced Text Formatting

If you completed the first four projects in this book, you have already learned about many options for formatting text, both locally and using styles. And yet, there are still more options, including more complex ones that meet very specific needs (such as formatting tabbed text), improving consistency from one document to another (such as importing styles from another InDesign document), and even automatically generating text from stored image data. As we mentioned very early in this book, InDesign gives you almost unlimited control over the text in your layout; this stage of the project introduces some of the more sophisticated options for doing just that.

IMPORT AND FLOW CLIENT-SUPPLIED TEXT

In the previous project you learned the basics of importing user-defined styles from a Microsoft Word file. When your clients use more sophisticated styles in their layouts, you need to understand what to do with those styles when you import the files into your InDesign layout.

1. **With letterfold_ireland.indd open, make the Page 4–6 spread visible in the document window.**

   Remember: you can double-click the page numbers below the page icons to show the entire spread in the document window.

2. **Choose File>Place. Navigate to brochure_copy.doc in your WIP>Ireland folder. Make sure the Show Import Options box is checked and click Open.**

   The Formatting section of the resulting Import Options dialog box shows that three conflicts exist between the styles in the Microsoft Word file and the styles in the InDesign file.

3. **Under Preserve Styles and Formatting from Text and Tables, make sure the Import Styles Automatically option is selected, and then choose Auto Rename in the Paragraph Style Conflicts menu. Click OK.**

   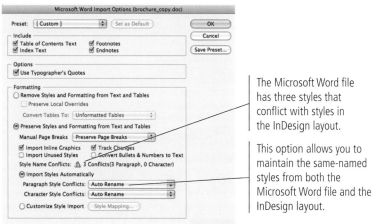

   The Microsoft Word file has three styles that conflict with styles in the InDesign layout.

   This option allows you to maintain the same-named styles from both the Microsoft Word file and the InDesign layout.

4. **If you see a Missing Font warning, review the information and then click OK.**

5. **In the document window, press Option/Alt and move the cursor over the text frame on Page 4.**

Normally, clicking with the loaded text cursor fills the current frame and leaves overset text as overset text. By pressing Option/Alt before clicking, however, you can keep overset text loaded in the cursor so you can choose the next frame where the story will thread; this is called **semi-automatic text flow**.

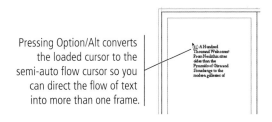

Pressing Option/Alt converts the loaded cursor to the semi-auto flow cursor so you can direct the flow of text into more than one frame.

Note:

Semi-automatic text flow works on one frame at a time, so you have to Option/Alt-click each frame to keep overset text loaded in the cursor. You can automatically flow an entire story by Shift-clicking with the loaded cursor. In this case, pages are added as necessary to accommodate the entire story.

6. **While holding down the Option/Alt key, click in the text frame on the middle page of the spread to place more of the story.**

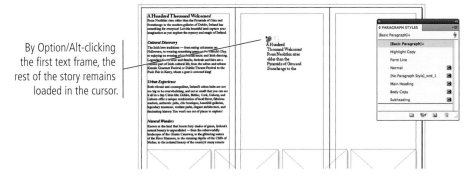

By Option/Alt-clicking the first text frame, the rest of the story remains loaded in the cursor.

7. **Click the third frame to place the rest of the story.**

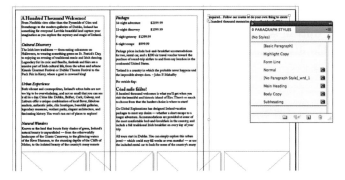

8. **Highlight all text including and after the paragraph "For outside flap:".**

In some cases, you might want to thread text across multiple frames (as you just did for the inside of the brochure). In other cases, it is better to break a single story into multiple stories to prevent text from accidentally flowing into the wrong place.

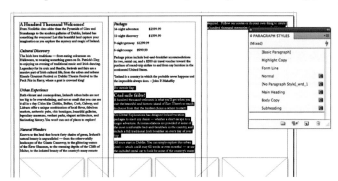

Note:

This kind of notation is common in client-supplied text.

9. **Cut the text from the frame (Edit>Cut or Command/Control-X).**

   As in many applications, when you cut text from a story, the text is stored in the Clipboard so you can paste it somewhere else.

10. **Using the Type tool, click the empty text frame on Page 1 (on the outside spread) to place the insertion point and then paste the text you just cut (Edit>Paste or Command/Control-V).**

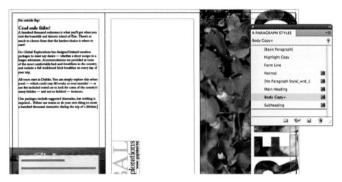

11. **Highlight the entire first paragraph in the frame ("For outside flap:", including the paragraph-return character) and press Delete/Backspace.**

    Pressing Delete/Backspace removes the selected text from the story; the deleted text is not stored in the Clipboard.

12. **Save the file and continue to the next exercise.**

 ## IMPORT InDESIGN STYLES

In many instances, the styles you need for a particular job have already been created for another job. For example, a particular client likes to use 12-pt Garamond with 14-pt leading for the main body copy in every job. If you've already spent the time to create styles once, you can simply import them into your current file instead of repeatedly redefining the same styles.

1. **With letterfold_ireland.indd open, choose Load All Text Styles from the Paragraph Styles panel Options menu.**

   You could also choose Load Paragraph Styles, but the Load All Text Styles allows you to access both character and paragraph styles in a single pass, instead of requiring two steps to import the two different types of styles.

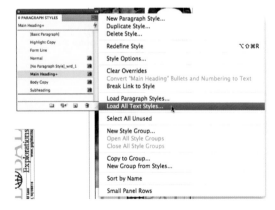

2. **Navigate to the file `gg_styles.indd` in the WIP>Ireland folder and click Open.**

   This file contains several styles that were used when your agency created other printed products for the client; for consistency, the client would like to use the same styles in this brochure.

   The Load Styles dialog box shows all styles available in the gg_styles.indd file. By default, the incoming style definitions will override the existing style definitions. You can choose Auto-Rename in the Conflict with Existing Style menu to maintain both versions of a same-named style.

   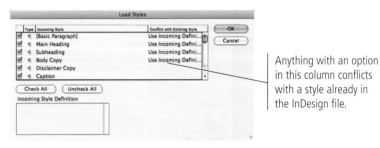

   Anything with an option in this column conflicts with a style already in the InDesign file.

3. **Click the box to the left of [Basic Paragraph] to uncheck that style.**

   By unchecking the style, it will not be imported into the active InDesign file.

4. **Click OK to import the selected styles (eight paragraph and three character).**

   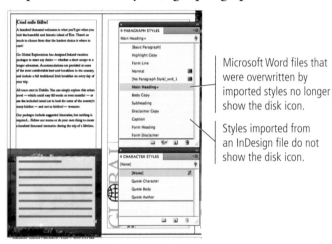

   Microsoft Word files that were overwritten by imported styles no longer show the disk icon.

   Styles imported from an InDesign file do not show the disk icon.

5. **Select all the text in the frame on Page 1 and then click the Clear Overrides button in the Paragraph Styles panel.**

   When you have conflicts between styles imported from Microsoft Word and styles in InDesign, it is fairly common to see the + indicator next to style names, indicating that something other than the style definition is applied. Clearing overrides solves this problem.

   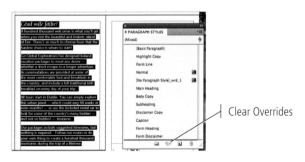

   Clear Overrides

   Note:

   Clearing overrides could also remove intentional formatting, such as a bold or italic word. Carefully review client-supplied text before making sweeping changes.

6. **On Page 4, place the insertion point in the first text frame and then choose Edit>Select All. Click the Clear Overrides button in the Paragraph Styles panel.**

With the story highlighted, you might notice another problem: some text in the story exists below the graphics frames and behind the green text frame. You can't see the text because the main text frames are below the green frame in the stacking order.

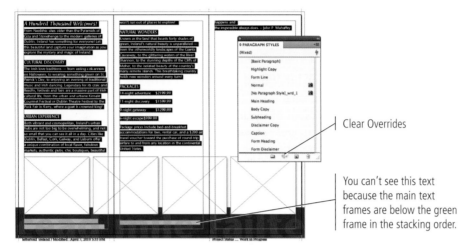

Clear Overrides

You can't see this text because the main text frames are below the green frame in the stacking order.

7. **Click the green text frame at the bottom of the spread. Using the Text Wrap panel, click the Wrap Around Bounding Box option.**

This forces the main copy to appear only above the four empty graphics frames.

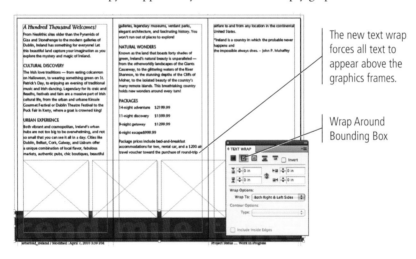

The new text wrap forces all text to appear above the graphics frames.

Wrap Around Bounding Box

8. **Save the file and continue to the next exercise.**

At times, you might want to show a specific part of an image instead of the entire image. You can accomplish this task in a number of ways, but the two most common methods involve using either Alpha channels or clipping paths stored in the image.

A **clipping path** is a vector-based path used to mask (cover) specific parts of an image; areas inside the path are visible, and areas outside the path are hidden. Because the clipping path is a vector-based object, clipping paths always result in hard edges on the clipped image.

An **Alpha channel** is a special type of image channel that masks specific parts of an image by determining the degree of transparency in each pixel. (In other words, a 50% value in the Alpha channel means that particular spot of the image will be 50% transparent). Alpha channels allow you to design with degrees of transparency; the soft edge created by a blended Alpha channel means you can blend one image into another, blend one layer into another, or blend an entire image into a background in a page-layout application.

1. With **letterfold_ireland.indd** open, make the inside spread visible in the document window; nothing should be selected in the layout.

2. Choose **File>Place**. Select **ireland_gem.tif** in the WIP>Ireland folder and then click Open.

3. Click to place the loaded image on the left page of the spread. Using the Control panel, place the image (based on the top-left reference point) at X: –1.4″, Y: –0.5″.

4. With the placed file selected, choose Object>Clipping Path>Options.

5. In the Clipping Path dialog box, choose Alpha Channel in the Type menu.

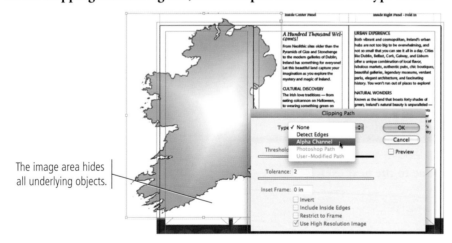

The image area hides all underlying objects.

6. **Check the Preview option to review the effect of applying the Alpha channel, and then click OK.**

   Applying the Alpha channel as a clipping path makes the white areas of the saved channel transparent; you can see the underlying objects behind those areas of the image.

Applying the Alpha channel reveals underlying objects that are outside of the channel area.

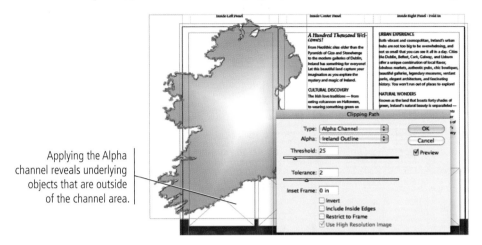

7. **Open the Text Wrap panel. Click the Wrap Around Object Shape option, and then choose Same As Clipping in the Contour Options Type menu.**

Applying the Same As Clipping contour type allows text to flow around the clipping path shape.

Wrap Around Object Shape

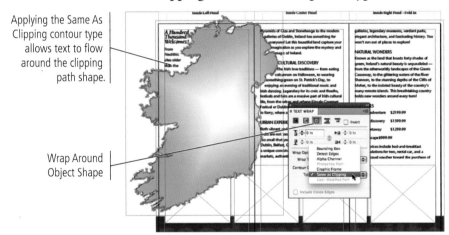

8. **Change the Top Offset field to 0.1875".**

   There are no "sides" to the non-standard shape, so you can only define a single offset value (using the Top Offset field).

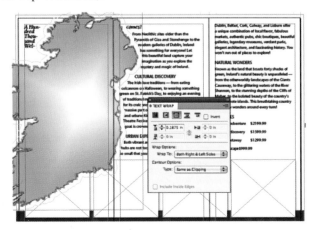

9. **Using the Layers panel, click the <ireland_gem.tif> item and drag it below the four <rectangle> items.**

The empty graphics frames are now entirely visible, on top of the placed Ireland image. Always remember that the Layers panel makes it very easy to rearrange the stacking order of objects without worrying about manually selecting anything in the layout.

Note:

You can use the Direct Selection and Pen tool variants to manually edit the text wrap in the document window. If you manually edit the clipping path, the Contour Options Type menu changes to show "User-Modified Path" and the Offset field becomes unavailable.

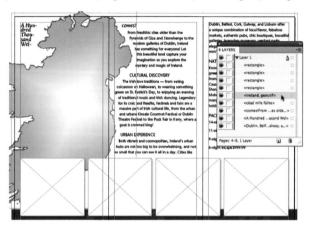

10. **In the Layers panel, click the rectangle to the right of the <A Hundred...> text frame to select that frame in the layout.**

The Layers panel also makes it easy to select objects that are entirely behind other objects, as is the case with the first main text frame and the frame that contains the Ireland graphic.

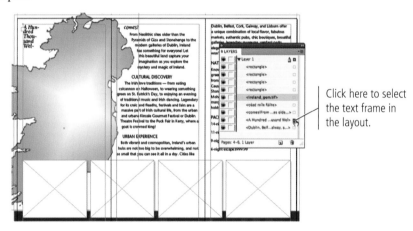

Click here to select the text frame in the layout.

11. **Press Delete/Backspace to remove the selected frame.**

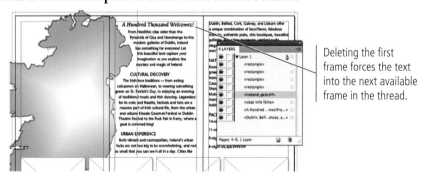

Deleting the first frame forces the text into the next available frame in the thread.

12. **Save the file and continue to the next exercise.**

Your client asked you to include a **pull quote**, which is a special visual treatment for text that is either pulled from the story (hence the name) or somehow supports the surrounding text. For the pull quote in this layout, you have been asked to use the following structure:

- Format the first character in the pull quote as a quotation mark using the Quote Character character style.

- Format the text of the quote with the Quote Copy character style. All quotes have one or more paragraphs.

- Format the author's name (preceded by an en dash) with the Quote Author character style.

You could simply format these elements in the layout, but nested styles allow you to create the structure once and apply it anywhere.

1. **With letterfold_ireland.indd open, click the text frame on Page 6 to select it.**

2. **Using the Selection tool, click the overset text icon to load the rest of the story into the cursor.**

3. **Click the pasteboard area to the right of the spread to place the remaining text in a new text frame.**

   When you work with a defined (and limited) space, it's common to have overset text that you need to place in other locations. Using the pasteboard as a temporary workspace is an easy way to review and access the remaining text.

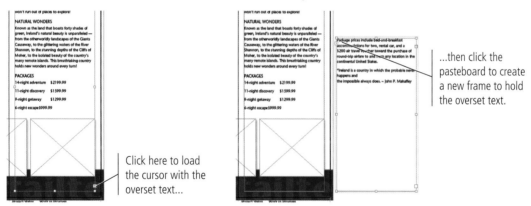

Click here to load the cursor with the overset text...

...then click the pasteboard to create a new frame to hold the overset text.

4. **Highlight the last paragraph in the copy and cut it (Edit>Cut or Command/Control-X).**

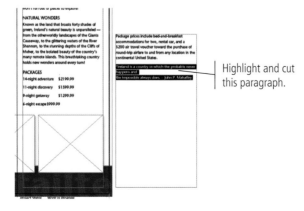

Highlight and cut this paragraph.

5. **Create a new text frame on the left page of the spread (over the Ireland picture), snapping to the margins. Paste the cut text into the new frame.**

The pasted text is affected by the image's text wrap.

6. **Select the new frame with the Selection tool and open the Text Frame Options dialog box. Check the Ignore Text Wrap option and then click OK.**

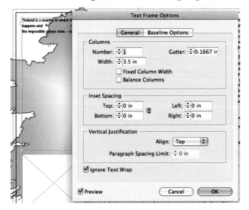

7. **Place the insertion point anywhere in the pasted text, and apply right paragraph alignment to the paragraph.**

8. **Highlight the en dash in the pasted text (before the author's name) and choose Edit>Copy.**

9. **With the insertion point anywhere in the quote paragraph, click the Create New Style button in the Paragraph Styles panel.**

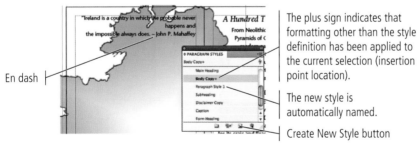

En dash

The plus sign indicates that formatting other than the style definition has been applied to the current selection (insertion point location).

The new style is automatically named.

Create New Style button

10. **Double-click Paragraph Style 1 in the panel to edit the style.**

Because the insertion point is flashing in the quotation text, the first click in the double-click applies the new style to the paragraph. The new style defaults to the formatting of the current insertion point (or selection, if any characters are highlighted).

11. **Change the style name to Pull Quote and make sure the Preview check box is active.**

12. Click Drop Caps and Nested Styles in the list of categories to display those options, and then click the New Nested Style button.

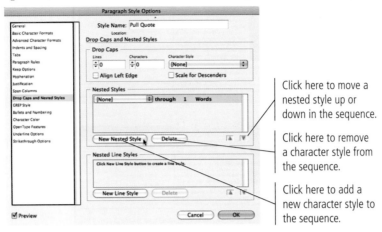

Click here to move a nested style up or down in the sequence.

Click here to remove a character style from the sequence.

Click here to add a new character style to the sequence.

13. Click the first menu (the one that says "[None]") and choose Quote Character in the list of available character styles.

When you imported the styles from the gg_styles.indd file, you imported three character styles that should be used to format pull quotes. In the next few steps, you will create a nested style that automatically applies those styles to the appropriate parts of the quote.

14. Click the Words menu and choose Characters from the list.

Nested styles can be applied up to or through a specific character sequence; if you choose the Through option, the character(s) you specify will be formatted with the character style you define. For this layout, the first character in any pull quote will be formatted with the Quote Character style; you can leave the default Through 1 option.

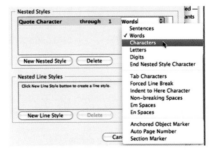

Because the Preview option is checked, the layout shows a dynamic preview of your choices. The nested styles apply the Quote Character character style to the first character in the paragraph.

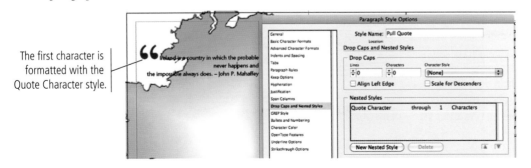

The first character is formatted with the Quote Character style.

InDesign supports three kinds of nested styles. The first is the basic parent/child relationship, in which one style is based on another. When you base one style on another, you change all related styles by changing the parent style.

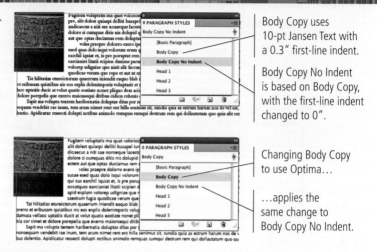

Body Copy uses 10-pt Jansen Text with a 0.3" first-line indent.

Body Copy No Indent is based on Body Copy, with the first-line indent changed to 0".

Changing Body Copy to use Optima…

…applies the same change to Body Copy No Indent.

The second type of nested style incorporates different character styles for specific parts of a paragraph. You can use nested character styles for drop caps, bulleted lists, and numbered lists.

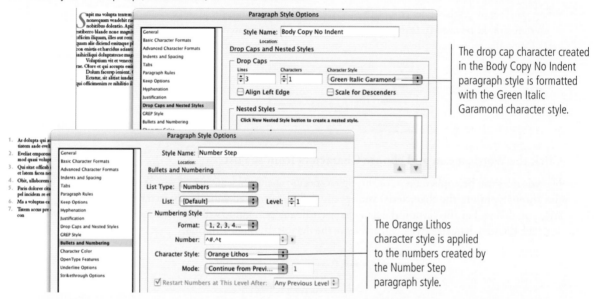

The drop cap character created in the Body Copy No Indent paragraph style is formatted with the Green Italic Garamond character style.

The Orange Lithos character style is applied to the numbers created by the Number Step paragraph style.

Nested Line Styles (at the bottom of the dialog box) affect the appearance of entire lines of text. You can define specific character styles to apply to a specific number of lines; the Repeat option allows you to continue a sequence of defined styles for the remainder of the paragraph. In this example, a paragraph style ("Chart") has been applied to the chart paragraph.

The first two items in the Nested Line Styles area tell InDesign to apply the Cyan Band character style to the first line of the paragraph, and then apply the Yellow Band character style to the second line of the paragraph. The third item in the list — [Repeat] — determines what to do with the remaining lines of the paragraph; in this example, InDesign will repeat the last 2 lines of the Nested Line Styles list.

The Chart paragraph style defines a sequence of two character styles that will be applied to every other line in the paragraph.

This entire chart is a single paragraph; each line is forced by a soft-return character.

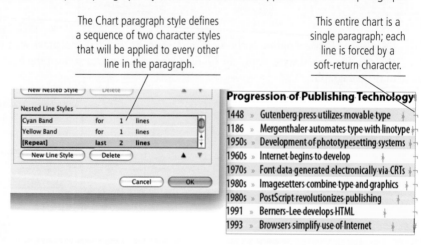

Progression of Publishing Technology

1448	»	Gutenberg press utilizes movable type
1186	»	Mergenthaler automates type with linotype
1950s	»	Development of phototypesetting systems
1960s	»	Internet begins to develop
1970s	»	Font data generated electronically via CRTs
1980s	»	Imagesetters combine type and graphics
1980s	»	PostScript revolutionizes publishing
1991	»	Berners-Lee develops HTML
1993	»	Browsers simplify use of Internet

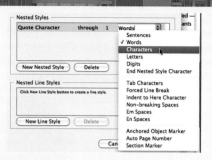

INDESIGN FOUNDATIONS

- **Sentences** applies the style up to or through the defined number of sentences. InDesign recognizes the end of a sentence as the location of a period, question mark, or exclamation point. (Quotation marks following punctuation are included as part of the sentence.)

- **Words** applies the style up to or through the defined number of words. InDesign recognizes the division of individual words by space characters.

- **Characters** applies the style up to or through the defined number of characters. Nonprinting characters (tabs, spaces, etc.) are included in the character count.

- **Letters** applies the style up to or through the defined number of letters.

- **Digits** applies the style up to or through the defined number of Arabic numerals (0–9).

- **End Nested Style Character** applies the style up to or through a manually added End Nested Style Here character (Type>Insert Special Character>Other>End Nested Style Here).

- **Tab Characters** applies the style up to or through a nonprinting tab character. (Choose Type>Show Hidden Characters to see tab characters in the text.)

- **Forced Line Break** applies the style up to or through a nonprinting forced line break character.

- **Indent to Here Character** applies the style up to or through a nonprinting Indent to Here character.

- **Non-Breaking Spaces**, **Em Spaces**, and **En Spaces** apply the style up to or through these space characters.

- **Anchored Object Marker** applies the style up to or through an inline graphic frame (which exists by default wherever you have an inline object in the text).

- **Auto Page Number** and **Section Marker** apply the style up to or through page or section markers.

15. **Add another nested style to the list, applying the Quote Body character style and using the Up To option instead of the Through option. Highlight the contents of the fourth menu and press Command/Control-V to paste the en dash that you copied in Step 8.**

    You can define a specific character by selecting the menu and typing the character.
    In this case, you're formatting all text up to the en dash preceding the author's name.

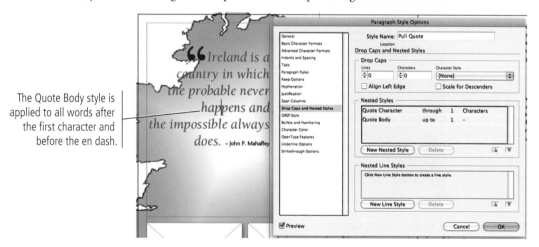

The Quote Body style is applied to all words after the first character and before the en dash.

Option/Alt-Hyphen is the key command for inserting an **en dash**, which is a special character typically used to separate ranges (as in 2–5 hours or January 13–15) in place of the word "through." Macintosh users can actually type the en dash in the dialog box field; this doesn't work for Windows users, who have to copy the character from the layout and paste it into the dialog box field.

16. **Add a third nested style to the list, applying the Quote Author character style up to one Tab character.**

    In this case, you want the style to go through the end of the paragraph. The Up To 1 Tab Character option means the Quote Author style will apply until the application encounters a Tab character; because the author information is the end of the text frame, there will never be a Tab character to interrupt the style.

The Quote Author style is applied to the en dash and all following text.

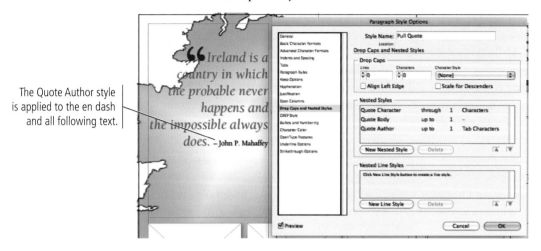

17. **Click OK to return to the document.**

18. **Place the insertion point before the en dash and press Shift-Return/Enter to force the author information onto a new line without starting a new paragraph.**

19. **Add another soft-return before the word "always" in the quote.**

20. **Adjust the top edge of the frame until you are satisfied with the position of the quote over the Ireland image.**

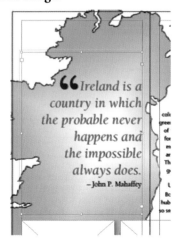

Note:

Remember, Shift-Return/Enter is the key command for a forced line break or "soft return," which starts a new line without starting a new paragraph.

21. **Save the file and continue to the next exercise.**

The final elements that need to be added to this layout are the four images at the bottom of the inside spread. The client wants to include captions to identify each location, but did not send any specific text for those captions; instead, they added titles to the various image files as metadata. In this exercise, you will generate captions directly in the layout based on the metadata that is defined for the placed images.

1. With **letterfold_ireland.indd** open, make the inside spread visible in the document window.

2. With nothing selected in the document, choose File>Place. In the resulting dialog box, press Command/Control to select **blarney.tif**, **doonagore.tif**, **malahide.tif**, and **moher.tif**.

3. Click Open to load the four selected images into the cursor.

4. Click in each of the four empty frames at the bottom of the spread to place the four loaded images.

5. Click the left image to select it, and then open the Links panel. Review the information in the lower half of the panel.

Files can include a wide range of metadata, including information about how and when the image was captured; file dimensions and resolution; color mode, and a number of other factors. You can also define custom metadata for a file, including a title, keywords, and descriptive text that make searching in a content management system easier. These images have all been assigned unique titles, which identifies the location shown in the image. You are going to use those titles to automatically generate captions in the layout.

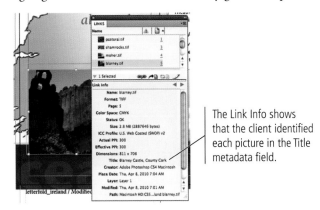

The Link Info shows that the client identified each picture in the Title metadata field.

6. **Choose Object>Captions>Caption Setup. In the resulting dialog box:**

- **Choose Title in the Metadata menu.**

    You can use the empty text fields to define specific text before and after the selected metadata.

- **Choose Below Image in the Alignment menu.**

    You can align the caption to the left, right, top, or bottom edge of the image frame.

- **Change the Offset field to 0.0625".**

    The offset determines how far the caption text appears from the image frame; it is applied as a text inset within the resulting caption frame.

- **Choose Caption in the Paragraph Style menu.**

    You can use any existing paragraph style to automatically format the resulting caption.

- **Check the Group Caption with Image option.**

    When this option is checked, the resulting caption frame is automatically grouped with the related image frame. When Group Caption is *not* checked, you can use the Layer menu to choose a specific layer where the resulting caption frames will be placed; this is useful, for example, if you want to add captions for development purposes (file name, color mode, etc.) that you want to see but should not be included in client proofs or final output.

7. **Click OK to close the dialog box.**

    Nothing yet appears in the layout because you haven't yet created the captions.

8. **With the left image selected, choose Object>Captions>Generate Live Caption.**

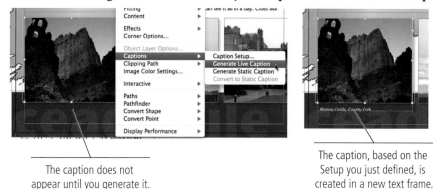

The caption does not appear until you generate it.

The caption, based on the Setup you just defined, is created in a new text frame.

9. **Repeat Step 8 for the remaining three images.**

    The second image caption shows a placeholder that indicates the placed image has no defined Title metadata. This is referred to as an **unresolved caption variable**, and can be flagged as an error using the Preflight panel.

The caption shows that the file does not include the necessary metadata.

10. **Double-click the second image to select only the image frame within the group.**

11. **Choose File>Place. Select `church.tif` in the dialog box, check the Replace Selected Item option, and click Open.**

    Because you used the Live Caption option, the existing caption automatically changes to show the Title metadata for the replacement image.

Note:

If you used the Static Caption option, the caption would not change when you replace the image.

The Live Caption option allows the caption to automatically update when you replace the image.

12. **Save the file and continue to the next exercise.**

 ## CONTROL TAB FORMATTING

Some people incorrectly rely on the spacebar for aligning columns of text, or they rely on the default tab stops (usually every half-inch in InDesign and Microsoft Word) and add as many tab characters as they need to align text. Both methods can be time consuming, and both are unnecessary to properly format tabbed text.

1. **With the inside spread of `letterfold_ireland.indd` visible, make sure hidden characters are showing (Type>Show Hidden Characters).**

2. **Click with the Type tool to place the insertion point in the first paragraph after the Packages heading.**

3. **Using the Control or Paragraph panel, change the Space After value to 0″.**

4. **If possible, make the top of the selected frame visible in the document window.**

5. **Choose Type>Tabs.**

    This is the only InDesign panel not accessed in the Window menu. If the top edge of the active text frame is visible, the Tabs panel will automatically appear at the top of the frame. If the top edge of the frame is not visible, the panel floats randomly on screen.

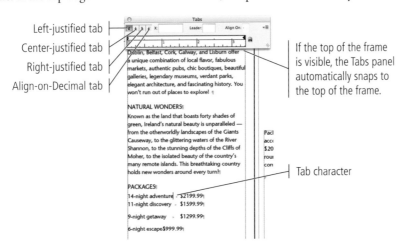

Left-justified tab
Center-justified tab
Right-justified tab
Align-on-Decimal tab

If the top of the frame is visible, the Tabs panel automatically snaps to the top of the frame.

Tab character

Note:

You can click the Snap Above Frame button to position the Tabs panel above the text frame.

 Snap Above Frame button

6. **Click the Align to Decimal tab marker in the Tabs panel, and then click the ruler to add a tab stop.**

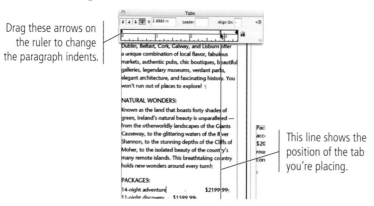

Drag these arrows on the ruler to change the paragraph indents.

This line shows the position of the tab you're placing.

Note:

If you use the Align-on-Decimal tab, you can define a different alignment character in the Align On field.

7. **With the stop you added in Step 6 selected on the ruler, change the X field to 3.125″.**

You can either drag markers on the ruler to adjust tab-stop positions, or you can use the X field to define a precise location.

8. **Type ". " (period space) in the Leader field, then press Return/Enter to apply the change.**

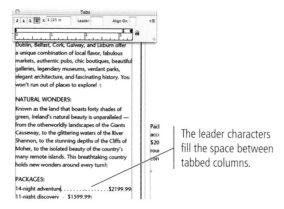

The leader characters fill the space between tabbed columns.

9. **With the insertion point still in the first price line, click the Create New Style button at the bottom of the Paragraph Styles panel.**

When you create a new style from scratch, the new style automatically adopts the settings of the current insertion point. In this case, the new style has all of the formatting that is defined in the paragraph you just edited — including the tab with its leader characters.

10. **Without moving the insertion point, double-click the new Paragraph Style 1 in the panel.**

As you already learned, the first click of the double-click applies the selected style to the active paragraph. The second click opens the Paragraph Style Options dialog box for the selected style, which automatically adopted the formatting of the insertion point when you created the style in Step 9.

11. In the resulting dialog box, type `Price Line` in the Style Name field. Click OK to return to the document window.

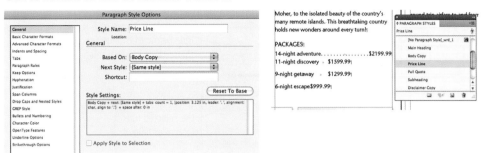

12. Select the remaining three lines of prices, then click the new Price Line style to apply it to those paragraphs.

Note:

Many client files will have multiple tab characters separating one bit of text from another. You should almost always remove extra tab characters and use tab-formatting options to create the appropriate columns.

13. Place the insertion point in the last paragraph of the story and then click the Disclaimer Copy style to apply it.

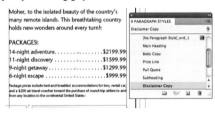

14. Save the file and continue to the next exercise.

 DEFINE PARAGRAPH RULES

The brochure layout is almost complete, with only a few remaining issues to address. In this exercise, you are going to use paragraph rules to add more visual weight to the subheadings in the body copy. You will then perform whatever clean-up tasks are required to finish the layout.

1. With **letterfold_ireland.indd** open, make sure the inside spread is visible.

2. Control/right-click the Subheading style in the Paragraph Styles panel and choose Edit "Subheading".

3. Click Paragraph Rules in the list of formatting categories and make sure the Preview option is checked.

Paragraph rules are simply lines that are attached to a specific paragraph. Rules can be placed above or below any paragraph (or above *and* below a paragraph) to add visual interest and importance to specific text elements.

4. **Choose Rule Below in the first menu, and then check the Rule On box.**

   If Rule Above appears in the menu, click to open the menu and choose Rule Below.

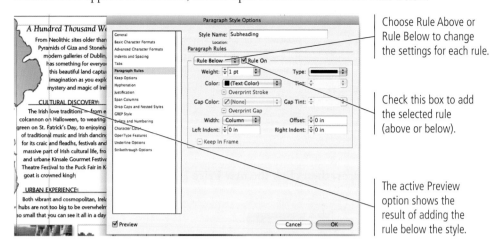

Choose Rule Above or Rule Below to change the settings for each rule.

Check this box to add the selected rule (above or below).

The active Preview option shows the result of adding the rule below the style.

5. **Change the rule weight to 6 pt. Change the rule color to C=89 M=38 Y=100 K=38 with a 15% tint.**

   This swatch is used by one of the styles you imported from another InDesign file in a previous exercise. When you import a style from one InDesign file to another, any other required assets — such as color swatches — are also imported into the current file.

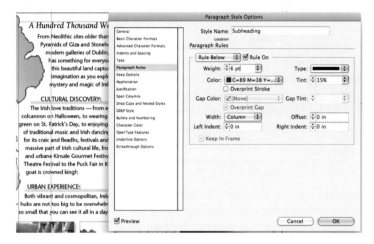

Note:

Paragraph rules do not need to be applied as part of a style. You can apply paragraph rules to paragraphs in the layout by placing the insertion point, and then choosing Paragraph Rules in the Paragraph panel Options menu.

6. **Change the Offset field to** `-0.0625"`**.**

   By default, paragraph rules align to the baseline of the text (the top edge of the rule touches the text baseline). The Offset value moves the position of the rule relative to the baseline; negative numbers move the rule up, and positive numbers move the rule down.

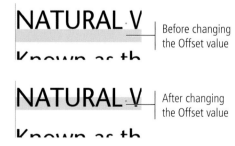

Before changing the Offset value

After changing the Offset value

The Width option defines whether the rule extends the length of the text in the paragraph or across the entire width of the column (or frame, if it's a one-column frame). You can also use the Left Indent and Right Indent fields to move the rule in from the column (or frame) edge by a specific distance.

7. **Click OK to close the dialog box and return to the layout.**

By editing the style definition, you simultaneously changed the appearance of all three paragraphs formatted with the Subheading style.

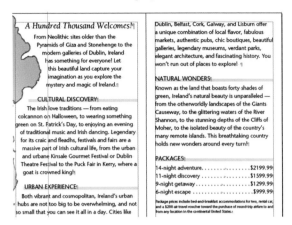

8. **Save the file and continue to the next exercise.**

 ## CLEAN AND FINISH THE FILE

Almost every job requires some amount of clean-up work at the end, even if only to optimize your file. In this exercise, you perform this last check before creating a PDF file for the output provider.

1. **With `letterfold_ireland.indd` open, make the inside spread visible in the document window.**

2. **Choose View>Fit Spread in Window to review the entire spread at once.**

As a general rule, objects on the pasteboard should be removed before the file is considered "final." Since this frame is empty, you can simply delete it.

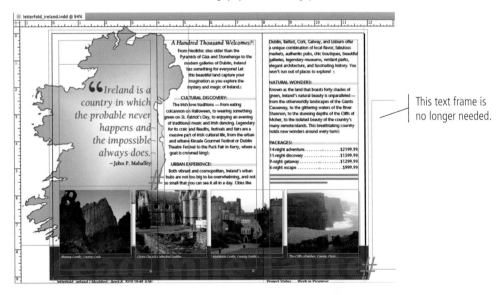

This text frame is no longer needed.

3. **Select the empty text frame on the right side of the pasteboard and press Delete/Backspace to remove it.**

4. **Navigate to the outside spread.**

Unlike the extraneous frame on the inside spread pasteboard, the outside spread has a very real problem — overset text in the form. You need to fix this problem before outputting the file.

This text frame has overset text.

5. **Zoom into the form at the bottom of Page 1.**

6. **Apply the style Form Heading to the first line in the form.**

7. **Place the insertion point at the beginning of the Zip paragraph. Press Delete/Backspace to make it part of the previous paragraph.**

Delete the paragraph return character that separates these two lines.

8. **Choose Type>Tabs to open the Tabs panel.**

9. **Choose the Left-Justified Tab marker and then click to place a new tab stop at 2″. Type an underscore character (_) in the Leader field and press Return/Enter.**

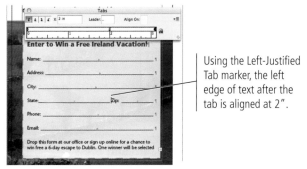

Using the Left-Justified Tab marker, the left edge of text after the tab is aligned at 2″.

10. **Apply the Form Disclaimer style to the last line in the frame.**

11. **Choose View>Fit Spread in Window, then save the file and continue to the final exercise.**

CHANGE THE CUSTOM TEXT VARIABLE

The Project Status variable that you defined in an earlier exercise allows you to monitor the status of the project while you work. As you finalize the project, you should change the variable to reflect the new status.

1. **With letterfold_ireland.indd open, choose Type>Text Variables>Define.**

2. **Select Project Status in the list and click Edit. In the Text field, change "Work In Progress" to** Finished.

3. **Click OK, and then click Done to return to the layout.**

   Because you placed the Project Status variable on each master page layout, changing the variable definition automatically changes all placed instances. Because you placed the variable instances on the master page layouts, the same change automatically reflects on the associated layout pages.

4. **Choose File>Export. Navigate to your WIP>Ireland folder, choose Adobe PDF (Print) in the Format/Save As Type menu, and click Save.**

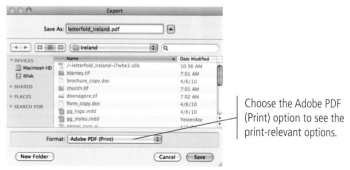

Choose the Adobe PDF (Print) option to see the print-relevant options.

5. **In the resulting dialog box, choose Press Quality in the Preset menu.**

6. **In the General pane, check the Spreads and View PDF After Exporting options.**

   Because you created each panel as a separate page, you need to export each entire spread as a single page in the resulting file.

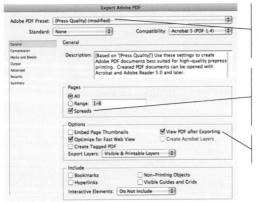

Start with the [Press Quality] preset; the [modified] indicator will appear when you change the Spreads option.

Check the Spreads option to output each side of the brochure as a single page in the PDF file.

Check this option to open the PDF when it is complete.

7. **In the Marks and Bleeds pane, check the Crop Marks option and change the Offset value to 0.125″. Check the Use Document Bleed Settings and Include Slug Area options.**

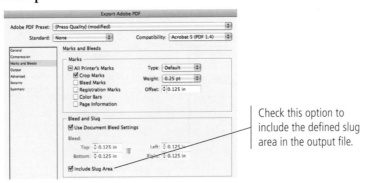

Check this option to include the defined slug area in the output file.

8. **Click Export to create the PDF file. Review the PDF file when it appears in Acrobat (or your default PDF reader application).**

   Text frames in the upper slug areas are not included because you checked the Nonprinting option in the Attributes panel when you created them.

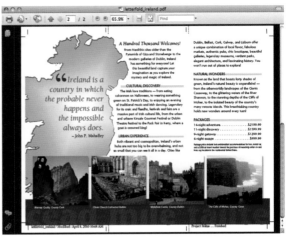

9. **Close the PDF file and return to InDesign. Save the layout file and close it.**

fill in the blank

1. A(n) _____ folds three times, resulting in four panels on each side of the sheet. The paper is folded in half, and then each half is folded in half toward the center so the two ends of the paper meet at the center fold.

2. A(n) _____ can be used to place information such as creation/modification date, file name, or custom text.

3. A(n) _____ is a spread with more than two pages.

4. You can use the _____ panel to define whether certain objects are printed when the job is output.

5. The _____ is used to modify the dimensions of a master page.

6. A(n) _____ is a special visual treatment for text that is either pulled from the story or somehow supports surrounding text.

7. A(n) _____ caption will not change if you replace one image with another in a layout.

8. A(n) _____ can be used to define multiple styles that will be used for different portions of the same paragraph, based on specific sequences of characters or markers.

9. A(n) _____ is used to format entire lines of text within a single paragraph.

10. A(n) _____ can be used to apply the same attributes (such as text wrap and stroke weight) to multiple text frames.

short answer

1. Briefly explain the rules of page geometry regarding panels that fold into other panels in a folding document.

2. Explain three different ways that text formatting styles might appear in an InDesign file.

3. Explain two scenarios in which multiple page sizes in a document might be useful.

Portfolio Builder Project

Use what you learned in this project to complete the following freeform exercise.
Carefully read the art director and client comments, then create your own design to meet the needs of the project.
Use the space below to sketch ideas; when finished, write a brief explanation of your reasoning behind your final design.

art director comments

The owner of Hollywood Sandwich Shoppe wants you to design new menus that can be printed every month at the local quick printer.

To complete this project, you should:

❏ Download the client-supplied files (in the **ID5_PB_Project5.zip** archive) from the Student Files Web page.

❏ Plan the overall layout of the piece using a letter-size sheet as the basic flat size, with no bleeds.

❏ If you decide to design the menu with folds, create a document grid that incorporates the necessary folding allowances.

❏ Import the client's text, then develop a text-formatting scheme (using styles) that will communicate the theme of the restaurant.

❏ Find supporting artwork or images that will support the restaurant's theme.

client comments

A menu is the single most important tool that a restaurant can develop to promote the business. Be creative, but also be sure that the menu is readable.

The cover needs to include the restaurant's logo, name, and address. We gave you the logo, and the address is in the menu text file.

Somewhere on the menu, you need to include space for a "special feature" that will include a description of the monthly special and a picture of the star that it's named after — we'll send this to you as soon as we finalize the first two months' specials. For now, can you just use placeholders?

Since we have to print new menus every month, we just take them to the local quick printer. We want something we can print on letter-size paper — nothing fancy or overly expensive. We might be willing to print in color if it's important, but black-only is much cheaper so we'll probably stick with that.

project justification

This project built on the skills you learned in previous projects. To begin the letterfold layout, you built a technically accurate folding guide by taking advantage of InDesign CS5's ability to incorporate multiple page sizes into a single layout. You also incorporated dashed fold guides and nonprinting text frames into the slug area. To speed up the process for the next time you need to build one of these common jobs, you saved your initial work as a template.

You also learned about several more options for improving workflow. Object styles allow you to store and apply multiple frame-formatting options (including nested paragraph styles) with a single click. Libraries store entire objects or groups of objects (including their formatting and even contents) so you can place as many instances as necessary on any page of any file.

Finally, you learned about a number of advanced text-formatting options, including importing styles from another InDesign document, creating a complex text wrap, converting text to frames, building a nested paragraph style, formatting tabs and paragraph rules, and even adding dynamic image captions based on information that is stored in a placed image.

Use type variables to define slug information

Use nonprinting objects as informational slugs

Convert text to outlines to create a complex frame shape

Use an imported object style to format a text frame

Create a library to store and access commonly used objects and groups

Remove an image background by calling an embedded alpha channel

Create a custom text wrap based on an object's clipping path

Use a nested style to format elements of a pull quote

Define an object style to format multiple image frames

Import styles from another InDesign file

Define paragraph rule settings

Define tab formatting

Create a new style based on the current insertion point

Define live captions based on image metadata

Manage font and image links in library items

Versioned Brochure

Your client produces a monthly brochure that is mailed to consumers throughout the eastern United States and Canada. The old brochure listed two prices for each product: one in U.S. dollars and one in Canadian dollars. The client now wants to produce two separate versions of the piece — one version with U.S. prices and one with Canadian prices.

This project incorporates the following skills:

❑ Managing color in placed images and layout files

❑ Controlling import options for a variety of image file types

❑ Searching and replacing text and special characters

❑ Searching and changing object attributes

❑ Controlling the language and checking the spelling in layout text

❑ Using conditional text to create multiple versions of a file

❑ Using layers to create multiple versions of a file

❑ Outputting a color-managed PDF file

client comments

We print a new brochure every month with a few featured products and sale information. The brochures drive a lot of traffic to our Web store, where we close the sales without needing to maintain a brick-and-mortar storefront.

After two years, we're starting to broaden our market. Our original name was VermontKids, but we changed it to ToyTrends so the company didn't seem so regional. We included our new logo with the files for this issue.

We do a lot of business in Canada. We used to print a single version of the brochure with both U.S. and Canadian prices, but that caused a lot of confusion from people who didn't understand why they had to "pay more" for the same product. That's why we decided to print two versions this year; now customers will see only the prices that apply to their country.

We want to print the basic flyer, but we also want to print two versions with special offers that will be mailed at the beginning of March and the beginning of April. Of course, each of those needs to have the U.S./Canadian variations.

art director comments

We build each issue of the brochure from a standard template to maintain the brand consistency the client prefers. Every issue of the brochure is printed in five-color — CMYK plus one of the three spot colors in the logo; this issue should use the blue spot color.

The client provided all of the pieces for the job — a text file with this issue's copy, as well as all product images. As the production artist, your job is to assemble the pieces, check the text and images for errors or technical problems, and create the final printable files.

You will ultimately be creating six different PDF files for the printer, but it can all be done in a single layout.

project objectives

To complete this project, you will:

❏ Define file color settings

❏ Place and control a variety of file types, including native Illustrator, native Photoshop, EPS, TIFF, PDF, JPEG, and native InDesign layouts

❏ Place multiple images at one time

❏ Check and correct spelling in the document and linked files

❏ Search and replace basic text and special characters, text formatting, and object attributes

❏ Create versions with conditional text

❏ Create and manage multiple layers

❏ Proof colors and separations on-screen

❏ Export a color-managed PDF file

Stage 1 Controlling Color for Output

You can't accurately reproduce color without some understanding of color theory, so we present a very basic introduction in the following pages. We highly recommend that you read this information. Be aware that there are entire, weighty books written about color science; we're providing the condensed version of what you absolutely must know to work effectively with color.

While it's true that color management science can be extremely complex and beyond the needs of most graphic designers, applying color management in InDesign is more intimidating than difficult. We believe this foundational knowledge of color management will make you a more effective and practically grounded designer.

Additive vs. Subtractive Color Models

The most important thing to remember about color theory is that color is light, and light is color. You can easily demonstrate this by walking through your house at midnight; you will notice that what little you can see appears as dark shadows. Without light, you can't see — and without light, there is no color.

The **additive color** model (RGB) is based on the idea that all colors can be reproduced by combining pure red, green, and blue light in varying intensities. These three colors are considered the additive primaries. Combining any two additive primaries at full strength produces one of the additive secondaries — red and blue light combine to produce magenta, red and green combine to produce yellow, and blue and green combine to produce cyan. Although usually considered a "color," black is the absence of light (and, therefore, of color). White is the sum of all colors, produced when all three additive primaries are combined at full strength.

Printing pigmented inks on a substrate is a very different method of reproducing color. Reproducing color on paper requires **subtractive color** theory, which is essentially the inverse of additive color theory. Instead of adding red, green, and blue light to create the range of colors, subtractive color begins with a white surface that reflects red, green, and blue light at equal and full strength. To reflect (reproduce) a specific color, you add pigments that subtract or absorb only certain wavelengths from the white light. To reflect only red, for example, the surface must subtract (or absorb) the green and blue light.

Remember that the additive primaries (red, green, and blue) combine to create the additive secondaries (cyan, magenta, and yellow). Those additive secondaries are also called the subtractive primaries because each subtracts one-third of the light spectrum and reflects the other two-thirds:

- Cyan absorbs red light, reflecting only blue and green light.

- Magenta absorbs green light, reflecting only red and blue light.

- Yellow absorbs blue light, reflecting only red and green light.

A combination of two subtractive primaries, then, absorbs two-thirds of the light spectrum and reflects only one-third. As an example, a combination of yellow and magenta absorbs both blue and green light, reflecting only red.

Note:

Additive color theory is practically applied when a reproduction method uses light to reproduce color. A television screen or computer monitor is black when turned off. When the power is turned on, light in the monitor illuminates at different intensities to create the range of colors that you see.

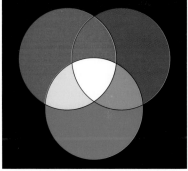

Additive color model

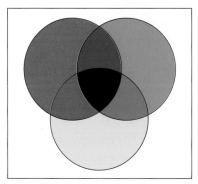

Subtractive color model

Color printing is a practical application of subtractive color theory. The pigments in the cyan, magenta, yellow, and black inks are combined to absorb different wavelengths of light. To create the appearance of red, the green and blue light must be subtracted or absorbed, thus reflecting only red. Magenta absorbs green light, and yellow absorbs blue light; combining magenta and yellow inks on white paper reflects only the red light. By combining different amounts of the subtractive primaries, it's possible to produce a large range (or gamut) of colors.

Because white is a combination of all colors, white paper should theoretically reflect equal percentages of all light wavelengths. However, different papers absorb or reflect varying percentages of some wavelengths, thus defining the paper's apparent color. The paper's color affects the appearance of ink colors printed on that paper.

Understanding Gamut

Different color models have different ranges or **gamuts** of possible colors. A normal human visual system is capable of distinguishing approximately 16.7 million different colors. Color reproduction systems, however, are far more limited. The RGB model has the largest gamut of the output models. The CMYK gamut is far more limited; many of the brightest and most saturated colors that can be reproduced using light cannot be reproduced using pigmented inks.

This difference in gamut is one of the biggest problems graphic designers face when working with color images. Digital image-capture devices (including scanners and digital cameras) work in the RGB space, which, with its larger gamut, can more closely mirror the range of colors in the original scene. Printing, however, requires images to be first converted or separated into the CMYK color space.

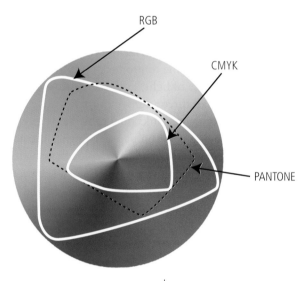

The usual goal in color reproduction is to achieve a color appearance equivalent to the original. Depending on the images, it is likely that at least some colors in the RGB model cannot be reproduced in the more limited gamut of the CMYK color model. These out-of-gamut colors pose a challenge to faithfully reproducing the original image. If the conversion from RGB to CMYK is not carefully controlled, color shift can result in drastic differences between the original and the printed images.

Color Management in Brief

Color management is intended to preserve color predictability and consistency as a file is moved from one color mode to another throughout the reproduction process. Color management can also eliminate ambiguity when a color is only specified by some numbers. For example, you might create a royal purple in the Swatches panel; but without color management, that same set of RGB numbers might look more lilac (or even gray) when converted to CMYK for printing. A well-tuned color management system can translate the numbers that define a color in one space to numbers that can better represent that same color in another space.

It's important to have realistic expectations of color management, and to realize that color management isn't a replacement for a thorough understanding of the color-reproduction process. Even at its best, color management can't fix bad scans or

Note:

Color shift can also result when converting from one CMYK profile to another (e.g., a sheetfed press profile to a web press profile), or (though less likely) from one version of RGB to another. Whatever models are being used, color management gives you better control over the conversion process.

bad photos — all it can do is provide consistency and predictability to a process that otherwise rarely has either.

Color management relies on color profiles, which are simply data sets that define the reproduction characteristics of a specific device. A profile is essentially a recipe that contains the ingredients for reproducing a specific color in a given color space. The color recipes in profiles are known as look-up tables (LUTs), which are essentially cross-reference systems for finding matching color values in different color spaces.

Source profiles are the profiles of the devices (scanners, digital cameras, etc.) used to capture an image. **Destination profiles** are the profiles of output devices. LAB (or L*a*b*, or CIELAB) is a device-independent, theoretical color space that represents the entire visible spectrum. The color management engine uses LAB as an intermediate space to translate colors from one device-dependent space to another.

The mechanics of color-managed conversions are quite simple. Regardless of the specific input and output spaces in question, the same basic process is followed for every pixel in the image:

1. The color-management engine looks up the color values of a pixel in the source (input-space) profile to find a matching set of LAB values.

2. The color-management engine looks up the LAB values in the destination (output-space) profile to find the matching set of color values that will display the color of that pixel as accurately as possible in the output space.

Note:

Color profiles are sometimes called "ICC profiles," named after the International Color Consortium (ICC), which developed the standard for creating color profiles.

Note:

Most professional-level devices come with profiles you can install when you install the hardware; a number of generic and industry-specific destination profiles are also built into InDesign.

Color Management in Theory and Practice

INDESIGN FOUNDATIONS

RGB and CMYK are very different entities. The two color models have distinct capabilities, advantages, and limitations. There is no way to exactly reproduce RGB color using the CMYK gamut because many of the colors in the RGB gamut are simply too bright or too saturated. Rather than claiming to produce an exact (but impossible) match from your monitor to a printed page, the true goal of color management is to produce the best possible representation of the color using the gamut of the chosen output device.

A theoretically ideal color-managed workflow looks like this:

- Image-capture devices (scanners and digital cameras) are profiled to create a look-up table that defines the device's color-capturing characteristics.

- Images are acquired using a profiled device. The profile of the capturing device is tagged to every image captured.

- You define a destination (CMYK) profile for the calibrated output device that will be used for your final job.

- InDesign translates the document and embedded image profiles to the defined destination profiles.

This ideal workflow mentions the word "calibrate," which means to check and correct the device's characteristics. Calibration is an essential element in a color-managed workflow; it is fundamentally important to consistent and predictable output.

Taking this definition a step further, you cannot check or correct the color characteristics of a device without having something to compare the device against. To calibrate a device, a known target — usually a sequence of distinct and varying color patches — is reproduced using the device. The color values of the reproduction are measured and compared to the values of the known target. Precise calibration requires adjusting the device until the reproduction matches the original.

As long as your devices are accurately calibrated to the same target values, the color acquired by your RGB scanner will match the colors displayed on your RGB monitor and the colors printed by your CMYK desktop printer. Of course, most devices (especially consumer-level desktop devices, which are gaining a larger market share in the commercial graphics world) are not accurately calibrated, and very few are calibrated to the same set of known target values.

Keeping in mind these ideals and realities, the true goals of color management are to:

- Compensate for color variations in the different devices
- Accurately translate one color space to another
- Compensate for limitations in the output process
- Better predict the final outcome when a file is reproduced

InDesign's color management options allow you to integrate InDesign into a color-managed workflow. This includes managing the color profiles of placed images, as well as previewing potential color problems on screen before the job is actually output.

There are two primary purposes for managing color in InDesign: previewing colors based on the intended output device, and converting colors to the appropriate space when a file is output (whether to PDF or an imagesetter for commercial printing).

1. **With no file open in InDesign, choose Edit>Color Settings.**

   The Color Settings dialog box defines default working spaces for RGB and CMYK colors, as well as general color management policies.

   The RGB working space defines the default profile for RGB colors and images that do not have embedded profiles. The CMYK working space defines the profile for the device or process that will be used to output the job.

2. **Choose North America Prepress 2 in the Settings menu.**

   InDesign includes a number of common option groups, which you can access in the Settings menu. You can also make your own choices and save those settings as a new preset by clicking Save, or you can import settings files created by another user by clicking Load.

   A working space is a specific profile that defines color values in the associated mode. Using Adobe RGB (1998), for example, means new RGB colors in the InDesign file and imported RGB images without embedded profiles will be described by the values in the Adobe RGB (1998) space.

3. **In the CMYK menu, choose U.S. Sheetfed Coated v2.**

   There are many CMYK profiles; each output device has a gamut unique to that individual device. U.S. Sheetfed Coated v2 is an industry-standard profile for a common type of printing (sheetfed printing on coated paper). In a truly color-managed workflow, you would actually use a profile for the specific press/paper combination being used for the job. (We're using one of the default profiles to show you how the process works.)

4. **In the Color Management Policies, make sure Preserve Embedded Profiles is selected for RGB, and Preserve Numbers (Ignore Linked Profiles) is selected for CMYK.**

   These options tell InDesign what to do when you open existing files, or if you copy elements from one file to another.

   - When an option is turned off, color is not managed for objects or files in that color mode.
   - **Preserve Embedded Profiles** maintains the profile information saved in the file; files with no profile use the current working space.
   - If you choose **Convert to Working Space**, files automatically convert to the working space defined at the top of the Color Settings dialog box.
   - For CMYK colors, you can choose **Preserve Numbers (Ignore Linked Profiles)** to maintain raw CMYK numbers (ink percentages) rather than adjusting the colors based on an embedded profile.

5. **Check all three options under the Color Management Policies menus.**

   The check boxes control InDesign's behavior when you open an existing file or paste an element from a document with a profile other than the defined working space (called a profile mismatch), or when you open a file that does not have an embedded profile (called a missing profile).

6. **If it is not already checked, activate the Advanced Mode check box (below the Settings menu).**

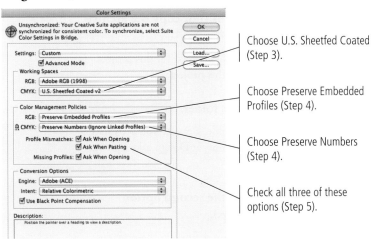

Choose U.S. Sheetfed Coated (Step 3).

Choose Preserve Embedded Profiles (Step 4).

Choose Preserve Numbers (Step 4).

Check all three of these options (Step 5).

   The Engine option determines the system and color-matching method for converting between color spaces:

   - **Adobe (ACE)**, the default, stands for Adobe Color Engine.
   - **Apple CMM** (Macintosh only) uses the Apple ColorSync engine.
   - **Microsoft ICM** (Windows only) uses the Microsoft ICM engine.

   The **Intent** menu defines how the engine translates source colors outside the gamut of the destination profile.

   When the **Use Black Point Compensation** option is selected, the full range of the source space is mapped into the full-color range of the destination space. This method can result in blocked or grayed-out shadows, but it is most useful when the black point of the source is darker than that of the destination.

7. **Click OK to apply your settings, then continue to the next exercise.**

Understanding Rendering Intents

LAB color has the largest gamut, RGB the next largest, and CMYK the smallest. If you need to convert an image from an RGB space to a more limited CMYK space, you need to tell the CMS how to handle any colors that exist outside the CMYK space. You can do this by specifying the **rendering intent** that will be used when you convert colors.

- **Perceptual** presents a visually pleasing representation of the image, preserving visual relationships between colors. All colors in the image — including those available in the destination gamut — are shifted to maintain the proportional relationship within the image.

- **Saturation** compares the saturation of colors in the source profile and shifts them to the nearest-possible saturated color in the destination profile. The focus is on saturation instead of actual color value, which means this method can produce drastic color shift.

- **Relative Colorimetric** maintains any colors in both the source and destination profiles; source colors outside the destination gamut are shifted to fit. This method adjusts for the whiteness of the media, and is a good choice when most source colors are in-gamut.

- **Absolute Colorimetric** maintains colors in both the source and destination profiles. Colors outside destination gamut are shifted to a color within the destination gamut, without considering the white point of the media.

ASSIGN COLOR SETTINGS TO AN EXISTING FILE

This project requires working on a file that has already been started, so some work has been completed before the file was handed off to you. To manage the process throughout the rest of this project, you need to make sure the existing file has the same color settings that you just defined.

1. Download **ID5_RF_Project6.zip** from the Student Files Web page.

2. **Expand the ZIP archive in your WIP folder (Macintosh) or copy the archive contents into your WIP folder (Windows).**

   This results in a folder named **Toys**, which contains the files you need for this project. You should also use this folder to save the files you create in this project.

3. **Open the file toys_spring.indd from the WIP>Toys folder.**

   The existing file has neither a defined RGB nor a CMYK profile. Because you activated the Ask When Opening option in the Color Settings dialog box, InDesign asks how you want to handle RGB color in the file.

4. **In the Profile or Policy Mismatch dialog box, select the second option (Adjust the document to match current color settings).**

   This option assigns the existing RGB color settings (which you defined in the previous exercise) to the existing file.

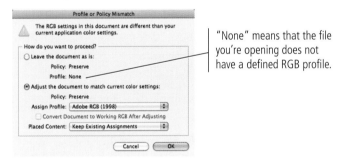

"None" means that the file you're opening does not have a defined RGB profile.

5. **Leave the remaining options at their default values and click OK.**

   Again, your choice in the Color Settings dialog box was to Ask When Opening if a file was missing a CMYK profile. Because the file does not have a defined CMYK profile, you see that warning now.

6. **In the second warning message, choose the second radio button (Adjust the document to match current color settings).**

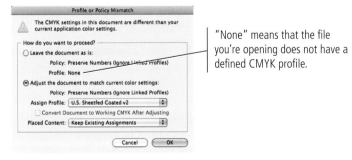

"None" means that the file you're opening does not have a defined CMYK profile.

7. **Click OK to open the file.**

This file contains the layout for a four-page folded brochure. The layout is designed with a 17 × 11″ page size; the flat size is 8.5 × 11″ when folded in the middle.

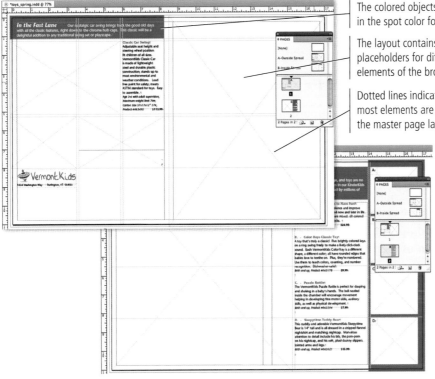

The colored objects will be output in the spot color for that issue.

The layout contains numerous placeholders for different elements of the brochure.

Dotted lines indicate that most elements are placed on the master page layouts.

Note:

Although you could design this file as four 8.5 × 11″ pages, this layout is a good example of when a file can be safely built with printer's spreads instead of reader's spreads. On Page 1 of the layout, the back (Page 4) faces the front (Page 1) of the brochure; on Page 2 of the layout, Page 2 of the brochure faces Page 3.

8. **Save the file and continue to the next stage of the project.**

Assigning and Converting Color Profiles

INDESIGN FOUNDATIONS

If you need to change the working RGB or CMYK space in a document, you can use either the Assign Profiles dialog box (Edit>Assign Profiles) or the Convert to Profile dialog box (Edit>Convert to Profile). Although these two dialog boxes have slightly different appearances, most of the functionality is exactly the same.

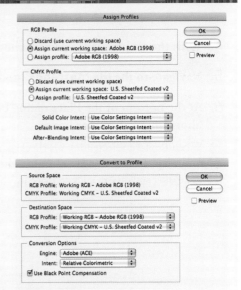

In the Assign Profiles dialog box:

- **Discard (Use Current Working Space)** removes the current profile from the document. This option is useful if you do not want to color manage the document. Colors will be defined by the current working space, but the profile is not embedded in the document.

- **Assign Current Working Space** embeds the working space profile in the document.

- **Assign Profile** allows you to define a specific profile other than the working space profile. However, colors are not converted to the new space, which can dramatically change the appearance of the colors as displayed on your monitor.

You can also define different rendering intents for solid colors, placed raster images, and transparent elements that result from blending modes, effects, or transparency settings. All three Intent menus default to use the intent defined in the Color Settings dialog box, but you can change any or all menus to a specific intent.

In the Convert to Profile dialog box, the menus can be used to change the RGB and CMYK destination spaces. This is basically the same as using the Assign Profile options in the Assign Profiles dialog box. You can also change the color management engine, rendering intent, and black point compensation options.

Stage 2 Placing and Controlling Images

Adobe InDesign supports a variety of graphics formats. The specific type of graphics you use depends on your ultimate output goal. For print applications such as the brochure you're building in this project, you should use high-resolution raster image files or vector-based graphics files.

Depending on what type of file you are importing, you have a number of options when you place a file. This stage of the project explores the most common file formats for print design workflows.

 ### REPLACE A NATIVE ILLUSTRATOR FILE

As part of the Adobe Creative Suite, InDesign supports native Adobe Illustrator files (with the ".ai" extension) that have been saved to be compatible with the PDF format. Illustrator files can include both raster and vector information (including type and embedded fonts), as well as objects on multiple layers in a variety of color modes (including spot colors, which are added to the InDesign Swatches panel when the AI file is imported).

1. **With toys_spring.indd open, double-click the A-Outside Spread icon in the master pages section of the Pages panel to show that layout.**

   Your client sent a new logo, which you need to use in the layout and template.

2. **Using the Direct Selection tool, click the logo on the page.**

3. **Open the Transform panel (Window>Object & Layout>Transform).**

   The options in the Transform panel are the same as those on the left side of the Control panel. As you can see, the selected graphic is scaled to 46.5% proportionally.

4. **With the graphic still selected, choose File>Place.**

5. **Navigate to the file toytrends logo.ai in the WIP>Toys folder.**

6. **At the bottom of the Place dialog box, check the Replace Selected Item and Show Import Options boxes.**

   When Replace Selected Item is checked, the file you choose replaces the selected item in the layout. If nothing is selected in the layout, the file you select is simply loaded into the cursor so you can click to place it.

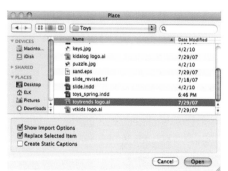

Note:

Artwork in an Illustrator file must be entirely within the bounds of the Artboard (page) edge. Anything outside the Artboard edge will not be included when you place the file into InDesign.

Note:

Make sure you use the Direct Selection tool to select the logo. If you use the Selection tool, the Transform panel shows the values for the frame instead of the graphic placed in the frame.

7. Click Open.

When Show Import Options is checked, the Place [Format] dialog box opens with the options for the relevant file format. Every file format has different available options.

When you place a native Illustrator file, the dialog box shows the Place PDF options because the PDF format is the basis of Illustrator files that can be placed into InDesign. (For an Illustrator file to be placed into InDesign, it must be saved from Illustrator with the Create PDF Compatible File option checked in the Illustrator Options dialog box.)

8. In the General tab, choose Art in the Crop To menu.

The Crop To menu determines what part of the file will import:

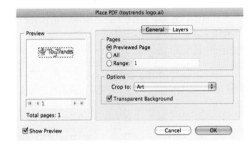

- **Bounding Box** places the file based on the minimum area that encloses the objects on the page. (You can also choose whether to include all layers or only visible layers in the bounding box calculation.)

- **Art** places the file based on the outermost dimensions of artwork in the file.

- **Crop** places the file based on the crop area defined in the file. If no crop area is defined, the file is placed based on the defined Artboard dimensions.

- **Trim** places the file based on trim marks defined in the placed file. If no trim marks are defined, the file is placed based on the defined Artboard size.

- **Bleed** places the file based on the defined bleed area. If no bleed area is defined, the file is placed based on the defined Artboard size.

- **Media** places the file based on the physical paper size (including printer's marks) on which the PDF file was created. This option is not relevant for native Illustrator files.

Note:

In the General tab, you can also define the specific PDF page or Illustrator Artboard of the file to place.

When the Transparent Background option is checked, background objects in the layout show through empty areas of the placed file. If this option is not checked, empty areas of the placed file knock out underlying objects.

9. Click the Layers tab to display those options.

PDF and native Illustrator files can include multiple layers. You can determine which layers to display in the placed file by toggling the eye icons on or off in the Show Layers list. In the Update Link Options menu, you can determine what happens when/if you update the link to the placed file.

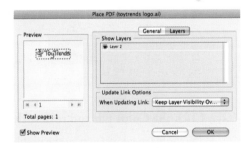

- **Keep Layer Visibility Overrides** maintains your choices regarding which layers are visible in the InDesign layout.

- **Use PDF's Layer Visibility** restores the layer status as saved in the placed file.

10. Click OK to place the file, then click the new image with the Direct Selection tool.

When you replace a selected file, the new file adopts the necessary scaling percentage to fit into the same space as the original. In this case, the new file is scaled to approximately 46.7% — the size that is necessary to fit the same dimensions as the original.

11. Save the file and continue to the next exercise.

Adobe Photoshop is also part of the Adobe Creative Suite; you can place native Photoshop files (with the extension ".psd") into an InDesign layout. You can control the visibility of Photoshop layers and layer comps, as well as access embedded paths and Alpha channels in the placed file. If a Photoshop file includes spot-color channels, the spot colors are added to the InDesign Swatches panel.

1. **With toys_spring.indd open, make Page 1 of the layout visible and make sure nothing is selected in the layout.**

2. **Choose File>Place. Select the file clowns.psd (in the WIP>Toys folder), and make sure the Show Import Options and Replace Selected Item options are checked.**

   The Place dialog box defaults to the last-used location, and the check boxes at the bottom of the dialog box also default to the last-used settings. Thus, if you continued directly from the previous exercise, you shouldn't have to make any changes.

3. **Click Open. In the resulting Image Import Options dialog box, click the Image tab and review the options.**

   If the Photoshop file includes clipping path or Alpha channel information, you can activate those options when you place the file.

   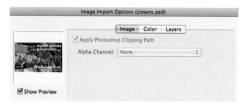

4. **Click the Color tab and review the options.**

   The Profile menu defaults to the profile embedded in the file. If the file was saved without an embedded profile, the menu defaults to Use Document Default. You can use the Profile menu to change the embedded profile (not recommended) or assign a specific profile if one was not embedded.

   The Rendering Intent menu defaults to Use Document Image Intent; you can also choose one of the four built-in options for this specific image.

   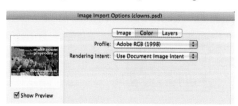

Note:

You can review and change the profile associated with a specific image by selecting the image in the layout and choosing Object>Image Color Settings. Keep in mind, however, that just because you can change the profile doesn't mean you should change it. If an image has an embedded profile, you should assume that the embedded profile is the correct one; don't make random profile changes in InDesign.

Note:

When you export the finished layout to PDF, you will use the PDF engine to convert the RGB images to CMYK. This profile tells InDesign how the RGB color is described in the file so it can be properly translated to the destination (CMYK) profile.

5. Click the Layers tab and review the options.

Photoshop files can include multiple layers and layer comps (saved versions of specific layer position and visibility). You can turn off specific layers by clicking the eye (visibility) icon for that layer. If the file includes layer comps, you can use the Layer Comp menu to determine which comp to place.

The Update Link Options you see here are the same as those in the Place PDF dialog box.

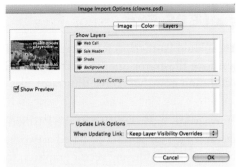

6. Click OK to load the image into the cursor.

Even though you checked the Replace Selected Item option in the Place dialog box, the image is loaded into the cursor because nothing was selected in the layout (in other words, there is nothing to replace).

Note:

Unless you know what the different layers contain, it is difficult to decide what you want to place, based on the very small preview image.

7. Click the loaded cursor in the middle frame on the left side of the page to place the image (as shown in the following screen shot).

As you can see, the text at the bottom of the image is set in both the Photoshop and InDesign files. You're going to turn off the related text layer in the Photoshop file because the client changed its company name and set up a new Web address to match the new name — and because InDesign is far better suited to setting type in a layout than Photoshop.

You should be working on Page 1, not on the A-Outside Spread master.

The same text is set in the Photoshop file and in the InDesign layout.

8. With the placed file selected, choose Object>Object Layer Options.

This dialog box contains the same options as the Layers tab in the Image Import Options dialog box.

9. Activate the Preview option, and then click the eye icon for the Web Call layer to turn off that layer. (If necessary, drag the dialog box out of the way so you can see the placed picture as well as the dialog box.)

When the Preview option is checked, your changes in the dialog box reflect in the placed image (behind the dialog box). This method makes it easy to experiment with different layer visibility options before finalizing your choices.

10. Click OK to close the Object Layer Options dialog box.

11. Save the file and continue to the next exercise.

The EPS (Encapsulated PostScript) format is commonly used for exporting vector graphics from Adobe Illustrator or other vector-based applications (although it is becoming les common now that native Illustrator files are supported by most other applications).

The EPS format uses an adaptation of the PostScript page-description language to produce a "placeable" file for PostScript-based artwork. Many vector graphics are saved as EPS files, but not all EPS files are vector graphics; the format supports both vector and raster information. Some Photoshop files — specifically, those with embedded clipping paths or spot color channels — also use the EPS format.

Because InDesign supports native Illustrator and Photoshop files, as well as PDF files, the EPS format is slowly disappearing from the graphics workflow.

1. **With toys_spring.indd open, select the placed clowns image on Page 1.**

2. **Choose File>Place and select the file sand.eps (in the WIP>Toys folder).**

3. **With the Show Import Options and Replace Selected Item options checked, click Open.**

This image should be selected.

This option should be checked.

4. **Review the options in the EPS Import Options dialog box.**

   The **Read Embedded OPI Image Links** option tells InDesign to read links from OPI comments for images included in the graphic. (OPI is a workflow that allows designers to work with low-resolution placement-only images in the layout; when the file is output, high-resolution versions are merged into the output stream, in place of the low-resolution proxies.)

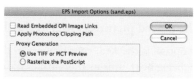

   The **Apply Photoshop Clipping Path** option applies a defined clipping path in a Photoshop EPS file. (If you turn off this option, you can later apply the clipping path by choosing Object>Clipping Path>Options.)

   The **Proxy Generation** options determine how the placed file will be viewed in the layout:

   • **Use TIFF or PICT Preview** shows the preview embedded in the file. If the file has no embedded preview, InDesign generates a low-resolution bitmap after rasterizing the PostScript data.

   • **Rasterize the PostScript** discards the embedded preview.

5. **Activate the Use TIFF or PICT Preview option and click OK to place the file.**

   Because the clowns image was selected and the Replace Selected Item option was checked, the sand image automatically appears in the selected frame.

6. **Choose Edit>Undo Replace.**

   If you accidentally replace a selected item, undoing the placement loads the last-placed image into the cursor.

Note:

The Undo command undoes the single last action. In this case, placing the image into the frame — even though it happened automatically — was the last single action.

Controlling Display Performance

INDESIGN FOUNDATIONS

By default, files display in the document window using the Typical display performance settings. In the Display Performance pane of the Preferences dialog box, you can change the default view settings (Fast, Typical, or High Quality), as well as change the definition of these settings. In the Adjust View Settings section, individual sliders control the display of raster images, vector graphics, and objects with transparency.

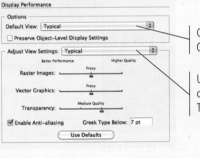

Choose Fast, Typical, or High Quality view as the default.

Use this menu to review and change the settings for Fast, Typical, and High Quality display.

In the layout, you can change the document display performance using the View>Display Performance menu. If **Allow Object-Level Display Settings** is checked in the View>Display Performance submenu, you can also change the preview for a single image in the layout (in the Object>Display Performance submenu or using the object's contextual menu).

You can turn object-level display settings on and off using the Allow Object-Level Display Settings toggle. To remove object-level settings, choose **Clear Object-Level Display Settings**. (Object-level display settings are maintained only while the file remains open; if you want to save the file with specific object-level display settings, check the **Preserve Object-Level Display Settings** option in the Display Performance pane of the Preferences dialog box.)

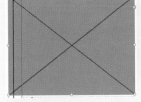

Fast displays gray boxes in place of images and graphics.

Typical shows the low-resolution proxy images.

High Quality shows the full resolution of placed files.

7. **Click the loaded cursor in the empty frame to the left of the clowns image.**

This is an easy fix if you accidentally replace an image — simply choose Edit>Undo Replace, and then click to place the loaded image in the correct location.

8. **Save the file and continue to the next exercise.**

 ## PLACE A TIFF FILE

The TIFF format is used only for raster images such as those from a scanner or digital camera. These files can be one-color (bitmap or monochrome), grayscale, or continuous-tone images.

1. **With toys_spring.indd open, make sure the placed sand image is selected in the layout and choose File>Place.**

2. **In the Place dialog box, select the file car.tif (in the WIP>Toys folder) and uncheck the Replace Selected Item option.**

This image should be selected.

This option should not be checked.

3. **Make sure the Show Import Options box is checked and click Open.**

In the Image Import Options dialog box, the Image and Color options for placing TIFF files are the same as the related options for placing native Photoshop files.

When you place a TIFF file into InDesign, you can access the clipping paths and Alpha channels saved in the files. InDesign does not allow access to the layers in a TIFF file; all layers are flattened in the placed file.

4. Click OK.

Although the placed sand image was selected when you reopened the Place dialog box, the car image is loaded into the cursor because you unchecked the Replace Selected Item option.

5. Click the loaded cursor in the empty frame above the sand image to place the car file.

6. Save the file and continue to the next exercise.

 ## PLACE A PDF FILE

PDF (Portable Document Format) files save layout, graphics, and font information in a single file. The format was created to facilitate cross-platform file-sharing so one file could be transferred to any other computer, and the final layout would print as intended. While originally meant for Internet use, PDF is now the standard in the graphics industry, used for submitting advertisements, artwork, and completed jobs to a service provider.

You can place a PDF file into an InDesign layout, just as you would place any other image. You can determine which page to place (if the file contains more than one page), which layers are visible (if the file has more than one layer), and the specific file dimensions (bounding box) to use when placing the file.

1. With toys_spring.indd open, choose File>Place.

2. In the Place dialog box, select car cover.pdf (in the WIP>Toys folder).

3. Make sure Show Import Options is checked and Replace Selected Item is not checked, and then click Open.

The options in the Place PDF dialog box are exactly the same as the options you saw when you placed the native Illustrator file. However, the options in the General tab are typically more important for PDF files than for Illustrator files.

Note:

Before placing a PDF file in an InDesign job, make absolutely sure it was created and optimized for commercial printing. Internet-optimized PDF files do not have sufficient resolution to print cleanly on a high-resolution output device; if these are used, they could ruin an otherwise perfect InDesign job.

PDF files can contain multiple pages; you can review the various pages using the buttons below the preview image. You can place multiple pages at once by choosing the All option, or you can select specific pages using the Range option.

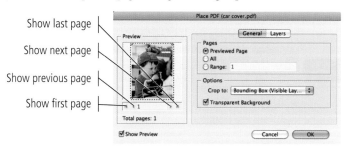

Show last page
Show next page
Show previous page
Show first page

Note:

If you place multiple pages of a PDF file, each page is loaded into the cursor as a separate object.

The Crop To options are also significant when placing PDF files. If the file was created properly, it should include a defined bleed of at least 1/8 inch and trim marks to identify the intended trim size.

4. Choose Bleed in the Crop To menu and click OK.

Note:

Import continuous pages by defining a page range, using a hyphen to separate the first page and last pages in the range. Import non-continuous pages by typing each page number, separated by commas.

5. Click the loaded cursor in the empty frame on the right side of Page 1 to place the loaded file.

6. Access the placed content by clicking the image with the Direct Selection tool or by clicking the Content Indicator icon with the Selection tool.

This file was created with 1/8″ bleeds on all four sides. In this layout, however, the left bleed allowance is not necessary. When you place the image into the frame, the bleed area on the left side causes the image to appear farther to the right than it should.

Note:

If you place an Illustrator file that contains multiple Artboards, you have the same options for choosing which Artboard (page) to place.

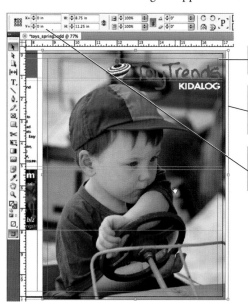

This is the placed PDF file.

When the content is selected, you can see the image edge beyond the frame edge.

The image is placed at X:0, Y:0 (based on the top-left reference point) in relation to the frame.

7. **With the placed file still selected, make sure the top-left reference point is selected, and then change the picture position (within the frame) to X+: –0.125″.**

The image bounding box now shows the extra bleed allowance extending beyond the left edge of the frame.

8. **Save the file and continue to the next exercise.**

 ## PLACE MULTIPLE JPEG IMAGES

The JPEG format is commonly used for raster images, especially images that come from consumer-level digital cameras. Originally used for Web applications only, the JPEG format is now supported by most commercial print-design applications (including InDesign).

The JPEG format can be problematic, especially in print jobs, because it applies a lossy compression scheme to reduce the image file size. If a high-resolution JPEG file was saved with a high level of compression, you might notice blockiness or other artifacts (flaws) in the printed image. If you must use JPEG files in your work, save them with the lowest compression possible.

1. **With toys_spring.indd open, navigate to Page 2 of the layout.**

2. **Choose File>Place. Navigate to the WIP>Toys folder and click the file bear.jpg to select it.**

3. **Press Command/Control and click blocks.jpg, keys.jpg, and puzzle.jpg to add those files to the selection.**

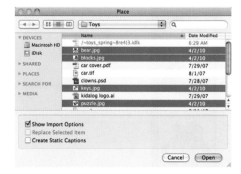

4. **With the Show Import Options box checked, click Open.**

When multiple images are selected, you will see the Image Import Options dialog box for each selected image. For JPEG images, the options are the same as for TIFF files.

5. **Click OK in each of the four Image Import Options dialog boxes.**

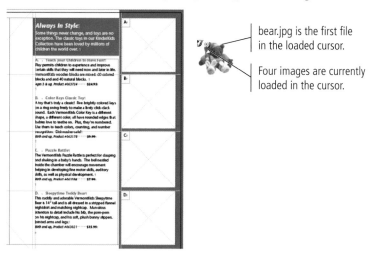

bear.jpg is the first file in the loaded cursor.

Four images are currently loaded in the cursor.

Note:

When multiple images are loaded into the Place cursor, you can use the Left Arrow and Right Arrow keys to change which image will be placed by clicking.

6. **Click in the empty frames to place the images in the appropriate spots.**

Use the cursor preview to verify which image is currently loaded, and use the brochure copy to match the products to the letters.

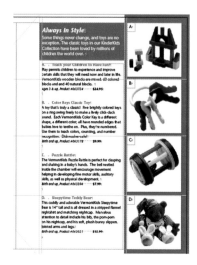

7. **Save the file and continue to the next exercise.**

Project 6: Versioned Brochure

PLACE AN INDESIGN FILE

In addition to the different types of image files, you can also place one InDesign layout directly into another InDesign file. As with PDF files, you can determine which page is placed (if the file contains more than one page), which layers are visible (if the file has more than one layer), and the specific file dimensions (bounding box) to use when the file is placed. Placed InDesign pages are managed as individual objects in the file where they are placed.

1. **With `toys_spring.indd` open, choose File>Place. In the Place dialog box, select `slide.indd` (in the WIP>Toys folder).**

2. **With the Show Import Options box checked, click Open.**

3. **In the General tab of the Place InDesign Document dialog box, choose Bleed Bounding Box in the Crop To menu.**

   The options for placing an InDesign file are mostly the same as for placing PDF files; the only exception is the Crop To menu. When you place an InDesign file into another InDesign file, you can place the page(s) based on the defined page, bleed, or slug, as described in the Document Setup dialog box.

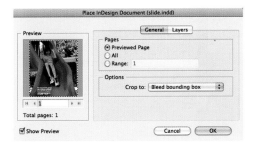

4. **Click OK. Read the resulting warning message and click OK.**

   To output properly, image links need to be present and up to date. Images placed in nested InDesign layouts are still links, so the link requirements apply in those files.

5. **Click the loaded cursor in the empty frame on the left side of Page 2 to place the file.**

   When you place one InDesign file into another, the Links panel lists images placed in the InDesign file (indented immediately below the placed InDesign file).

6. **Open the Links panel and click the arrow to the left of slide.indd to show the nested images.**

   The Links panel is more than just an informational tool; you can also use it to navigate to and edit selected images.

   - The **Relink** button opens a navigation dialog box, where you can locate a missing file or link to a different file.

   - The **Go to Link** button selects and centers the file in the document window.

   - The **Update Link** button updates modified links. If the selected image is missing, this button opens a navigation dialog box so you can locate the missing file.

   - The **Edit Original** button opens the selected file in its native application. When you save the file and return to the InDesign layout, the placed file is automatically updated.

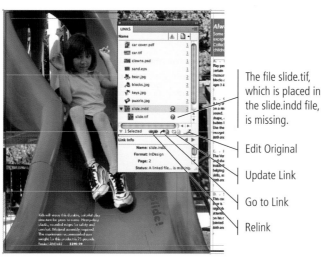

The file slide.tif, which is placed in the slide.indd file, is missing.

Edit Original

Update Link

Go to Link

Relink

7. **Click slide.indd in the Links panel, and then click the Edit Original button.**

   The Edit Original option opens the file selected in the Links panel. Because slide.indd is a placed InDesign file, that document opens in a new document window in front of toys_spring.indd.

   When you open any InDesign file, of course, you are first warned if any necessary source file is missing (which you already knew from the Links panel of the toys_spring.indd file).

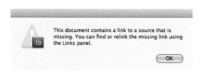

This document contains a link to a source that is missing. You can find or relink the missing link using the Links panel.

OK

8. **Click OK to dismiss the warning message.**

9. **In the resulting Profile or Policy Mismatch dialog box, choose the Adjust option and click OK.**

   Again, when you open any file, InDesign verifies the file's color based on your choices in the Color Settings dialog box.

   This file (slide.indd) was created with the U.S. Web Coated (SWOP) v2 CMYK working space, as you can see from the profile listed in the Leave Document As Is section. You are working with the U.S. Sheetfed Coated v2 working space, however, so you need to convert this file to the same CMYK working space as the main brochure file.

When the file opens, you see the missing image link in the Links panel — the reason you are editing the file.

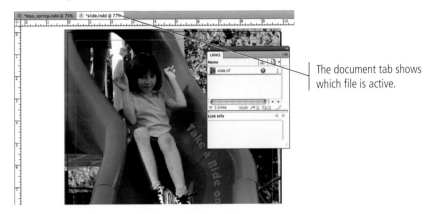

The document tab shows which file is active.

10. **In the Links panel for slide.indd, click the missing file to select it, and then click the Relink button at the bottom of the panel.**

11. **Navigate to slide_revised.tif in the WIP>Toys folder and click Open.**

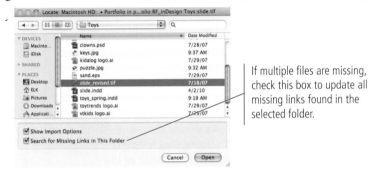

If multiple files are missing, check this box to update all missing links found in the selected folder.

12. **If the Image Import Options dialog box opens, click OK.**

13. **Save the slide.indd file and close it.**

    When you save and close the slide.indd file, the Links panel for toys_spring.indd automatically reflects the new placed file.

Note:

If you change a placed file without using the Edit Original option, the Links panel shows a Modified icon. In this case, you have to manually update the link.

14. **Save toys_spring.indd and continue to the next stage of the project.**

Stage 3 Controlling and Checking Text

As you learned in an earlier project, InDesign gives you extremely tight control over every aspect of the text elements in a layout. You can control the appearance and position of every single character, enabling you to create high-quality typographic elements. This high degree of precision is what separates the amateur from the professional designer.

Some text issues, however, have little to do with typography and more to do with "user malfunction" — common errors introduced by the people who created the text (most often, your clients). Regardless of how knowledgeable or careful you are, some problems will inevitably creep into the text elements of your layouts. Fortunately, InDesign has the tools you need to correct those issues.

ENABLE TRACK CHANGES

In many cases, multiple users collaborate on a single document — designers, editors, content providers, and clients all go back and forth throughout the design process. Each person in the process will request changes, from changing the highlight color in a document to rewriting the copy to fit in a defined space. Because the words in a design are a vital part of communicating the client's message, tracking text changes throughout the process can be useful to make sure that all changes are accurate and approved before the job is finalized.

1. **With toys_spring.indd open, use the Type tool to place the insertion point in any story.**

2. **Choose Type>Track Changes>Enable Tracking in All Stories.**

   The Track Changes feature can be activated to monitor text editing during development. This allows multiple users to edit the text without permanently altering that text until the changes have been reviewed and approved or rejected. (After you have made all the changes in this stage of the project, you will review and finalize those changes.)

3. **Open the Track Changes pane of the Preferences dialog box.**

   Make sure the Added Text, Deleted Text, and Moved Text options are checked.

4. **Choose Red in the Deleted Text Background Color menu.**

   The Text Color options define the color of highlighting that will identify each type of change. All three options default to the same color; changing the color for Deleted Text will make it easier to identify this type of change when you review the corrections at the end of this stage of the project.

Note:

Remember, preferences are accessed in the InDesign menu on Macintosh or in the Edit menu on Windows.

5. **Check the option to Include Deleted Text When Spellchecking.**

   It is very easy to make a mistake when spellchecking, so it's a good idea to include those changes in the tracking.

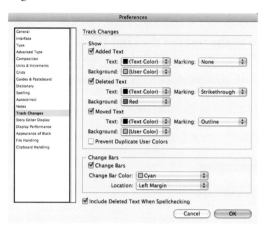

6. **Click OK to return to the document, then save the file and continue to the next exercise.**

FIND AND CHANGE TEXT

You will often need to search for and replace specific elements in a layout — a word, a phrase, a formatting attribute, or even a specific kind of object. InDesign's Find/Change dialog box allows you to easily locate exactly what you need, whether your layout is two pages or two hundred. For this brochure, you can use the Find/Change dialog box to correct the client's typing errors.

1. **With toys_spring.indd open, choose Edit>Find/Change.**

2. **Place the insertion point in the Find What field and press the Spacebar twice.**

3. **Press Tab to highlight the Change To field and press the Spacebar once.**

4. **In the Search menu, choose Document.**

   When the insertion point is placed, you can choose to search the entire Document, All [open] Documents, only the active Story, or only text following the insertion point in the selected story (To End of Story).

Note:

If the insertion point is not currently placed, you can only choose to search the active Document or All Documents.

5. **Click Change All. When you see the message that 14 replacements were made, click OK.**

6. **Highlight the content of the Find What field (the two space characters).**

   Because you can't see the space characters in the field, it can be easy to forget about them. If you forget to highlight the space characters, the new content will be added to the space characters instead of replacing them.

7. **Choose End of Paragraph in the menu to the right of the Find What field.**

   Use this menu to place common special characters in the dialog box fields. When you choose a special character in the menu, the code for that character is entered in the field.

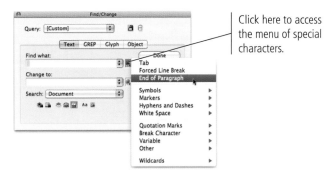

Click here to access the menu of special characters.

Note:

In real-world jobs, you might need to do these replacements several times to remove all double spaces and paragraph returns from text received from clients.

8. **Choose End of Paragraph from the menu again to search for all instances of two consecutive paragraph returns.**

9. **Highlight the Change To field and choose End of Paragraph from the associated menu.**

   You are replacing all instances of two paragraph returns with a single paragraph return.

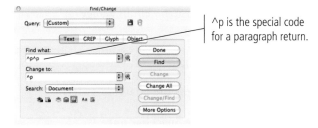

^p is the special code for a paragraph return.

10. **Click Change All, and then click OK to close the message box.**

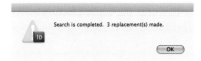

11. **Change all instances of the word "VermontKids" to ToyTrends.**

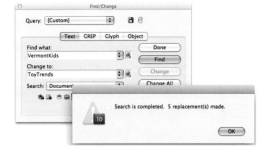

12. **Click OK to dismiss the message about the number of changes, then click Done to close the Find/Change dialog box.**

13. **Save the file and continue to the next exercise.**

Entering Special Characters in Dialog Boxes

You can enter special characters in InDesign dialog boxes using the following special codes, called metacharacters. (Note that these metacharacters are case specific; for example, "^n" and "^N" refer to different special characters.)

Character	Code (Metacharacters)
Symbols	
Bullet (•)	^8
Caret (^)	^^
Copyright (©)	^2
Ellipsis (…)	^e
Paragraph	^7
Registered Trademark (®)	^r
Section (§)	^6
Trademark (™)	^d
Dashes and Hyphens	
Em Dash (—)	^_
En Dash (–)	^=
Discretionary hyphen	^-
Nonbreaking hyphen	^~
White Space Characters	
Em space	^m
En space	^>
Third space	^3
Quarter space	^4
Sixth space	^%
Flush space	^f
Hair space	^| (pipe)
Nonbreaking space	^s
Thin space	^<
Figure space	^/
Punctuation space	^.
Quotation Marks	
Double left quotation mark	^{
Double right quotation mark	^}
Single left quotation mark	^[
Single right quotation mark	^]
Straight double quotation mark	^"
Straight single quotation mark	^'
Page Number Characters	
Any page number character	^#
Current page number character	^N
Next page number character	^X
Previous page number character	^V

Character	Code (Metacharacters)
Break Characters	
Paragraph return	^p
Forced line break (soft return)	^n
Column break	^M
Frame break	^R
Page break	^P
Odd page break	^L
Even page break	^E
Discretionary line break	^j
Formatting Options	
Tab character	^t
Right indent tab character	^y
Indent to here character	^i
End nested style here character	^h
Nonjoiner character	^k
Variables	
Running header (paragraph style)	^Y
Running header (character style)	^Z
Custom text	^u
Last page number	^T
Chapter number	^H
Creation date	^S
Modification date	^o
Output date	^D
File name	^| (lowercase L)
Markers	
Section marker	^x
Anchored object marker	^a
Footnote reference marker	^F
Index marker	^I
Wildcards	
Any digit	^9
Any letter	^$
Any character	^?
White space (any space or tab)	^w
Any variable	^v

In addition to the tools you use in this project, the Find/Change dialog box has a number of options for narrowing or extending a search beyond the basic options. The buttons below the Search menu are toggles for specific types of searches:

- When **Include Locked Layers and Locked Objects** is active, the search locates instances on locked layers or individual objects that have been locked; you can't replace locked objects unless you first unlock them.

- When **Include Locked Stories** is active, the search locates text that is locked; you can't replace locked text unless you first unlock it.

- When **Include Hidden Layers** is active, the search includes frames on layers that are not visible.

- When **Include Master Pages** is active, the search includes frames on master pages.

- When **Include Footnotes** is active, the search identifies instances within footnote text.

As you have seen, the Text tab allows you to search for and change specific character strings, with or without specific formatting options. The Object tab identifies specific combinations of object formatting attributes, such as fill color or applied object effects.

The GREP tab is used for pattern-based search techniques, such as finding phone numbers in one format (e.g., 800.555.1234) and changing them to the same phone number with a different format (e.g., 800/555-1234). Adobe's video-based help system (www.adobe.com) provides some assistance in setting up an advanced query.

The Glyph tab allows you to search for and change glyphs using Unicode or GID/CID values. This is useful for identifying foreign and pictographic characters, as well as characters from extended sets of OpenType fonts.

You can also save specific searches as queries, and you can call those queries again using the Query menu at the top of the Find/Change dialog box. This option is useful if you commonly make the same modifications, such as changing Multiple Return to Single Return (this particular search and replacement is so common that the query is built into the application).

- When **Case Sensitive** is active, the search only finds text with the same capitalization as the text in the Find What field. For example, a search for "InDesign" will not identify instances of "Indesign," "indesign," or "INDESIGN."

- When **Whole Word** is active, the search only finds instances where the search text is an entire word (not part of another word). For example, if you search for "old" as a whole word, InDesign will not include the words "gold," "mold," or "embolden."

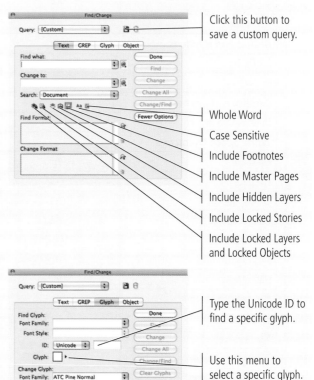

Click this button to save a custom query.

Whole Word

Case Sensitive

Include Footnotes

Include Master Pages

Include Hidden Layers

Include Locked Stories

Include Locked Layers and Locked Objects

Type the Unicode ID to find a specific glyph.

Use this menu to select a specific glyph.

FIND AND CHANGE TEXT FORMATTING ATTRIBUTES

In addition to finding and replacing specific text or characters, you can also find and replace formatting attributes for both text and objects. For this project, you need to use the blue spot color as the accent, replacing the red spot color from the template. You can't simply delete the red spot color from the Swatches panel, however, because that color is used in the placed logo file. The Find/Change dialog box makes this kind of replacement a relatively simple process.

1. With **toys_spring.indd** open, choose Edit>Find/Change. Delete all characters from the Find What and Change To fields.

    You only want to change the formatting, not the text that is formatted. To accomplish this result, you have to delete all characters from both fields.

2. Highlight the Find What field. Click the associated menu and choose Any Character from the Wildcards submenu.

    Wildcards allow you to search for formatting attributes, regardless of the actual text. In addition to searching for Any Character, you can also narrow the search to Any Digit, Any Letter, or Any White Space characters.

    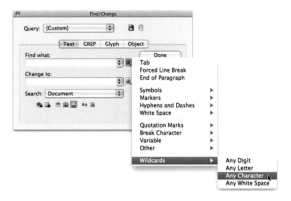

3. Click the More Options button to show the expanded Find/Change dialog box.

    When more options are visible, you can find and replace specific formatting attributes of the selected text.

    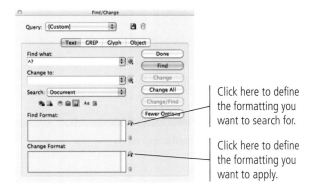

    Click here to define the formatting you want to search for.

    Click here to define the formatting you want to apply.

4. Click the button for the Find Format field to open the Find Format Settings dialog box.

    You can search for and replace any character formatting option (or combination of options) that can be applied in the layout.

5. **Show the Character Color options and click the Pantone 186 C swatch.**

6. **Click OK to return to the Find/Change dialog box.**

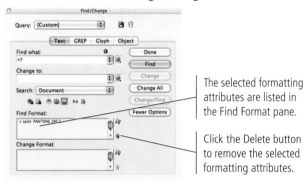

The selected formatting attributes are listed in the Find Format pane.

Click the Delete button to remove the selected formatting attributes.

7. **Click the button for the Change Format field to open the Change Format Settings dialog box.**

8. **Show the Character Color options and click the Pantone Blue 072 C swatch.**

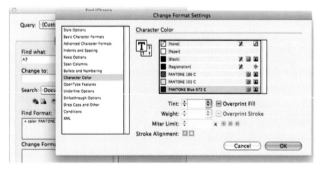

9. **Click OK to return to the Find/Change dialog box.**

10. **Make sure Document is selected in the Search menu and click Change All. Click OK to close the message about the number of replacements.**

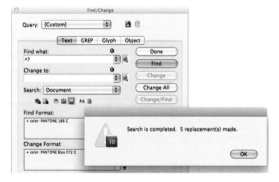

11. **In the Find/Change dialog box, click the Delete buttons to remove the formatting options from the Find Format and Change Format fields.**

It can be easy to forget to remove these formatting choices. However, if you leave them in place, your next search will only find the Find What text with the selected formatting. It's a good idea to clear these formatting choices as soon as you're done with them.

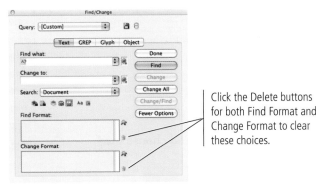

Click the Delete buttons for both Find Format and Change Format to clear these choices.

12. **Save the file and continue to the next exercise.**

 FIND AND CHANGE OBJECT ATTRIBUTES

In addition to searching for specific text formatting attributes, you can also find and replace specific object formatting attributes. In this exercise you will replace all red-filled frames with the blue spot color for this issue of the brochure.

1. **With toys_spring.indd open, open the Find/Change dialog box.**

2. **Click the Object tab to display those options, and make sure Document is selected in the Search menu.**

When you search objects, you can search the current document, all documents, or the current selection.

3. **In the Type menu, choose All Frames.**

You can limit your search to specific kinds of frames, or search all frames.

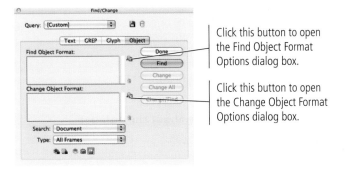

Click this button to open the Find Object Format Options dialog box.

Click this button to open the Change Object Format Options dialog box.

4. **Click the button to open the Find Object Format Options dialog box.**

You can find and change any formatting attributes that can be applied to a frame.

5. **Display the Fill options and click the Pantone 186 C swatch.**

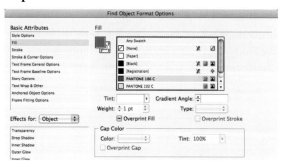

Note:

*Selected formatting options are cumulative. If you added the stroke color to the Find options, the search would only identify objects that have a red fill **and** a red stroke. To find **either** of these options, you have to perform two separate searches.*

6. **Click OK to return to the Find/Change dialog box.**

7. **Open the Change Object Format Options dialog box and choose the Pantone Blue 072 C swatch in the Fill options.**

8. **Click OK to return to the Find/Change dialog box.**

9. **Click the Include Master Pages icon to activate that option.**

   Because some frames exist only on the master pages for this file, you need to activate the Include Master Pages option to successfully replace the fill color in all frames.

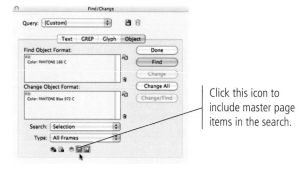

Click this icon to include master page items in the search.

10. **Click Change All, then click OK to dismiss the message about the number of changes.**

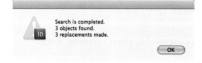

Search is completed.
3 objects found.
3 replacements made.

OK

11. **Click the Delete buttons for both the Find Object Format and Change Object Format options to clear your choices.**

12. **Click Done to close the Find/Change dialog box, and then review the layout.**

Elements of placed Illustrator, EPS, and PDF files are not affected by the Find/Change function. Placed InDesign files are only affected by the search if those files are also open when you initiate the search and if you specified All Documents in the Search menu. Because the slide.indd file was not already open, the red spot-color text in the placed InDesign file was not affected; you now have to open the placed InDesign file and manually change the red text.

 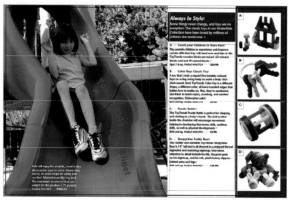

13. **On Page 2, click the placed slide.indd file with the Selection tool to select the frame. Control/right-click the selected object and choose Edit Original from the contextual menu.**

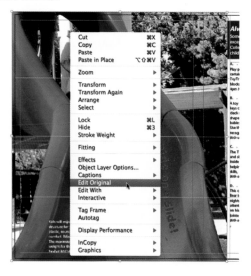

14. In the linked file, change the red text (along the curved path) to a fill of Paper. Save the slide.indd file and close it.

It makes more visual sense to change the red type to white (Paper) rather than placing blue type on a blue image. When you return to the toys_spring file, the change will automatically reflect in the placed file.

15. Save toys_spring.indd and continue to the next exercise.

 CHECK DOCUMENT SPELLING

In Project 3 you learned about preflighting and how to verify that required elements (graphics and fonts) are available. This simple process prevents potential output disasters such as font replacement or low-resolution preview images in the final print.

Many designers understand these issues and carefully monitor the technical aspects of a job. It is all too common, however, to skip another important check — for spelling errors. Misspellings and typos creep into virtually every job despite numerous rounds of content proofs. These errors can ruin an otherwise perfect print job.

1. With toys_spring.indd open, open the Dictionary pane of the Preferences dialog box.

InDesign checks spelling based on the defined language dictionary — by default, English: USA. You can choose a different language dictionary in the Language menu.

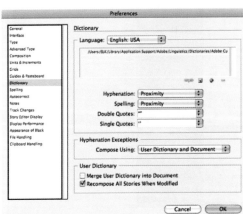

Note:

You might not (and probably won't) create the text for most design jobs, and you aren't technically responsible for the words your client supplies. However, you can be a hero if you find and fix typographical errors before a job goes to press; if you don't, you will almost certainly hear about it after it's too late to fix. Remember the cardinal rule of business: the customer is always right. You simply can't brush off a problem by saying, "That's not my job" — at least, not if you want to work with that client in the future.

2. **Make sure English: USA is selected in the Language menu and click OK.**

3. **Choose Edit>Spelling>Dictionary.**

   When you check spelling, you are likely to find words that, although spelled correctly, are not in the selected dictionary. Proper names, scientific terms, corporate trademarks, and other custom words are commonly flagged even though they are correct. Rather than flagging these terms every time you recheck spelling, you can add them to a custom user dictionary so InDesign will recognize them the next time you check spelling.

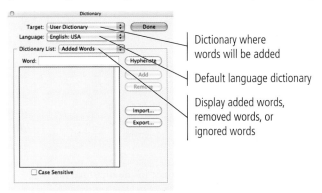

Dictionary where words will be added

Default language dictionary

Display added words, removed words, or ignored words

4. **In the Target menu, choose toys_spring.indd.**

   By default, the user dictionary is associated with all documents. You can define custom words for a specific file using the Target menu; when you change the user dictionary for a specific file, words you add for that file will still be flagged in other files.

5. **In the Word field, type** `ToyTrends`.

   Your client's company name is not a real word (even though it is a combination of two real words). If you know that certain words will be flagged, you can manually add those words to the user dictionary at any time.

   By adding this word to the file's dictionary (not the language dictionary), you prevent potential errors that might arise if you work on a project that uses the term in a more generic sense. For example, a magazine article about "Toy Trends in Middle America" should result in an error if the first two words are not separated by a space.

6. **Check the Case Sensitive option at the bottom of the dialog box, and then click Add.**

   If Case Sensitive is not checked, InDesign will not distinguish between ToyTrends (which is correct) and toytrends (which is incorrect).

7. **Click Done to close the Dictionary dialog box.**

8. With nothing selected in the layout, choose Edit>Spelling>Check Spelling.

As soon as you open the Check Spelling dialog box, the first flagged word is highlighted in the layout. The same word appears in the Not in Dictionary field of the Check Spelling dialog box.

If you are using a shared computer, it is possible that another user might have already added this word to the user dictionary (not the current file's dictionary). In this case, this word will not be flagged for your file; continue to Step 9.

Use this menu to search the current document or search all documents.

The flagged word (Burlington) is the name of a city. Although it is not in the dictionary, it is spelled correctly.

9. Activate the Case Sensitive option and click Add to add the word "Burlington" to the user dictionary.

Spellings added to the User Dictionary apply to all InDesign files; if you want to define a spelling for only a specific file, you have to add it to the dictionary for the active file (as you will do in Step 12).

The layout immediately changes to show the next flagged word — the sole capital letter "B." Many single letters will be flagged when you check spelling.

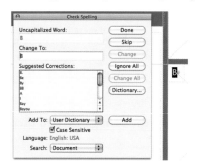

10. Click Skip.

In context, this single letter is used as an identifier, so it is correct. However, other instances of the single letter B might be errors. Clicking Skip moves to the next flagged word without adding the word to the user dictionary.

11. Review the next flagged word ("playscape").

The word "playscape" is the name of a product, and it is spelled correctly according to your client.

12. **Click the Dictionary button in the Check Spelling dialog box. Choose toys_spring.indd in the Target menu and click Add.**

When you add words in the Check Spelling dialog box, the words are added to the default user dictionary. When you open the Dictionary dialog box from the Check Spelling dialog box, you can choose the file-specific dictionary in the Target menu and click Add to add the word to the dictionary for the selected file only.

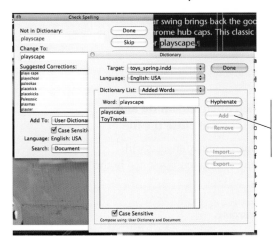

Click Add to remember the word "playscape" as a correct spelling in this document.

13. **Click Done to close the Dictionary dialog box and return to the Check Spelling dialog box. Click Skip.**

When you return to the Check Spelling dialog box, playscape still appears in the Word field. You have to click Skip to find the next suspect word.

14. **With ASTM highlighted, click Ignore All.**

When you click Ignore All, the word is added to a special list in the user dictionary so it will not be flagged again.

15. **Continue checking the spelling in the document. Make the following choices when prompted:**

37x17x12	**Skip**
KinderKids	**Add to toys_spring.indd dictionary**
and and	**Click "and" in the Suggested Corrections list and click Change**
Sleepytime	**Add to toys_spring.indd dictionary**
Marvalous	**Click "Marvelous" in the Suggested Corrections list and click Change**
www.toytrends.biz	**Ignore all**
B	**Skip**

Note:

InDesign checks spelling based on the defined language dictionary. In addition to misspellings, however, InDesign also identifies repeated words (such as "the the"), uncapitalized words, and uncapitalized sentences. These options can be turned off in the Spelling pane of the Preferences dialog box.

Note:

There seems to be some inconsistency about when Web addresses are flagged on different operating systems, depending on the specific Web address and type (e.g., .biz, .com, .edu, etc.).

If the Web address is flagged in your file, you don't want to add the Web address to the user dictionary, but you also don't want InDesign to repeatedly flag it as an error.

16. When you see the green check mark at the top of the dialog box, click Done to close the Check Spelling dialog box.

17. Using the Edit Original function in the Links panel, open slide.indd and check spelling in the file. Correct any errors, then save and close the file.

As with the Find/Change function, the Check Spelling function only interacts with nested files if those files are already open and the All Documents option is selected in the Search menu.

18. Save toys_spring.indd and continue to the next exercise.

Using Dynamic Spelling

You can turn on dynamic spelling (Edit>Spelling>Dynamic Spelling) to underline potential spelling and capitalization errors in a document without opening the Check Spelling dialog box. You can use the Spelling pane of the Preferences dialog box to assign a different-color underline for each of the four potential problems.

If you type directly into InDesign, you can turn on the Autocorrect feature (Edit>Spelling>Autocorrect) to correct misspelled words as you type. Of course, automatic corrections are not always correct; software can't always select the correct word within the context of the layout, and it might produce some very strange results for words that aren't in the active dictionary (technical or corporate terms, for example). To avoid the potential for fixing "errors" that aren't really errors, you can define what misspellings to replace and what spelling should replace those specific errors.

In the Autocorrect pane of the Preferences dialog box, you can click Add to define a specific misspelling, as well as the correct spelling to use. The Autocorrect List is maintained for the specified language dictionary.

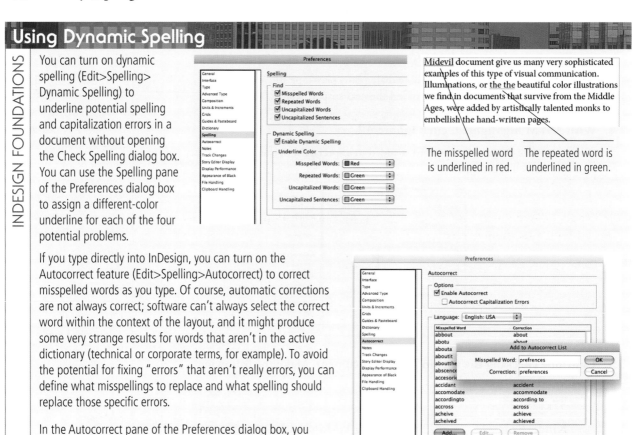

Midevil document give us many very sophisticated examples of this type of visual communication. Illuminations, or the the beautiful color illustrations we find in documents that survive from the Middle Ages, were added by artistically talented monks to embellish the hand-written pages.

The misspelled word is underlined in red.

The repeated word is underlined in green.

REVIEW TRACKED CHANGES

At the beginning of this stage of the project, you enabled the Track Changes feature for all stories in this document. You might have noticed, however, that there is no visual indication of those changes in the layout. Tracking editorial changes is useful for monitoring changes in the text, but displaying those changes in the layout would make it impossible to fit copy and accurately format the text in a layout. To avoid this confusion, changes are tracked in a special utility called the Story Editor, which more closely resembles a word-processor screen.

1. **With `toys_spring.indd` open, place the insertion point in the text frame of the right half of Page 2.**

2. **Choose Edit>Edit in Story Editor.**

   The Story Editor opens in a separate window, showing only the current story. (A **story** in InDesign is the entire body of text in a single frame or string of linked frames.)

Note:

If your deleted text is not highlighted red, you missed a step in the earlier exercise where you enabled the Track Changes feature (see page 338). You can open the Track Changes pane of the Preferences dialog box and change the highlight options now.

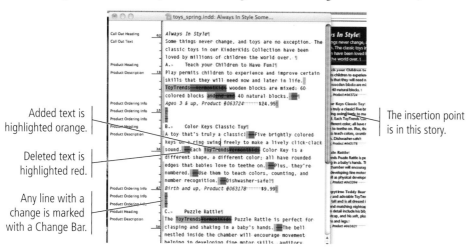

Added text is highlighted orange.

Deleted text is highlighted red.

Any line with a change is marked with a Change Bar.

The insertion point is in this story.

3. **Click at the top of the story editor to place the insertion point anywhere above the first marked change.**

4. **Choose Type>Track Changes>Next Change.**

   The first change is highlighted after you choose the menu command. Although you replaced VermontKids with ToyTrends using a single action in the Find/Change dialog box, adding and deleting are technically two separate changes that are highlighted and reviewed individually.

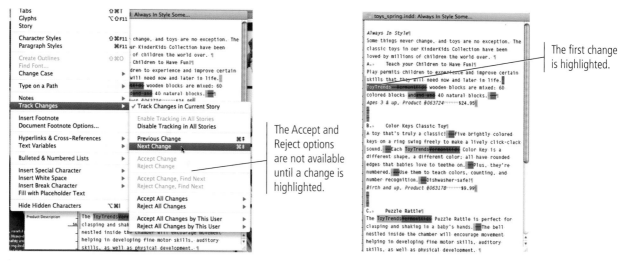

The Accept and Reject options are not available until a change is highlighted.

The first change is highlighted.

5. **Choose Type>Track Changes>Accept Change, Find Next.**

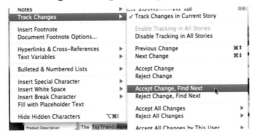

After implementing this command, the ToyTrends addition is no longer highlighted; the deleted VermontKids is the next change in the story, so it becomes highlighted.

6. **Choose Type>Track Changes>Accept All Changes>In This Story.**

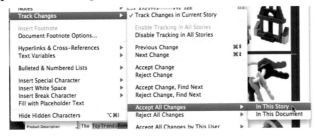

7. **Click OK to dismiss the Warning dialog box and accept the changes.**

Accepting all changes without reviewing them essentially defeats the purpose of tracking changes. However, you were conscientious in making these changes through this project; we are telling you that, in this case, it is safe to simply accept all the changes. In a real-world workflow — and especially if more than one person has been working on the same document — you should be sure to carefully review all tracked changes before finalizing the job.

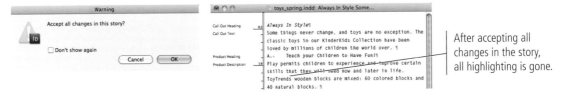

After accepting all changes in the story, all highlighting is gone.

8. **Close the Story Editor window.**

9. **Choose Type>Track Changes>Accept All Changes>In This Document.**

In Step 7 you only accepted the changes in the active story; other stories in the layout still have tracked changes that should be reviewed. Again, we are telling you it is safe to simply accept those changes. In a real-world environment, you should open each story and review the changes carefully.

10. **Click OK to dismiss the Warning dialog box and accept the changes.**

11. **Save the file and continue to the next stage of the project.**

Stage 4 Versioning Documents

The concept of versioning is a growing segment of graphic design. Clients are using a single base document, then adding varying content for different users based on specific demographics — geographic region, age, gender, or any other factor that differentiates one group from another. Other reasons for versioning include producing special editions of documents with content that does not appear on all copies; customization based on known information about past purchases or preferences; and even individual personalization using variable data to target individual users.

InDesign offers two utilities that make it possible to create multiple versions of a document in a single file rather than saving different layout files for each required version. To complete this project, you will use both conditional text and layers to accomplish the stated goals of the project.

CREATE VARIATIONS WITH CONDITIONAL TEXT

In this exercise, you create multiple "regionalized" versions of the job so recipients in Canada are not misguided by prices in American dollars. To create these variations, you will use conditional text rather than saving a separate layout file for each version.

1. With **toys_spring.indd** open, navigate to Page 2.

2. Control/right-click the placed **slide.indd** file in the layout and choose Edit Original from the contextual menu.

3. In the external file, select the text frame on the page and choose Edit>Cut.

In slide.indd...

...select and cut this frame to the Clipboard.

4. Save the **slide.indd** file and close it.

5. In the **toys_spring.indd** file, choose Edit>Paste, and then move the frame to the same approximate location where it appeared in the external file.

In toys_spring.indd, paste the cut frame and drag it into position.

6. Open the Conditional Text panel (Window>Type & Tables>Conditional Text).

7. Click the New Condition button at the bottom of the panel. In the New Condition dialog box, type American Prices in the Name field and then click OK.

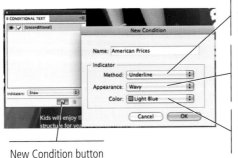

Use this menu to change the style of indicators from an underline to a highlight.

Use this menu to change the conditional indicator from the default Wavy style to the Solid or Dashed style.

Use this menu to change the color of indicators for the specific condition.

New Condition button

8. Click the New Condition button again. In the New Condition dialog box, type Canadian Prices in the Name field and then click OK.

9. In the text frame that you pasted in Step 5, place the insertion point to the right of the existing price and type $359.99.

Both prices exist in the frame.

No conditions are yet applied.

10. Highlight the first price, then click American Prices in the Conditional Text panel.

Applying a condition is as simple as selecting the targeted text and choosing the appropriate condition in the panel. In this case, you created the price as a condition so you can turn it off when you need to display the Canadian prices.

1 condition has been applied to the selected text.

11. Highlight the second price, then click Canadian Prices in the Conditional Text panel.

12. Using the same basic process, add the Canadian prices (listed here) to the remaining items on Page 2, and apply the appropriate conditions to each price:

Blocks	$29.99
Keys	$11.99
Rattle	$9.99
Teddy bear	$18.99

13. Navigate to Page 1.

Because the text frame in this case has little room for additional text, typing a new price will cause overset text and make it hard to work with. You can use the ability to show and hide specific conditions to add the new price information.

14. Highlight the existing price and apply the American Prices condition.

15. Click the Eye icon to the left of the American Prices condition.

Click this column to toggle the visibility of specific conditions.

This nonprinting character indicates hidden conditional text.

16. Click to place the insertion point after the conditional text indicator, then type $139.99. Highlight the new price, then apply the Canadian Prices condition.

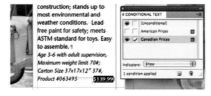

17. Click the visibility icon for the Canadian Prices condition to hide the related text, then click the empty space to the left of the American Prices condition to show those prices.

When you have multiple conditions in a file, only the visible conditions will be included in the output. By default, the conditional indicators do not appear on the output.

The color of conditional indicators matches the color of the item in the panel.

These lines are conditional-text indicators. They do not appear in the output unless you choose Show and Print in the Indicators menu of the Conditional Text panel.

Note:

You can print conditional indicators by choosing Show and Print in the Indicators menu of the Conditional Text panel.

18. Save the file and continue to the next exercise.

InDesign layers offer a powerful option for controlling the objects that make up your layouts. You can use the Layers utility to create multiple versions of the same layout. This is particularly useful if you need different versions with different objects.

When you use layers to create multiple versions of a document, the first step is to determine how many layers you need. Elements that will appear in all versions should exist on one layer. Each different version that you need to create requires its own layer to hold those elements that will change from one version to the next. In this exercise, you use InDesign layers to create variations that include special offers that appear on the versions that are mailed in March and then again in April.

1. **With toys_spring.indd open, navigate to Page 1 of the layout.**

2. **In the Layers panel (Window>Layers), double-click the Layer 1 name to open the Layer Options dialog box.**

   The default in every file is named "Layer 1", which is not terribly useful when you use multiple layers. Descriptive names are far better for any asset — including layers.

3. **Change the Name field to Common Elements and review the other options.**

   • The **Color** menu determines the color of frame edges and bounding box handles for objects on that layer. You can choose a different color from the menu, or you can choose Custom at the bottom of the menu and define your own color.

   • If **Show Layer** is checked, the layer contents are visible in the document window. You can also change this attribute by toggling the eye icon in the Layers panel.

   • If **Lock Layer** is checked, you can't select or change objects on that layer.

   • If **Print Layer** is checked, the layer will output when you print or export to PDF.

   • The **Show Guides** option allows you to create and display different sets of guides for different layers; this is a more versatile option than showing or hiding all guides (which occurs with the View>Grids & Guides>Show/Hide Guides toggle).

   • The **Lock Guides** option allows you to lock and unlock guides on specific layers.

   • If **Suppress Text Wrap When Layer is Hidden** is checked, text on underlying layers reflows when the layer is hidden.

4. **Click OK to close the Layer Options dialog box.**

5. **Using the Type tool, create a new text frame with the following parameters:**

   X: –0.125″   W: 3.5″

   Y: 10″   H: 0.6″

6. **Fill the frame with Pantone Blue 072 C, and apply a 0.0625″ inset (in the Text Frame Options dialog box) to all four sides.**

7. **In the new frame, type:**

   Order by April 1 and save 15%!
   Use code TTMAR2010 when ordering.

Note:

Layers are also useful for designing die-cut documents, which are cut in non-rectangular shape or contain an area cut out within the page. The tab on a manila folder and a folded carton are two examples of die-cut jobs.

8. **Format the first line with the Offer Main paragraph style, and format the second line with the Offer Subtext paragraph style.**

The layer shows its new name.

9. **Click the Create New Layer button at the bottom of the Layers panel.**

New layers are added above the currently selected layer; each new layer is added as Layer [N] (where "N" is a sequential number). In this case, the new layer is "Layer 2".

The Pen icon indicates the layer where new objects will be created.

10. **Double-click Layer 2 in the Layers panel. Change the layer name to** March Offer **and click OK.**

11. **In the Layers panel, click the arrow to the left of the Common Elements layer to expand it.**

12. **Click the item that represents the special-offer text frame, and drag until a line appears between the March Offer and Common Elements layers.**

Because you need to be able to output this file without any special offer, you need to move the text frame to a layer that can be independently hidden.

This line indicates that you are moving the selected item to the March Offer layer.

The frame borders and bounding box handles are now red, matching the color of the March Offer layer.

13. **Control/right-click the March Offer layer and choose Duplicate Layer in the contextual menu.**

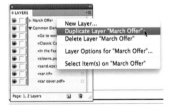

14. **Double-click the new March Offer Copy layer. Rename the layer April Offer and choose Green in the Color menu, then click OK.**

Duplicating a layer applies the same layer color to the duplicate. So you can better see where an object resides, you should change the layer to use a different color.

Note:

Two layers of the same color defeat the purpose of unique layer identifiers. When you duplicate a layer, it's a good idea to change the layer color for the duplicate.

15. In the Layers panel, click the visibility icon for the March Offer layer to hide that layer.

The text frame is still visible because it also exists on the duplicate layer.

16. In the visible text frame, change the offer text to:

Order by May 1 and get free shipping!
Use code TTAPR2010 when ordering.

17. Save the file and continue to the next exercise.

Controlling Text Wrap on Different Layers

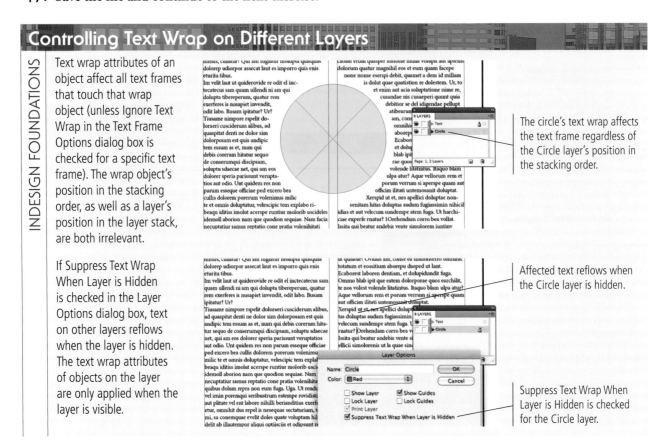

Text wrap attributes of an object affect all text frames that touch that wrap object (unless Ignore Text Wrap in the Text Frame Options dialog box is checked for a specific text frame). The wrap object's position in the stacking order, as well as a layer's position in the layer stack, are both irrelevant.

If Suppress Text Wrap When Layer is Hidden is checked in the Layer Options dialog box, text on other layers reflows when the layer is hidden. The text wrap attributes of objects on the layer are only applied when the layer is visible.

The circle's text wrap affects the text frame regardless of the Circle layer's position in the stacking order.

Affected text reflows when the Circle layer is hidden.

Suppress Text Wrap When Layer is Hidden is checked for the Circle layer.

PREVIEW SEPARATIONS

To be entirely confident in color output, you should check the separations that will be created when your file is output to an imagesetter. InDesign's Separations Preview panel makes this easy to accomplish from directly within the application workspace.

1. **With toys_spring.indd open, choose Window>Output>Separations Preview.**

2. **In the View menu of the Separations Preview panel, choose Separations.**

   When Separations is selected in the View menu, all separations in the current file are listed in the panel. You can turn individual separations on and off to preview the different ink separations that will be created:

   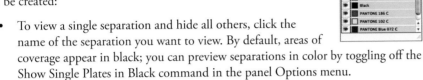

   - To view a single separation and hide all others, click the name of the separation you want to view. By default, areas of coverage appear in black; you can preview separations in color by toggling off the Show Single Plates in Black command in the panel Options menu.

   - To view more than one separation at the same time, click the empty space to the left of the separation name. When viewing multiple separations, each separation is shown in color.

   - To hide a separation, click the eye icon to the left of the separation name.

   - To view all process plates at once, click the CMYK option at the top of the panel.

3. **Click Pantone 186 C in the Separations Preview panel, and then click the empty space to the left of Pantone 102 C to review where those two colors are used in the layout.**

   The placed logos on Page 1 use both selected Pantone colors.

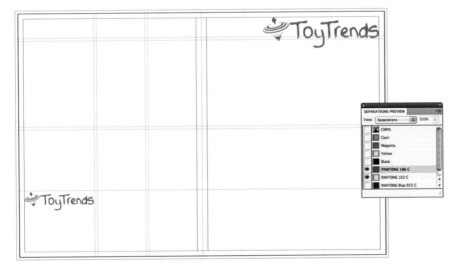

4. **Click Pantone Blue 072 C in the Separations Preview panel to see where that color is used.**

As your client stated, the brochure should use a single spot color — for this issue, the blue spot color in the logo. By reviewing the separation, you can see that the blue from the logo is also used for the accent elements on both pages of the layout.

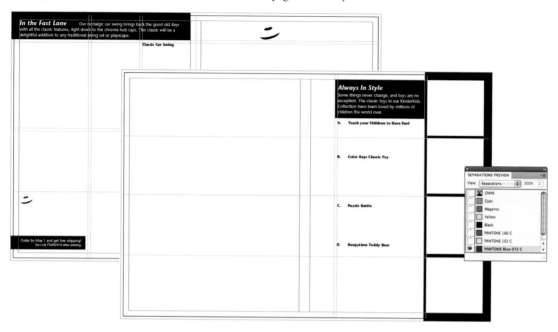

5. **Click the empty space left of CMYK in the Separations Preview panel to view the CMYK separations in addition to the Pantone Blue 072 C separation.**

You can't simply delete the other two spot colors because they are used in the client logo. You could convert them for output only, but if you need to output more than once you would have to convert the colors again each time you output the file. In this case, the most efficient option is to convert the unwanted spot colors to process colors before you output the file.

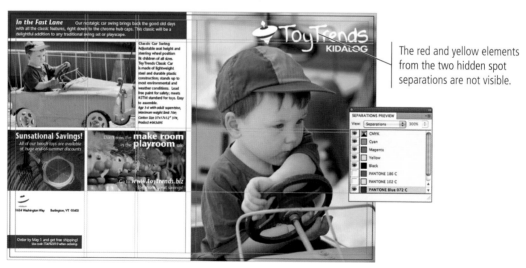

The red and yellow elements from the two hidden spot separations are not visible.

6. **In the Swatches panel, double-click Pantone 186 C to open the Swatch Options dialog box.**

7. Change the Color Type menu to Process and click OK.

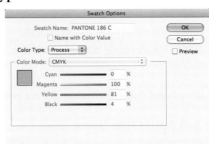

Note:

Be careful when changing spot colors to process. One reason for using spot colors is to reproduce colors that are outside the CMYK gamut; when spot colors are converted to their nearest possible CMYK equivalents, some (possibly drastic) color shift will occur.

After converting the Pantone 186 C swatch to process color, the separation is removed from the Separations Preview panel.

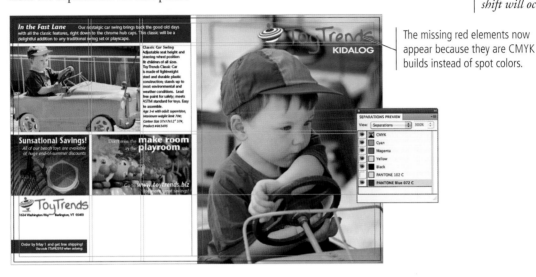

The missing red elements now appear because they are CMYK builds instead of spot colors.

8. Repeat Steps 6–7 for the Pantone 102 C swatch.

The Separations Preview panel now shows the correct number of separations for this file.

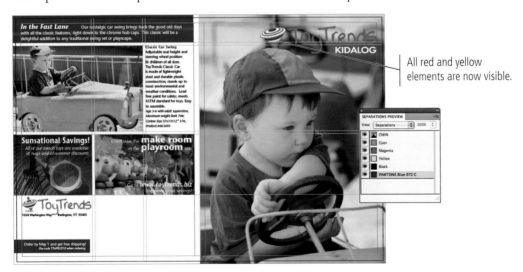

All red and yellow elements are now visible.

9. Save the file and continue to the final exercise.

EXPORT COLOR-MANAGED PDF FILES

The file is now complete and ready for output. To create the various versions of the file, you have to output the same file a number of times, selecting different layers and conditions for each version.

1. **With toys_spring.indd open, open the Layers and the Conditional Text panels.**

2. **In the Layers panel, hide the March Offer and April Offer layers.**

3. **In the Conditional Text panel, show the American Prices condition and hide the Canadian Prices condition.**

4. **Choose File>Export. Change the file name to toys_spring_nooffer_us.pdf, and choose Adobe PDF (Print) in the Format/Save As Type menu. Click Save.**

5. **Choose [High Quality Print] in the Preset menu.**

6. **In the General options, make sure Visible & Printable Layers is selected in the Export Layers menu.**

   When you output a file with layers, you can choose All Layers (including hidden and non-printable layers), Visible Layers (regardless of printable status), or Visible & Printable Layers.

7. **Uncheck the View PDF after Exporting option.**

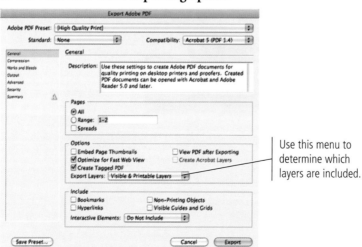

Use this menu to determine which layers are included.

Note:

These options are also available in the Print dialog box.

8. **In the Marks and Bleeds pane, turn on Crop Marks with a 0.125″ offset, and activate the Use Document Bleed Settings option.**

9. **In the Output options, choose Convert to Destination in the Color Conversion menu.**

You have several options for converting colors when you output a file:

- **No Color Conversion** maintains all color data (including placed images) in its current space.

- **Convert to Destination** converts colors to the profile selected in the Destination menu.

- **Convert to Destination (Preserve Numbers)** converts colors to the destination profile if the applied profile does not match the defined destination profile. Objects without color profiles are not converted.

The Destination menu defines the gamut for the output device that will be used. (This menu defaults to the active destination working space.) Color information in the file (and placed images) is converted to the selected Destination profile.

Note:

Spot-color information is preserved when colors are converted to the destination space.

10. **Choose Include Destination Profile in the Profile Inclusion Policy menu.**

The **Profile Inclusion Policy** menu determines whether color profiles are embedded in the resulting PDF file. (Different options are available, depending on what you selected in the Color Conversion menu.)

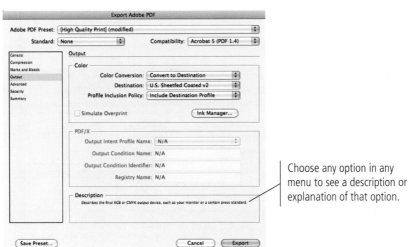

Choose any option in any menu to see a description or explanation of that option.

11. **Click the Save Preset button at the bottom of the Export Adobe PDF dialog box. In the resulting Save Preset dialog box, name the preset** `Toy Brochure PDF` **and click OK.**

    You're going to export this file six times; creating a preset means you need to make your export choices only once.

12. **Click Export to create the PDF file.**

13. **When you return to the layout, hide the American Prices condition and show the Canadian Prices condition.**

14. **Choose File>Export. Change the file name to** `toys_spring_nooffer_cdn.pdf` **and then click Save.**

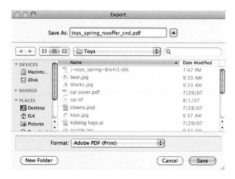

INDESIGN FOUNDATIONS

Using the Ink Manager

The Ink Manager, primarily used by experienced commercial output providers, offers control over specific inks at output time. Changes in this dialog box affect the current output, not how the colors are defined in the document. (You can access this dialog box by clicking the Ink Manager button in the Output pane of the Print or Export Adobe PDF dialog box.)

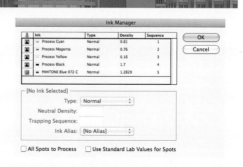

If a process job includes a spot color, a service provider can open the document and change the spot color to the equivalent CMYK process color. If a document contains two similar spot colors when only one is required, or if the same spot color has two different names, a service provider can map the two colors to a single separation. Finally, the service provider can also control the ink density for trapping purposes, as well as the sequence in which inks are printed and trapped.

15. **Make sure Toy Brochure PDF is selected in the Adobe PDF Preset menu and click Export.**

When you reopen the Export Adobe PDF dialog box, the Toy Brochure PDF preset should be already selected; the menu remembers the last-used settings. The preset calls all the same options that you already defined.

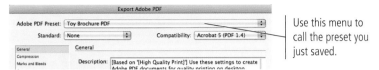

Use this menu to call the preset you just saved.

16. **When you return to the layout, show the March Offer layer.**

17. **Export a PDF file with the name `toys_spring_march_cdn.pdf`, using the Toys Brochure PDF preset.**

Continue exporting the remaining three versions by showing and hiding the appropriate layers and conditions. Use descriptive file names so you will recognize each version without opening them.

18. **Save and close the toys_spring file.**

Monitoring Ink Limits

In CMYK color, shades of gray are reproduced using combinations of four printing inks. In theory, a solid black would be printed as 100% of all four inks, and pure white would be 0% of all four inks. This, however, does not take into consideration the limitations of mechanical printing.

Paper's absorption rate, the speed of the printing press, and other mechanical factors limit the amount of ink that can be placed on the same area of a page. If too much ink is applied, the result is a dark blob with no visible detail; heavy layers of ink also result in drying problems, smearing, and a number of other issues.

Total area coverage (also called **total ink coverage**) is the largest percentage of ink that can be safely printed on a single area. This number varies according to the ink/paper/press combination being used for a given job. The Specifications for Web Offset Printing (SWOP) indicates a 300% maximum. Many sheetfed printers require 280% maximum, while the number for newspapers is usually around 240% because the lower-quality paper absorbs more ink. You should ask your service provider what TAC value is appropriate for a specific job.

In the Separations Preview panel, you can choose Ink Limit in the View menu and define the TAC value for the file. You can then preview the layout to find elements that exceed the defined limit; if color is critical, those images should be corrected in Photoshop to be within the defined CMYK working space and ink limits.

Although trapping should typically be left to experienced professionals in the output provider's prepress department, if you understand these concepts, you will be better able to prevent potential output problems when you build a layout.

Trapping Theory and Terminology

In process-color printing, the four process colors (Cyan, Magenta, Yellow, and Black) are imaged or separated onto individual printing plates; each color separation is printed on a separate unit of a printing press. When printed on top of each other in varying percentages, the semitransparent inks produce the range of colors in the CMYK gamut. Spot colors are printed using specially formulated inks as additional color separations.

Because printing is a mechanical process, some variation between the different units of the press is possible (if not likely). Paper moves through the units of a press at considerable speed, and some movement from side to side is inevitable. Each printing plate has one or more **registration marks** (crosshairs) that are used to monitor the alignment of each color. If the units are in **register**, the crosshairs from each color plate print exactly on top of each other.

Misregistration can cause a noticeable gap of uninked paper between adjacent elements, particularly when these elements are made up of different ink colors. When a press is out of register, the individual overlapping colors are discernible.

Misregister results in a visible gap between objects.

Misregister

If any misregister occurs, type can become blurry or virtually unreadable. Any time multiple inks are placed on top of each other, you run the risk of misregister.

Trapping is the compensation for misregister of the color plates on a printing press. Trapping minimizes or eliminates these errors by artificially expanding adjacent colors so small areas of color on the edge of each element overlap and print on top of one another. If sufficiently large, this expansion of color, or trap, fills in the undesirable inkless gap between elements. Trapping procedures differ based upon your workflow; most service providers will perform trapping before generating film or plates. The specific amount of trapping to be applied varies, depending on the ink/paper/press combination that will be used for the job.

A **knockout** is an area of background color that is removed so a lighter foreground color is visible. To achieve white (paper-colored) type on a black background, for example, the black background is removed wherever the type overlaps the black. Any time a lighter color appears on top of a darker color, the area of the lighter color is knocked out of the background.

Overprint is essentially the opposite of knockout. A darker-color foreground object is printed directly on top of a lighter-color background, which means that slight variation in the units of the press will not be as noticeable, especially if the darker color is entirely contained within the lighter color. Black is commonly set to overprint other colors, as are some special colors that are printed using opaque inks. Black is particularly effective when overprinted since it becomes visually richer when other process colors — especially cyan — are mixed with it.

Overprint   Knockout

When a color is set to knock out, anything beneath that color will not be printed. If the black knocks out the cyan, any misregistration can result in a paper-colored gap where the two objects meet. Setting black to overprint eliminates the possibility of a gap caused by misregistration. (The dashed lines in the graphic are for illustration only.)

A **choke** means that the edge of the background color is expanded into the space in which the foreground color will be printed. A **spread** means that the edge of the foreground color is expanded to overprint the edge of the background color. As a general rule, the lighter object should be trapped into the darker area. This rule helps determine whether you should choke or spread.

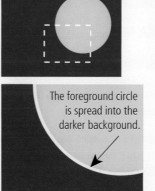
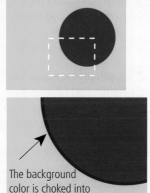

- If the background is darker than the foreground object, the lighter color of the foreground object should be spread to overprint the darker background.

- If the foreground color is darker than the background color, the lighter background color is choked so it overprints the darker foreground color.

The foreground circle is spread into the darker background.

The background color is choked into the darker foreground.

If adjacent elements share a large percentage of one or more common colors, trapping between those elements is unnecessary. If both elements contain a lot of magenta, for example, the continuity of the magenta between the two objects will mask any gaps that occur between the other process colors in the two images; this makes trapping unnecessary. The general rule is that if two adjacent elements share one process color that varies by less than 50%, or if two elements share two or more process colors that vary by less than 80%, don't bother with trapping — the continuous layer of the inks common to both elements will effectively mask any gaps.

C: 85
M: 50
Y: 0
K: 0

C: 0
M: 50
Y: 80
K: 0

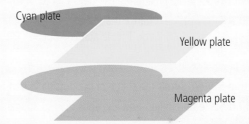

Cyan plate

Yellow plate

Magenta plate

Using the Attributes Panel

An **overprint** prevents underlying objects from being knocked out, so overprint elements don't need to be trapped. As a general rule, overprinting should only be used for dark objects, or objects that are output in opaque spot-color inks. You can overprint the stroke and/or fill of a selected object using the Attributes panel (Window>Attributes). The Overprint Gap option is only available if the stroke style has gaps between elements of the stroke (such as dashed lines or double-stroke lines). You can also set the overprint attributes of frame contents (such as text) by selecting the relevant contents with the Direct Selection tool.

Controlling the Appearance and Overprint Attributes of CMYK Black

The black inks that are used in process-color printing might not produce a pure opaque black. (You used a rich black in Project 2 to improve the appearance of solid black areas.) On screen or on a desktop inkjet printer, however, 100% black typically looks as black as black can be. This discrepancy can cause problems when you don't get what you expect in the final printed job. To solve the problem, you can change the appearance of black in the Appearance of Black preferences. You can define how blacks appear on-screen and in output.

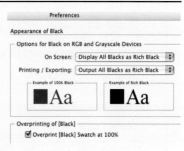

- **Display All Blacks Accurately** shows 100% CMYK black as dark gray on screen.

- **Display All Blacks As Rich Black** shows 100% CMYK black as pure black (R=0 G=0 B=0) on screen.

- **Output All Blacks Accurately** outputs CMYK blacks based on the actual numbers in the color definition. This allows you to see the difference between pure black and rich black on non-PostScript desktop printers.

- **Output All Blacks As Rich Black** outputs all blacks as pure black (R=0 G=0 B=0) when printing to a non-PostScript desktop printer.

By default, [Black] is set to overprint other colors. If you want to knock out [Black] elements, you have to uncheck the Overprint [Black] Swatch at 100% option.

InDesign applies trapping using Trap Presets, or defined collections of trapping settings. The Trap Presets panel (Window>Output>Trap Presets) allows you to create, edit, and apply trap presets to specific pages in a layout. If you don't apply a specific trap preset to a page, that page will use the [Default] trap preset.

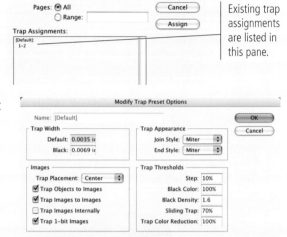

If you choose Assign Trap Preset in the panel Options menu, you can assign an existing preset to all pages or a specific range of pages. Clicking Done simply closes the dialog box; you have to click the Assign button to change the preset for the selected pages.

If you edit the Default trap preset, you open the Modify Trap Preset Options dialog box. If you create a new trap preset, you open the New Trap Preset dialog box. In either case, you have the same choices; the only difference is the availability of the Name field (you can't rename the Default trap preset option).

Existing trap assignments are listed in this pane.

Trap Width. Different types of paper and inks, as well as different output devices, require different amounts of trapping. The two fields in this section define the amount of overlap that will be created in the traps.

- **Default** defines the trap width for all colors except those with 100% Black. The default value is 0.0035" (1/4 point).

- **Black** defines the distance that other colors will spread into colors with 100% Black. The default is 0.0069" (1/2 point).

Trap Appearance. These menus determine the shape of joins (where two trap edges meet) and ends in trap lines.

- **Join Style** controls the shape of the outside join of two trap segments (Miter, Round, and Bevel).

- **End Style** determines how the ends of lines appear when three different trap lines intersect.

Images. InDesign is able to trap placed raster images; each option handles imported graphics differently.

- **Trap Placement** determines where the trap falls when you trap vector objects to bitmap images. Center creates a trap that straddles the edge between objects and images. Choke causes objects to overlap abutting images. Neutral Density applies the same trapping rules as used elsewhere in the document. Spread causes images to overlap abutting objects.

- **Trap Objects To Images** forces vector objects (e.g., frame strokes) to trap to images using the Trap Placement settings.

- **Trap Images To Images** enables trapping along the edges of two overlapping raster images.

- **Trap Images Internally** enables trapping within an individual raster image. This option should be used with caution for only high-contrast images; it does not produce good results for photographic (continuous-tone) images.

- **Trap 1-Bit Images** enables trapping for 1-bit (bitmap or line art) images.

Trap Thresholds. These values determine when trapping will be applied.

- **Step** specifies the threshold at which a trap is created, or the percentage that adjacent component colors must be different before trapping occurs. Higher Step percentages require greater variance in adjacent colors; lower percentages make the application more sensitive to color differences, resulting in more traps.

- **Black Color** defines the minimum percentage of black ink required before the Black trap-width setting is applied.

- **Black Density** defines a neutral density value at which InDesign treats an ink as black. Any inks with a neutral density at or above this value will use the Black trap-width setting.

- **Sliding Trap** determines when traps start to straddle the centerline of the color edges. The value refers to the proportion of the lighter color's neutral density to that of adjacent darker colors; using the default value (70%), the trap will be applied at the centerline when the lighter color's neutral density is more than 70% of the darker color's neutral density (lighter color's neutral density divided by darker color's neutral density > 0.70).

- **Trap Color Reduction** defines the degree to which components from adjacent colors are used to reduce the trap color. A Trap Color Reduction lower than 100% lightens the color of the trap; Trap Color Reduction of 0% makes a trap with the same neutral density as the darker color.

1. A(n) _____ describes the color reproduction characteristics of a particular input or output device.

2. _____ is the range of possible colors within a specific color model.

3. _____ are the four component colors in process-color output.

4. When importing an Adobe Illustrator file, the Crop To _____ option places the file based on the defined Artboard size.

5. When placing a native Photoshop file, you can check the _____ option in the Place dialog box to be able to control layer visibility before the file is placed.

6. The appearance of all images in a layout is controlled in the _____ menu.

7. When you place a PDF file, the _____ option in the Place PDF dialog box determines which area of the file (trim, bleed, etc.) is imported.

8. When placing images into a layout, press _____ to select multiple, non-contiguous files in the Place dialog box.

9. The _____ lists all files that are placed in a layout, including the location and status of each placed file.

10. The _____ can be used to review tracked changes.

1. Briefly explain the difference between additive and subtractive color.

2. Briefly explain the concept of color management, as it relates to building a layout in InDesign.

3. Briefly explain two options for versioning content.

Portfolio Builder Project

Use what you learned in this project to complete the following freeform exercise.
Carefully read the art director and client comments, then create your own design to meet the needs of the project.
Use the space below to sketch ideas; when finished, write a brief explanation of your reasoning behind your final design.

art director comments

Your client, the Miami/Equatorial Travel Agency, wants to create a graphics-rich brochure to promote travel and tourism in Costa Rica.

To complete this project, you should:

❏ Design two versions of the brochure using the client's die-cut template. Make sure to incorporate bleed allowance outside the template edges.

❏ Flip the template horizontally on the second page so the front and back of the piece line up properly.

❏ Create different layers for the English and Spanish versions of the brochure.

❏ Use the die template, images, and text for both languages from the **ID5_PB_Project6.zip** archive on the Student Files Web page.

client comments

We want this brochure to be unique. Our printer gave us a die-cut template that we'd like to use for this job. The printer said to just place the file as a template on its own layer in the file, and treat the template lines like page edges.

We want the brochure to focus on images — sunsets, beaches... the kind of images that make someone say, "I want to go there." We've given you some of those, but feel free to find other images that will convey this same message.

There is very little text. The words "Costa Rica" should appear on the front, back, and inside of the piece. Otherwise, we have a blurb about how to contact us, which has to be included in the final piece, and some quotes that you can use or not.

Here in Miami, many of our customers are fluent in Spanish. Even though there is very little text for the brochure, we're going to create two versions of the brochure — one in English and one in Spanish.

project justification

Project Summary

As you have seen, placing pictures into an InDesign layout is a relatively easy task, whether you place them one at a time or load multiple images at once and then simply click to place the loaded images into the appropriate spots. InDesign allows you to work with all of the common image formats (including PDF), as well as placing one InDesign layout directly into another. The Links panel is a valuable tool for managing images, from updating file status, to replacing one image with another, to opening an external file in its native application so you can easily make changes in placed files.

Fine-tuning a layout requires checking for common errors — both technical (such as low-resolution images) and practical (such as spelling errors). You learned in Project 3 how to use InDesign's preflighting tools; the Check Spelling utility is just as important in creating high-quality, professional designs.

Finally, you should understand how the InDesign conditional text and layers utilities make it very easy to create versioned documents — whether as basic as changing some prices, or as complex as using entirely new images for a specific demographic audience.

Place and control a PDF file

Place and control a TIFF file

Place and control a layered Photoshop file

Place and control an EPS file

Place and control a native Illustrator file

Place and control a native InDesign file

Load and place multiple images at one time

Edit a placed image using the Links panel

Find and replace elements with specific formatting attributes

Find and replace text strings, with and without specific formatting attributes

Check for and correct spelling errors

Create multiple versions of the layout using layers and conditional text

National Parks Info Pieces

Your client is the marketing manager for the National Parks Service (NPS). She wants to create a series of collateral pieces that will be used at tourism centers to lure potential visitors. She hired you to produce a one-sheet flyer that will be distributed in print and online, a rack card that can be placed in area hotels, and a postcard that will be given away to park visitors.

This project incorporates the following skills:

❑ Using placeholder objects to design an initial layout concept

❑ Adjusting a layout concept to suit content provided by a client

❑ Creating an XML file using tagged frames and content

❑ Building a layout from imported XML content

❑ Controlling the structure of a layout to merge XML content into tagged frames

❑ Defining hyperlinks to link layout elements to an external Web page

❑ Creating interactive buttons with multiple states

❑ Exporting PDF files without interactive elements for print distribution

❑ Exporting PDF files with interactive elements for digital distribution

client comments

We want to create several pieces to promote tourism in the national parks. Each piece should include two images, which we'll provide as soon as we decide which ones we want to use. We haven't written any of the content yet, but we can tell you it will include the park name, one paragraph of historical copy, a list of four or five "fun facts" about the park, and directions to the park.

For each park, we want you to create two documents — a flyer and a rack card — with the same content. The flyer will be sent to tourism boards and agencies as a handout; the rack card will be placed in hotels near the park for potential visitors. We also want to create a postcard that we can give away as a souvenir to visitors; this piece will include some (but not all) of the content from the other two pieces.

We'd also like to offer the flyers digitally, both as downloads from our Web site and as attachments to emails. In the digital version, we would like to add buttons that link to the parks' home pages on the NPS Web site and to our basic informational email address.

art director comments

The client promised to give us actual content for at least one park by the end of the week. While you're waiting, I want you to start experimenting with a layout. You know all the elements that need to be included, so you can use placeholders to play with various options.

There are more than 350 national parks, monuments, and other protected areas in the national park system. When the flyer layout is finalized, save it as a template so you can use it again later when we get the content for the different parks.

Because each piece is going to include the same content, you can use InDesign's XML tools to share the content between the pieces. This way, if the client decides to change something, you can modify only one instance, and then update the XML file in all other documents.

When you create the interactive elements, build them into the flyer file that will be used for print. InDesign makes it easy to control whether those elements will be included in a PDF file, so there is no need to create two versions of that document.

project objectives

To complete this project, you will:

❏ Use text and picture placeholders to design a layout concept

❏ Experiment with glyphs to find suitable bullet characters

❏ Create styles based on formatting in the layout

❏ Redefine styles based on local formatting overrides

❏ Sample colors from a placed image to unify the completed layout

❏ Tag frames and content for XML

❏ Generate a structured XML file from layout content

❏ Create additional layouts from imported XML content

❏ Create hyperlinks and buttons to add user interactivity

❏ Export multiple PDF files for different distribution methods

Stage 1   Experimenting with Layout Options

Many InDesign projects start with little more than an idea. Although templates, master pages, and styles are invaluable tools when implementing a layout, in many cases you simply need to open a blank document and start experimenting. When you have to design a project from scratch, InDesign makes it easy to create and format objects, experiment with different options, and then create masters and styles when you are satisfied with your work.

USE TEXT PLACEHOLDERS TO STRUCTURE A LAYOUT

It's always a good idea to begin a project as soon as possible after getting the assignment. When working with clients, however, you will often find that the idea for a project comes before the actual content — sometimes long before the client has finalized the text or provided the promised images. Rather than waiting until the client's content is ready — which is sometimes the day before a project is due — you can design a layout using placeholders to mark the location of pictures and text frames, and even experiment with the appearance of different elements of the text.

The pieces in this project will include the same basic elements:

- Two images
- The park name
- One paragraph of historical copy about the park
- A short list of "fun facts" about the park
- Directions to the park from major landmarks

The main piece of this project is the so-called "one-sheet," or a single-page flyer printed on one side of the sheet. You'll create that file first.

1. **Download ID5_RF_Project7.zip from the Student Files Web page.**

2. **Expand the ZIP archive in your WIP folder (Macintosh) or copy the archive contents into your WIP folder (Windows).**

   This results in a folder named **Parks**, which contains the files you need for this project. You should also use this folder to save the files you create in this project.

3. **Create a new 1-page letter-size document for print, using portrait orientation. Define 1/4″ margins on the top and bottom, 3/8″ margins on the left and right, and 1/8″ bleeds on all four sides. Use non-facing pages and no master text frame.**

4. **Create a text frame anywhere on the page, and type** `Black Canyon of the Gunnison National Park`.

In some cases, certain text elements will be made clear in the initial project description. Your client stated that the one-sheets should identify the park name, so you can use actual text to plan the appearance of this element.

When you're working with placeholders, it's a good idea to design around the longest possible content. The words "Black Canyon of the Gunnison" have the most characters of all national parks, so this is a good representation of the possible text that can appear in this area.

5. **Apply right paragraph alignment to the park name paragraph.**

6. **Click the frame with the Selection tool and then rotate it 90° counterclockwise.**

7. **Drag the rotated frame so it snaps to the top and left bleed guides, change the frame height to 0.875″, and drag the left frame edge to Y: 6.875″.**

The Selection tool is active, so you can access frame options and bounding box handles.

When a frame is rotated, the frame height is still based on the original top edge of the frame.

The left edge of the rotated frame is at the visual bottom.

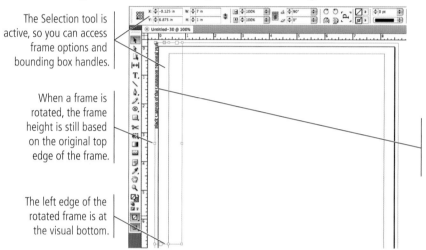

With no inset spacing values, most of the text is outside the page edge.

8. **Control/right-click the text frame and choose Text Frame Options from the contextual menu.**

9. **Apply 0.375″ inset on the right edge of the frame and 0.125″ inset on the top edge. Change the Align menu to Center, then click OK.**

The top inset allows you to center the frame content vertically based on the visible area, excluding the bleed.

The new inset spacing values align to the left page edge and the top margin.

The Center vertical alignment option aligns the text vertically within the area defined by the inset values.

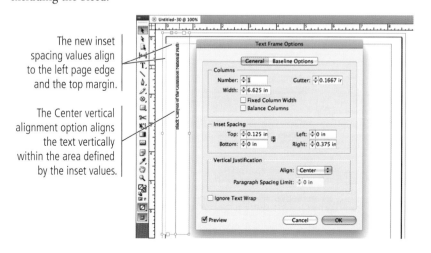

Note:

A bit of creative thinking might be required to find the longest possible text for a specific element. To identify the longest national park name, we searched the Internet for a list of all parks, formatted the list in a monospace font, and simply looked for the one that extended farthest to the right.

Note:

It isn't always possible to determine the longest possible content for a particular editorial element. In that case, use your judgment when planning a layout. In other words, don't try to format a main heading with only one or two words of placeholder text.

Note:

It is unnecessary — and, in fact, poor technical form — to place multiple text frames on top of one another to achieve the text-inset effect.

10. **Fill the text frame with the Black swatch, and change the type color in the frame to the Paper swatch.**

    You don't need to select the text to change its color. You can use the Formatting Affects Text button at the top of the Swatches panel to change the attributes of the text in the frame.

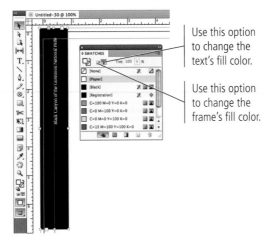

Use this option to change the text's fill color.

Use this option to change the frame's fill color.

11. **Create another text frame with the following dimensions:**

X: 0.375″	W: 7.75″
Y: 8″	H: 2.75″

12. **Open the Text Frame Options dialog box for the new frame. Change the frame to 3 columns with a 0.2″ gutter, and then click OK.**

Note:

If the options are visible on your system, you can also change the frame's number of columns and gutter width in the Control panel.

13. **With the text frame selected, choose Type>Fill with Placeholder Text.**

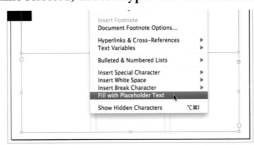

    This command fills the selected text frame with nonsense or **lorem text** (so called because it is Greek nonsense) using the default text-format settings.

    Lorem placeholder text is valuable for experimenting with the appearance of paragraph text; these random words give you a better idea of what text will look like when real content is placed in the layout.

Note:

If a text frame is linked to other text frames, the placeholder text fills the entire series of linked text frames.

Note:

The placeholder text is randomly generated, so the exact words in your layout probably do not match what you see in our screen shot. However, the exact words are irrelevant; the important point is that you have placeholder text to work with while you experiment with formatting options.

14. **Save the file as** **flyer.indd** **in your WIP>Parks folder and continue to the next exercise.**

The best place to begin experimenting is to define the basic font for the layout. Rather than simply selecting the text in a frame and adjusting it locally, you can change the [Basic Paragraph] style to affect the default appearance of all text in the layout.

As you design a layout, it's important to realize that nothing is permanent — including styles — until the job is printed. Of course, some methods for changing a design are better than others. Because changing a style applies the same change to any text formatted with that style, it's better to do as much work as possible with styles.

1. **With flyer.indd open, Control/right-click [Basic Paragraph] in the Paragraph Styles panel and choose Edit "[Basic Paragraph]" from the contextual menu.**

2. **In the Basic Character Formats options, change the font to ATC Oak Normal, and change the type size to 9 pt. In the Indents and Spacing options, change the Space After value to 0.0625″. Click OK to apply the change.**

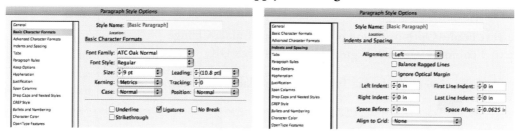

Because you changed the default formatting, the placeholder text no longer fills the frame.

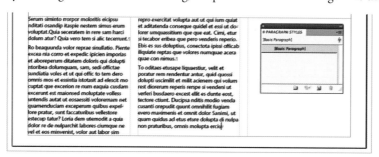

3. **If hidden characters are not visible, choose Type>Show Hidden Characters.**

4. **In the three-column text frame, place the insertion point near the end of the first column and press Return/Enter to add a paragraph break.**

Press Return/Enter to break the placeholder text and start a new paragraph at the top of the column.

5. **Type Did You Know... and press Return/Enter.**

In this case, you know the actual heading that will be used, so you can enter the actual text as the placeholder.

6. **Highlight this new subheading paragraph and change the text to 11-pt ATC Oak Bold.**

Subheads like this one should typically be related to either the body copy or the main headings. Remember that professional-looking designs do not use 15 different fonts on a page. Try to stick with two or three primary fonts, and use variants of those fonts for emphasis and visual interest. (Of course, rules were made to be broken, but don't break from design conventions unless you have a good reason for doing so.)

7. **In the text after the subheading, break or combine the placeholder text so you have four paragraphs of three lines each. Delete all remaining text.**

In this experimentation phase of development, these paragraphs represent the "fun facts" that will appear in the final copy. The actual text in these lines (including capitalization) is irrelevant because you are using them for formatting purposes only.

8. **Highlight all text in the second column, copy the text, and paste it at the end of the existing story. Change the second subhead to Directions... .**

9. **Place the insertion point in the Directions subhead. Open the Paragraph panel Options menu and choose Keep Options. In the resulting dialog box, choose In Next Column in the Start Paragraph menu, and then click OK.**

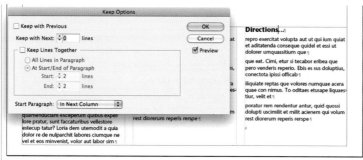

10. **In the rotated frame, highlight the park name. Change the font to ATC Oak Bold and apply the All Caps type style.**

11. **Press Command/Control-Shift-> four times to increase the type size to 17 pt.**

   By default, this key command increases the type size by 2 points. You can change this increment in the Units and Increments pane of the Preferences dialog box.

Note:

Add Option/Alt to the basic keyboard shortcut to increase or decrease the type size by five times the defined increment.

12. **Save the file and continue to the next exercise.**

Navigating and Selecting Text with Keyboard Shortcuts

Keyboard shortcuts can be helpful, especially in early stages when you are still experimenting with text formatting options.

	Macintosh	Windows
Move left one character*	Left Arrow	Left Arrow
Move right one character*	Right Arrow	Right Arrow
Move up one line*	Up Arrow	Up Arrow
Move down one line*	Down Arrow	Down Arrow
Move left one word*	Command-Left Arrow	Control-Left Arrow
Move right one word*	Command-Right Arrow	Control-Right Arrow
Move to start of line*	Home	Home
Move to end of line*	End	End
Move to previous paragraph*	Command-Up Arrow	Control-Up Arrow
Move to next paragraph*	Command-Down Arrow	Control-Down Arrow
Move to start of story*	Command-Home	Control-Home
Move to end of story*	Command-End	Control-End
Select current line	Command-Shift-\	Control-Shift-\
Select characters from insertion point	Shift-click	Shift-click
Select entire story	Command-A	Control-A
Select previous frame	Command-Option-Page Up	Control-Alt-Page Up
Select next frame	Command-Option-Page Down	Control-Alt-Page Down
Select first frame	Command-Option-Shift-Page Up	Control-Alt-Shift-Page Up
Select last frame	Command-Option-Shift-Page Down	Control-Alt-Shift-Page Down
Delete word in front of insertion point (Story Editor)	Command-Delete	Control-Backspace
*Add Shift to select text between the previous and new location of the insertion point.		

INDESIGN FOUNDATIONS

Formatting Text with Keyboard Shortcuts

Keyboard shortcuts can be helpful, especially in early stages when you are still experimenting with text formatting options.

	Macintosh	Windows
Bold type style	Command-Shift-B	Control-Shift-B
Italic type style	Command-Shift-I	Control-Shift-I
Normal type style	Command-Shift-Y	Control-Shift-Y
Underline type style	Command-Shift-U	Control-Shift-U
Strikethrough type style	Command-Shift-/	Control-Shift-/
All Caps type style (on/off)	Command-Shift-K	Control-Shift-K
Small Caps type style (on/off)	Command-Shift-H	Control-Shift-H
Superscript type style	Command-Shift-Plus sign	Control-Shift-Plus sign
Subscript type style	Command-Option-Shift-Plus sign	Control-Alt-Shift-Plus sign
Reset horizontal scale to 100%	Command-Shift-X	Control-Shift-X
Reset vertical scale to 100%	Command-Option-Shift-X	Control-Alt-Shift-X
Align left	Command-Shift-L	Control-Shift-L
Align right	Command-Shift-R	Control-Shift-R
Align center	Command-Shift-C	Control-Shift-C
Justify all lines (all but last line)	Command-Shift-J	Control-Shift-J
Justify all lines (all lines)	Command-Shift-F	Control-Shift-F
Increase point size*	Command-Shift->	Control-Shift->
Decrease point size*	Command-Shift-<	Control-Shift-<
Increase point size by 5 times the defined increment*	Command-Option-Shift->	Control-Alt-Shift->
Decrease point size by 5 times the defined increment*	Command-Option-Shift-<	Control-Alt-Shift-<
Increase leading*	Option-Up Arrow	Alt-Up Arrow
Decrease leading*	Option-Down Arrow	Alt-Down Arrow
Increase leading by 5 times the defined increment*	Command-Option-Up Arrow	Control-Alt-Up Arrow
Decrease leading by 5 times the defined increment*	Command-Option-Down Arrow	Control-Alt-Down Arrow
Auto leading	Command-Option-Shift-A	Control-Alt-Shift-A
Align to grid (on/off)	Command-Option-Shift-G	Control-Alt-Shift-G
Auto-hyphenate (on/off)	Command-Option-Shift-H	Control-Alt-Shift-H
Increase kerning and tracking	Option-Right Arrow	Alt-Right Arrow
Decrease kerning and tracking	Option-Left Arrow	Alt-Left Arrow
Increase kerning and tracking by 5 times	Command-Option-Right Arrow	Control-Alt-Right Arrow
Decrease kerning and tracking by 5 times	Command-Option-Left Arrow	Control-Alt-Left Arrow
Increase kerning between words*	Command-Option-\	Control-Alt-\
Decrease kerning between words*	Command-Option-Delete	Control-Alt-Backspace
Clear all manual kerning and reset tracking to 0	Command-Option-Q	Control-Alt-Q
Increase baseline shift*	Option-Shift-Up Arrow	Alt-Shift-Up Arrow
Decrease baseline shift*	Option-Shift-Down Arrow	Alt-Shift-Down Arrow
Increase baseline shift by 5 times	Command-Option-Shift-Up Arrow	Control-Alt-Shift-Up Arrow
Decrease baseline shift by 5 times	Command-Option-Shift-Down Arrow	Control-Alt-Shift-Down Arrow

*The default increment for type size, leading, and baseline shift is 2 points. The default kerning tracking value is 20/1000 of an em. You can change these values in the Units & Increments pane of the Preferences dialog box.

The Glyphs panel offers an easy way to review and select specific characters in available fonts. When experimenting with type formatting, the Glyphs panel is an excellent way to search through extended, symbol, and pictographic characters that you can't easily preview in the document layout.

1. **With flyer.indd open, place the insertion point at the beginning of the first "fun fact" placeholder in the second column of the three-column text frame.**

2. **Choose Window>Type & Tables>Glyphs.**

3. **In the menu at the bottom of the Glyphs panel, choose a pictographic font such as Zapf Dingbats or Wingdings.**

Insertion point

Use this menu to view the characters in a specific font.

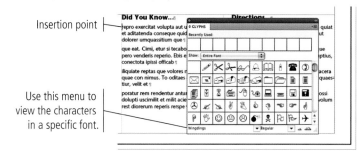

Note:

You can also open the Glyphs panel by choosing Type>Glyphs.

4. **Scroll through the panel and find a character that matches the theme of the document.**

We found a character in the Wingdings font that looks like a compass crosshair. You can use any character from any font that you feel works with the "outdoors" theme of many national parks.

The important point to remember is that you can use the Glyphs panel to look at all available characters in the selected font; this is an excellent way to explore and experiment when you want to use type characters to create visual interest.

5. **When you find a character you like, double-click that glyph in the panel.**

Double-clicking inserts the selected character at the location of the insertion point.

The character is added at the location of the insertion point.

The character you add into the layout appears in the Recently Used area of the Glyphs panel.

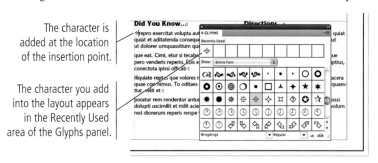

Note:

Decorative fonts can be useful for adding visual interest without the need for linked graphics.

6. **Make note of the font that includes the character you selected.**

7. **Select all "fun facts" paragraphs. In the Paragraph panel Options menu, choose Bullets and Numbering.**

   The options you see here are the same options you used to define styles with bullets in Project 4. Anything that can be applied in a style can also be applied as a local formatting option.

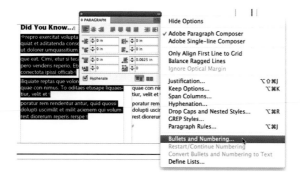

8. **Check the Preview option, then choose Bullets in the List Type menu.**

9. **Change the Left Indent field to 0.15″, the First Line Indent field to –0.15″, and the Tab Position field to 0.15″.**

   A negative first-line indent is called a **hanging indent**.

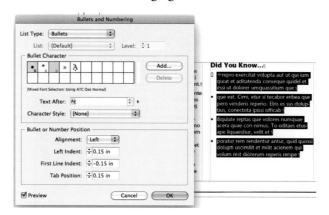

10. **Click the Add button. In the Add Bullets dialog box, select the same font you noted in Step 6. Find and select the character you chose for the bullets and click OK.**

   You could have skipped Steps 2–6, but we believe it's easier to use the Glyphs panel for exploring and experimenting with different characters. Once you know what character you want to use, it's easy to add that character in the formatting of a bulleted list.

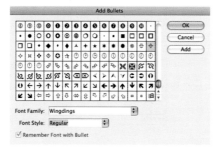

The OpenType font format enables you to use the same font files on both Macintosh and Windows computers; it provides storage capacity for more than 65,000 glyphs in a single font. In many cases, these extra glyphs are alternative formatting for other characters (such as ligatures and fractions). You can also use these glyphs for special formatting needs.

OpenType features are treated as a character-formatting attribute. You can apply OpenType features to specific text using the OpenType menu in the Character panel Options menu.

Adobe Garamond is not an OpenType font.

OpenType attributes are bracketed if they are unavailable for the currently selected font.

It's important to understand that OpenType attributes can be applied even if they aren't available for the font you are currently using. For example, you can apply the Fractions attribute to a list of ingredients; as you experiment with different fonts, the Fractions attribute will be applied if it's available in the applied font.

When an OpenType font is used, the Fractions attribute is applied if the font includes the appropriate glyphs.

Warnock Pro is an OpenType font.

It's also important to realize that OpenType attributes change the appearance of glyphs, but do not change the actual text in the layout. When the Fractions attribute replaces "1/2" with "½", the text still includes three characters; the OpenType Fractions attribute has simply altered the glyphs that represent those three characters to display a styled fraction. You can turn off OpenType attributes by toggling off the option in the Character panel Options menu. With OpenType attributes turned off, the styled characters return to their basic appearance.

Exploring OpenType Fonts in the Glyphs Panel

You can also use the Glyphs panel to explore the different character sets available for a specific font. The Show menu allows you to access different character sets, including extended character sets such as symbols and OpenType alternative character sets. If you select a specific character in the panel, you can also review possible alternatives for the selected character only.

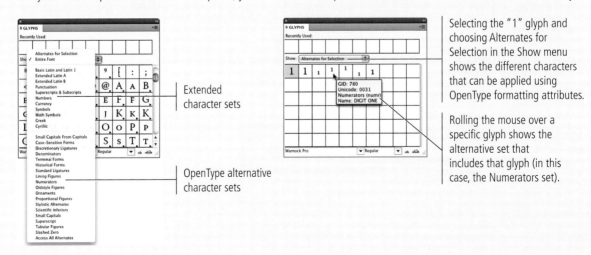

Extended character sets

OpenType alternative character sets

Selecting the "1" glyph and choosing Alternates for Selection in the Show menu shows the different characters that can be applied using OpenType formatting attributes.

Rolling the mouse over a specific glyph shows the alternative set that includes that glyph (in this case, the Numerators set).

11. Select the newly added glyph in the Bullet Character area. Click OK to finalize your changes.

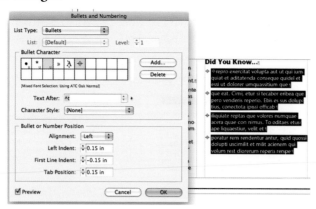

12. Delete the extra bullet character from the first bulleted paragraph.

This is the bullet you added from the Glyphs panel. It is unnecessary now that the same character has been added by the applied bullet formatting.

13. If adding the bullets results in a fourth line for any of the bulleted paragraphs, delete enough of the text from the bulleted paragraphs so all four bulleted items fit into the middle column of the frame.

Delete the extra bullet character you manually added at the beginning of the first paragraph.

Delete as much text as necessary so all four bulleted items fit into the column.

14. Save the file and continue to the next exercise.

 CREATE STYLES FROM EXPERIMENTAL FORMATTING

When you are satisfied with the appearance of your sample text, it's a good idea to convert that formatting into styles, which have the obvious benefit of dynamically changing text by updating the applied style definition. Styles can also be easily applied, they can be imported into other documents, and they can be mapped to different elements in an XML layout (which you will do in Stage 2 of this project).

1. With flyer.indd open, place the insertion point in the paragraph that contains the park name.

Remember, a plus sign next to the style name (in the Paragraph Styles panel) indicates that some local formatting has been applied to override the style definition.

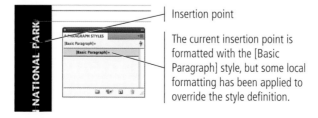

Insertion point

The current insertion point is formatted with the [Basic Paragraph] style, but some local formatting has been applied to override the style definition.

2. **Click the Create New Style button at the bottom of the Paragraph Styles panel.**

3. **Control/right-click the new style and choose Edit "Paragraph Style 1" from the contextual menu.**

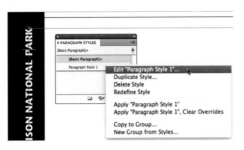

4. **Name the new style `Park_Name` and click OK.**

   Make sure you use the underscore in the style name; this will be very important in Stage 2.

When you return to the layout, you see that the new style has not yet been applied to the selected paragraph.

5. **In the Paragraph Styles panel, click the Park_Name style to apply it to the selected text.**

6. **Place the insertion point in the first paragraph of the three-column frame, then click the Create New Style button at the bottom of the Paragraph Styles panel.**

7. **Double-click the new Paragraph Style 1 to open the Paragraph Style Options dialog box. Change the style name to `Body_Copy` and click OK.**

Note:

If you are building a project that will (or might) be used for XML, it's a good idea to follow XML-based naming conventions, which prohibit spaces in element names.

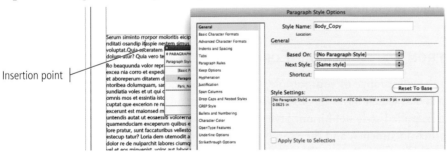

Insertion point

To apply a style to a paragraph, you simply select the paragraph and click the style name. When you double-click the style name, the first click applies the style to the selected text.

This is a very important distinction — Control/right-clicking allows you to edit the style without applying the style. Double-clicking allows you to edit the style and applies the style to the selected text, as well. Each method is useful in different circumstances; be certain that you use the correct method, based on what you are trying to accomplish.

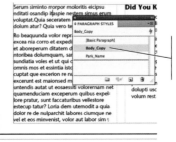

The Body_Copy style is already highlighted (applied).

8. **Using the double-click method, define additional styles from the existing formatting. Use the following image as a guide; make sure your style names exactly match what you see in our image:**

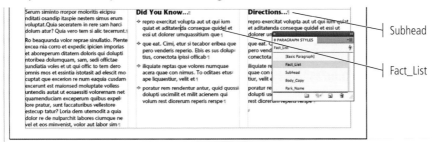

For the Subhead style, make sure you base it on the "Directions" paragraph because that paragraph has the Keep instruction to force the subhead into the next column. (The "Did You Know…" subhead does not yet include the Keep formatting.)

9. **Save the file and continue to the next exercise.**

 ## EXPERIMENT WITH GRAPHICS PLACEHOLDERS

To plan image placement, you can simply create and manipulate empty frames. You can even predefine some attributes of the images that will be placed, including applied effects and content-fitting options.

1. **With flyer.indd open, create a new rectangular graphics frame. Align the left edge at X: 0.75", extend the top and right edges to the bleed guides, and change the frame height to 8".**

2. **Fill the empty graphics frame with the C=100 M=0 Y=0 K=0 swatch.**

   When designing an initial layout, it can be a good idea to fill empty picture boxes with a color. This serves as a visual cue so you can quickly identify the areas that will be filled with the actual content.

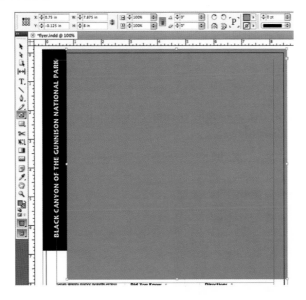

3. Create another empty graphics frame with the following dimensions:

    X: –0.125″   W: 3″
    Y: 6.1″   H: 3″

4. Apply a 5-pt black stroke to the frame, and fill the frame with the C=100 M=0 Y=0 K=0 swatch.

5. Using the Text Wrap panel, apply a 0.0625″ text wrap to all four sides of the frame.

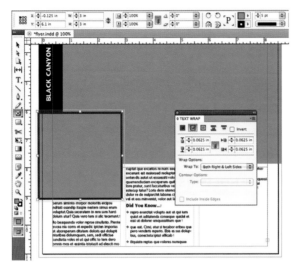

6. Click the frame with the Selection tool, then click the yellow square (on the top-right edge of the frame) to enter Live Corner Effects edit mode.

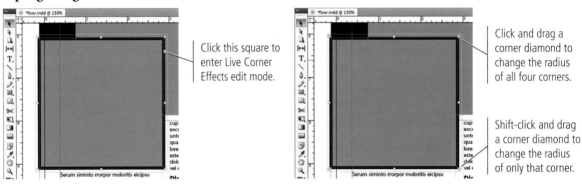

Click this square to enter Live Corner Effects edit mode.

Click and drag a corner diamond to change the radius of all four corners.

Shift-click and drag a corner diamond to change the radius of only that corner.

7. Press Shift, then click the diamond on the top-right corner and drag left until the cursor feedback shows a radius of 0.25″.

Pressing Shift allows you to affect only one corner of the frame without changing the other corners.

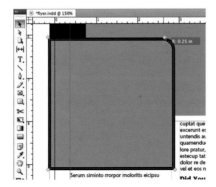

8. **Repeat Step 7 for the bottom-right corner.**

9. **Edit the Park_Name style to 15.5 pt so the placeholder (the longest possible variant) fits on a single line.**

    You will frequently make this kind of change while designing an initial layout concept.

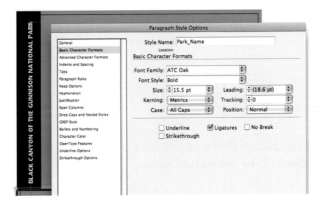

10. **Save the file and continue to the next exercise.**

 ## SAVE THE FINAL TEMPLATE

Now that the layout is finished, you should make the template as user-friendly as possible. The template currently includes a specific park name that might be easy to overlook; it also includes a lot of nonsense text that must be deleted every time you use the template. In this exercise, you modify the template to require as little setup as possible each time you use it to create a new layout.

1. **With flyer.indd open, select the park name text and type Park Name.**

    Changing the text to a generic description can be helpful to designers who later use the template, reminding them to type the actual park name.

2. **Select all text in the three-column frame and delete it.**

    When hidden characters are showing, you can see (if you look closely) that the end-of-story character appears at the location of the insertion point. The formatting of that character becomes the default formatting for the text frame.

Because you did not format the end-of-story character with one of the styles you defined, it will use the [Basic Paragraph] style.

3. **With the insertion point flashing in the empty frame, click the Body_Copy style in the Paragraph Styles panel (if it is not already selected).**

By applying the style to the insertion point in the empty frame, you define the default formatting options for any text that is later entered into the frame.

Applying the Body_Copy style to the insertion point/ end-of-story character defines the default style for text in this frame.

4. **Using the Selection tool, Control/right-click the large graphics frame and choose Fitting>Frame Fitting Options in the contextual menu.**

In this case, you know how much space is available, but you don't yet know the size of the images that are intended to fill the space. You can use the Frame Fitting options to determine what will happen when you place any image into the existing frames.

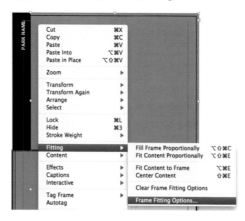

5. **In the Frame Fitting Options dialog box, activate the Auto-Fit option. Choose Fill Frame Proportionally, choose the center point in the Align From proxy, and click OK.**

When an image is placed into this frame, it will fill the entire frame and the aspect ratio of the image will be maintained.

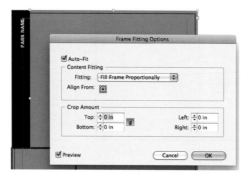

6. **Repeats Steps 4–5 for the smaller graphics frame.**

7. **Save the flyer.indd file (File>Save), then choose File>Save As.**

8. **Save the file as a template named flyer.indt in your WIP>Parks folder, close the file, and then continue to the next exercise.**

ADJUST THE LAYOUT TO SUPPLIED CONTENT

InDesign provides all of the tools you need to experiment with and plan a basic layout structure. However, the best-laid plans (or planned layouts) always require some adjustment when you place the actual content into the document. Fortunately, nothing in a layout is final until it's printed; until a job leaves your desk, you can change anything in the document.

1. **Open the flyer.indt template file (from your WIP>Parks folder) using the Open Normal option to create a new file.**

2. **Click with the Type tool to place the insertion point in the three-column text frame.**

3. **Choose File>Place and navigate to the file bryce.txt in your WIP>Parks folder. Deselect the Show Import Options check box, select the Replace Selected Item check box, and then click Open.**

Insertion point

Because the Replace Selected Item option is checked, the text automatically flows into the frame at the location of the insertion point. Nothing is selected, so nothing (other than the insertion point) is replaced.

A text-only file (with the extension ".txt") includes no formatting information; all placed text is formatted with the Body_Copy style, which you defined as the default style for the frame in the previous exercise.

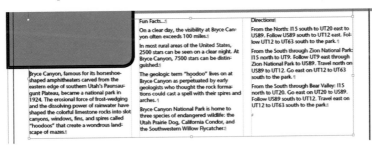

4. **Apply paragraph styles as shown in the following image:**

Subhead

Fact_List

Note:

If the Replace Selected Item option is not checked, the imported text loads into the cursor instead of into the selected frame.

Note:

Placing text that is already formatted — whether copied from another InDesign text frame or imported from a file that includes formatting — overrides the formatting you applied to the empty frame's insertion point.

5. **Deselect everything in the layout, then choose File>Place.**

6. Select **bryce1.tif** and **bryce2.tif** (in your WIP>Parks folder) and click Open.

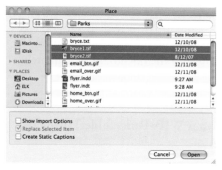

7. Click to place bryce1.tif in the large graphics frame, and then click to place bryce2.tif in the smaller graphics frame.

8. Use the Selection tool/Content Indicator icon or the Direct Selection tool to select the placed bryce1.tif image. Review the Control panel.

The image is reduced to approximately 98% because you changed the empty frame settings to fill the frame proportionally with whatever image is placed into the frame.

Be careful when you use this type of setting because an image might need to be enlarged to fill the frame. Remember the rules of effective resolution — enlarging an image's physical dimensions has a proportional negative effect on the image's resolution.

The Control panel shows the position of the image relative to the frame, as well as its scale percentage.

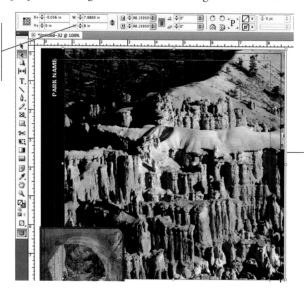

This line marks the actual edge of the image.

9. Select the smaller image and review its scale percentage.

Note:

You might notice that the park name is currently incorrect. You will fix this in a later exercise.

10. Save the file as **flyer_bryce.indd** in your WIP>Parks folder and continue to the next exercise.

CREATE SWATCHES FROM SAMPLED COLORS

You worked with the Eyedropper tool to sample colors from images and apply them locally to selected objects in the layout. In this exercise, you will use the same sampling technique to choose colors, but then save those colors as custom swatches.

1. With flyer_bryce.indd open, deselect everything in the layout and open the Swatches panel (Window>Color>Swatches).

2. Choose the Eyedropper tool in the Tools panel and make sure the Fill box is active.

3. Click the Eyedropper cursor in a dark orange area of the larger image.

   The Eyedropper tool allows you to sample a color from any layout element, including placed images. Selecting a color in this way does not define a swatch in the file. The color only exists for the active attribute (fill or stroke).

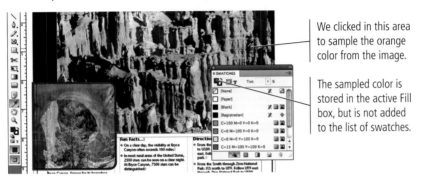

We clicked in this area to sample the orange color from the image.

The sampled color is stored in the active Fill box, but is not added to the list of swatches.

4. Click the Create New Swatch button at the bottom of the Swatches panel.

   The new swatch is created based on the current color in the active attribute (the fill). Notice, however, that the new swatch is named based on its RGB components. This occurred because the placed image — from which the color was sampled — is in the RGB color mode.

The new swatch uses the RGB color mode.

Note:

Your color name might be slightly different than ours, depending on the specific location you sampled with the Eyedropper tool.

5. Double-click the new RGB swatch in the Swatches panel to edit the color.

6. Choose CMYK in the Color Mode menu of the Swatch Options dialog box.

   When you change the color mode, notice the difference in the preview swatch. Changing RGB colors to process colors can result in color shift, which might be significant if the original color is far outside the CMYK gamut.

Note:

If you sample colors from placed images, make sure they are in the correct color mode.

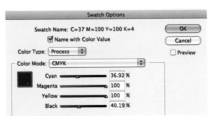

7. Click OK to return to the layout.

8. **Using the Type tool, highlight the Fun Facts heading, and then click the new orange swatch in the Swatches panel.**

This paragraph is formatted with the Subhead paragraph style. Changing the color of the selected text (instead of changing the style definition) is called local formatting or style override. Of course, local formatting is exactly that — local to the selected text. The other Subhead paragraph ("Directions" in the second frame) remains unchanged.

9. **With the insertion point in the Fun Facts heading, Control/right-click the Subhead style in the Paragraph Styles panel and choose Redefine Style from the contextual menu.**

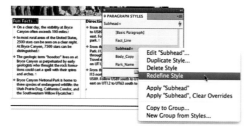

You no longer see the plus sign next to the Subhead style because the Subhead style now uses the orange character color. The redefined style formatting also applies to the other subhead.

10. **Save the file and continue to the next stage of the project.**

Stage 2 Working with XML

In Project 6, you worked with versioning, where the same layout hosts different content for different users. Repurposing content — placing the same content into different layouts — is another common task. InDesign uses XML (Extensible Markup Language) to enable content repurposing.

For many designers, XML is an intimidating concept among the alphabet soup of industry-related acronyms. Despite all the complexities that underlie this programming language, InDesign makes it very easy to implement XML in your layout documents.

As you know, styles define the appearance of content. All paragraphs formatted with the Subhead style display the characteristics defined for that style, regardless of the actual content in those headings.

XML, on the other hand, describes the content marked with a specific tag. In other words, the heading is the actual text identified by the XML Heading tag, regardless of the formatting applied to those words.

In the following exercises, you create an XML file from the flyer content, and then use that XML file to generate two additional layouts — a rack card and a postcard.

TAG FRAMES FOR XML

The first step in creating an XML file is to identify the elements that make up the document content, each of which will be enclosed within tags as shown below:

<Heading>Much Ado About Nothing</Heading>

The first tag, <Heading>, is the opening tag; it identifies the beginning of the content. The second tag, </Heading>, is the closing tag; it identifies the end of the content.

When the XML file is imported into a layout, InDesign places the content from the Heading tag into the appropriate location.

To create the XML file for this project, you first have to define and apply tags for the different elements of the layout.

> **Note:**
>
> *When InDesign reads an XML file, it finds the content within tags, and places that content into the appropriate locations in the layout.*

1. **With flyer_bryce.indd open from your WIP>Parks folder, choose Window>Utilities>Tags to open the Tags panel.**

   The Tags panel allows you to create and manage XML tags within an InDesign layout. One tag, "Root," exists by default in every file; it is the basic container tag that encloses all other tags in the document.

2. **Using the Selection tool, select the larger image in the layout.**

3. **In the Tags panel, click the Autotag button.**

   The Image tag is automatically created and applied to the selected frame.

4. **If your image is not bordered and overlaid with a purple color, choose View>Structure>Show Tagged Frames.**

   The border and overlay color are for identification purposes. They only appear while you are working in the file; they do not appear when the file is output.

Note:

If you click the New Tag button to create a tag, that new tag is not automatically applied to the selected object.

5. **In the Tags panel, double-click the Image tag to open the Tag Options dialog box.**

6. **Change the Name field to Main_Img and click OK.**

   Because you want to identify two different images, you have to assign a unique name to each tag. If you use the basic Image tag for both images, it will be difficult to control image placement when the XML file is imported into a different InDesign layout.

Note:

Tag names cannot include spaces, so you must use the underscore character to separate words in the tag name.

7. **Using the same method, tag the other image frame with a tag named Sub_Img.**

8. **Select the text frame with the park name placeholder and click the Autotag button in the Tags panel.**

   Text frames are automatically tagged with the Story tag. You need to identify two different stories in this job, so you should use a unique tag for each.

Note:

You might notice that the park name is currently incorrect. You will fix this in a later exercise.

9. **Double-click the Story tag and change the name to** `Park_Name`. **Click OK to close the Tag Options dialog box.**

   This is the same name as the paragraph style applied to the text; using the same name for both elements allows you to map the tagged content to styles of the same name (which you will do later).

10. **Select the three-column text frame. Create and apply a tag named** `Main_Text`.

    The file now has four tagged frames, each identified by a unique tag.

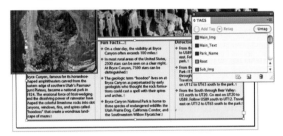

11. **Save the file and continue to the next exercise.**

 REVIEW DOCUMENT STRUCTURE

In addition to tagging frames, you can also tag specific content within frames. Doing so enables you to automatically format XML content in other layouts, and allows you to access specific content when necessary.

1. **With `flyer_bryce.indd` open, highlight the first paragraph in the three-column text frame (excluding the paragraph return), and then click the New Tag button at the bottom of the Tags panel.**

   The new Tag1 is automatically added and highlighted.

2. With the tag name highlighted, type `Body_Copy` and press Return/Enter to finalize the name change.

The new tag has been renamed, but it has not yet been applied to the selected text.

3. With the paragraph still selected in the layout, click the new Body_Copy tag to apply it.

4. Click in the paragraph to place the insertion point and remove the text highlighting.

5. If you don't see brackets around the paragraph, choose View>Structure> Show Tag Markers.

Like the overlay and border on tagged frames, these brackets will not appear in the printed piece.

Brackets indicate that the text is tagged.

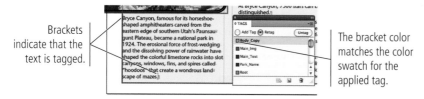

The bracket color matches the color swatch for the applied tag.

6. Highlight the Fun Facts heading (excluding the ending paragraph return). Create and apply a tag named `Subhead`.

7. Highlight the bulleted paragraphs below the subhead. Create and apply a tag named `Fact_List`.

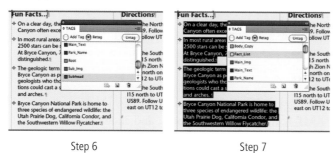

Step 6   Step 7

8. Highlight the Directions heading and apply the Subhead tag.

9. Highlight the paragraphs after the Directions heading and apply the Fact_List tag.

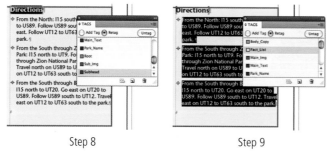

Step 8   Step 9

10. Save the file and continue to the next exercise.

REVIEW XML STRUCTURE AND ATTRIBUTES

XML files allow you to share content across multiple files, using either a structured or an unstructured method. Using the unstructured method (which you will utilize to create the postcard in a later exercise), you can simply import the XML into a document, and then drag elements into the layout. Structured repurposing requires more planning, but allows you to merge tagged XML content into tagged frames in another layout.

1. **With flyer_bryce.indd open, choose View>Structure>Show Structure. In the Structure pane, click the arrow to the left of Root to expand the structure.**

   The Structure pane appears in the left side of the document window, showing the hierarchical order of tagged elements in the file. Elements appear in the order in which they were created; any element with an arrow next to its name can be expanded to show nested elements and associated attributes (we explain those attributes shortly).

2. **If you don't see the words "Park Name" to the right of the Park_Name element, open the Structure pane Options menu and choose Show Text Snippets.**

   When snippets are visible, the first 32 characters of text in that element display in the pane.

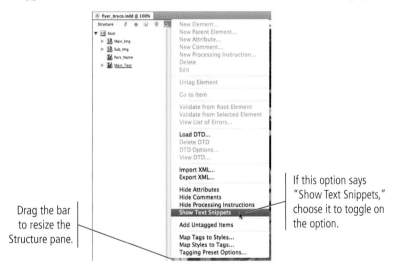

Drag the bar to resize the Structure pane.

If this option says "Show Text Snippets," choose it to toggle on the option.

3. **In the Structure pane, click the Main_Img element and drag it to the bottom of the list.**

   XML follows a linear, top-down structure. Although the elements are listed in the order you create them, you should modify the structure to more accurately reflect the order they appear in the layout.

The tagged element will be placed at the location of the heavy black line.

These are text snippets (toggled on in Step 2).

4. Expand all elements by clicking the arrow to the left of each element.

The Main_Text element contains additional tagged elements.

When expanded, the two image elements show the path to the placed image, with the "href" prefix. This path is an attribute of the image element, defining the location of the content placed within the element. This path information tells InDesign which image to use when the file is imported into another layout.

Note:

Attributes are identified in the Structure pane by a large bullet character

Identifying Structure Pane Icons

INDESIGN FOUNDATIONS

Use the following as a guide to the different icons in the Structure pane.

Icon	Name	Use
‹›	Root element	Every document includes one root element at the top, which can be renamed but not moved or deleted
	Story element	Tagged story (one or more linked frames)
	Text element	Tagged text within a frame
	Graphic element	Tagged frame that includes a placed image; includes an href attribute that defines the path or URL to the linked file
	Unplaced text element	Unplaced text element not yet associated with a page item
	Unplaced graphic element	Unplaced graphic element not yet associated with a page item
	Table element	Table
	Header cell element	Cell in the header row of a table
	Body cell element	Cell within the body of a table
	Footer cell element	Cell in the footer row of a table
⊠	Empty element	An empty frame is associated with this element
•	Attribute	Metadata, such as keywords or location of a linked image (href attribute)
	Comment	Comments that appear in the XML file, but not the InDesign document
	Processing instruction	Instruction to trigger an action in applications that can read instructions
	DOCTYPE element	Tells InDesign which DTD file to use when validating the XML file

5. **Save the InDesign file.**

6. **Choose File>Export and navigate to your WIP>Parks folder as the target destination.**

7. **Choose XML in the Format/Save As Type menu and remove flyer_ from the file name. Click Save.**

8. **Make sure no boxes are checked in either tab of the Export XML dialog box that appears, and then click Export.**

9. **Continue to the next exercise.**

Options for Exporting XML

INDESIGN FOUNDATIONS

You can control a number of options when you export an XML file from an InDesign layout. The following options are available in the General tab:

- **Include DTD Declaration** exports a reference to the defined DTD (if any) along with the XML file. This option is only available if a DOCTYPE element is showing in the Structure pane.

- **View XML Using** opens the exported file in the defined browser or editing application.

- **Export From Selected Element** starts exporting from the currently selected element in the Structure pane.

- **Export Untagged Tables As CALS XML** exports untagged tables in CALS XML format. (CALS is an extension of XML, designed by the U.S. Department of Defense Continuous Acquisition and Life-Cycle Support project.)

- **Remap Break, Whitespace, and Special Characters** converts special characters to their XML code equivalents (if equivalents exist).

- **Apply XSLT** applies a style sheet from the XML file or from an external file. (XSLT stands for Extensible Stylesheet Language Transformation.)

- **Encoding** defines the encoding mechanism for representing international characters in the XML file.

In the Images tab, you can move images identified in the XML code to a folder created during the export process. (This is similar to the Links folder created when you use the Package utility.)

- **Original Images** copies the original image file into an Images subfolder.

- **Optimized Original Images** optimizes and compresses the original image files, and places the optimized versions in an Images subfolder.

- **Optimized Formatted Images** permanently applies transformations (rotation, scaling, etc.) in the optimized images that are placed in the Images subfolder.

Using either Optimized option, you can choose the format (GIF or JPEG) to use in the Image Compression menu. You can also define the optimization options for each format. The Optimized options are more useful if you are repurposing the XML content into a Web layout; GIF and JPEG are not recommended for print layout design.

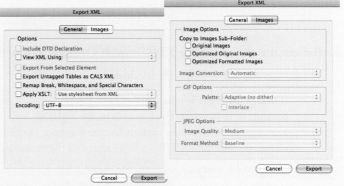

PLACE UNSTRUCTURED XML CONTENT

As we mentioned earlier, you can use either an unstructured or a structured method for applying tagged XML content into a new layout. The unstructured method is easiest because you can simply drag the content from the Structure pane and place it into your new document.

1. **Open the file postcard.indt from the WIP>Parks folder to create a new file.**

   We created this basic postcard template with placeholders for the same two images, park name, and body copy elements that you already used in designing the single-sheet flyer.

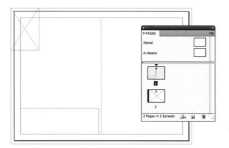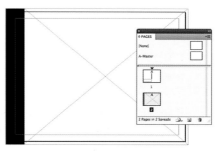

2. **Open the Structure pane for the postcard layout. In the Structure pane Options menu, choose Import XML.**

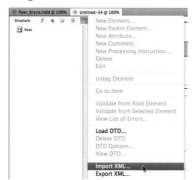

Note:

You can also simply choose File>Import XML.

3. **Navigate to the file bryce.xml in your WIP>Parks folder. Make sure the Show XML Import Options box is checked and click Open.**

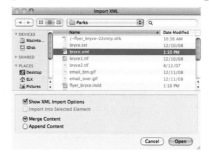

Note:

The Merge Content and Append Content radio buttons are available in the Import XML dialog box because you need to make this choice even if you don't review the other import options.

4. **Review the choices in the XML Import Options dialog box.**

   The most important option is the Mode menu:

   - If **Merge Content** is selected, the XML content will be placed into the Root element of the current file. Content in the XML file will be automatically placed into tagged frames in the current layout. If frames in the layout are not tagged, elements from the XML file will be added to the Structure pane.

   - If **Append Content** is selected, the entire XML file will be placed into the Root element of the current document, *after* any elements that already exist.

5. **Make sure Merge Content is selected in the Mode menu and check the Create Link option.**

   The **Create Link** option maintains a dynamic link to the XML file, just as a placed image is linked to the original image file. If content in the XML file changes, you can update the layout to automatically reflect the same changes.

6. **Click OK to import the XML file into the postcard document. In the Structure pane, expand all items.**

   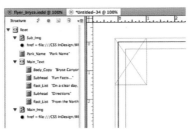

7. **With Page 1 of the postcard showing in the document window, drag the Sub_Img element from the Structure pane onto the empty frame in the top-left corner.**

   Adding content is as easy as dragging it into the layout. If you drag an element into an empty area, a frame is automatically created.

   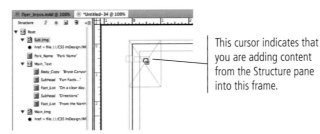

   This cursor indicates that you are adding content from the Structure pane into this frame.

Import XML Options

When importing and placing XML data using the Merge Content option, the XML Import Options dialog box offers the following options:

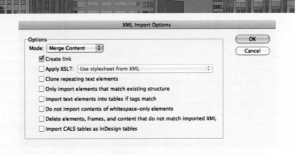

- **Create Link** links to the XML file so, if the XML file is changed, the XML data in the InDesign document is automatically updated.

- **Apply XSLT** defines a style sheet that transforms XML data from one structure to another.

- **Clone Repeating Text Elements** replicates the formatting applied to tagged placeholder text for repeating content (for example, formatting applied to different elements of an address placeholder).

- **Only Import Elements That Match Existing Structure** filters imported XML content so only elements from the imported XML file with matching elements in the document are imported. When this option is unchecked, all elements in the XML file are imported into the Structure pane.

- **Import Text Elements Into Tables If Tags Match** imports elements into a table if the tags match the tags applied to the placeholder table and its cells.

- **Do Not Import Contents Of Whitespace-only Elements** leaves existing content in place if the matching XML content contains only whitespace (such as a paragraph return character).

- **Delete Elements, Frames, and Content That Do Not Match Imported XML** removes elements from the Structure pane and the document layout if they don't match any elements in the imported XML file.

- **Import CALS Tables As InDesign Tables** imports any CALS tables in the XML file as InDesign tables.

When you release the mouse button, the frame is automatically tagged with the Sub_Img tag.

This icon indicates a graphic element that has been placed in the document.

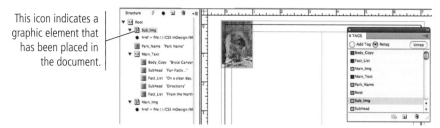

8. **Drag the Body_Copy element from the Main_Text element to the empty text frame at the bottom of Page 1.**

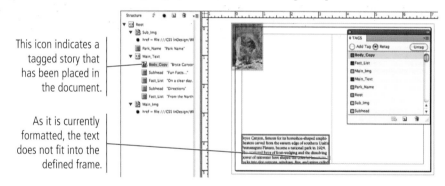

When you release the mouse button, the content of the selected Body_Copy element is placed into the frame. The paragraph doesn't fit in the assigned space.

This icon indicates a tagged story that has been placed in the document.

As it is currently formatted, the text does not fit into the defined frame.

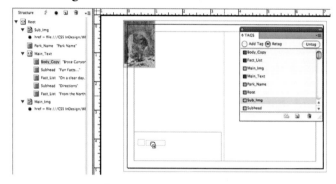

9. **In the Structure pane Options menu, choose Map Tags to Styles.**

This dialog box allows you to assign specific styles to specific elements.

10. Click the Map by Name button at the bottom of the dialog box.

Using the same names for tags and styles allows you to easily format different elements with the appropriate style. The Park_Name tag matches the style of the same name, so it is properly mapped to that style. Notice, however, that the Body_Copy tag is not mapped to a style.

11. Click the words "[Not Mapped]" to the right of the Body_Copy tag and choose Body Copy from the menu.

This menu lists all styles defined in the layout. Paragraph, character, table, cell, and object styles are all listed because any of these five might apply to a specific type of tag.

Note:

The difference between the name of the XML tag and the style is the underscore character.

12. Click OK to apply the defined formatting to the XML tags.

All element text now fits within the available space.

13. On Page 2 of the layout, drag the XML elements into the layout as shown in the following image.

The text element is automatically formatted because you already mapped that tag (Park_Name) to the existing document style (Park_Name).

XML does not communicate the appearance of the different elements, just the content. After mapping the tags to the postcard styles (which we defined in the provided template file), the Park_Name text is placed with the ATC Oak Normal font with no type styles — as defined by the Park_Name style in the postcard template — instead of ATC Oak Bold with All Caps that is used in the flyer style.

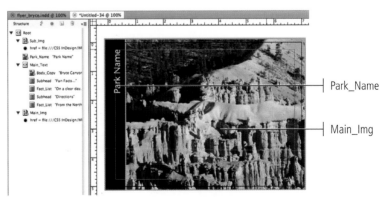

Park_Name

Main_Img

14. Save the file as `postcard_bryce.indd` in your WIP>Parks folder, then continue to the next exercise.

UPDATE LINKED XML DATA

When you placed the XML file into the postcard layout, you checked the Create Link option. This means that changes to the XML file can easily be updated in the postcard layout, just as you would update a placed image.

1. **Make sure flyer_bryce.indd is open and active.**

2. **In the page heading, change the words "Park Name" to Bryce Canyon National Park.**

The flyer file is active.

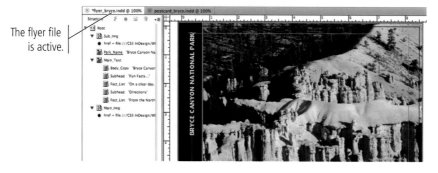

3. **Save the file.**

4. **Choose File>Export and navigate to the WIP>Parks folder as the target. Make sure XML is selected in the Format/Save As Type menu and the file name is bryce.xml, then click Save.**

5. **When asked if you want to overwrite the existing file, click Replace/Yes.**

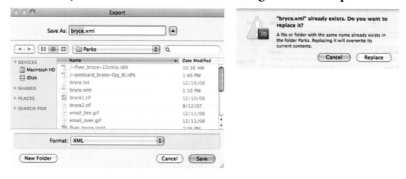

6. **Click Export in the resulting dialog box to rewrite the XML file.**

7. **Make postcard_bryce.indd the active file, and then display the Links panel.**

The XML file is linked to the document, so it appears (appropriately) in the Links panel. The Warning icon indicates that the file was changed since being imported.

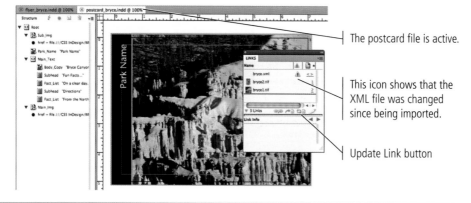

The postcard file is active.

This icon shows that the XML file was changed since being imported.

Update Link button

8. **Select bryce.xml in the Links panel and click the Update Link button.**

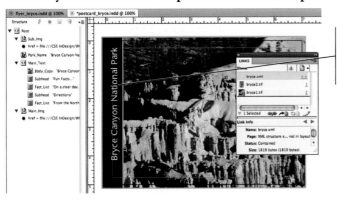

When the linked XML file is updated, the text change is automatically reflected in the postcard.

9. **Save the postcard file and close it.**

10. **Continue to the next exercise.**

 ## IMPORT STRUCTURED XML

With some advance planning, you can build a layout with tagged frames to automatically contain elements when the XML file is imported. For this process to work correctly, keep the following points in mind:

- The tag names must be exactly the same in the document file as in the XML data. (You can load tags from one InDesign file to another to be sure the names match.)

- You can automatically format imported XML content by mapping tag names to styles. (Style names need to exactly match the tag names.)

- The tagged layout should have the same structure as the data in the XML file. (Remember, the structure in the XML file is based on the order of elements in the Structure pane.)

1. **Create a new file by opening the rack.indt template in the WIP>Parks folder.**

This layout includes two pages with placeholder frames for all the same elements used in the flyer. To prepare these frames for XML import, you have to tag those frames with the same tag names used in the XML file you want to import.

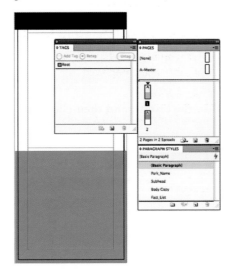

2. **In the Tags panel Options menu, choose Load Tags.**

3. **Navigate to flyer_bryce.indd in your WIP>Parks folder and click Open.**

   You used this file to generate the XML file, so its tags match those in the XML file. This method of loading tags ensures that the tags you add in the rack card file exactly match the tags in the flyer (and thus, in the XML file).

4. **Open the Structure pane for the rack card file (View>Structure>Show Structure).**

   Adding tags to the file does not automatically add elements to the structure. Elements aren't added to the structure until you attach the loaded tags to frames in the layout.

5. **Place the Tags panel next to the Paragraph Styles panel and compare the two lists.**

   Remember, for tags to correctly map to styles, the names of the styles must exactly match the names of the tags.

   The space character in the Body Copy style means the style name does not exactly match the tag name (the underscore is missing).

6. **Control/right-click the Body Copy paragraph style and choose Edit "Body Copy" from the contextual menu.**

7. **In the Paragraph Style Options dialog box, change the style name to Body_Copy and click OK.**

   The style name now matches the tag name.

8. **Select the black frame at the top of Page 1 in the layout, and then click the Park_Name tag in the Tags panel.**

   After the frame is tagged, the element is added to the Structure pane.

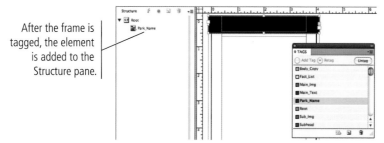

Note:

Tag names can't have spaces but style names can, so you will probably see this type of mismatch frequently throughout your career.

9. Using the same method, assign the Main_Text tag to the large text frame, and assign the Sub_Img tag to the cyan graphics frame on Page 1 of the layout.

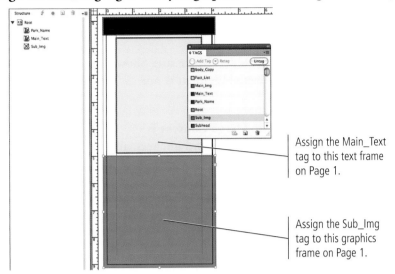

Assign the Main_Text tag to this text frame on Page 1.

Assign the Sub_Img tag to this graphics frame on Page 1.

10. On Page 2 of the layout, assign the Main_Img tag to the cyan graphics frame.

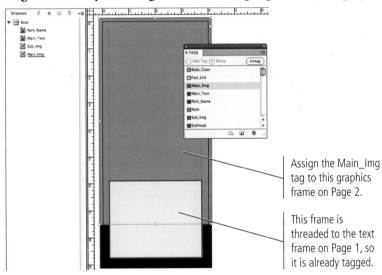

Assign the Main_Img tag to this graphics frame on Page 2.

This frame is threaded to the text frame on Page 1, so it is already tagged.

11. Make sure flyer_bryce.indd is open. Choose the 2-Up (side-by-side) document arrangement in the Application/Menu bar.

To be sure the XML will import properly, the tagged document structure should exactly match the structure in the XML file. The two Structure panes show that the Sub_Img element is not in the same order; you need to fix this before importing the XML file.

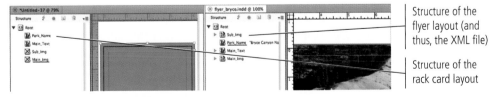

Structure of the flyer layout (and thus, the XML file)

Structure of the rack card layout

12. In the rack card Structure pane, drag the Sub_Img element to the top of the list.

13. **Return to the single-document arrangement and make the rack card file active.**

14. **With the rack card document active, choose File>Import XML.**

    This is the same as choosing the Import XML option in the Structure pane Options menu.

15. **Navigate to the file bryce.xml in your WIP>Parks folder. Make sure Show XML Import Options is checked, Import Into Selected Element is not checked, and then click Open.**

16. **In the XML Import Options dialog box, make sure Merge Content is selected in the Mode menu. Check the Create Link option and uncheck all other options.**

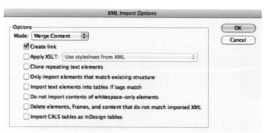

Validating Structure with a DTD

INDESIGN FOUNDATIONS

In the previous exercise, you loaded tag names and modified the element structure in the rack card to match the structure in the XML file. Because the XML file was created from another InDesign file, it was easy to compare the tag names and structures in the two files, ensuring the import process would work correctly. In many cases, however, different applications will be involved in the repurposing process, whether generating the XML file or reading the XML file generated from InDesign. When other applications are involved, you need a mechanism to verify that the structure is correct.

A DTD (Document Type Definition) file defines the required structure for an XML document. Using a DTD, you can ensure that the structure in a print layout matches the structure in a Web layout file (for example). You can also verify that both layouts match the structure that exists in the XML file being used to transfer content. A DTD file also provides a set of elements and attributes, ensuring consistency of the tag names in different documents.

For example, the DTD file may require the Park_Name element to be a child of a story element (in the case of this project, the story element is named Main_Text). If a document tags a title without tagging the story in which it appears, the DTD file marks the title element as invalid. (The process of comparing a document structure to a specific DTD is called validation.)

You can load a DTD into an InDesign file using the Options menu in the Structure pane or the Tags panel. When you load a DTD, the element names from the DTD appear in the Tags panel so you can tag elements with the correct names. Elements imported with a DTD are locked, so you can't delete or rename them unless you delete the DTD file as well.

If you have loaded a DTD into your InDesign file, you can verify that your layout meets the requirements defined in the DTD. In the Structure pane Options menu, you can validate from the Root element or the selected element.

After validating the file, problems are listed in red in the Structure pane. The bottom section of the Structure pane provides more information about specific errors, including suggestions for fixing them.

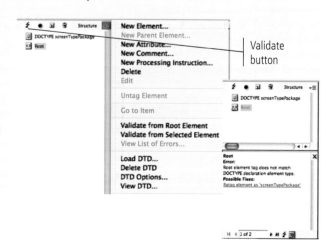

17. **Click OK to import the XML file into the rack card layout and merge the data into the tagged frames.**

The tagged elements are all placed into the matching tagged frames, but they do not yet show the appropriate style settings.

18. **In the Structure pane Options menu, choose Map Tags to Styles.**

19. **In the resulting dialog box, click Map by Name, and then click OK.**

Because you took the time to define style names that exactly matched the tag names, the mapping process requires no additional intervention.

20. **Choose View>Structure>Hide Tagged Frames and View>Structure>Hide Tag Markers to turn off the nonprinting visual indicators.**

21. **Save the rack card file as `rack_bryce.indd` in your WIP>Parks folder, and then close the file.**

Of course, XML can be far more complex than what you applied in these short documents; in fact, entire books have been written on the subject. The point of this project is to introduce you to the concepts of XML, and show you how InDesign's XML capabilities make it relatively easy to work with XML data. With some careful planning, you can set up multiple files to read the same information and repurpose content into whatever physical format is necessary.

22. **Continue to the next stage of the project.**

Note:

To learn more about the capabilities of XML, we encourage you to explore www.xml.org. This site offers a wealth of information about XML from experts and standards organizations in multiple industries.

Stage 3 Working with Interactive Elements

As we discussed earlier, the PDF format is now an industry standard for transmitting high-resolution files to an output provider. The format was originally created to share files electronically, preserving the appearance of a document regardless of the creating application or platform.

When files are shared on the Internet, they often include interactive elements such as live hyperlinks and buttons that make a digital document more user-friendly. Why force users to retype a Web address, for example, when you could enable them to simply click the text that already appears in the document?

In the final stage of this project, you add interactivity to elements that will appear in the digital version of the PDF flyer file. InDesign includes a number of tools for adding interactive elements — specifically hyperlinks and buttons — that can be useful in digitally distributed PDF files.

Note:

InDesign includes an option to export XHTML for a Web page. However, InDesign is not a Web design application. Just as there are technical requirements for designing print layouts, a number of standards and limitations govern the correct way to design and implement a Web page. We highly recommend using a Web design application such as Adobe Dreamweaver rather than trying to design a Web page layout in InDesign.

Define Hyperlinks

Hyperlinks are the most basic — and the most common — interactive elements in digital documents. Every hyperlink has two parts — the hyperlink object (which can be text) and the destination. The destination is the document, specific place in the file, or other location that is called by clicking the hyperlink. InDesign's Hyperlinks panel makes it very easy to create and apply hyperlinks to elements of a layout.

1. **With flyer_bryce.indd open, choose View>Structure>Hide Tagged Frames and View>Structure>Hide Tag Markers (if necessary) to hide the non-printing visual indicators.**

2. **Create a new text frame at the top of the smaller image frame.**

3. **Open the Text Frame Options dialog box for the new frame and check the Ignore Text Wrap option. Click OK to apply the change.**

   By default, text wrap attributes apply to any overlapping object, regardless of stacking order.

4. **In the frame, type the following:**

   For complete park information, [soft return]
   go to www.nps.gov/brca/.

5. **Select all the text and change it to 10-pt ATC Oak Normal, filled with the Paper swatch.**

6. **Open the Hyperlinks panel (Window>Interactive>Hyperlinks).**

7. **Highlight the Web address you just typed in the text frame (including the final forward slash but not the period at the end of the sentence).**

8. **Choose New Hyperlink from URL in the Hyperlinks panel Options menu.**

    The New Hyperlink dialog box defines the type and destination of the link, as well as the default appearance of the link in the layout. The highlighted text is automatically entered in the Name field.

    The New Hyperlink from URL option automatically creates a URL destination based on the selected text.

    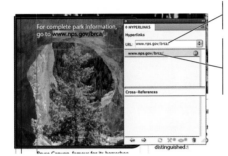

    Defined destinations are available in this menu.

    After applying the hyperlink destination, the applied hyperlink appears in the panel.

> **Note:**
>
> *You are only adding this link because not linking the text would seem to be an omission to users who assume that any instance of a Web site should be clickable. In the next exercise, you add hyperlink buttons that clearly provide interactive functionality.*

9. **With the new hyperlink selected in the panel, choose Hyperlink Options in the panel Options menu.**

    By default, hyperlinks in a print layout have no visual identification. You can use the Appearance section of this dialog box to change the invisible rectangle to a visible rectangle. (In this case, the layout will be exported for both print and Web, so you want the hyperlink to be invisible in the layout.)

    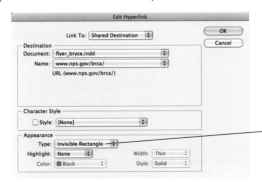

    If necessary, use this menu to turn on a visible outline of the hyperlink.

> **Note:**
>
> *If you use the Invisible Rectangle option, there will be no visual indication that the text is a hyperlink. It will be up to users to accidentally stumble onto the interactivity, which basically defeats the purpose of adding interactivity.*

10. **Click Cancel to close the dialog box.**

11. **Save the file and continue to the next exercise.**

If you are designing a document for digital distribution, you can incorporate interactive buttons for the user to initiate specific behaviors (such as opening a Web site or sending an email). InDesign buttons are created with the Button tool and managed in the States panel.

1. With **flyer_bryce.indd** open, choose File>Place and navigate to your WIP>Parks folder (if necessary). Select **email_btn.gif** and **home_btn.gif**, then click Open.

2. Click twice in the empty area in the bottom-right corner of the layout to place each loaded image in a new frame.

3. Align the top edges of the two images, and position them as shown here.

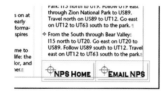

4. Open the Buttons panel (Window>Interactive>Buttons).

5. Click the NPS Home image to select the frame, then click the Convert Object to Button icon at the bottom of the Buttons panel.

An InDesign button can have three states, based on the position of the user's mouse cursor. The default Normal state displays when the cursor is not touching the button.

Note:

When the selected obect is already a button, the Convert Object to Button icon becomes the Convert Button to Object icon.

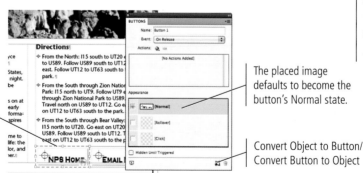

The button object is identified by a dashed (nonprinting) border.

The placed image defaults to become the button's Normal state.

Convert Object to Button/ Convert Button to Object

6. Click the Content Indicator icon in the frame to select the frame content (the placed image).

7. In the Buttons panel, click the [Rollover] state to select it.

8. Choose File>Place. Navigate to the file **home_over.gif**, make sure the Replace Selected Item option is checked, and click Open.

You have to select the placed content (not the frame) to be able to replace the image in a different button state.

When an alternative state is selected in the panel, you can place an additional image into the frame.

This image (the rollover state) will display when a user's mouse cursor moves over the button area.

9. In the Buttons panel, click the [Click] state to select it.

10. Click the Content Indicator icon in the frame to access the placed image, then choose File>Place. Navigate to the file **home_over.gif** and click Open.

This image — the click state — displays when the user clicks the button.

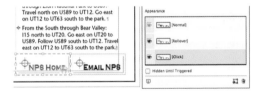

11. Using the same techniques, convert the Email NPS image to a button; define **email_over.gif** (WIP>Parks) as the Rollover and Click states.

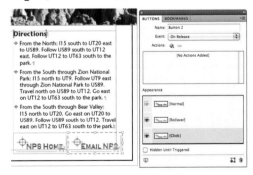

12. Save the file and continue to the next exercise.

The two buttons in your file will both cause something to happen when clicked; the "something" that happens is called an action. You can define various behaviors for different events (also called triggers) that cause a behavior (action) to occur, such as when the mouse moves over the button or when the button is clicked.

1. **With flyer_bryce.indd open, click the NPS Home button with the Selection tool.**

2. **Type Link to NPS Home Page in the Name field of the Buttons panel.**

   As with a hyperlink, the button name is used for identification purposes only. It does not appear in the actual layout or output.

3. **Make sure On Release is selected in the Event menu.**

   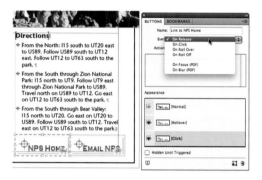

   InDesign supports six different types of events:

   - **On Release** triggers when the mouse button is released after clicking.
   - **On Click** triggers as soon as the mouse button is clicked.
   - **On Roll Over** triggers when the cursor enters the button area.
   - **On Roll Out** triggers when the cursor leaves the button area.
   - **On Focus** triggers when pressing the Tab key highlights the button (called "being in focus").
   - **On Blur** triggers when pressing the focus moves to another button.

4. **Click the "+" button in the Buttons panel and choose Go To URL in the Actions menu.**

   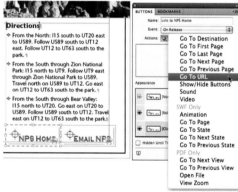

   When the user clicks and then releases the mouse button, an action occurs. The specific action that occurs is defined in this menu:

   - **Go To Destination** navigates to a specific bookmark or anchor.
   - **Go To [First/Last/Next/Previous] Page** navigates to the specified page in a file.
   - **Go To URL** opens a Web page in the user's default browser.
   - **Show/Hide Buttons** toggles between showing and hiding specified buttons in the exported file.
   - **Sound** allows you to play, pause, stop, or resume a sound file that is placed in the document.
   - **Video** allows you to play, pause, stop, or resume a movie file that is placed in the document.
   - **Animation** lets you play, pause, stop, or resume to selected animation.
   - **Go To Page** navigates to the page that you specify in a defined SWF file.
   - **Go To State** navigates to a specific state in a multi-state object.
   - **Go To Next/Previous State** navigates to the next or previous state in a multi-state object. These options are especially useful for clicking through a slideshow.
   - **Go To Next View** navigates to a page after going to the previous view (similar to the Forward button in a browser).
   - **Go To Previous View** navigates to the most recently viewed page in the PDF file, or returns to the last-used zoom size (similar to the Back button in a browser).
   - **Open File** opens the specified file in the file's native application (if possible).
   - **View Zoom** displays the page according to the zoom option you specify.

Note:

You can control the properties of placed movie files by choosing Object>Interactive> Movie Options.

You can control the properties of placed sound files by choosing Object>Interactive> Sound Options.

5. **In the URL field, place the insertion point after the "http://" prefix and type www.nps.gov/, and then press Return/Enter to finalize the URL.**

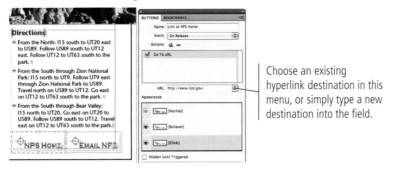

Choose an existing hyperlink destination in this menu, or simply type a new destination into the field.

6. **Select the second button and change its name to Email NPS Staff.**

7. **Define an On Release event with the Go To URL behavior. In the URL field, delete the "http://" prefix and type mailto:info@nps.gov, and then press Return/Enter to finalize the URL.**

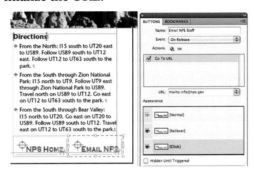

Note:

The "mailto:" prefix is the correct code to open a new message that is already targeted to the defined email address.

8. **Save the file and continue to the next exercise.**

Export Multiple PDF Files

Your layout now has two interactive buttons and one hyperlink that is not visually identified in the layout (although it will work if a user clicks the address text). The final step of this project is to output your files to the necessary formats.

1. **With flyer_bryce.indd open, choose File>Export. If necessary, navigate to your WIP>Parks folder as the target location for saving.**

2. **Choose Adobe PDF (Print) in the Format/Save As Type menu. Change the file name to flyer_bryce_print.pdf, and then click Save.**

3. **In the Export Adobe PDF dialog box, choose [Press Quality] in the Adobe PDF Preset menu.**

4. **In the General options, make sure Do Not Include is selected in the Interactive Elements menu.**

   You can use this menu to include the appearance of interactive elements in the resulting PDF file; the interactivity of the buttons, however, will not be included unless you use the Adobe PDF (Interactive) format option.

5. **In the Marks and Bleeds options, add crop marks with a 0.125″ offset and activate the Use Document Bleed Settings option.**

6. **Click the Save Preset button and save these settings as Print with Bleed.**

   You need to export two other layouts using the same settings; creating a preset now will save time later.

7. **Click OK to close the Save Preset dialog box, and then click Export to create the PDF file for print.**

8. When the export process is complete, choose File>Export again. Choose Adobe PDF (Interactive) in the Format/Save As Type menu, change the file name to flyer_bryce_web.pdf, and click Save.

9. In the Export to Interactive PDF dialog box, uncheck the View After Exporting option. Choose Fit Page in the View menu. In the Buttons and Media area, make sure the Include All option is selected, then click OK.

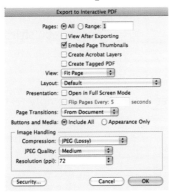

10. Click Export. When the export process is complete, open both PDF files in Acrobat. Test the buttons and hyperlink in the Web file.

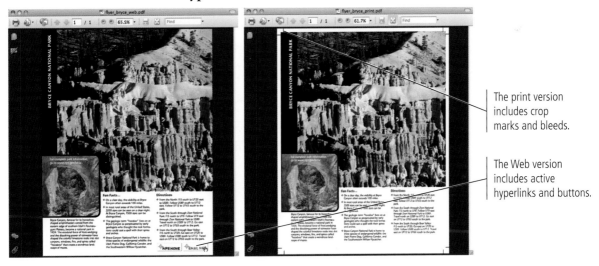

The print version includes crop marks and bleeds.

The Web version includes active hyperlinks and buttons.

11. Close the PDF files and return to InDesign. Save and close the flyer file.

12. Open the postcard and rack card files from your WIP>Parks folder. Export PDF files for print using the Print with Bleed preset.

13. Save and close both InDesign files.

1. You can edit the _____ settings to change the default text formatting for all new text frames.

2. The _____ panel shows every character in the selected font. You can view the entire font, or sort by specific defined sets.

3. The _____ option changes a style definition to include local formatting that has been applied to currently selected text.

4. The _____ format can store thousands of characters in a single font file.

5. You can _____ to edit a paragraph style without applying that style to the selected text.

6. You can change the _____ settings to change the physical appearance of a rounded rectangle.

7. _____ can be used to build a sample layout and test the appearance of paragraph styles before you have the final job text.

8. In an empty text frame, you can apply a style to the _____ to define the default style for unformatted text that is imported into that frame.

9. You can use the _____ tool to sample colors from placed images.

10. You can use the _____ to review the content and hierarchy of tagged frames.

1. Briefly explain why styles can be beneficial when experimenting with a page design.

2. Briefly explain two advantages of the OpenType format.

3. Briefly explain the difference between XML tags and styles.

Use what you learned in this project to complete the following freeform exercise.
Carefully read the art director and client comments, then create your own design to meet the needs of the project.
Use the space below to sketch ideas; when finished, write a brief explanation of your reasoning behind your final design.

art director comments

The client is very pleased with the pieces you have designed to promote tourism in the national parks. Before she presents the project to her director for approval, she would like to have the same pieces for at least one other park.

To complete this project, you should:

❏ Create the flyer, rack card, and postcard layouts for Yosemite National Park. Use the images and text that are provided in the **ID5_PB_Project7.zip** archive on the Student Files Web page.

❏ Create one additional layout for a letterfold brochure that will include the same content as the other pieces. The inside of the brochure should have only the park name and space for a map of the park.

❏ If you completed Project 5, you can use the same basic 4×9″ template that you created in that project.

client comments

These pieces are exactly what I had in mind. I would like to see one additional layout — redesigning our park map brochure to include this same content, but also with a large map of the specific park. We already have the maps, but I'll have to find the files for you; for now just leave space on the inside of the brochure.

When I pitch the project to my superiors, I want to be able to show them the pieces for at least two different parks. That way the committee will see how different colors and pictures will affect the individual pieces, but still have a consistent look and feel. I've sent you the text and images for Yosemite for this second set of files.

I'm thinking about combining the flyers for all the parks (when they're done) into a booklet that we might be able to sell. I'm going to include this in my presentation as a potential source of income to justify the cost of the overall project. Having more than one flyer finished will help to explain this part of the project.

project justification

_____
_____
_____
_____
_____
_____
_____
_____
_____
_____
_____
_____
_____
_____
_____

To complete this project, you started with the very basics — defining a new document — and worked all the way through complex content repurposing using XML. You should realize that you have virtually unlimited creative control as you experiment with an initial layout concept, but that creating a unified design sometimes requires minor adjustments based on the actual content that will be placed in the layout.

You used unstructured XML to drag specific types of content into a layout, and you used a more structured approach to automatically place content into tagged frames of a different layout. By maintaining a link to the XML file, you were able to automatically update the placed content to reflect changes in the text. Repurposing the same content in multiple different layouts — both for print and digital distribution — is becoming increasingly common in the design world; using InDesign's XML capabilities makes the process far easier than manually creating each different version.

Experiment with text formatting based on placeholder text before actual content is ready

Define frame fitting options for a graphics placeholder frame

Change the corner style of an existing frame

Create a swatch based on colors sampled from an image

Redefine a style based on local formatting overrides

Create new styles based on existing text formatting

Create interactive buttons for electronic versions

Repurpose content using imported XML content

Bryce Canyon National Park

Bryce Canyon, famous for its horseshoe-shaped amphitheaters carved from the eastern edge of southern Utah's Paunsaugunt Plateau, became a national park in 1924. The erosional force of frost-wedging and the dissolving power of rainwater have shaped the colorful limestone rocks into slot canyons, windows, fins, and spires called "hoodoos" that create a wondrous landscape of mazes.

Fun Facts...

» On a clear day, the visibility at Bryce Canyon often exceeds 100 miles.

» In most rural areas of the United States, 2500 stars can be seen on a clear night. At Bryce Canyon, 7500 stars can be distinguished.

» The geologic term "hoodoo" lives on at Bryce Canyon as perpetuated by early geologists who thought the rock formations could cast a spell with their spires and arches.

» Bryce Canyon National Park is home to three species of endangered wildlife: the Utah Prairie Dog, California Condor, and the Southwestern Willow Flycatcher.

park information, ps.gov/brca/

Fun Facts...

◆ On a clear day, the visibility at Bryce Canyon often exceeds 100 miles.

◆ In most rural areas of the United States, 2500 stars can be seen on a clear night. At Bryce Canyon, 7500 stars can be distinguished.

◆ The geologic term "hoodoo" lives on at Bryce Canyon as perpetuated by early geologists who thought the rock formations could cast a spell with their spires and arches.

◆ Bryce Canyon National Park is home to three species of endangered wildlife: the Utah Prairie Dog, California Condor, and the Southwestern Willow Flycatcher.

Directions

From the North: I15 south to UT20 east to US89. Follow US89 south to UT12 east. Follow UT12 to UT63 south to the park.

From the South through Zion National Park: I15 north to UT9. Follow UT9 east through Zion National Park to US89. Travel north on US89 to UT12. Go east on UT12 to UT63 south to the park.

From the South through Bear Valley: I15 north to UT20. Go east on UT20 to US89. Follow US89 south to UT12. Travel east on UT12 to UT63 south to the park.

⊕ NPS HOME   ⊕ EMAIL NPS

Multi-Chapter Booklet

Your client, Against The Clock (ATC), publishes books related to the computer graphics industry. In addition to application-specific books, they are also creating a series of "companion" titles that discuss the concepts underlying the use of digital software — basic design principles, type, color, and so on. You were hired to build an "excerpt" booklet of the companion titles, which ATC will use for marketing purposes.

This project incorporates the following skills:

❏ Combining multiple InDesign files into a single book

❏ Synchronizing the assets in multiple files to ensure consistency from one piece to the next

❏ Building a unified table of contents for the entire book

❏ Building an index that covers all chapters of the book

❏ Using variable data to build a personalized letter

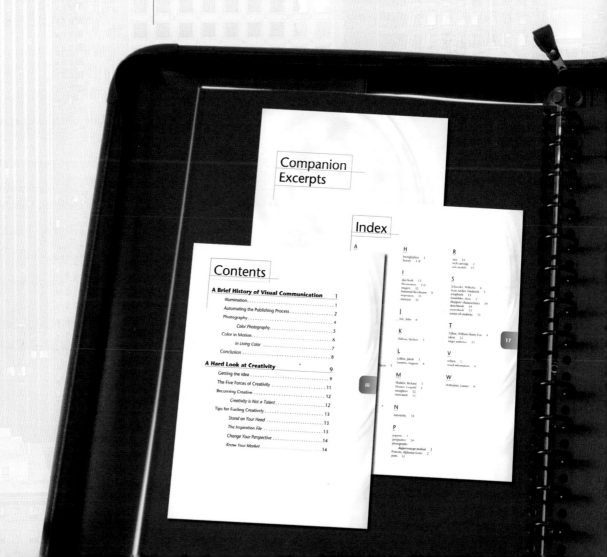

client comments

We are launching a new series of books that will complement our application-specific books. We want to use the existing InDesign files to create a sample excerpt booklet that we can use in digital and print advertising.

We sent you the files for the first chapter from two of the books. Unfortunately, the file from the *Color Companion* seems to be one version behind — we can't find the version that was tagged for the book's index. We want the sample booklet to include a representative index, though, so we'd like you to tag a few entries in the *Color Companion* chapter and build a mini-index for the sample. The booklet should also have its own self-cover, title page, and table of contents.

The first set of these booklets will be printed and mailed to 50 clients that we selected from our database. We're asking these clients to review the sample chapters and provide quotes that we can use in marketing materials. We provided you with a comma-delimited data file that was exported from our database. We also sent you the text for a thank-you letter we want to include with the booklet.

art director comments

Long documents such as books (especially non-fiction) require several special elements, including a table of contents and an index. Many publishers spend countless hours manually composing these elements; they literally flip through pages and hand-write every entry in a spreadsheet. Fortunately, InDesign has built-in tools that make this process far easier.

If you use styles consistently, you can build a table of contents based on the styles in the chapters. Unfortunately, the index is a bit more complicated. Although the tools for tagging and compiling an index make the process a bit easier, indexing remains a largely manual process; there is no software smart enough to to decide exactly what to include in an index.

The advantage of using these tools is that you complete the process only once. Using the old methods, changes late in the process — which happen almost every time — meant manually re-compiling the table of contents and index. Using InDesign's built-in tools, you can easily re-compile both elements as often as necessary, and you can format them automatically using other styles.

project objectives

To complete this project, you will:

- ❏ Create an InDesign book file
- ❏ Manage different files as chapters of a single book
- ❏ Control section and page numbering across multiple chapter files
- ❏ Synchronize assets in all files of the book
- ❏ Build a table of contents based on styles
- ❏ Tag index entries in each file of the book
- ❏ Compile the index for all book chapters at once
- ❏ Create a variable-data letter addressed to previous ATC clients

Stage 1 Combining Documents into Books

Publication design is a unique subset of graphic design. Attention to detail is critical. You must ensure that subhead formatting in early chapters matches the subhead formatting in later chapters, that captions are all set in the same font, that body copy is the same size throughout the document, and so on. Regardless of whether one or several designers work on the project, consistency is essential from the first page of the book to the last. To make long-document design easier, InDesign allows you to create a special type of book file for combining and managing multiple chapters as a single unit.

Long documents are frequently split into multiple files during the conception and design phases, and then combined at the end of the process to create the final job. This workflow offers several advantages:

- Layouts with numerous images can become very large; dividing these layouts into pieces helps keep the file size smaller.

- If a long document is divided into multiple stand-alone files, several designers can work on different files of the same book without the risk of accidentally overwriting another designer's work.

- If a long document is split into several files, you won't lose the entire job if a single file becomes corrupt.

Before digital book-building utilities were introduced, working with multiple files required extreme care and attention to detail to maintain consistency from one file to the next. InDesign's book-building tools make the process much easier by automating many of the tasks that were previously done manually. (Of course, even though the InDesign book utilities automate much of the process, you must still — and always — pay close attention to the details of your work.)

Note:

When a single design project is made up of several files, it is even more important to maintain consistency from one file to the next. If the font is slightly different from one issue of a newsletter to the next, few people are likely to spot the difference. That difference is far more noticeable, however, when two or more files are bound together in the same publication.

BUILD AN INDESIGN BOOK

An InDesign book is simply a container file into which multiple InDesign files are placed for easier organization and file management. The InDesign book utility offers several benefits, including:

- Synchronizing styles, colors, and other assets to the book's master file;

- Monitoring page and section numbering of each individual file in the book, and the book as a whole;

- Building a table of contents and index from all book files at once; and

- Printing or exporting the entire book, or outputting only selected chapters.

1. **Download ID5_RF_Project8.zip from the Student Files Web page.**

2. **Expand the ZIP archive in your WIP folder (Macintosh) or copy the archive contents into your WIP folder (Windows).**

   This results in a folder named **Companions**, which contains the files you need for this project. You should also use this folder to save the files you create in this project.

3. **With nothing open in InDesign, choose File>New>Book. Navigate to your WIP>Companions folder as the target location.**

   Unlike creating a new file, creating a new book requires you to immediately name and save the book file.

Note:

When you work with book files, you frequently open, save, and close the chapters of the book files; in fact, some operations happen without your direct intervention. Book chapter files need to be stored on a writable disk as long as you are still working on the book.

4. **Change the book name to `excerpts.indb` and click Save.**

   The correct extension is automatically added for you, but if you accidentally remove it, add it to the file name.

Note:

You can open a book file the same way you open a regular document file (File>Open).

Clicking Save opens the Book panel; the file name that you defined ("Excerpts") appears in the panel tab. By default, the Book panel floats in the workspace; you can drag it anywhere you prefer (including into a specific panel group, whether docked or not).

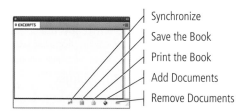

Note:

You can save a book with a different name by choosing Save Book As from the panel Options menu.

5. **Windows users: If the Welcome Screen is open, move or close it so you can see the new Book panel. Click the Book panel title bar and drag it away from the center of the workspace.**

   On Windows, the new Book panel opens behind the Welcome screen; this is an apparent bug in the software. Once you have revealed the panel, dragging it to a different location allows the panel to remain visible even when the Welcome Screen reopens.

6. **Continue to the next exercise.**

 ADD BOOK CHAPTERS

Once the book file has been defined, adding chapters is easy. The first chapter you add becomes (by default) the style source chapter, to which other chapters can be synchronized.

1. **With the `excerpts` book file open, click the Add Documents button at the bottom of the Book panel.**

2. **Navigate to `color1.indd` in your WIP>Companions folder and click Open.**

   Depending on the size of the chapter, it might take a few seconds to process the file.

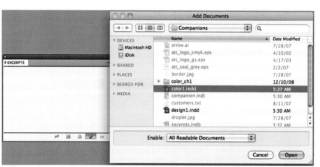

Note:

Don't worry about making these decisions early in the project. You can change the specific file to which the book is synchronized later; you will do this in a later exercise.

When the process is complete, the file name appears in the Book panel.

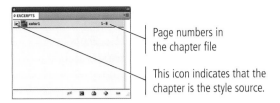

Page numbers in the chapter file

This icon indicates that the chapter is the style source.

Note:

You can change the style source for the book by clicking the empty space to the left of a specific chapter.

3. **Click the Add Documents button again. Navigate to design1.indd in your WIP>Companions folder and click Open.**

   New files are automatically added below the previously selected chapter. If no chapter is selected in the panel, new files are added to the end of the book.

   If you haven't changed the section or page numbering options for the files you add, new book chapters are automatically numbered sequentially from one file to the next.

Note:

You can remove a file from a book by clicking the Remove Documents button at the bottom of the Book panel. Once you remove a chapter from a book, you can't undo the deletion. The file still exists in its original location, however, so you can simply add the file back into the book, if necessary.

4. **Create a new file by opening companion.indt from your WIP> Companions folder.**

   This is the template from which the companion chapters were created. Although the two excerpt chapters are already laid out, you need to create a front matter document that will hold a title page and the table of contents for the combined excerpts.

5. **In the Pages panel, drag the F-Title Page master page icon onto the Page 1 icon.**

   The front matter document will include the title page and table of contents — both conventional parts of book design, which have been planned for in the existing master page layouts. By dragging the F-Title Page master onto Page 1, you're applying the existing master page to the first page of the front matter file.

Note:

If you get a Profile or Policy Mismatch warning at any point in this project, select the option to leave the document as is and click OK.

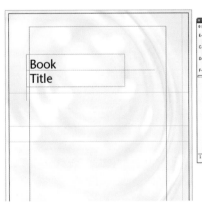

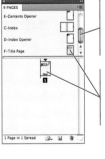

Scroll through the master page area (if necessary) to find the F-Title Page master at the bottom of the available layouts.

Drag the F-Title Page master onto the Page 1 icon in the lower section of the Pages panel.

6. **Press Command/Control-Shift and click the Book Title text frame to detach only that object from the master page.**

   The text frame for the book title is placed on the master page; to change the text and enter the actual book title, you either have to make the change on the master page or detach the master items on the regular layout page.

7. **Using the Type tool, highlight the text "Book Title" in the text frame and type `Companion Excerpts`.**

8. **Drag the right-center handle of the text frame until the word "Excerpts" moves to the second line and the right edge of the frame is approximately 1/8″ from the edge of the text.**

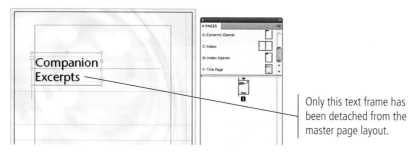

Only this text frame has been detached from the master page layout.

Note:

Front matter *typically refers to the information that precedes the main content of a book, including a title page, table of contents, copyright information, acknowledgments, and other important elements.*

9. **Save the file as `excerpts front.indd` in your WIP>Companions folder, and then close the file.**

10. **In the `excerpts` Book panel, click the Add Documents button.**

11. **Navigate to the `excerpts front.indd` file you just created and add it to the book file.**

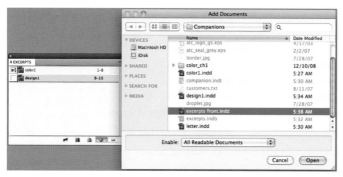

Managing Book Chapters

INDESIGN FOUNDATIONS sidebar

When you place a file into a book, the book file acts as a container; this process is very similar to placing an image into a layout. An InDesign layout stores the path to a placed image as a reference. Books use the same methodology, storing references to the files contained within the book; the book file does not contain the actual chapter files, only links to those chapters.

If the chapter files have been moved since being added to the book, the Book panel shows a missing-link warning icon. When you double-click a missing book chapter, InDesign asks if you want to replace the missing file; clicking Yes opens a navigation dialog box so you can locate the missing file or identify a replacement file. (You can also select a missing file in the panel and choose Replace Document from the Book panel Options menu.)

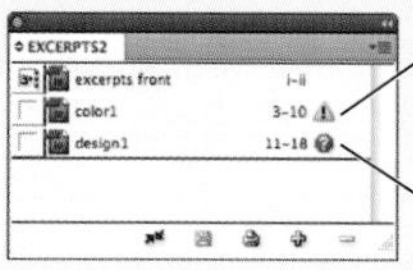

This chapter was modified outside the context of the book.

This chapter file is not in the same location as when it was placed in the book.

If you open a chapter using the Book panel, changes automatically reflect in the containing book. When you open a book chapter outside the context of the book, the Book panel displays a modified-link icon for that file.

You can update a modified book chapter by simply double-clicking the file in the panel to open it. When you save the chapter and close it, InDesign updates the book chapter link to reflect the most current version of the file. Once a chapter has been added to a book file, it is best to make changes only within the context of the book.

design1.indd is missing. Do you want to replace it with a new document?

No   Yes

430   Project 8: Multi-Chapter Booklet

12. **Click `excerpts front` in the panel and drag up until a heavy black line appears above `color1` in the panel.**

When you release the mouse button, excerpts front becomes the first chapter in the book. However, color1 is still the style source; the style source does not need to be the first chapter in the book.

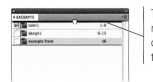

This line indicates the new position of the chapter (when you release the mouse button).

color1 is still the style source for the book file.

Note:

When you drag a file within a book, align the thumb on the cursor icon with the location where you want to place the file.

13. **Click the Save the Book button at the bottom of the panel.**

14. **Continue to the next exercise.**

 ## CONTROL SECTION AND PAGE NUMBERING

After moving the front matter chapter in front of the color chapter, the page numbers for each chapter automatically change to reflect their new position in the book. The problem, however, is that the second file (color1) begins on Page 2 and the third file (design1) begins on Page 10. Even-numbered pages are left-facing pages, but book design conventions dictate that book chapters begin on right-facing (odd-numbered) pages.

1. **With the `excerpts` book file open, choose Book Page Numbering Options from the Book panel Options menu.**

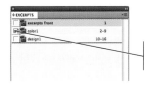

Note:

Although some book designs intentionally break from convention and begin chapters on left-facing pages, this is not the norm. Right-facing chapter-starts are so common, in fact, that InDesign's long-document tools include the ability to force chapters to begin on the right side of the spread.

2. **In the Book Page Numbering Options dialog box, choose the Continue on Next Odd Page option.**

You can use this dialog box to control exactly where new chapter files begin:

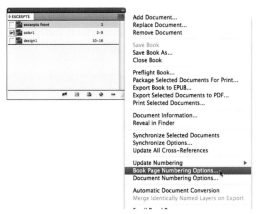

- **Continue from Previous Document**, the default option, allows new chapters to pick up numbering from the end of the previous file. This option allows new chapters to begin on odd- or even-numbered pages.

- **Continue on Next Odd Page** forces new chapter files to begin on odd-numbered pages. If your layouts use facing pages, this means new chapters will always begin on right-facing pages.

- **Continue on Next Even Page** forces new chapter files to begin on even-numbered pages. If your layouts use facing pages, this means new chapters will always begin on left-facing pages.

3. **Check the Insert Blank Page option and leave the Automatically Update option checked.**

   The Insert Blank Page option adds a blank page into any file where the defined page order leaves a blank space in the page numbering. When the Automatically Update option is checked (as it is by default), files in the book automatically adjust to reflect additional choices in this dialog box.

4. **Click OK to apply your changes.**

   The second and third files in the book now begin on odd-numbered (right-facing) pages. Blank pages have been added as necessary to fill empty spaces caused by moving the chapters to the appropriate side of the spread.

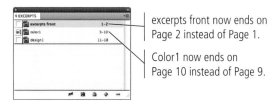

   excerpts front now ends on Page 2 instead of Page 1.

   Color1 now ends on Page 10 instead of Page 9.

5. **In the Book panel, click the `excerpts front` file to select it.**

6. **Open the Book panel Options menu, choose Document Numbering Options.**

   In addition to controlling the page numbering from one file to another, you can also control the page numbering for a specific file. This option is useful if, for example, you want the front matter of a book to be numbered separately from the main body of the document.

   To change document-specific settings such as page numbering and sections, the document must be open. When you choose Document Numbering Options in the Book panel Options menu, the selected file automatically opens so you can make changes.

Understanding Book Page Numbering

If you had not checked Insert Blank Pages in the Book Page Numbering Options dialog box, each chapter in your book would begin on a right-facing (odd-numbered) page. However, the last page in each file would remain unchanged. The image here shows the original pagination (on the left) in comparison to the renumbered pages; the first page of each file is highlighted in pink. In the middle version — the result of the steps you just took — blank pages are highlighted in yellow.

The third version (on the right) shows what would have happened if you had not selected the Insert Blank Pages option. Although the second and third files would have begun on odd-numbered (right-facing) pages, the blank pages would not have been added to fill the space. This could cause significant problems when the book is imposed into printer's spreads for commercial printing. (Refer to Project 4 for an explanation of printer's spreads.)

Original pagination		Pagination after modifying numbering (inserting blank pages)		Pagination without inserting blank pages	
	1		1		1
2	3	2	3		3
4	5	4	5	4	5
6	7	6	7	6	7
8	9	8	9	8	9
10	11	10	11	10	11
12	13	12	13		13
14	15	14	15	14	15
16		16	17	16	17
		18		18	

7. **In the Document Numbering Options dialog box, choose lowercase Roman numerals in the Page Numbering Style menu.**

This is another convention in book design and layout — the front matter is numbered separately from the main part of the book, commonly in lowercase Roman numerals.

The excerpts front file is selected in the Book panel.

Choosing Document Numbering Options in the Book panel Options menu opens the selected file.

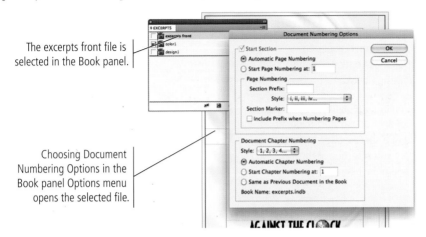

8. **Click OK to apply the change, save the open layout, and then close the file.**

In the Book panel, the excerpts front file reflects the new numbering style. The problem, however, is that the first content chapter still begins on Page 3 (even though this file is still numbered with Arabic numerals).

9. **Double-click color1 in the Book panel.**

Double-clicking a file in the Book panel automatically opens that file.

10. **Control/right-click the Page 3 icon in the Pages panel and choose Numbering & Section Options.**

This command opens a dialog box similar to the Document Numbering Options dialog box. The primary difference is that this dialog box provides options for controlling a specific page (Page 3, which you Control/right-clicked to access the dialog box).

When you use the Document Numbering Options command, InDesign automatically applies your choices, beginning with the first page of the selected file. Using the Numbering & Section Options command, you can change the options for any page in the document.

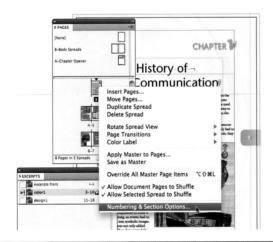

Section and Page Numbering in a Single File

Although there are distinct advantages to maintaining long documents in separate chapter files, there are times when you want to work with an entire booklet or other project in a single InDesign file. In this case, it is important to realize that you can change the page and section numbering options for any page in the layout; these options are not restricted to files placed in an InDesign book.

Sections allow you to create different page numbering sequences within a single file. For any section start page, you can restart page numbering at a specific page number, change the style of page numbers in the section, define a section marker for the section, and/or include the section prefix in the page number.

You can change the page and section options for any specific page by Control/right-clicking the page in the Pages panel and choosing Numbering & Section Options from the contextual menu.

When you choose Numbering & Section Options for a page that isn't already a section start, the New Section dialog box opens with the Start Section option automatically checked. When you click OK in the New Section dialog box, the selected page is designated as a section start.

If you choose Numbering & Section Options for an existing section start page, the Numbering & Section Options dialog box opens. The choices in this dialog box are exactly the same as those in the New Section dialog box; the only differences are the title bar and the choices already selected when you open the dialog box.

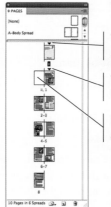

The first page in the file is a section start by default.

The triangle above the page icon indicates a section start.

Pages between two section starts are part of the preceding section.

Adding Section Prefixes

If you use the Page Number markers (Type> Insert Special Character>Markers>Current/Next/ Previous Page Number), you can add a section prefix to page numbers in the layout by checking the Include Prefix when Numbering Pages option. Whatever you type in the Section Prefix field is added in front of the page number.

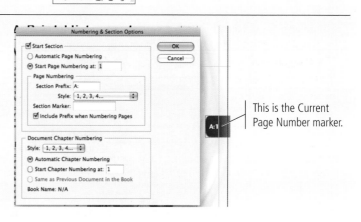

This is the Current Page Number marker.

11. In the Numbering & Section Options dialog box, choose the Start Page Numbering At option and change the number in the field to 1.

InDesign's default behavior — the Automatic Page Numbering option — causes pages to number sequentially from one file to the next in the book. By choosing the Start Page Numbering At option, you can override the default page numbering and determine the exact page number of any file in the book.

Note:

If you are using facing pages, changing an even-numbered page to an odd-numbered page moves the page to the other side of the spread. Remember from earlier chapters that this can cause objects to appear out of position in relation to the page's new location.

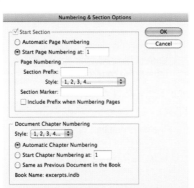

Section and Chapter Numbering in Depth (continued)

INDESIGN FOUNDATIONS

Adding Section Markers

Section markers are a type of variable. You can define the Section Marker text for a specific section, and then place the marker into the layout (Type>Insert Special Character>Markers>Section Marker).

The Section Marker special character displays the text in the Section Marker field of the Numbering & Section Options dialog box. If a section has no defined Section Marker text, the special character displays nothing. You can also change all instances of the section marker within a section by re-opening the dialog box for the section start page and changing the text in the Section Marker field.

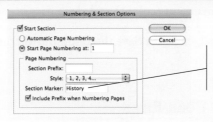

The word "History" is the defined Section Marker text for this section.

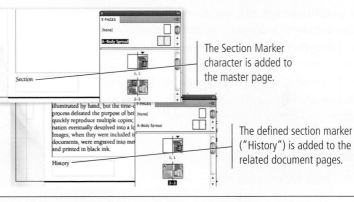

The Section Marker character is added to the master page.

The defined section marker ("History") is added to the related document pages.

Chapter Numbering

When you work with book files, you can also define Document Chapter Numbering options, which is basically section numbering for files. If you define a specific chapter number in the Numbering & Section Options dialog box, you can place the built-in Chapter Number variable (Type> Text Variables>Insert Variable>Chapter Number) in the layout to reflect the current chapter number.

If nothing appears in the Insert Variable submenu, the document was probably created in an earlier version of InDesign. Several predefined variables — including Chapter Number — were added in InDesign CS3. In this case, you can either define your own Chapter Number variable (see Project 5) or load the variables from a file created in InDesign CS3 or later.

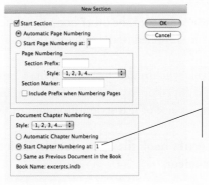

This number is placed anywhere the Chapter Number variable is used in the file.

12. **Click OK to apply the new page number to the first page of the color1 file.**

    Because you haven't changed the numbering options for the design1 file (or any specific page in that file), it is still automatically numbered in sequence with the color1 file.

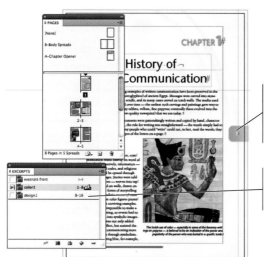

This object is placed using the Current Page Number marker. It reflects the correct page number relative to the entire book.

The page numbers for design1 change to reflect the new overall book page numbering.

13. **Save the open document (color1) and close it.**

14. **In the Book panel, click the Save the Book button, and then continue to the next exercise.**

SYNCHRONIZE BOOK FILES

Layout designers frequently manipulate, tweak, and even cheat to force-fit text into a desired amount of space, to make a runaround work correctly, or to achieve a specific effect. When the files are combined into the final book, these adjustments can cause problems if the variation is noticeable from one chapter to the next. A primary advantage of using the InDesign book-building functionality is the ability to easily synchronize various assets — swatches, styles, etc. — across multiple chapter files to ensure consistency thoughout a publication.

When a book is synchronized, assets in the style source file are applied to all other files in the book. (The synchronization process does not affect elements that are not in the style source file.)

- If an asset in the Style Source file does not exist in other book files, it is simply added to the other files.

- If an asset already exists in the other book files, the element definition from the Style Source file is applied to the same-named element in the other files.

In this exercise, you synchronize the assets in the Companion Excerpts files to make sure the highlight color has the same definition in all files, and to ensure consistency in the appearance of text styles throughout the document.

1. **With the excerpts book file open, double-click the excerpts front file to open that document.**

2. **Open the Swatches panel, and then open the Swatch Options dialog box for the Companion Color swatch.**

Note:

The page numbering of a book relies on the Current Page Number marker. When you use the Current Page Number marker in book chapter files, those markers reflect the correct page number in relation to the entire book.

Note:

You can close a book just as you would close any other panel — click the "X" button in the Book panel tab. If you haven't manually saved the book file, you are asked to save before closing the file.

Note:

The tool tip name for the Synchronize button — Synchronize Styles and Swatches with the Style Source — is deceptively non-inclusive. Because you can synchronize far more than just these two elements, we refer to this button as simply "Synchronize."

Note:

Synchronizing a book does not delete any element from any file, but can override changes that you made to a particular file.

3. **Change the swatch definition to C=70 M=100 Y=0 K=0 and make sure the Name with Color Value option is not checked.**

Each book in the Companion series was printed with a different highlight color. When combining chapters from different books in the series, the highlight color needed to be unifed for consistency throughout the "combo" document. In this excerpt booklet, the client decided to use a purple shade as the highlight color.

This is an instance where there is good reason to break from the color-naming convention based on color definition. The swatch is different in all companion books, but the swatch is named the same in all files of all books. By synchronizing the color in all book files to this new definition, you can change the Companion Color swatch in multiple files at one time.

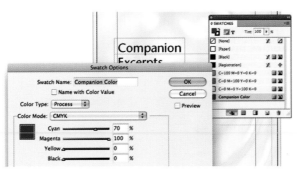

4. **Click OK to close the Swatch Options dialog box, save the document and close it, but leave the book file open.**

5. **In the Book panel, click the empty space to the left of the excerpts front file to redefine the style source.**

Since the front matter file now has the Companion Color swatch definition that you want to use for the entire document, you need to synchronize other files in the book to the excerpt front file.

You can change the style source at any time by clicking in this space.

6. **Click in the empty area at the bottom of the Book panel to deselect all files.**

If nothing is selected in the Book panel, all chapter files will be synchronized to the style source file. You can also synchronize specific files by selecting them in the Book panel before clicking the Synchronize button. (Of course, synchronizing only certain files defeats the purpose of synchronizing, but the option is available nonetheless.)

7. **In the Book panel Options menu, choose Synchronize Options.**

Click in this space to deselect all chapters in the book.

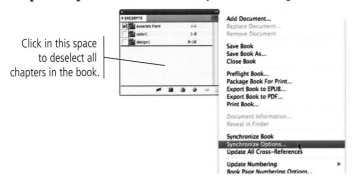

8. **In the Synchronize Options dialog box, uncheck everything except Character Styles, Paragraph Styles, and Swatches.**

In this simple project, your primary concern is consistency of appearance between existing files from the same series of books. The three selected options are sufficient for this project. In other cases where you combine radically different files from a variety of designers, it might be useful — or, in fact, vital — to synchronize the other types of assets as well.

9. **Click OK to close the dialog box.**

10. **In the Book panel, click the Synchronize button.**

11. **Click OK in the resulting warning.**

As we mentioned, synchronizing book files can cause problems. InDesign is smart enough to recognize and warn you about one of the most common and serious problems — overset text.

Smart Matching Style Groups

The Smart Match Style Groups option is useful if you use groups (folders) to organize styles in your layout files. The following images show the results of synchronizing styles that are stored in style groups.

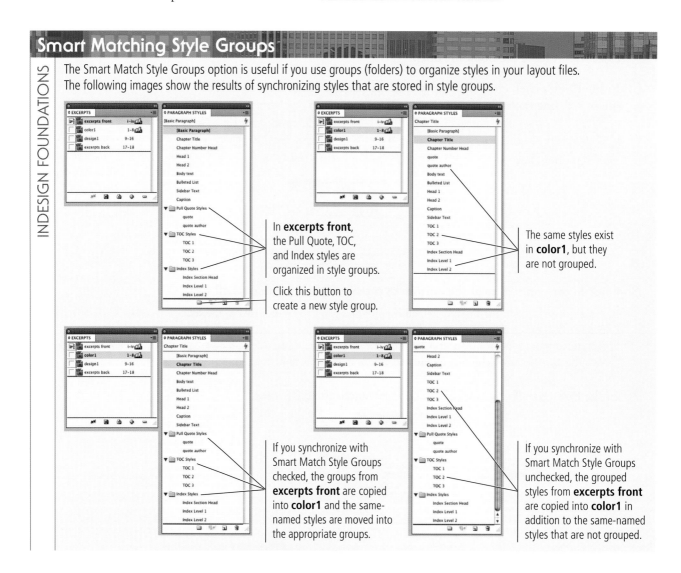

In **excerpts front**, the Pull Quote, TOC, and Index styles are organized in style groups.

Click this button to create a new style group.

The same styles exist in **color1**, but they are not grouped.

If you synchronize with Smart Match Style Groups checked, the groups from **excerpts front** are copied into **color1** and the same-named styles are moved into the appropriate groups.

If you synchronize with Smart Match Style Groups unchecked, the grouped styles from **excerpts front** are copied into **color1** in addition to the same-named styles that are not grouped.

12. When the process is complete, click OK to dismiss the resulting message.

This message warns you of the potential problem we mentioned earlier — documents might have changed. When you synchronize book files — especially if you did not create the original files — you should carefully review the pages to be sure the content is still where it belongs.

13. Double-click color1 in the Book panel to open that file, and navigate to Page 8.

When you synchronize files, you often have no idea what caused the problem — but you still need to fix it. You have several options:

- Edit the text to fit the overset line in the available space. Of course, this assumes you have permission to edit text, which you usually do not.
- Add text frames to the chain. This typically assumes you can add pages to a file, which you often can't.
- Change style definitions to fit text into the available space. If you synchronize again later, your changes will again be overwritten.
- Adjust local formatting of specific text to make the layout work properly.

After synchronizing styles, the last two lines of the last paragraph on Page 7 reflow onto Page 8.

The reflowed text causes the overset text icon to appear.

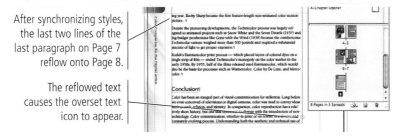

14. On Page 7 of the file, place the insertion point in the "In Living Color" head. Change the Space Before Paragraph setting for this paragraph only to 0.1".

After changing the Space Before Paragraph setting for the heading, the last two lines of this paragraph again fit on Page 7.

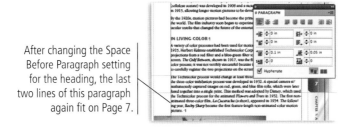

15. Navigate to Page 8 and review the text.

The end-of-story character now shows, and the overset text icon no longer appears in the frame's out port.

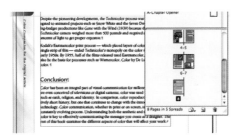

16. Save the document and close it.

17. Save the book file and continue to the next stage of the project.

Note:

If you change a style — to fit text onto a page, for example — synchronizing the book to the master file overwrites the changes, and the text no longer fits the same way.

Note:

In case you were wondering, the Space Before Paragraph setting for the head 2 style was reduced in the original color1 file to fit the text in eight pages, instead of placing only two lines of text on Page 9 and inserting a blank Page 10.

Note:

If you absolutely must adjust text in a particular file of a book, we recommend you manipulate the selected text and not the style.

Stage 2 Building a Table of Contents

Before desktop-publishing software automated the document-design process, tables of contents and other lists (figures, tables, etc.) were created manually from page proofs — by turning each page and writing down the appropriate text and page number, and then sorting and typesetting those hard-copy lists into the final document. The process was extremely time-consuming and required precise attention to detail. If the document changed after the lists were completed, the entire piece had to be rechecked, one page at a time.

Fortunately, InDesign includes a Table of Contents feature that automates this process, greatly improving production time and making it easier to maintain accuracy. InDesign tables of contents are based on the paragraph styles used in a layout. If you are conscientious about applying styles when you build a layout, you can easily create a thorough, accurate table of contents based on those styles.

You can define the styles that will be included in the compiled table of contents. For example, a table of contents might include Heading 1, Heading 2, and Heading 3 paragraph styles; any text set in those styles will appear in the list.

You can also determine the styles that will be used to format different elements in the compiled table of contents. Using the same example, TOC1 can be assigned to Heading 1 list items, TOC2 to Heading 2 items, and so on. When you compile the table of contents into the file, it is formatted automatically.

DEFINE A TABLE OF CONTENTS STYLE

A table of contents can be defined and applied in a single process. You can also create and save table of contents styles, which you can apply as needed in the active file, as well as import into and apply in other files. Because of the versatility allowed by styles of all types (paragraph, table, object, etc.), we recommend creating table of contents styles rather than defining a single-case table of contents.

1. **With the excerpts book file open, double-click the excerpts front file in the panel to open that file.**

2. **Drag the E-Contents Opener master page to the right of the Page ii icon.**

    When the new page is added, another blank page is also added because of your choices (Insert Blank Page) in the Book Page Numbering Options dialog box.

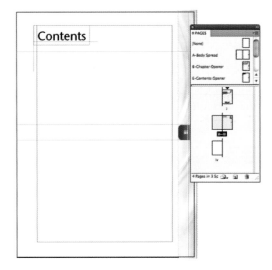

3. **Choose Layout>Table of Contents Styles.**

   You can create new styles, edit or delete existing styles, or load styles from other files.

4. **Click New. In the resulting New Table of Contents Style dialog box, type Companion Contents in the TOC Style field.**

   The TOC Style field defines the style name. It is basically the same as a paragraph style name (an identifier).

5. **Delete the text from the Title field.**

   The Title field, on the other hand, is actual text that is included at the top of the compiled table of contents. Because the "Contents" title for this layout is built into the master page, you should not include a title in the compiled table of contents.

6. **If necessary, click the More Options button on the right side of the dialog box.**

   When More Options are showing, you can control the appearance of page numbers in the table of contents.

   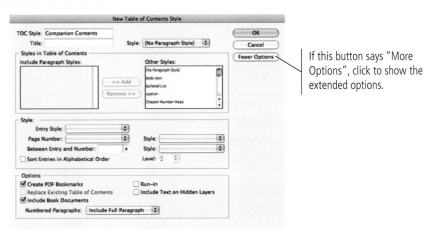

   If this button says "More Options", click to show the extended options.

7. **Scroll though the Other Styles list, select Chapter Title, and click the Add button.**

8. **In the middle section of the dialog box, choose TOC 1 in the Entry Style menu.**

9. **Choose After Entry in the Page Number field, and choose TOC Page Number in the associated Style menu. Leave all other options at their default settings.**

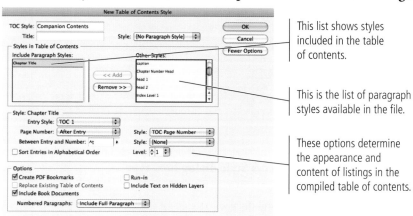

This list shows styles included in the table of contents.

This is the list of paragraph styles available in the file.

These options determine the appearance and content of listings in the compiled table of contents.

You can define a number of options for each style included in a table of contents:

- **Entry Style** defines the paragraph style that will be applied to those entries in the compiled list.

- **Page Number** determines where the page number will be included for each entry (After Entry or Before Entry). You can also choose No Page Number to add the list entry without the associated page number.

- **Between Entry and Number** defines the character(s) that are placed between the list entry and the associated page number. The default option (^t) is the code for a Tab character. The attached menu includes a number of common special characters, or you can type the code for a specific special character (see Project 6 for details).

- You can use the Style menus in the right column to define separate character styles for the page number and the character between the entry and page number. If you don't choose a character style in one or both of these menus, that element will be formatted with the paragraph style settings defined for the list entry.

- If the **Sort Entries in Alphabetical Order** option is checked, the compiled list entries will appear in alphabetical order rather than page-number order.

- By default, each new style in the Include pane is added one level lower than the previous style. You can use the **Level** menu to change the hierarchy of styles in the list.

10. **In the Other Styles list, highlight head 1 and click Add. In the Style section of the dialog box, choose TOC 2 in the Entry Style menu. Choose After Entry in the Page Number field, and choose TOC Page Number in the associated Style menu.**

This label shows the active style, for which you are defining formatting options.

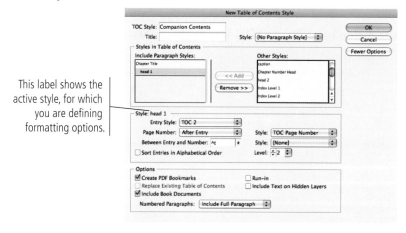

11. **In the Other Styles list, highlight head 2 and click Add. In the Style section of the dialog box, choose TOC 3 in the Entry Style menu. Choose After Entry in the Page Number field, and choose TOC Page Number in the associated Style menu.**

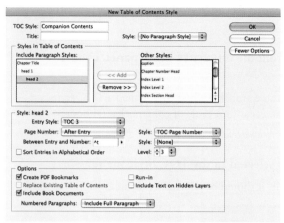

12. **In the Options area, check the Create PDF Bookmarks and Include Book Documents options.**

- **Create PDF Bookmarks** tags the table of contents entries to appear in the Bookmarks panel of Adobe Acrobat or Adobe Reader (when the document is exported to PDF).

- **Replace Existing Table of Contents** is only available if a table of contents has already been built in the open file. This option is more relevant when you build the table of contents than when you define a table of contents style.

- **Include Book Documents** allows you to build a single table of contents for all files in an InDesign book file. This option is only available if the open file is part of an InDesign book.

- **Run-in** builds a list in which all entries run into a single paragraph; individual entries are separated by a semicolon.

- **Include Text on Hidden Layers** adds list entries even if the text is on a hidden layer. This option is unchecked by default, and it should almost always remain that way — unless you have a very specific reason for listing elements that do not actually appear in the document.

- The **Numbered Paragraphs** menu determines whether the list entry includes the full numbered paragraph (number and text), only the numbers, or only the text.

13. **Click OK to return to the Table of Contents Styles dialog box.**

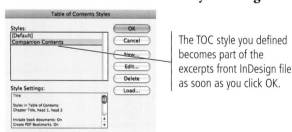

The TOC style you defined becomes part of the excerpts front InDesign file as soon as you click OK.

14. **Click OK to close the Table of Contents Styles dialog box and return to the document window.**

15. **Save the file and continue to the next exercise.**

Note:

Different types of projects call for different types of lists. Although called the Table of Contents utility, you can build a list of any editorial element formatted with a paragraph style. For example, some publications call for a separate table of contents for illustrations. If you define and apply a Figure Heading paragraph style, you can create a list of all entries formatted with that style.

BUILD AND UPDATE A TABLE OF CONTENTS

Once a list is defined, whether for a single file or a book, you can build it into the layout very easily. In fact, when you build a table of contents, the compiled list loads into the cursor; you can click to place the loaded list just as you would place any other text element.

1. **With excerpts front.indd open from the excerpts Book panel, choose Layout>Table of Contents.**

   This dialog box has the same options as those available when you defined a TOC style. The only difference is that here you define a one-time table of contents list (although you can click the Save Style button to create a style based on your choices).

2. **Make sure Companion Contents is selected in the TOC Style menu.**

   Because it is the only style in the open file, it should be selected by default.

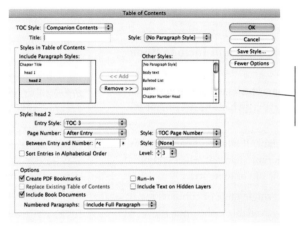

All options in this dialog box reflect your choices from when you defined the TOC style in the previous exercise.

3. **Click OK.**

   When the list is ready, it loads into the cursor. This process might take a little while to complete, depending on the size of your book, so don't panic or try to force-quit the application after a minute or two. If you're working on a very large book (such as this 400-plus-page Portfolio Series book), now is probably a good time for a coffee break.

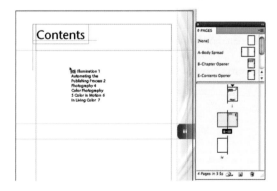

4. **Click the loaded cursor in the middle of Page iii to place the TOC into the text frame on the page.**

That's all there is to building a table of contents — whether for a single file or for multiple documents combined in an InDesign book file. After a TOC is built into a document, it is a static block of text. The applied styles can be changed like any other styles, and you can change the text box in which a list is placed. You can change or delete items from the list without affecting the main layout.

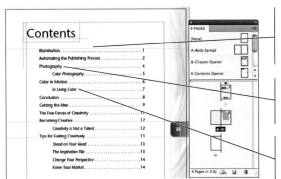

Each item is automatically formatted with the styles you assigned when you defined the Table of Contents style.

Text elements formatted as "head 1" in the book are formatted with the TOC 2 style.

Text elements formatted as "head 2" in the book are formatted with the TOC 3 style.

The table of contents built for this file reveals one potential problem: text that exists on the master page only (i.e., where the layout page hasn't been detached from the master) is not included in the compiled lists. The text frames for each chapter title have not been detached from the master pages, so the chapter titles do not appear in the compiled list.

5. **Double-click color1 in the Book panel to open the file, and navigate to Page 1. Command/Control-Shift-click the frame containing the document title to detach that frame from the master page.**

6. **Save the file and close it.**

7. **Repeat Steps 5–6 on the first page of the design1 file to detach the title text frame from the master page.**

8. **With Page iii of the excerpts front file showing, place the insertion point anywhere within the current table of contents and then choose Layout>Update Table of Contents. Click OK in the resulting message.**

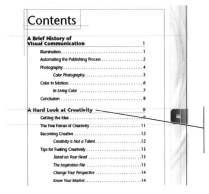

When the update process is complete, the chapter titles appear in the compiled list.

9. **Save your changes and close the document.**

10. **Save the book file and continue to the next stage of the project.**

Note:

Be careful when building a table of contents for an InDesign book. For a book TOC to function properly, the styles must be consistent in every chapter file. In other words, you shouldn't format second-level headings with "Head 2" in one chapter, "H2" in another chapter, and "Heading 2" in other chapters. If you do, the TOC has to include all three of those styles as separate list items.

Capitalization counts, too; when building a table of contents, "Head 2" is not the same as "head 2."

Stage 3 Building an Index

An index is a map to a publication's contents, providing the reader with an easy reference to specific content. As with tables of contents and other lists, creating an index used to be an extremely time-consuming and labor-intensive process. A professional indexer was hired to read each hard-copy page of a document, write down index entries and page numbers, manually compile the final alphabetized list, and typeset that list into the document. Any changes after the index was finished meant the entire document had to be rechecked manually.

InDesign includes an Index tool that manages and automates part of the indexing process, improving the production workflow and saving considerable time when changes are inevitably made.

Despite the manual nature of the process, some advance planning can make your indexing life easier. Indexing involves a number of styles, which you *should* plan in advance (although you can always change the style definitions later in the process):

- Paragraph styles for index headings (if you decide to use them).

- Paragraph styles for up to four levels of index entries. If you don't define these styles in advance, they will be automatically created for you when you generate the index.

- Character styles for the page numbers of each index entry (if you want them to be formatted differently than the paragraph style used for the index entry).

- Character styles for cross-references (if you want them to be formatted differently than the index entry).

TAG BASIC AND REVERSED INDEX TOPICS

1. **Double-click color1 in the excerpts Book panel to open that document.**

2. **Choose Window>Type & Tables>Index to open the Index panel.**

Go to Selected Marker
Update Preview
Generate Index
Create New Index Entry
Delete Selected Entry

3. **On Page 1 of the open document, highlight the word "hieroglyphics" in the middle of the second line of text.**

Note:

Reference mode (the default) is used to add index entries in a layout. Topic mode is used to define a list of topics and review the hierarchy of included topics before compiling the index.

4. **Click the Create New Index Entry button at the bottom of the Index panel.**

   The New Page Reference dialog box shows the highlighted text in the first Topic Levels field.

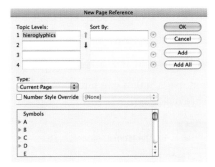

5. **Make sure the Type menu is set to Current Page and click OK.**

   You can define a number of different types of index entries; the Current Page option adds a reference to the page number where the text is currently highlighted.

   When you close the New Page Reference dialog box, you see that the highlighted text is preceded by a large carat character. This nonprinting character is an **index marker** — it indicates the location of a tagged reference, but it will not appear in the output job.

6. **In the Index panel, click the arrow to the left of the "H", and then click the arrow to the left of the word "hieroglyphics".**

   You can see that the topic was added using the text in the Topic Levels field, and the reference was added with the Current Page number of the highlighted text.

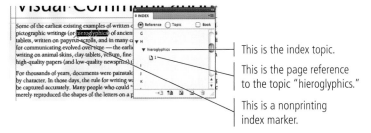

This is the index topic.

This is the page reference to the topic "hieroglyphics."

This is a nonprinting index marker.

7. **Click the arrow to collapse the "H" section of the Index panel.**

8. **Highlight the word "papyrus" in the next line and press Command-Option-Shift-[(Macintosh) or Control-Alt-Shift-[(Windows).**

   Using this key command, you can add a new Current Page reference without opening the New Page Reference dialog box.

9. **In the Index panel, expand the "P" list and the "papyrus" topic.**

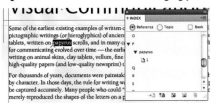

Note:

If text is highlighted, Command-Option-Shift-[(Macintosh) or Control-Alt-Shift-[(Windows) adds the highlighted text to the topic list and places an index marker for the selected text, without opening the New Page Reference dialog box.

10. **Create new Current Page references to "rock carvings", "clay tablets", and "vellum" in the same paragraph.**

11. **On Page 2 of the document, highlight the words "Johannes Gutenberg" in the second line of the first paragraph after the "Automating…" heading.**

12. **Press Command-Option-Shift-] or Control-Alt-Shift-] to add a reversed topic reference to this name.**

13. **In the Index panel, expand the "G" list and the nested index topic.**

    The reference for index markers is always the current page, unless you intentionally change the reference type in the New Page Reference dialog box.

The highlighted text was added in reverse order (last word, first word).

14. **On Page 4 of the layout, highlight the words "William Henry Fox Talbot" in the first line of the second paragraph.**

15. **Press Command-Option-Shift-] or Control-Alt-Shift-] to add a reversed topic reference to this name. Review the entry in the Index panel.**

    Only the last word of the highlighted text is placed before the comma in the index topic.

    In this case, the index topic is technically correct because some people might look for the last name "Talbot" to find information about this person. Others, however, might look for his full last name ("Fox Talbot"), so you should add another index entry for the same text.

16. **In the text, highlight the space character between the words "Fox" and "Talbot". Choose Type>Insert White Space>Nonbreaking Space.**

17. **Highlight the entire name again and press Command-Option-Shift-] or Control-Alt-Shift-] to add a reversed topic reference to this name. Review the entry in the Index panel.**

^S is the special code for a nonbreaking space. InDesign properly translates this code when it builds an index.

Nonbreaking space character

Note:

The key command for a nonbreaking space is Command-Option-X/ Control-Alt-X.

18. **Scan the text of the document and add Current Page index entries to all people mentioned in the chapter. Add all names in reverse order, using nonbreaking spaces as necessary to keep compound last names together.**

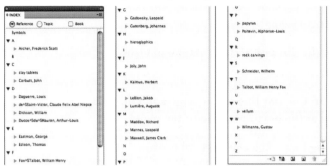

19. **Save the document and continue to the next exercise.**

Changing Topic Sort Order

The Sort By field allows you to change the alphabetical order of an index topic in the built index. When the index is built, the entries will appear in the list based on the Sort By text, but the entry text will still be the text defined in the Topic Levels field.

This option is particularly useful for indexing abbreviations and proper names. In the examples shown here, the abbreviated text "Mt." will be alphabetized according to the full word "Mount". The name "Benjamin Franklin" will appear in the index under F instead of B —alphabetized by last name but appearing in the text in standard first name/last name order.

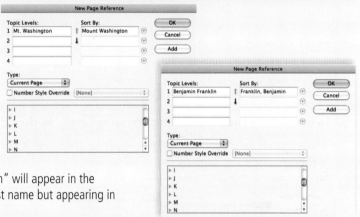

Reversing Index Entries

In addition to changing the sort order of a name, you can also change the actual order of the highlighted words when you add an entry to the index. When text is selected, pressing Command-Option-Shift-] (Macintosh) or Control-Alt-Shift-] (Windows) adds a reversed index entry without opening the New Page Reference dialog box. Using this key command, the highlighted text is added as an entry with the format "last word, comma, all other words".

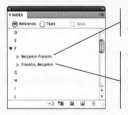

This entry was added with the text reversed in the Sort By field.

This entry was added by highlighting the text and pressing Command-Option-Shift-] (Macintosh) or Control-Alt-Shift-] (Windows).

If the text "Benjamin Franklin" is highlighted, for example, using this key command will add a reference to the term "Franklin, Benjamin." In this case, the added topic will appear in the built index with the reversed text instead of simply re-alphabetized based on the reversed Sort By text.

Compound nouns that are not hyphenated can cause problems. "Martin Luther King Jr.", for example, would be added as "Jr., Martin Luther King". Very few people would look for this reference in the "J" section of an index, and the point of an index is to be useable. To prevent this type of reference, you can change the text to a nonbreaking space between two words in the selection. With the nonbreaking space between "King" and "Jr.", the reversed index entry would be "King Jr., Martin Luther".

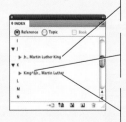

This entry was added in reverse without changing the highlighted text.

^S is the special code for a nonbreaking space. InDesign properly translates this code when it builds an index.

To create this entry, we replaced the standard space between "King" and "Jr." with a nonbreaking space.

ADD MULTIPLE PAGE REFERENCES

In some cases, you need to add multiple references to a specific index topic. Rather than searching through the text to find every instance of the topic, you can use the Add All button in the New Page Reference dialog box.

1. **With the color1 file open from the excerpts Book panel, navigate to Page 3 of the layout.**

2. **Highlight the word "Printing" in the first line of the page and click the Create New Index Entry button at the bottom of the Index panel.**

3. **In the New Page Reference dialog box, click the Add All button.**

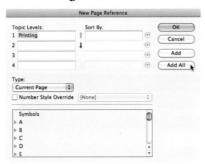

Note:

After you click Add or Add All in the New Page Reference dialog box, the OK button changes to Done.

4. **Click Done to close the New Page Reference dialog box.**

5. **In the Index panel, expand the "Printing" topic in the "P" list.**

    When creating an index, topics are case-sensitive. "Printing" is not the same as "printing". The word "Printing" is capitalized only once in the layout, so the Add All function added only one reference to the topic "Printing".

Lowercase instances of the topic were not tagged.

6. **Highlight the word "printing" in the first line of the second paragraph and click the Create New Index Entry button.**

7. **In the New Page Reference dialog box, click the Add All button and then click Done.**

8. **Review the new topic and references in the Index panel.**

    Your index now includes two references to the same term, one capitalized and one lowercase. This is not good practice, so you need to combine the two terms.

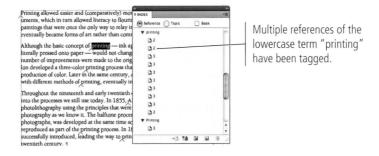

Multiple references of the lowercase term "printing" have been tagged.

9. **In the Index panel, double-click the capitalized "Printing" topic.**

   Double-clicking a term in the panel opens the Topic Options dialog box.

10. **In the pane at the bottom of the dialog box, expand the "P" list.**

    This pane shows all topics currently used in the document or book. In this case, you are working with an InDesign book; topics defined in the other book files (such as "Perspective") are also included in the topic list.

11. **Double-click "printing" in the topic list.**

    Double-clicking an existing topic changes the text in the Topic Levels field.

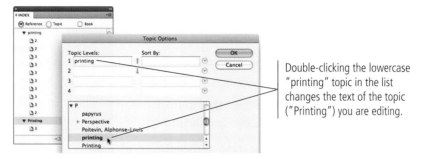

Double-clicking the lowercase "printing" topic in the list changes the text of the topic ("Printing") you are editing.

This method of choosing an existing topic also works in the New Page Reference dialog box. When you double-click a topic in the list at the bottom of the dialog box, text in the Topic Levels field changes to reflect the topic you double-click. The index marker will be placed at the location of the highlighted text, but the reference will be added for whatever was shown in the Topic Levels field.

12. **Click OK to close the dialog box, and then review the "P" list in the Index panel.**

    Your index now includes a single reference to the term "printing." The page reference for the previously capitalized term has been merged into the references for the lowercase term.

13. **Save the file and continue to the next exercise.**

ADD PAGE-RANGE REFERENCES

Index references are not limited to single page numbers. You can use the Type menu in the New Page Reference dialog box to define a number of reference types.

✓ Current Page
To Next Style Change
To Next Use of Style
To End of Story
To End of Document
To End of Section
For Next # of Paragraphs
For Next # of Pages
Suppress Page Range

See [also]
See
See also
See herein
See also herein
[Custom Cross-reference]

- **Current Page** includes a single-page reference for the index entry.

- **To Next Style Change** creates a page-range reference that starts at the location of the insertion point and ends at the first point where a different paragraph style has been applied in the text.

- **To Next Use of Style** creates a page-range reference that starts at the location of the insertion point and ends at the first instance in the story where a specific paragraph style has been applied in the text. When you choose this option, you can select the style that will end the range.

- **To End of Story** creates a page-range reference that starts at the location of the insertion point and ends at the last page of the current story.

- **To End of Document** creates a page-range reference that starts at the location of the insertion point and ends at the last page of the current document.

- **To End of Section** creates a page-range reference that starts at the location of the insertion point and ends at the last page of the current section.

- **For Next # of Paragraphs** creates a page-range reference that starts at the location of the insertion point and ends after the defined number of paragraphs.

- **For Next # of Pages** creates a page-range reference that starts at the location of the insertion point and ends after the defined number of pages.

- **Suppress Page Range** creates a topic reference with no associated page number.

1. With the `color1` file open from the `excerpts` Book panel, navigate to Page 1 of the layout.

2. Highlight the word "History" in the chapter title and click the Create New Index Entry button in the Index panel.

3. In the New Page Reference dialog box, change the capital "H" in the first Topic Levels field to a lowercase "h".

4. Choose To End of Document in the Type menu and click the Add button.

5. **Click Done to close the dialog box, and then review the new topic and reference in the Index panel.**

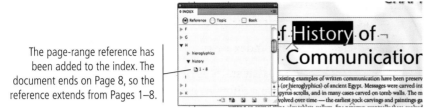

The page-range reference has been added to the index. The document ends on Page 8, so the reference extends from Pages 1–8.

6. **Highlight the word "Illumination" in the heading on Page 1 and click the Create New Index Entry button.**

7. **In the Type menu, choose To Next Use of Style. In the related Style menu, choose head 1.**

   This heading is formatted with the head 1 style. You are adding a reference that spans all text between this heading and the next instance of the head 1 style.

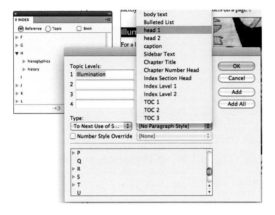

8. **Click Add, and then click Done to close the dialog box.**

9. **Review the new topic and reference in the Index panel.**

The new reference points to the current page only, instead of to the true next instance of the head 1 style.

   This problem highlights an apparent bug in the software, or at least something that does not work intuitively. When you highlight text formatted with the same style defined in the To Next Use of Style menu, InDesign identifies the highlighted text as the next use of the style — the reference points to the location of the highlighted text only. Solving this problem requires a workaround.

10. **In the Index panel, click the "1" reference to the "Illumination" topic and click the panel's Delete button.**

11. **In the resulting message, click Yes to confirm the deletion.**

12. **In the document, highlight the word "For" at the beginning of the paragraph after the Illumination heading.**

13. **Click the Create New Index Entry button in the Index panel.**

14. **In the lower half of the dialog box, expand the "I" list of topics and double-click the word "Illumination" in the list of topics.**

    As in the Topic Options dialog box, this method changes the current text in the Topic Levels field to the topic you double-click in the list.

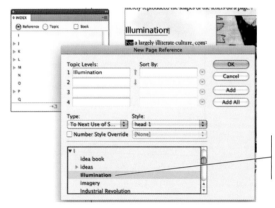

In Step 10 you deleted the reference to this topic, but you did not delete the topic itself.

15. **In the Type menu, choose To Next Use of Style. In the related Style menu, choose head 1.**

16. **Click Add, and then click Done to close the dialog box.**

17. **Review the new topic and reference in the Index panel.**

    The new reference shows the correct range between the selected text and the next instance of the head 1 paragraph style (on Page 2 of the document).

18. **Save the file and continue to the next exercise.**

Note:

If you use this workaround technique, you can simply type to replace the text in the Topic Levels field with the topic you want to reference. For this technique to work correctly, you can — but don't have to — select from the existing topics.

Note:

You can delete an entire topic from the index by selecting it in the panel and clicking the Delete button. If you delete a term from the index, all references to that term are also deleted.

ADD MULTIPLE-LEVEL REFERENCES

You might have noticed that the New Page Reference dialog box includes four fields in the Topic Levels area. These fields allow you to created multi-level or nested index entries. You can create up to four levels of nested index entries, depending on the complexity a particular project requires.

1. **With the `color1` file open through the `excerpts` Book panel, navigate to Page 4 of the layout.**

2. **Highlight the words "daguerreotype method" in the second line of the first paragraph. Click the Create New Index Entry button in the Index panel.**

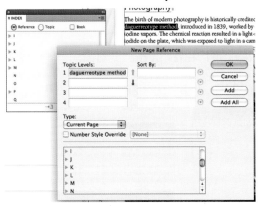

3. **In the New Page Reference dialog box, click the down-arrow button in the Topic Levels area.**

   This button moves the selected term down one level to become a second-level index term. Of course, when you add a second-level term, you also need to define the parent term for that nested entry.

Adding Cross-References in an Index

A cross-referenced item refers the reader to another index entry. For example, the index entry for "CIELAB" might say, "See LAB color." If you choose to create an entry as a cross-reference, you also need to define the type of notation. The Referenced field defines the topic to which a cross-reference will point; you can type in the field or drag an existing topic into the field from the list at the bottom of the dialog box.

- **See [also]** allows InDesign to choose the appropriate cross-reference method — "See" if the topic has no page references of its own, or "See also" if the topic includes page numbers.

- **See** refers the reader to another topic or topics; the entry has no page number, only text listing the cross-referenced topic. For example, if the index entry is "Dogs", the cross-reference might be "See Canine".

- **See also** directs attention to the current topic, as well as other information elsewhere in the index. For example, an index item called "Dogs" may have its own list of page numbers, and then a cross-reference to "See also Pets".

- **See herein** and **See also herein** refer the reader to entries within the current index entry. For example, if the main (Level 1) index entry is "Dogs", you might want to direct the index to a subentry (Level 2 or Level 3 item) that might not be expected under this heading, such as "See herein Wolf".

- **[Custom Cross-Reference]** allows you to define the text that will be used as the cross-reference, such as "Go to" or some similar text.

4. **Click the first Topic Levels field and type** `photographs`.

You can select an existing topic as the first level or type a new term in the field.

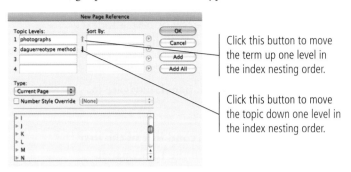

Click this button to move the term up one level in the index nesting order.

Click this button to move the topic down one level in the index nesting order.

5. **Click OK to add the term and reference to the index.**

6. **In the Index panel, expand the "photographs" entry in the "P" list.**

7. **Within the "photographs" entry, expand the "daguerreotype method" entry.**

This second-level term will be listed under the new first-level "photographs" term.

This is the page number reference for the second-level "daguerreotype method" entry.

8. **Save the color1 file and close it.**

9. **Save the book file and continue to the next exercise.**

 BUILD THE BOOK'S INDEX

Building an index into a document is very similar to building a table of contents. Once the index has been generated, it is loaded into the cursor so you can place it in the layout. When you are working with a book file, you can build the index into an existing chapter file, or you can add a separate back matter file to hold the index.

1. **Open the `companion.indt` template from the WIP>Companions folder to create a new file.**

2. **Drag the D-Index Opener master page onto the Page 1 icon.**

3. **Save the file as `excerpts back.indd` in your WIP>Companions folder and close the file.**

4. **In the `excerpts` Book panel, make sure nothing is selected in the panel and click the Add Documents button.**

5. **Navigate to the file `excerpts back.indd` file in your WIP>Companions folder and click Open.**

Note:

Back matter *is anything that comes after the primary chapters of a document, such as appendices and an index.*

6. **Open the Synchronize Options dialog box from the Book panel Options menu.**

7. **Deselect everything but the Swatches check box and click OK.**

   You can use the main check boxes (Other and Styles and Swatches) to deselect all items in the group, and then check only the Swatches check box.

8. **Make sure no files are selected in the Book panel and click the Synchronize button at the bottom of the panel. Click OK to acknowledge that the synchronization is complete.**

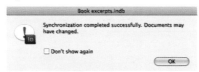

9. **Double-click the excerpts back file in the Book panel to open the file.**

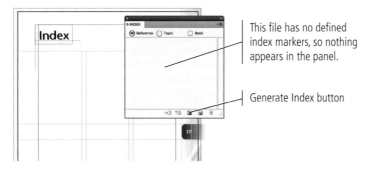

This file has no defined index markers, so nothing appears in the panel.

Generate Index button

Note:

You can preview all index entries in a book file by opening the individual chapter files and checking the Book option at the top of the Index panel. (The panel only shows entries for files that are currently open.)

10. **At the bottom of the Index panel, click the Generate Index button.**

11. **In the Generate Index dialog box, delete the word "Index" from the Title field.**

    The Title and Title Style options are the same as the related options for building a table of contents. Because the master page you're using already includes the title "Index", you should not include a title in the built index.

12. **Select the Include Book Documents option.**

    Even though there are no index references in this back-matter file, it is part of the book with files that have index markers.

13. If the third button on the right reads "More Options", click the button to expand the dialog box.

14. Review the available options. Click the Following Topic menu and choose Em Space as the character that will appear between the entry text and the associated references.

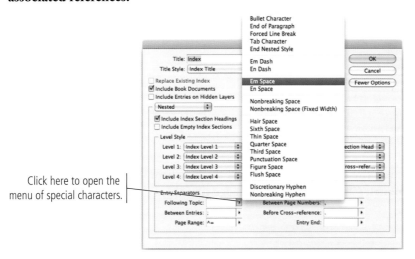

Click here to open the menu of special characters.

Options for Generating an Index

When you generate an index, you have a number of options for automatically formatting the compiled list. In many cases, the default settings will work perfectly well, but you can change any or all of the following options as necessary:

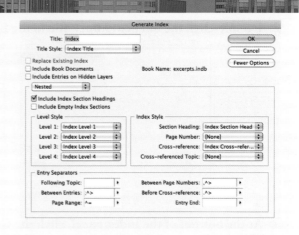

- The **Nested** or **Run-in** menu determines how individual entries in the index are placed. Nested creates each entry on its own line. Run-In forces all index entries to run together in the same paragraph.

- If **Include Index Section Headings** is checked, alpha-betical headings (A, B, C, etc.) are added to the index.

- If **Include Empty Index Sections** is checked, all letter headings are added to the built index, even if that letter has no associated terms.

- The **Level Style** menu defines paragraph styles used to format different levels of index entries. If you don't choose different styles in these menus, the default op-tions (Index Level 1, etc.) are created and applied to the headings. (If you define your own style named "Index Level 1," your settings are applied in the built index.)

- The **Section Heading** menu defines paragraph styles used to format the section headings in the index. If you don't choose a different style, the default Index Section Head is created and applied to the headings. (If you define your own style named "Index Section Head," your settings are applied in the built index.)

- The **Page Number** menu defines the character style applied to page numbers in the generated index.

- The **Cross-Reference** menu defines the character style applied to the cross-references in the index (for example, the "See also" part of "See also LAB color").

- The **Cross-Referenced Topic** menu defines the char-acter style applied to the text of a cross-reference (for example, the "LAB color" part of "See also LAB color").

- The **Entry Separators** area defines the characters used in specific parts of the index:

  - **Following Topic** is used between the entry text and the entry page references.

  - **Between Page Numbers** is used between individual page references.

  - **Between Entries** is used between entries in a run-in index.

  - **Before Cross-reference** is used before the text of a cross-reference.

  - **Page Range** separates numbers in a page range.

  - **Entry End** is added at the end of individual entries.

15. **Click OK to generate the index. Click the loaded cursor in the three-column text frame to place the index.**

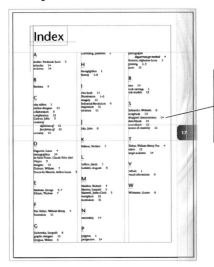

Some of these entries are from the second chapter (the file from the Design Companion); these tags were already created in the file provided by the publisher.

Note:

Your index might be slightly different than our example, depending on which names you added in the previous exercise.

16. **Save the file and close it.**

17. **Save the book file and continue to the next stage of the project.**

Stage 4 Exporting Book Files

Another advantage of combining multiple files is the ability to output those files all at once — choosing print or export settings once, instead of opening each file and changing the print or export settings individually. Using the Book panel, you can output all chapter files simultaneously, or you can output specific selected chapters.

EXPORT PDF FILES FOR PRINT AND DIGITAL DISTRIBUTION

Your client asked for two separate files — one that can be printed at high quality and one that can be posted on the company's Web site and sent via email. Because you're working with a single file for the entire book, you can easily create these two output files in a few steps.

1. **With the excerpts Book panel open, click the empty area at the bottom of the panel to deselect all files in the book.**

2. **Choose Export Book to PDF in the panel Options menu.**

Note:

If any files are selected, the menu option changes to Export Selected Documents to PDF.

3. **Navigate to your WIP>Companions folder as the target and change the file name to** `excerpts print.pdf`. **Choose Adobe PDF (Print) in the Format/ Save As Type menu, and then click Save.**

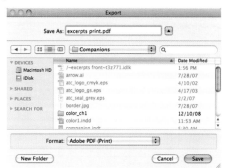

4. **In the Export Adobe PDF dialog box, choose [High Quality Print] in the Adobe PDF Preset menu.**

5. **In the Marks and Bleeds options, check the Crop Marks option. Change the Offset field to 0.125″, and change all four Bleed fields to 0.125″.**

6. **Click Export.**

Exporting a book does not occur in the background. You have to wait for the export process to finish.

7. **When the export process is complete, choose Export Book to PDF in the Book panel Options menu.**

8. **Make sure Adobe PDF (Print) is selected in the Format/Save As Type menu. Name the second file** `excerpts digital.pdf` **and click Save.**

If you completed Project 4, you know that the Adobe PDF (Interactive) option automatically exports every spread as a single page. You want each page in the resulting file to be separate, so you are using the Adobe PDF (Print) option to generate a low-resolution PDF file that will be suitable for digital distribution.

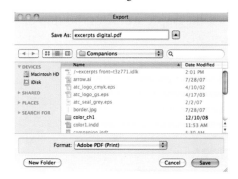

Note:

In Project 4 you used the Print Booklet command to output a booklet as printer's spreads for proofing purposes. In most commercial printing workflows, however, the output provider will create the necessary printer's spreads from the individual pages in your exported PDF file. Always consult with your output provider about what you need to supply to efficiently achieve the best possible result.

9. **Choose [Smallest File Size] in the Adobe PDF Preset menu.**

10. **In the General pane, activate the Hyperlinks option.**

    When the Hyperlinks option is selected, table of contents and index entries are exported as hyperlinks that navigate to the appropriate locations in the file.

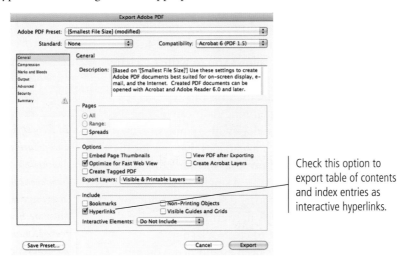

Check this option to export table of contents and index entries as interactive hyperlinks.

11. **Click Export. If you get a warning about transparency settings, click OK to dismiss the warning.**

    Using the book utility, you now have two complete PDF files for different purposes — created in only a few easy steps.

12. **Save the book file and then close it.**

    If your Book panel is floating independently, click the panel Close button to close it.

    You can also Control/right click the panel tab and choose Close from the contextual menu (as you would for any other panel).

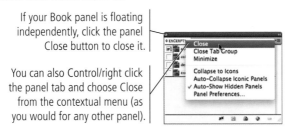

13. **Continue to the next stage of the project.**

For the final stage of this project, you need to create a thank-you note from the publisher to previous clients. This note will be included with the printed copies of the Excerpts booklet when the sample is mailed to the clients. Your client provided a comma-delimited file with the client mailing addresses; this file also identifies which book each client purchased.

Data merge is a fairly sophisticated utility in most word-processing applications; it allows you to combine text with information stored in a database or spreadsheet (such as a Microsoft Excel file). For example, data merge allows you to write one letter, click a few buttons, and print or export 147 copies of the letter, each with a different mailing address. InDesign's Data Merge capabilities can be used for this type of personal letter generation, but — with a bit of advance planning — it can also be used for more sophisticated database-driven layouts such as catalogs with graphics.

Personalized printing uses data to produce items such as catalogs that specifically target your interests. Other applications for personalized printing include newspaper inserts for a specific region. A national company might create a single weekly sale advertisement with one page that varies according to the local distribution; why, for example, would a company want to advertise snow shovels in southern California?

InDesign's Data Merge feature makes it fairly simple to create a layout incorporating variable data. Once the data source file has been established, you can create any layout you want, add the data, and create multiple versions of a finished layout in one action.

> *Note:*
>
> *Variable database printing is currently one of the hottest topics in the graphic design and printing industries. Marketing specialists have spent millions to determine that you are far more likely to open a piece of mail with your name on it than one addressed to "Resident."*

The Data Source File

INDESIGN FOUNDATIONS

If you have a contact manager anywhere on your computer, you are familiar with the idea of a simple database. A database is made up of **fields** that contain information. Each field has a **field name**, which is usually descriptive text that defines the contents of the field. Each listing in a database is called a **record**; each record contains every field in the database (even if a particular field contains no information for a given record).

In the following example, Name, Address, and Telephone are all fields. The first line of the file contains the field names "Name," "Address," and "Telephone Number." Each record appears on a separate line.

Name	Address	Telephone Number
James Smith	123 Anywhere St., Someplace, MI 99999	800-555-0000
Susan Jones	3208 Street Ct., Small Town, ID 55555	800-555-8888

InDesign's Data Merge feature does not interact directly with a database application. Data must first be exported from a database into a tab- or comma-delimited ASCII text file.

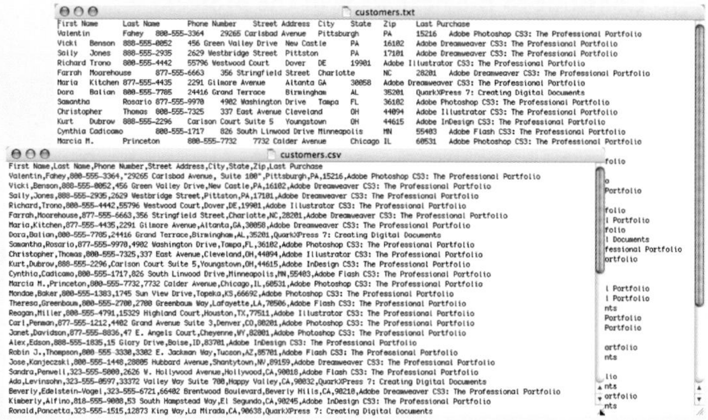

In the text file, the information in each field (called a **text string**) is separated by the delimiter (comma or tab), which tells the software that the next text string belongs in the next field. Records are separated by a paragraph return, so each record begins on a new line.

If a particular text string requires one of the delimiter characters — for example, a comma within an address — that string is surrounded by double quotation marks in the text file.

A comma contained within quotation marks is treated as a text character, not as a delimiter.

The first line of the text file should list the field names. If your database application does not export field names as the first line of the text-only file, you need to open the file in a text editor and add the field name line at the beginning.

CREATE THE MERGED DOCUMENT AND LOAD THE SOURCE DATA

The target document for a data merge needs to include placeholders, or locations where the data will appear after the data merge is complete. Once you have established the data source for the InDesign file, you can easily create these placeholders anywhere in the document.

1. **Open the file letter.indd from your WIP>Companions folder.**

   Your client wrote this letter using her InDesign letterhead template. She used all capital letters to indicate where she wants database information to be added in the letter text.

2. **Choose Window>Utilities>Data Merge to open the Data Merge panel.**

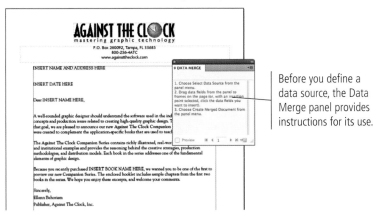

Before you define a data source, the Data Merge panel provides instructions for its use.

3. **Open the Data Merge panel Options menu and choose Select Data Source.**

4. **Navigate to the file customers.txt in your WIP>Companions folder and click Open.**

   When the file is processed, the available fields (defined by the first line in the data file) are listed in the Data Merge panel.

The T icons indicate that these fields are text strings.

5. **In the document, turn on hidden characters (Type>Show Hidden Characters).**

6. **Highlight the first line in the letter (excluding the paragraph return character), and then double-click the First Name item in the Data Merge panel.**

Highlight this line of placeholder text (excluding the paragraph return character).

Double-clicking an item in the Data Merge panel replaces the highlighted text with a placeholder for that data field.

Note:

Like a text variable, a placeholder is treated as a single character in the layout.

7. **Click to place the insertion point after the placeholder. Press the Spacebar, and then double-click the Last Name item in the Data Merge panel.**

Cleaning up Data

Placeholders are made up of the field name enclosed within double brackets, such as <<Name>>, inserted anywhere in the target document.

> <<Name>>
> <<Address>>
>
> Dear <<Name>>,
>
> *Congratulations! We are writing to inform you that your house at <<Address>> has been selected for a free facelift!*

Once data from the source file has been merged into the document, it looks like this:

> *James Smith*
> *123 Anywhere St., Someplace, MI 99999*
>
> *Dear James Smith,*
>
> *Congratulations! We are writing to inform you that your house at 123 Anywhere St., Someplace, MI 99999 has been selected for a free facelift!*

The same document is reproduced for every record in the text file, personalizing each copy of the letter for the intended recipient.

Notice that the address is entirely on one line of text, and that the "Dear" line includes the person's whole name — not a tremendous improvement over "Dear Occupant."

You should make sure your data includes the exact information you need. The previous example would benefit greatly from a different arrangement:

> *First_Name,Last_Name,Street_Address,City,State,Zip*
>
> *James,Smith, "123 Anywhere St.",Someplace,MI,99999*

The target file can then appear much more personal. Placeholders can be positioned with text characters (including spaces) in between to make the document more personal:

> <<First_Name>> <<Last_Name>>
> <<Street Address>>
> <<City>>, <<State>> <<Zip>>
>
> Dear <<First_Name>>,
>
> *Congratulations! We are writing to inform you that your house at <<Street_Address>> has been selected for a free facelift!*

Once data from the source file has been merged into this version, it looks like this:

> *James Smith*
> *123 Anywhere St.*
> *Someplace, MI 99999*
>
> *Dear James,*
>
> *Congratulations! We are writing to inform you that your house at 123 Anywhere St. has been selected for a free facelift!*

You could also include a title field, which would allow you to address the letter as "Dear <<title>> <<last name>>", which would result in "Dear Mr. Smith" instead of the less-formal "Dear James".

8. **Press Return/Enter to start a new paragraph in the document, and then double-click the Street Address item in the Data Merge panel.**

9. **Press Return/Enter again. Add the City, State, and Zip fields on the third line, separated by the appropriate punctuation and spaces.**

10. **Highlight the All Caps text in the salutation line, and then replace it with the First Name data field placeholder.**

Note:

Highlighting a few letters in any field name (in the document) automatically highlights the entire field name, including the brackets.

11. **In the third paragraph of the letter, replace the All Caps text with the Last Purchase data field placeholder.**

12. **With the Last Purchase placeholder selected, change the font to ATC Pine Italic.**

   After placeholders have been entered in the document, you can apply text and paragraph formatting as you would for any other text element.

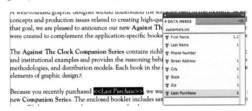

Note:

If you were going to re-use this letter, you might consider using a type variable for the date instead of typing an actual date.

13. **Highlight the text "INSERT DATE HERE" and type today's date.**

14. **Save the file and continue to the next exercise.**

Working with Long Text Fields

INDESIGN FOUNDATIONS

A text placeholder can be inserted anywhere in a document. Keep in mind, however, that if you attach a placeholder to a text frame, the frame must be large enough to hold the longest piece of data that exists for that field. Frames will not automatically enlarge or shrink to match the content.

When you preview the records, you can see how the formatting will apply once the data merge is complete. Even if the text for one record fits into a defined frame, that doesn't mean that all records will necessarily fit. Make sure a text frame is large enough to fit the longest possible record field.

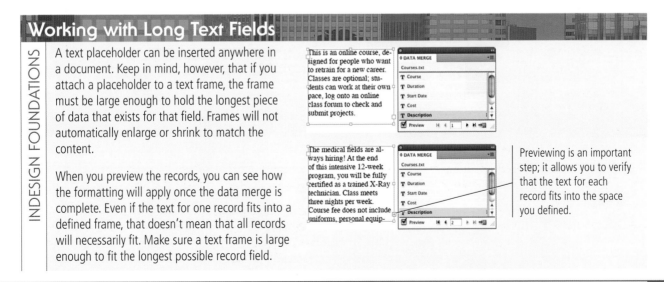

Previewing is an important step; it allows you to verify that the text for each record fits into the space you defined.

Incorporating Images in a Data Merge

A data source file is not limited to text; you can also incorporate images in the data source file to create variable images in a layout. If you want to incorporate graphics or images in your data merge, your data source file must include a field that contains the full path to the image, beginning with the drive name where the image resides (called an **absolute path**). In the field names, the name of the image field should start with the "@" symbol (for example, "@image").

The absolute path for an image tells the Data Merge processor where to find the necessary file. On a Macintosh, the components in the path name are separated by colons:

> Hard Drive:Pictures:image.tif   Mac:Catalog Files:Pictures:sweater.tif

On a Windows computer, the path name begins with the drive letter:

> C:\My Documents\Pictures\image.tif   D:\Vector files\graph.eps

The only spaces in the path name are those that exist in the name of a file or folder; no spaces should separate any of the backslash or colon characters.

Creating and Controlling Image Placeholders

When a data source includes an image field, the Data Merge panel shows a small picture icon for that field. You can attach an image placeholder to any graphics frame by selecting the frame in the layout and double-clicking the image item in the Data Merge panel.

When you use images from a data source file, you can choose Content Placement Options in the Data Merge panel Options menu to predetermine the appearance of the image in relation to the placeholder frame.

The image placeholder holds the images defined in the image data field.

- The **Fitting** menu includes the same options that are available for fitting placed images in a graphics frame.

- If **Center in Frame** is checked, the image is centered within the placeholder frame after the Fitting option has been applied.

- The **Link Images** check box, active by default, links the data source images to the layout that's created when you generate the merged document. If this option is not checked, the images are embedded in the resulting file. (Embedding images drastically increases file size; as a general rule, you should leave the Link Images box checked.)

You can preview variable images just as you preview text. If an image path is incorrect or a file is not in the path defined in the data, you will see a warning when you try to preview that record.

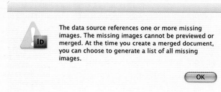

The data source references one or more missing images. The missing images cannot be previewed or merged. At the time you create a merged document, you can choose to generate a list of all missing images.

COMPLETE THE MERGED DOCUMENT

Once you have created your target document and formatted all the elements, you can preview the data and create the merged document. InDesign uses the data source file and the target layout to create a third document — the merged file. This third file is not linked to the data source; any changes you make to the data are not applied to the merged document. If you change the data file, you have to repeat the merge of the original layout file with the changed data.

1. **With letter.indd open from your WIP>Companions folder, activate the Preview check box at the bottom of the Data Merge panel.**

   You can preview your document at any time by activating the Preview check box in the Data Merge panel. The arrows to the left and right of the record number allow you to move through each record in the merged document.

When Preview is turned on, the actual data from the source file replaces the placeholder elements.

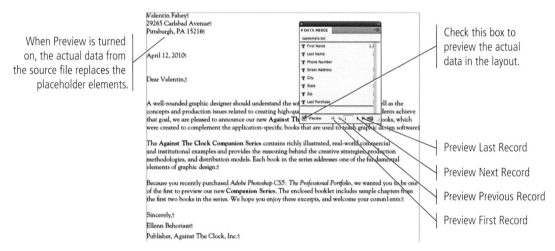

Check this box to preview the actual data in the layout.

Preview Last Record

Preview Next Record

Preview Previous Record

Preview First Record

2. **Choose Export to PDF in the Data Merge panel Options menu.**

   In the Create Merged Document dialog box, you can define specific options for your merged document. The Records tab determines which records (all, one single record, or a specified range) will be included in the merged document.

   The two check boxes at the bottom of the dialog box provide feedback after you create the data merge. Checked by default, these important options allow you to make sure all your data is available and fits into the spaces you defined.

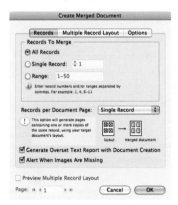

3. **Click OK in the Create Merged Document dialog box.**

Note:

If you choose Create Merged Document, the merge process results in an InDesign file with the necessary number of copies. The Export to PDF option skips this intermediary step.

Note:

The Records per Document Page option allows you to place multiple records on a single page in the merged document. This option can be useful for creating catalog listings, multiple labels, or other projects with more than one database record on a single page.

4. **Choose the [High Quality Print] preset in the Export Adobe PDF dialog box and click Export.**

5. **In the resulting dialog box, navigate to your WIP>Companions folder as the target location, and then click Save.**

6. **When you see the message that the data merge resulted in no overset text, click OK.**

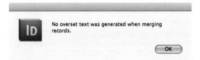

Managing Empty Data Fields

When you merge data, you should be aware that one or more fields for a specific record might be empty. For example, a specific record might not include a company name. If your target document includes a company name placeholder, the merged document might end up with an empty line where that placeholder appears.

In the example shown below, the record for Sally Jones doesn't include a company name or a phone number. In the merged document, these lines are blank.

In the Options tab of the Create Merged Document dialog box, the Remove Blank Lines for Empty Fields option solves this potential problem. (The same option is available in the Content Placement Options dialog box, which you can access in the Data Merge panel Options menu.) In the merged document, placeholders are ignored for fields that have no content.

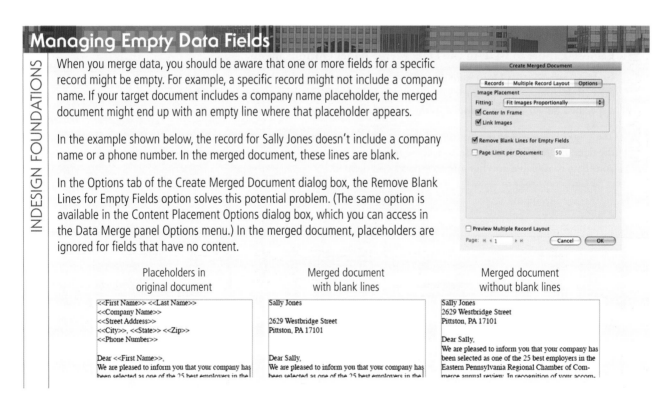

Placeholders in original document	Merged document with blank lines	Merged document without blank lines
<<First Name>> <<Last Name>> <<Company Name>> <<Street Address>> <<City>>, <<State>> <<Zip>> <<Phone Number>> Dear <<First Name>>, We are pleased to inform you that your company has been selected as one of the 25 best employers in the	Sally Jones 2629 Westbridge Street Pittston, PA 17101 Dear Sally, We are pleased to inform you that your company has been selected as one of the 25 best employers in the	Sally Jones 2629 Westbridge Street Pittston, PA 17101 Dear Sally, We are pleased to inform you that your company has been selected as one of the 25 best employers in the Eastern Pennsylvania Regional Chamber of Commerce annual review. In recognition of your accom-

7. On your desktop, find and double-click the **letter.pdf** file (in your WIP>Companions folder) to open it in Adobe Acrobat or Adobe Reader.

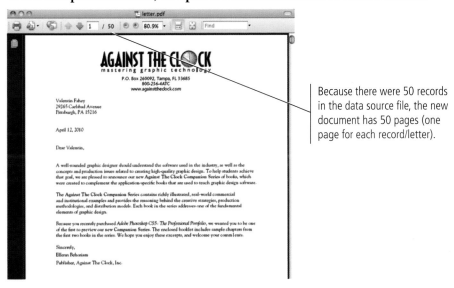

Because there were 50 records in the data source file, the new document has 50 pages (one page for each record/letter).

8. Close the PDF file, return to InDesign, and then save and close the letter.indd file.

Merging Multiple Records on a Single Page

INDESIGN FOUNDATIONS

You can merge more than one record onto a single page by selecting Multiple Records in the Records per Document Page menu. When this option is selected, the Multiple Record Layout tab determines how records are placed and separated in the merged document.

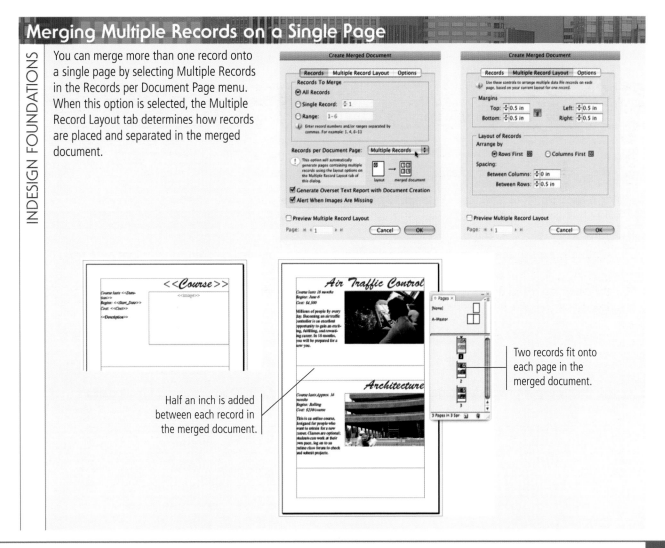

Half an inch is added between each record in the merged document.

Two records fit onto each page in the merged document.

Project Review

1. The _____ is used to organize and manage multiple chapter files in a book.

2. If a chapter file shows a _____ icon, it has been edited outside the context of the InDesign book.

3. Book chapters typically begin on _____-numbered, _____-facing pages.

4. _____, typically including a title page and table of contents, is the content preceding the main body of a book.

5. _____, typically containing indexes and appendices, appears after the primary content of a book.

6. The _____ option can be used to renumber any specific page in a document.

7. You can change the _____ of an index entry to rearrange its alphabetical position in the compiled index.

8. Clicking the _____ button in the New Page Reference dialog box is case-sensitive. "Printing" will not be tagged if the topic is "printing".

9. A(n) _____ is useful for tagging references to people based on their last names without changing the text in the document.

10. You can delete a(n) _____ without deleting its parent topic from the Index panel. The reverse is not true; deleting a parent topic deletes all _____ for that topic.

1. Describe three conventions that relate to and govern long-document design.

2. Briefly explain the concept of synchronization, including potential problems that might arise from it.

3. Briefly explain two advantages and two disadvantages of the InDesign indexing functionality.

Portfolio Builder Project

Use what you learned in this project to complete the following freeform exercise.
Carefully read the art director and client comments, then create your own design to meet the needs of the project.
Use the space below to sketch ideas; when finished, write a brief explanation of your reasoning behind your final design.

Every professional designer needs a portfolio of their work. If you've completed the projects in this book, you should now have a number of different examples to show off your skills using InDesign CS5.

The eight projects in this book were specifically designed to include a broad range of *types* of projects; your portfolio should use the same principle.

Using the following suggestions, gather your best work and create printed and digital versions of your portfolio:

❏ Include as many different types of work as possible — one-page layouts, folding brochures, multi-page booklets, etc.

❏ Print clean copies of each finished piece that you want to include.

❏ For each example in your portfolio, write a brief (one or two paragraph) synopsis of the project. Explain the purpose of the piece, as well as your role in the creative and production process.

❏ Design a personal promotion brochure — create a layout that highlights your technical skills and reflects your personal style.

❏ Create a PDF version of your portfolio so you can send your portfolio via email, post it on job sites, and keep it with you on a CD at all times — you never know when you might meet a potential employer.

_____
_____
_____
_____
_____
_____
_____
_____
_____
_____
_____
_____
_____
_____
_____

As you completed the exercises in this project, you learned to use InDesign tools to define special formatting, combine multiple files, build tables of contents and indexes, and merge variable data into a page layout.

Consistency is the key to effective long-document design. InDesign's book utility allows you to combine multiple chapter files into a single book, and to synchronize those files so related elements remain consistent from page to page and chapter to chapter. This book-building functionality works equally well for combining single-page documents or lengthy chapters with many pages.

By automating (as much as possible) the process of building tables of contents and indexes — which used to require days of manual checking and rechecking if even a single page in the layout changed — InDesign greatly improves the efficiency of your workflow. Effectively implementing styles throughout a long document makes it relatively easy to compile a thorough table of contents that includes every heading from Page 1 to the final page in the document.

Although no software is "smart" enough to identify which terms are important enough to appear in a document's index, the ability to store index markers in a document means compiling and recompiling the final index is far simpler than building and compiling the list by hand.

These skills are relatively rare in the graphics marketplace. Your ability to master them makes you much more marketable as a professional graphic designer.

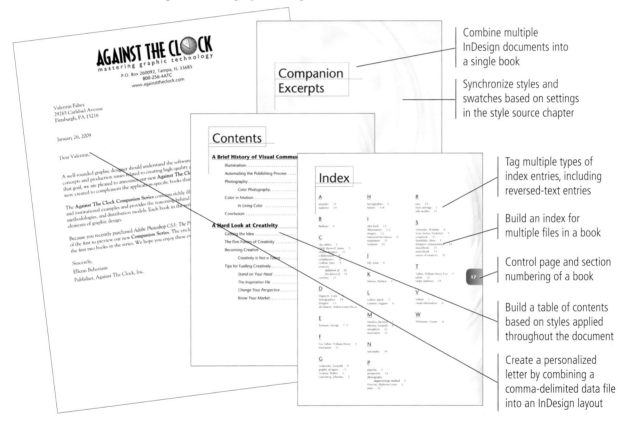

Combine multiple InDesign documents into a single book

Synchronize styles and swatches based on settings in the style source chapter

Tag multiple types of index entries, including reversed-text entries

Build an index for multiple files in a book

Control page and section numbering of a book

Build a table of contents based on styles applied throughout the document

Create a personalized letter by combining a comma-delimited data file into an InDesign layout

Index

Use our portfolio to build yours.

The Against The Clock Professional Portfolio Series walks you step-by-step through the tools and techniques of graphic design professionals.

Order online at www.againsttheclock.com
Use code **PFS710** for a 10% discount

Go to **www.againsttheclock.com** to enter our monthly drawing for a free book of your choice.

AGAINST THE CLOCK
mastering graphic technology